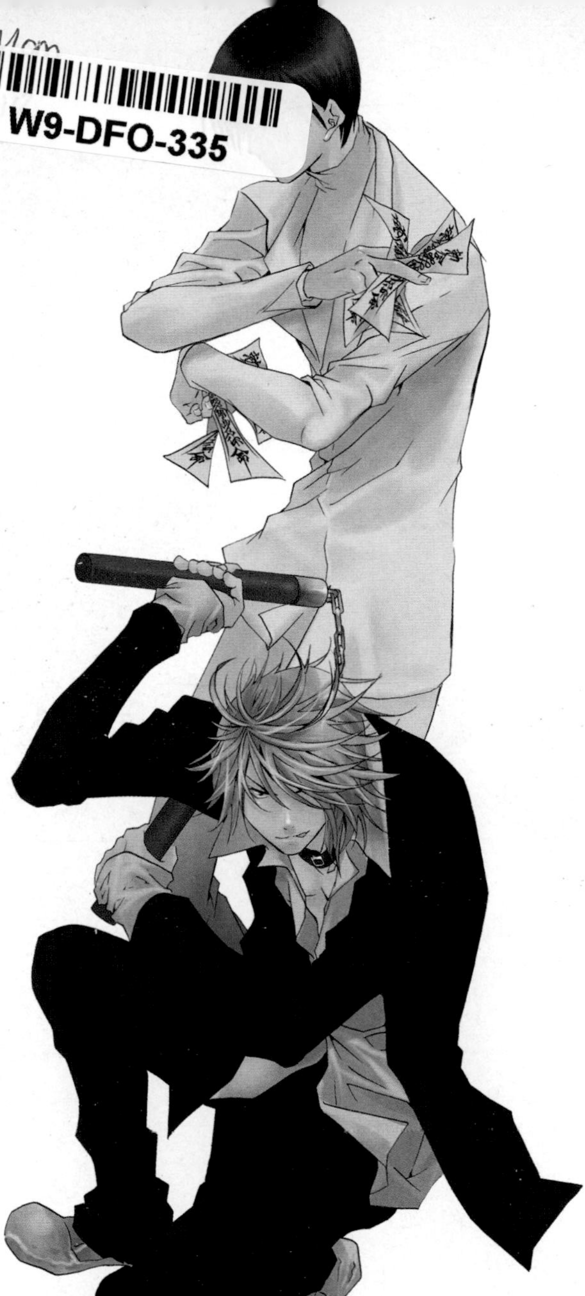

ZOMBIE-LOAN 10 PEACH-PIT

CONTENTS

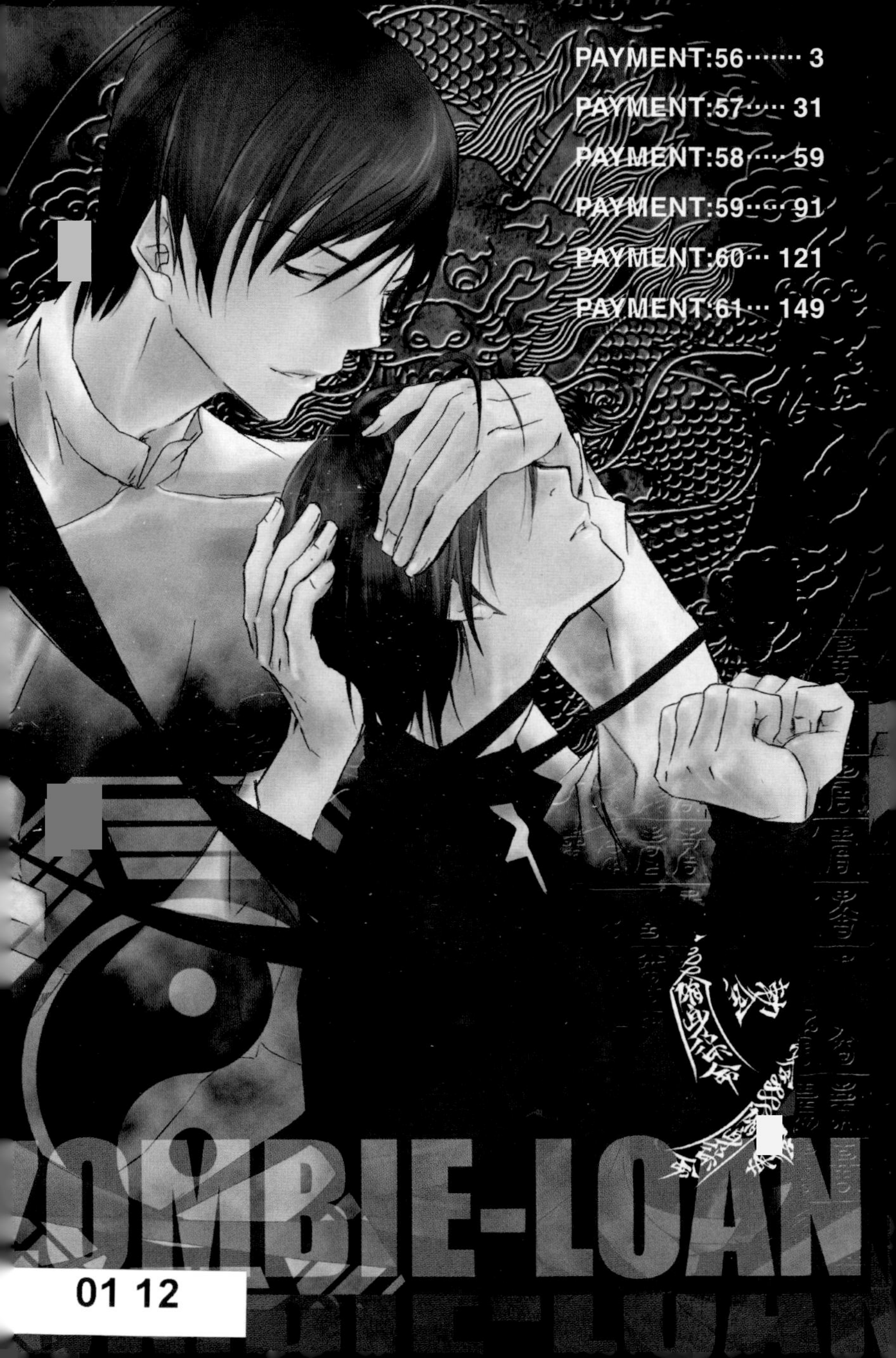

ZOMBIE-LOAN

PAYMENT:56

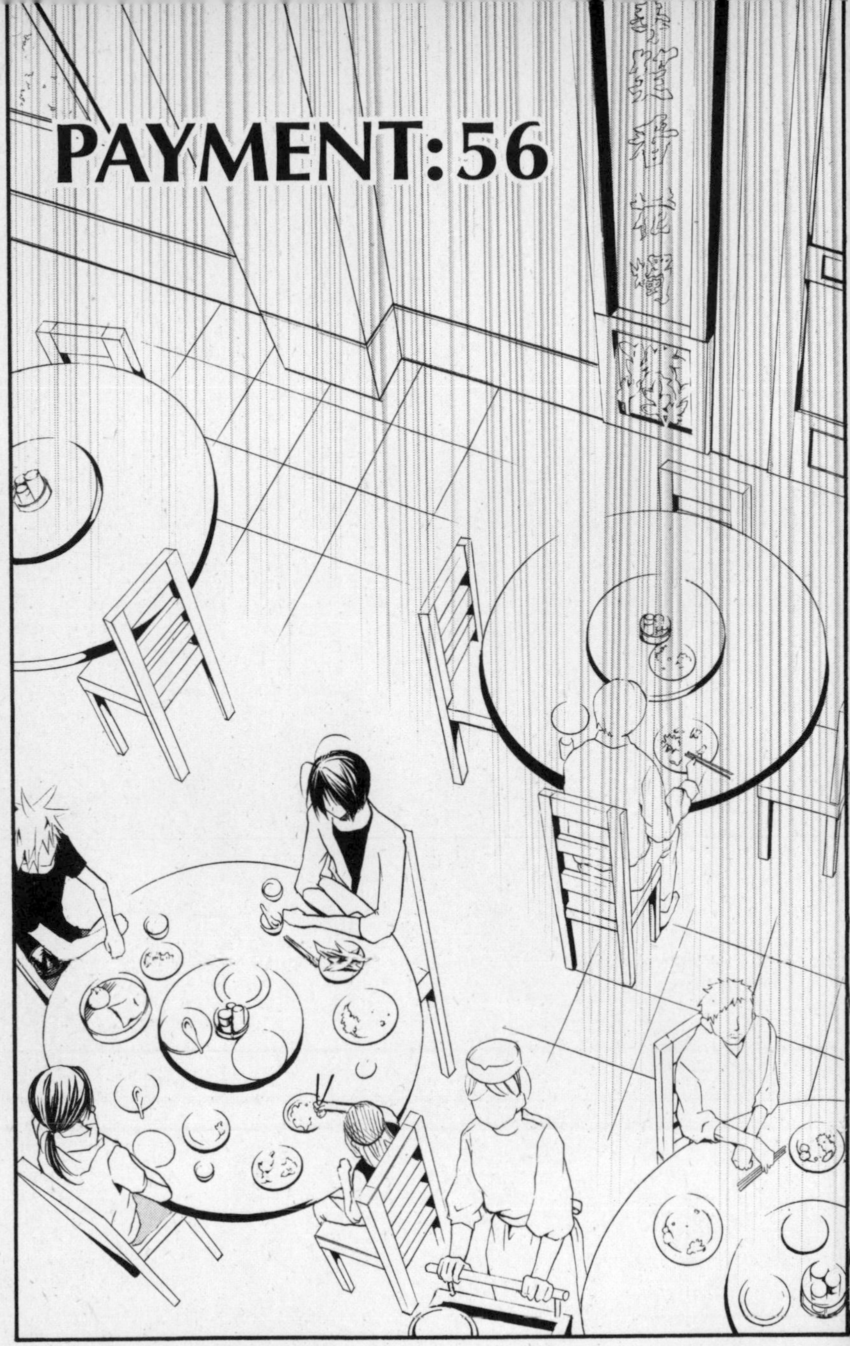

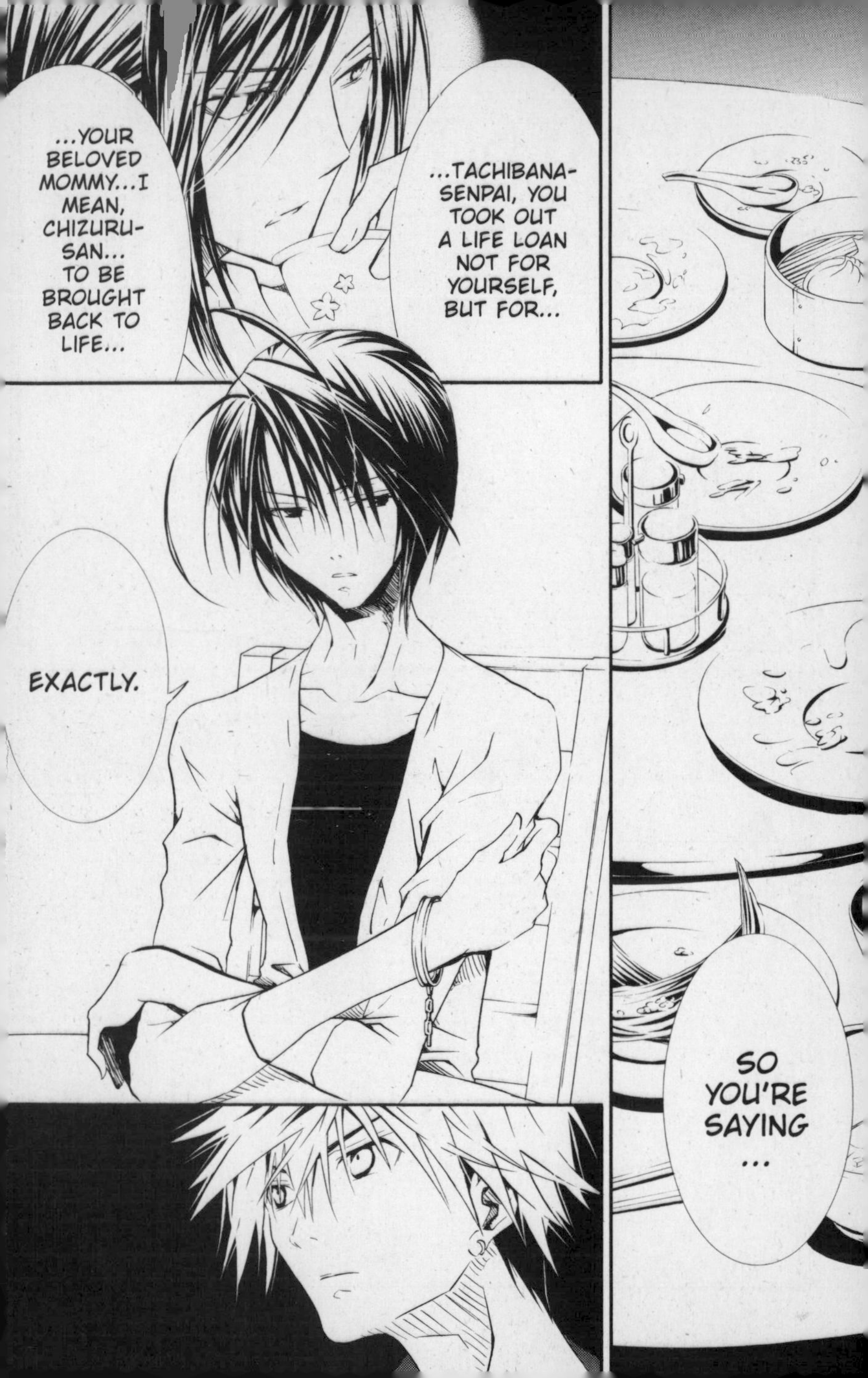
SO YOU'RE SAYING ...
...TACHIBANA-SENPAI, YOU TOOK OUT A LIFE LOAN NOT FOR YOURSELF, BUT FOR...
...YOUR BELOVED MOMMY...I MEAN, CHIZURU-SAN... TO BE BROUGHT BACK TO LIFE...
EXACTLY.

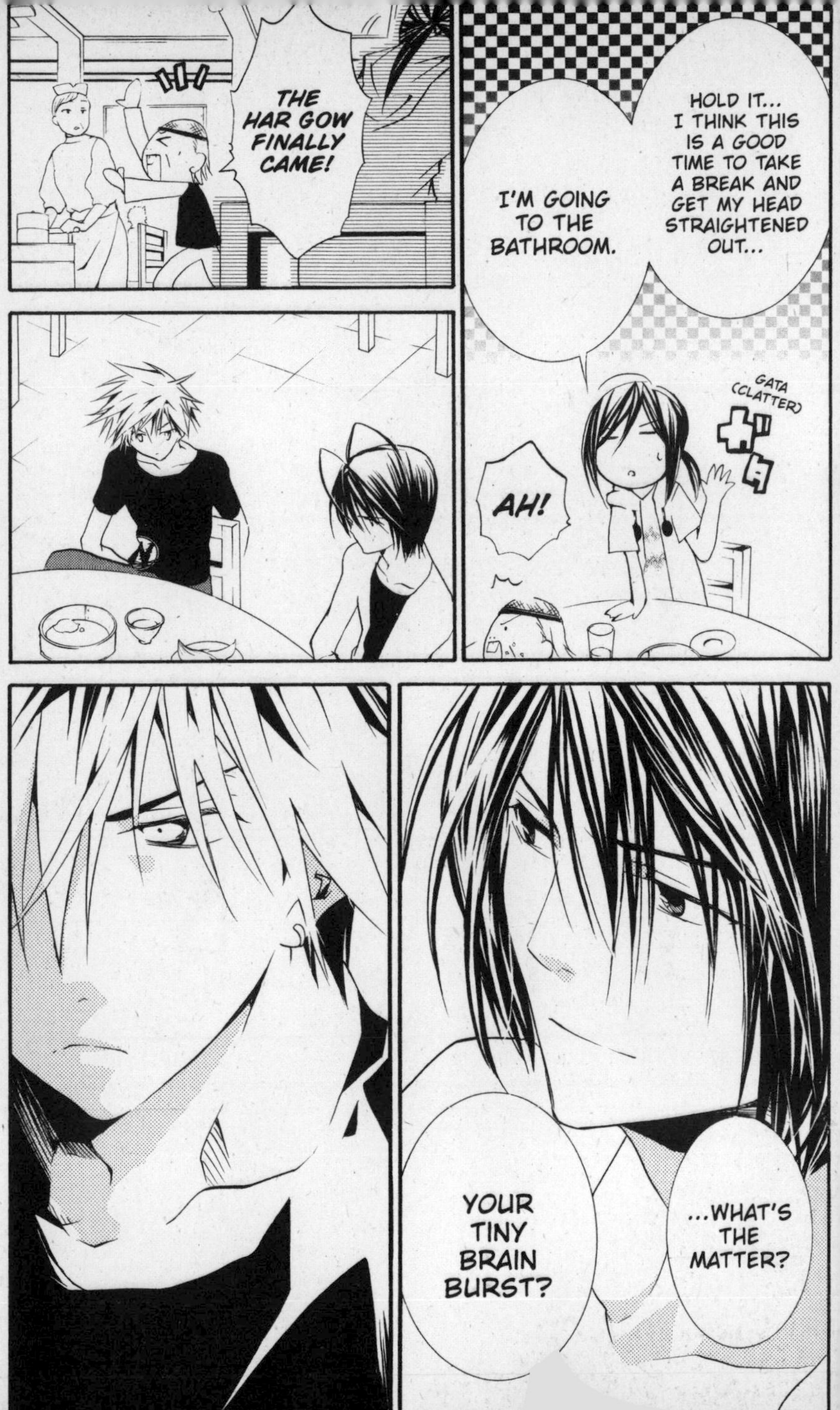
HOLD IT... I THINK THIS IS A GOOD TIME TO TAKE A BREAK AND GET MY HEAD STRAIGHTENED OUT...
I'M GOING TO THE BATHROOM.
GATA (CLATTER)
AH!
THE HAR GOW FINALLY CAME!
...WHAT'S THE MATTER?
YOUR TINY BRAIN BURST?

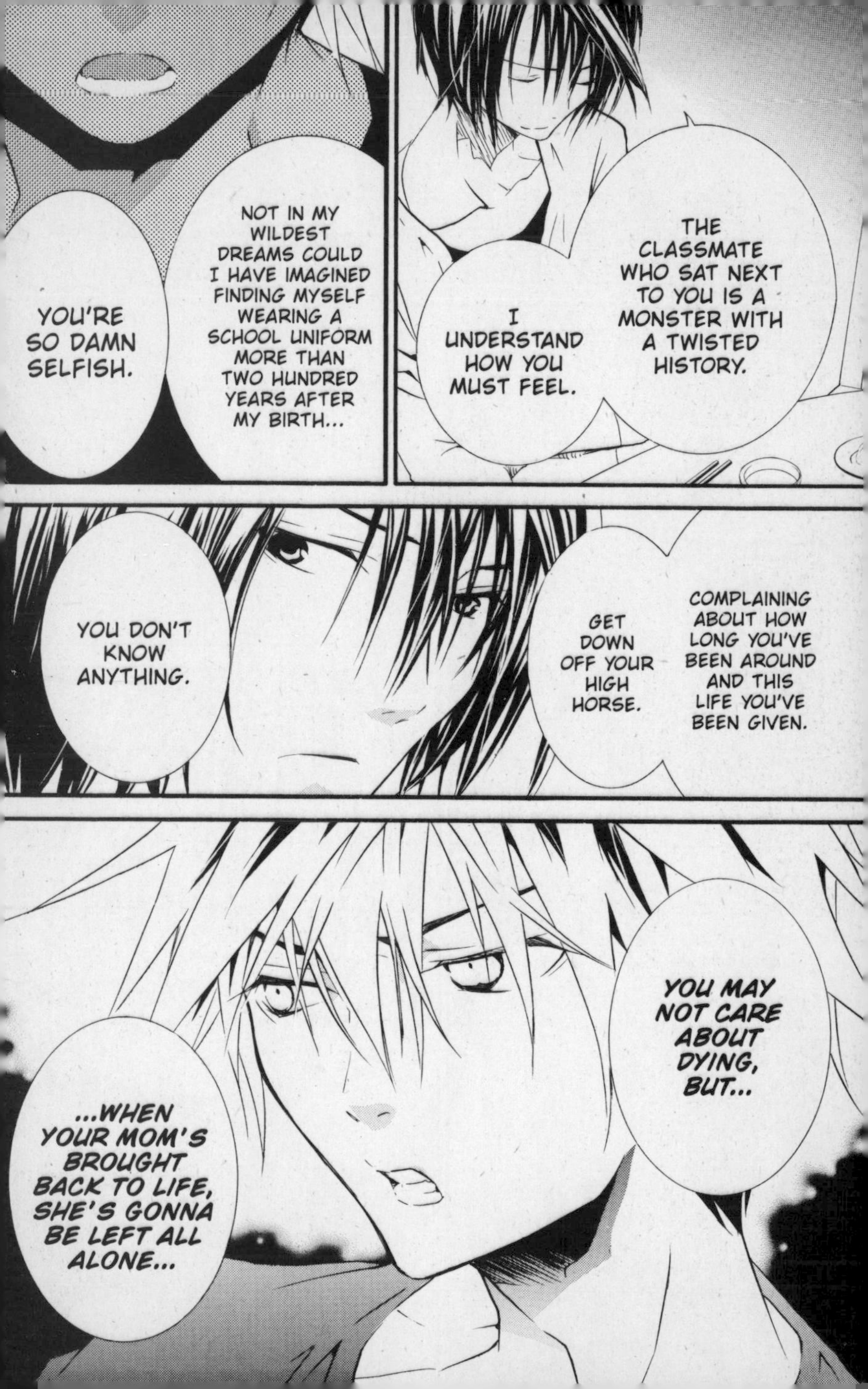
THE CLASSMATE WHO SAT NEXT TO YOU IS A MONSTER WITH A TWISTED HISTORY.
I UNDERSTAND HOW YOU MUST FEEL.
NOT IN MY WILDEST DREAMS COULD I HAVE IMAGINED FINDING MYSELF WEARING A SCHOOL UNIFORM MORE THAN TWO HUNDRED YEARS AFTER MY BIRTH...
YOU'RE SO DAMN SELFISH.
GET DOWN OFF YOUR HIGH HORSE.
COMPLAINING ABOUT HOW LONG YOU'VE BEEN AROUND AND THIS LIFE YOU'VE BEEN GIVEN.
YOU DON'T KNOW ANYTHING.
YOU MAY NOT CARE ABOUT DYING, BUT...
...WHEN YOUR MOM'S BROUGHT BACK TO LIFE, SHE'S GONNA BE LEFT ALL ALONE...

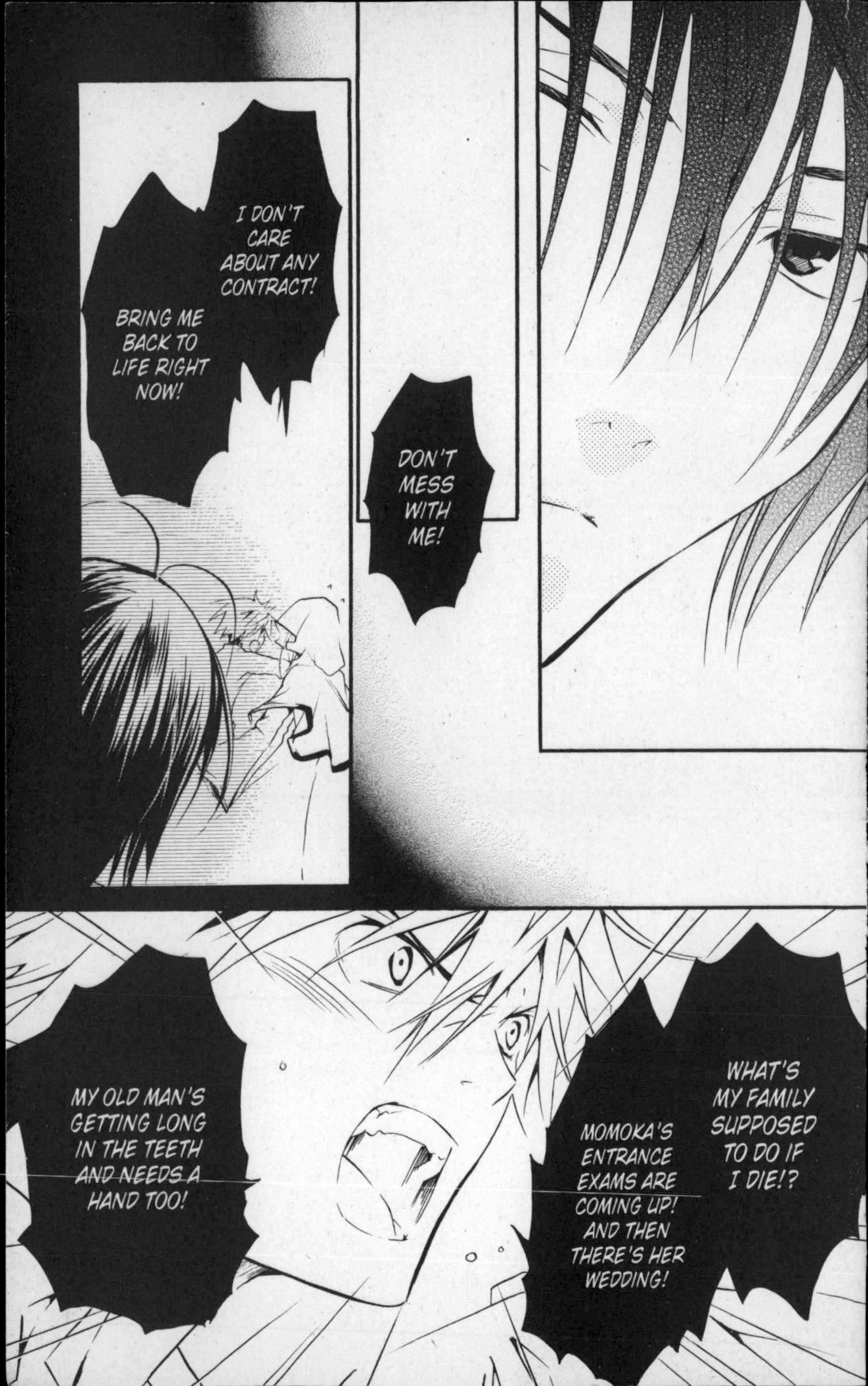
DON'T MESS WITH ME!
I DON'T CARE ABOUT ANY CONTRACT!
BRING ME BACK TO LIFE RIGHT NOW!
WHAT'S MY FAMILY SUPPOSED TO DO IF I DIE!?
MOMOKA'S ENTRANCE EXAMS ARE COMING UP! AND THEN THERE'S HER WEDDING!
MY OLD MAN'S GETTING LONG IN THE TEETH AND NEEDS A HAND TOO!

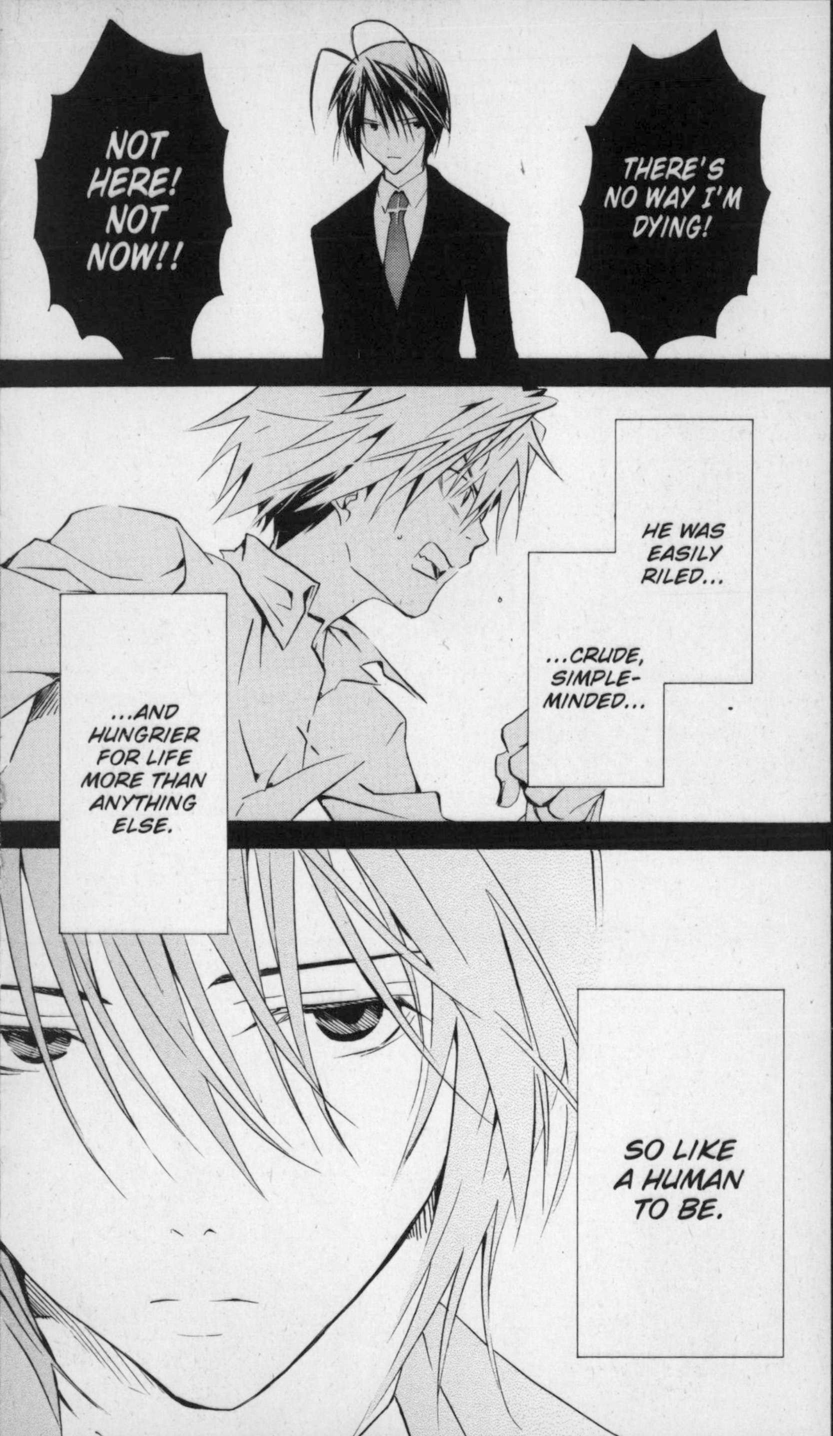
THERE'S NO WAY I'M DYING!
NOT HERE! NOT NOW!!
HE WAS EASILY RILED...
...CRUDE, SIMPLE-MINDED...
...AND HUNGRIER FOR LIFE MORE THAN ANYTHING ELSE.
SO LIKE A HUMAN TO BE.

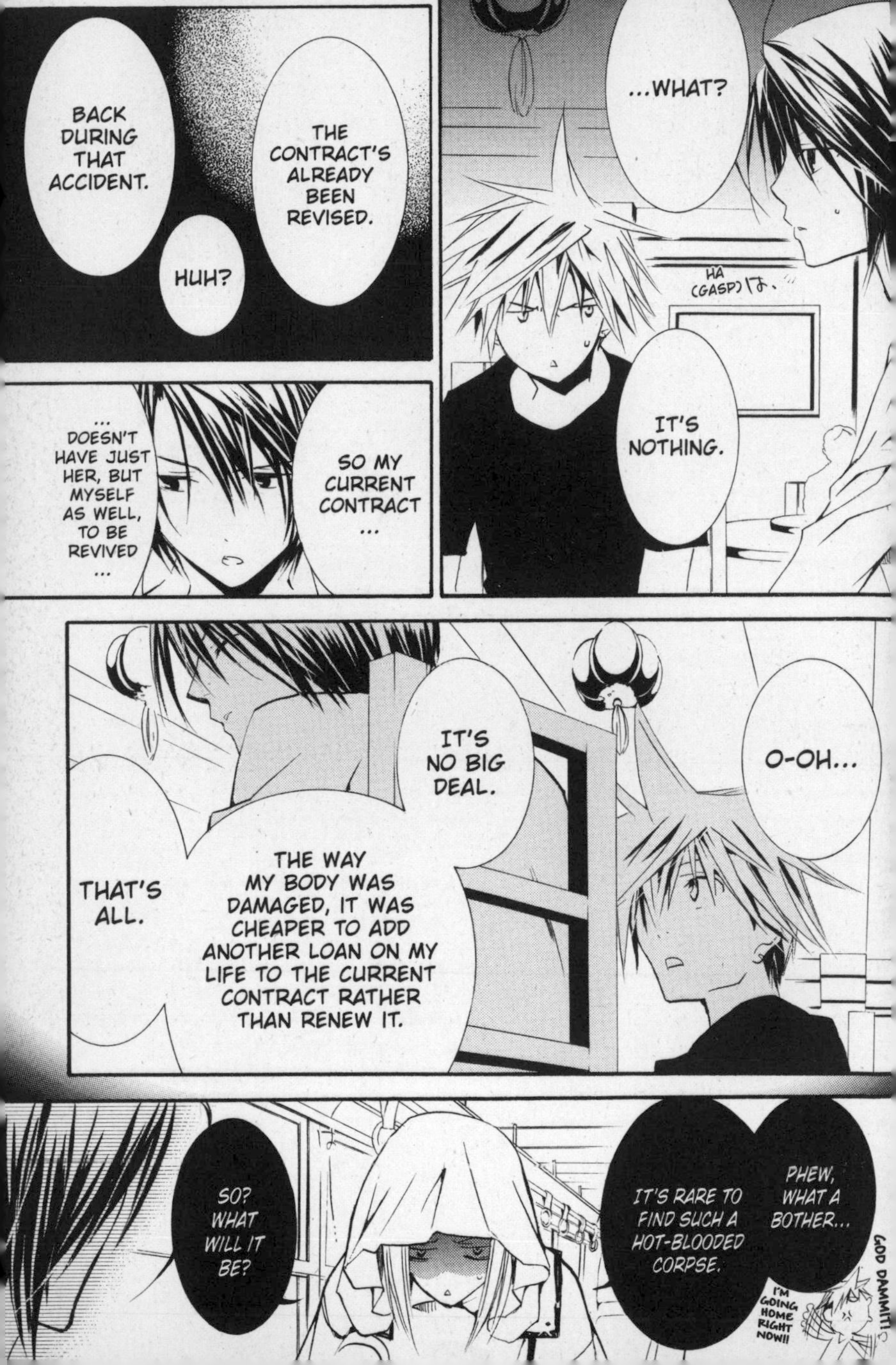
...WHAT?
HA (GASP) は。
IT'S NOTHING.
THE CONTRACT'S ALREADY BEEN REVISED.
BACK DURING THAT ACCIDENT.
HUH?
SO MY CURRENT CONTRACT ...
... DOESN'T HAVE JUST HER, BUT MYSELF AS WELL, TO BE REVIVED ...
O-OH...
IT'S NO BIG DEAL.
THE WAY MY BODY WAS DAMAGED, IT WAS CHEAPER TO ADD ANOTHER LOAN ON MY LIFE TO THE CURRENT CONTRACT RATHER THAN RENEW IT.
THAT'S ALL.
PHEW, WHAT A BOTHER...
IT'S RARE TO FIND SUCH A HOT-BLOODED CORPSE.
GOD DAMMIT!!
I'M GOING HOME RIGHT NOW!!
SO? WHAT WILL IT BE?

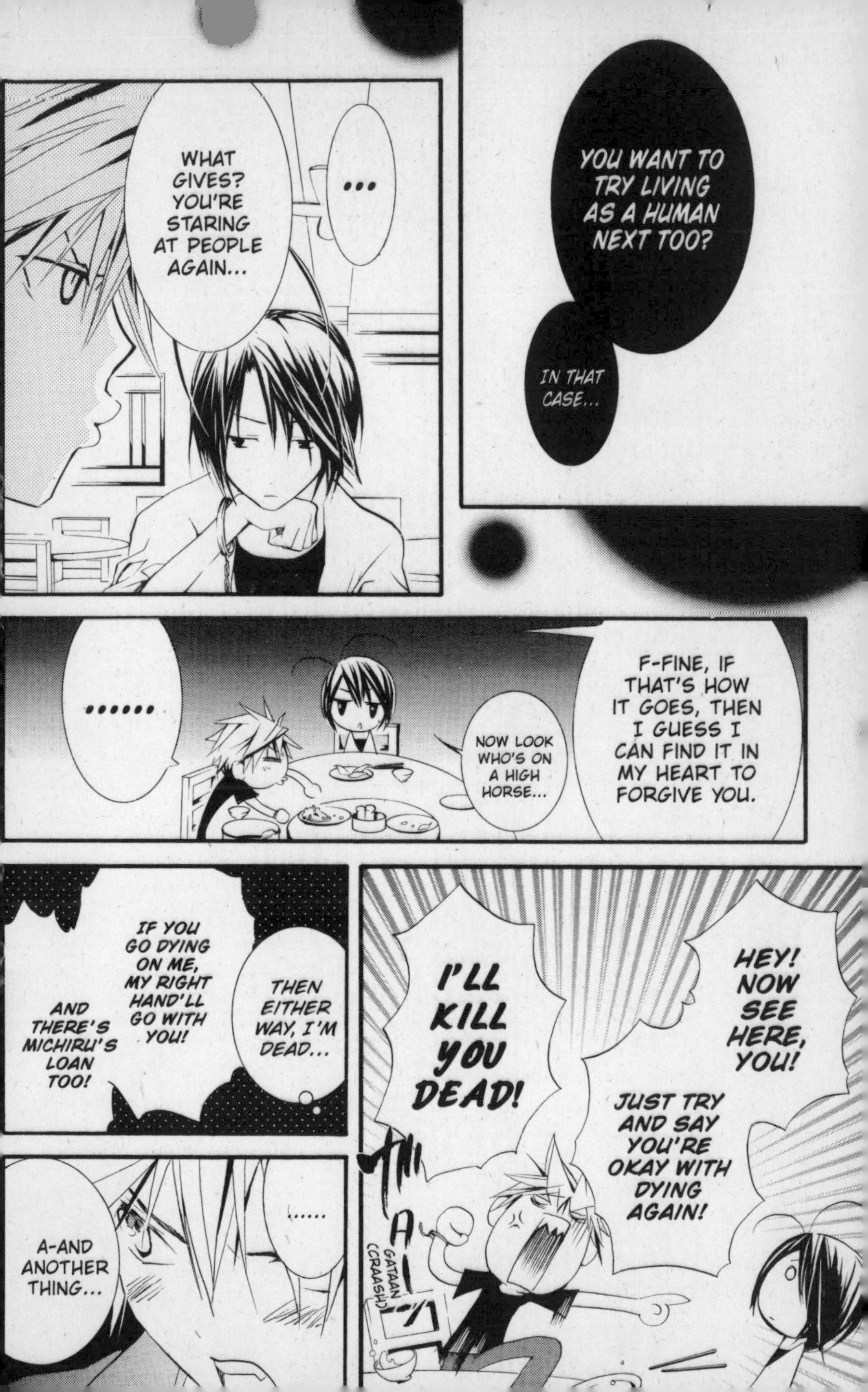
YOU WANT TO TRY LIVING AS A HUMAN NEXT TOO?
IN THAT CASE...
...
WHAT GIVES? YOU'RE STARING AT PEOPLE AGAIN...
F-FINE, IF THAT'S HOW IT GOES, THEN I GUESS I CAN FIND IT IN MY HEART TO FORGIVE YOU.
NOW LOOK WHO'S ON A HIGH HORSE...
......
HEY! NOW SEE HERE, YOU!
I'LL KILL YOU DEAD!
JUST TRY AND SAY YOU'RE OKAY WITH DYING AGAIN!
GATAAN (CRAASH)
THEN EITHER WAY, I'M DEAD...
IF YOU GO DYING ON ME, MY RIGHT HAND'LL GO WITH YOU!
AND THERE'S MICHIRU'S LOAN TOO!
......
A-AND ANOTHER THING...

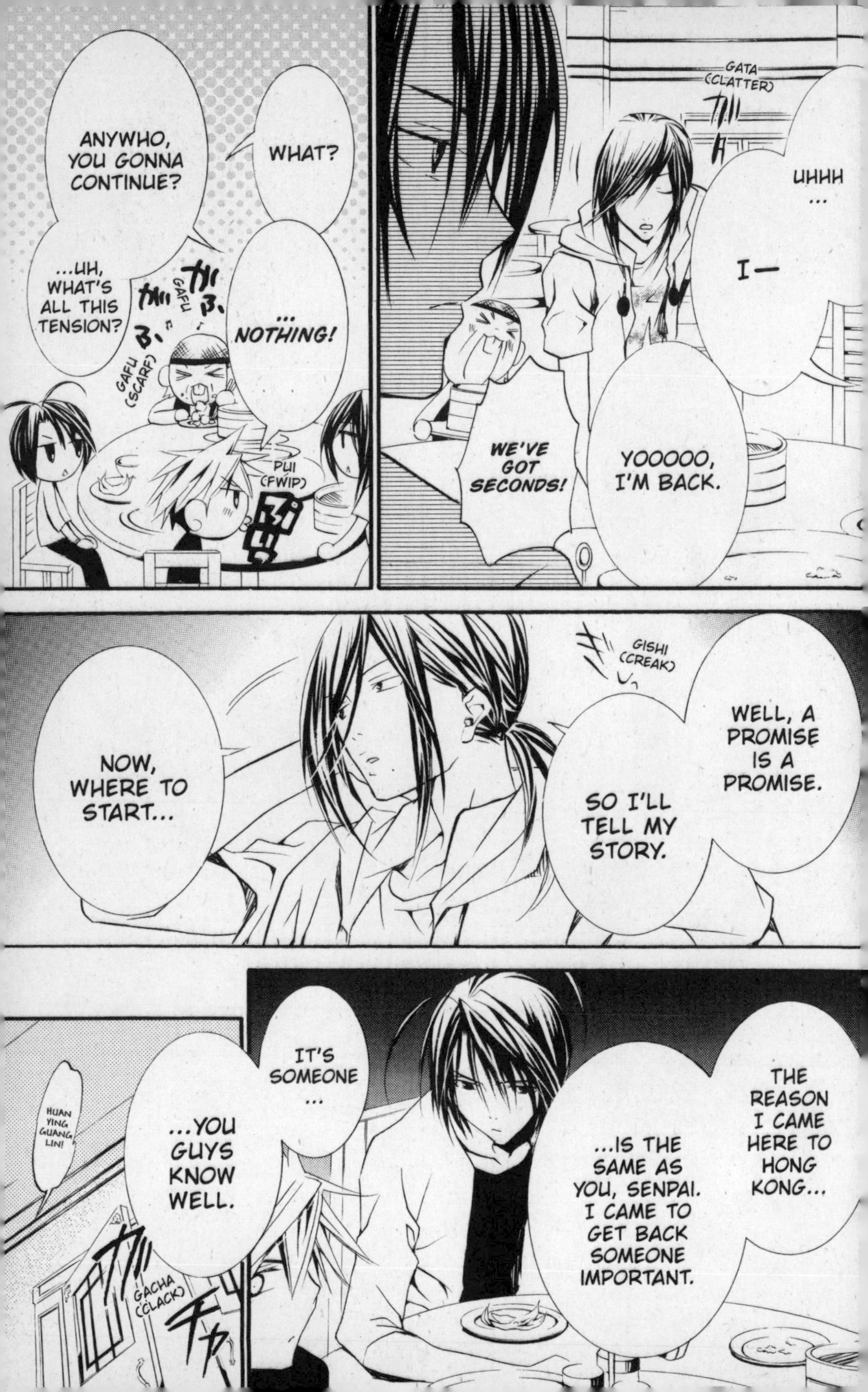
GATA (CLATTER)
UHHH ... I—
YOOOOO, I'M BACK.
WE'VE GOT SECONDS!
WHAT?
ANYWHO, YOU GONNA CONTINUE?
... NOTHING!
GAFU
...UH, WHAT'S ALL THIS TENSION?
GAFU (SCARF)
PUI (FWIP)
GISHI (CREAK)
WELL, A PROMISE IS A PROMISE.
SO I'LL TELL MY STORY.
NOW, WHERE TO START...
THE REASON I CAME HERE TO HONG KONG...
...IS THE SAME AS YOU, SENPAI. I CAME TO GET BACK SOMEONE IMPORTANT.
IT'S SOMEONE ...
...YOU GUYS KNOW WELL.
HUAN YING GUANG LIN!
GACHA (CLACK)

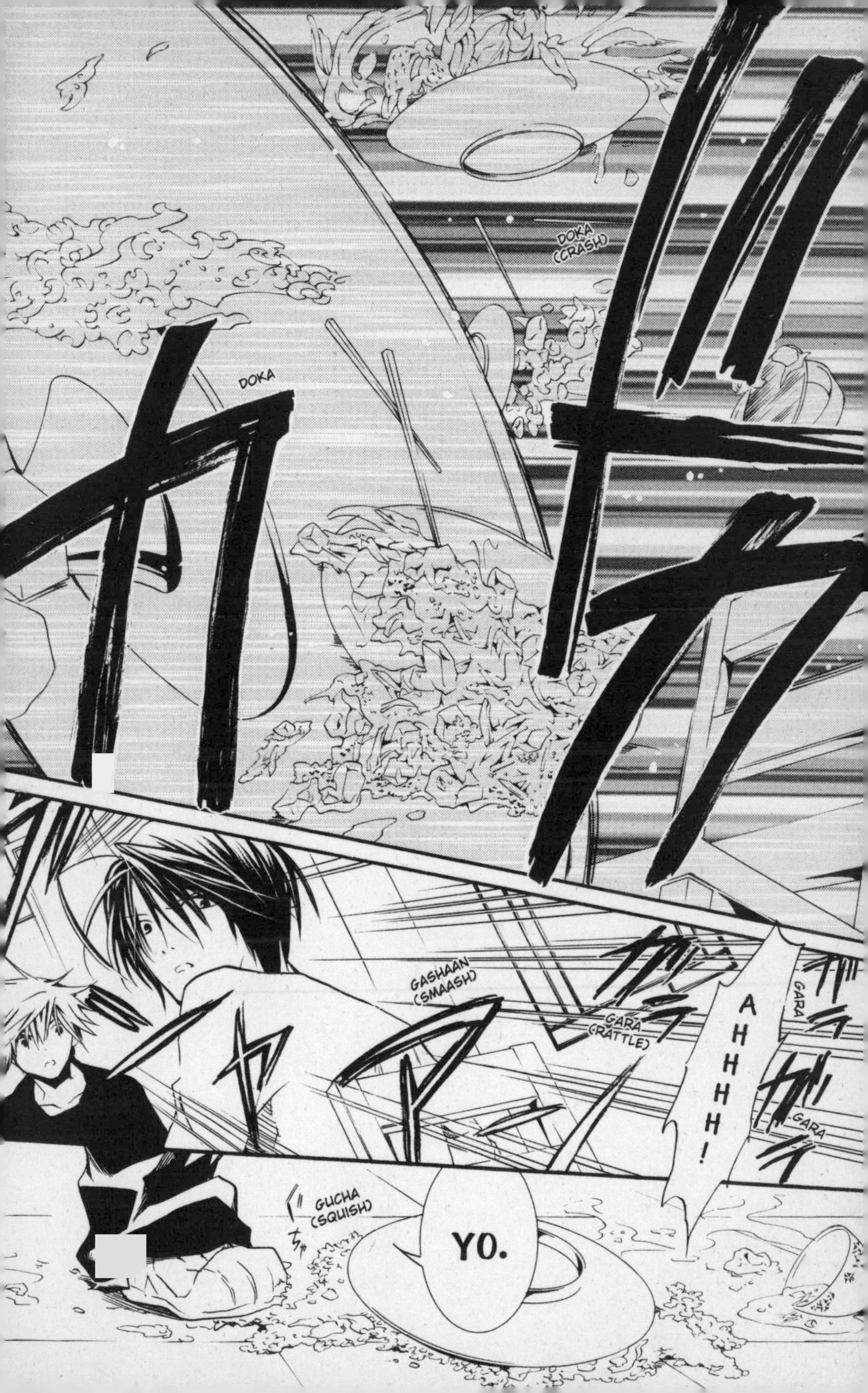
DOKA (CRASH)
DOKA
GARA
AHHHH!
GARA (RATTLE)
GASHAAN (SMAASH)
GARA
YO.
GUCHA (SQUISH)

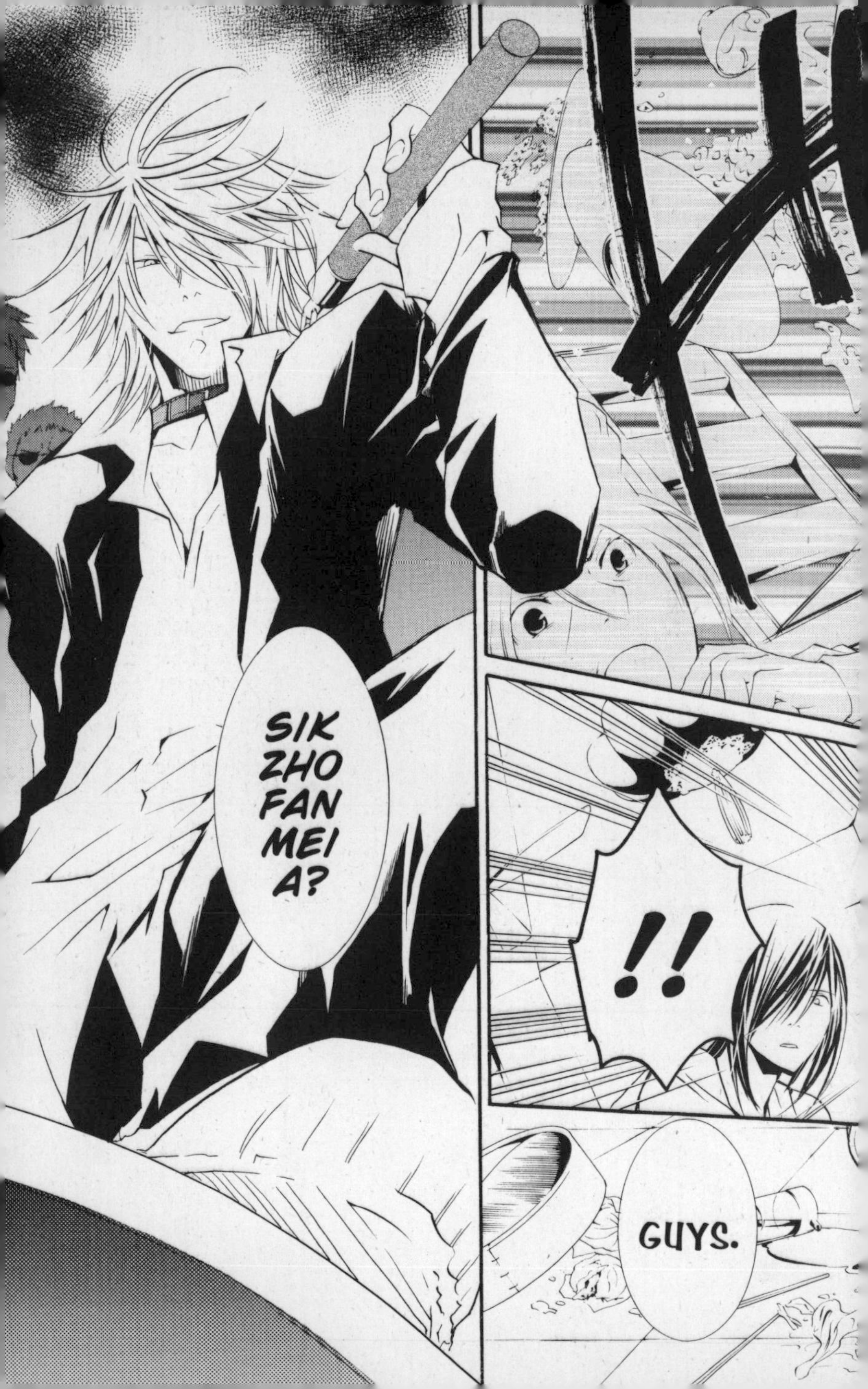
!!
GUYS.
SIK ZHO FAN MEI A?

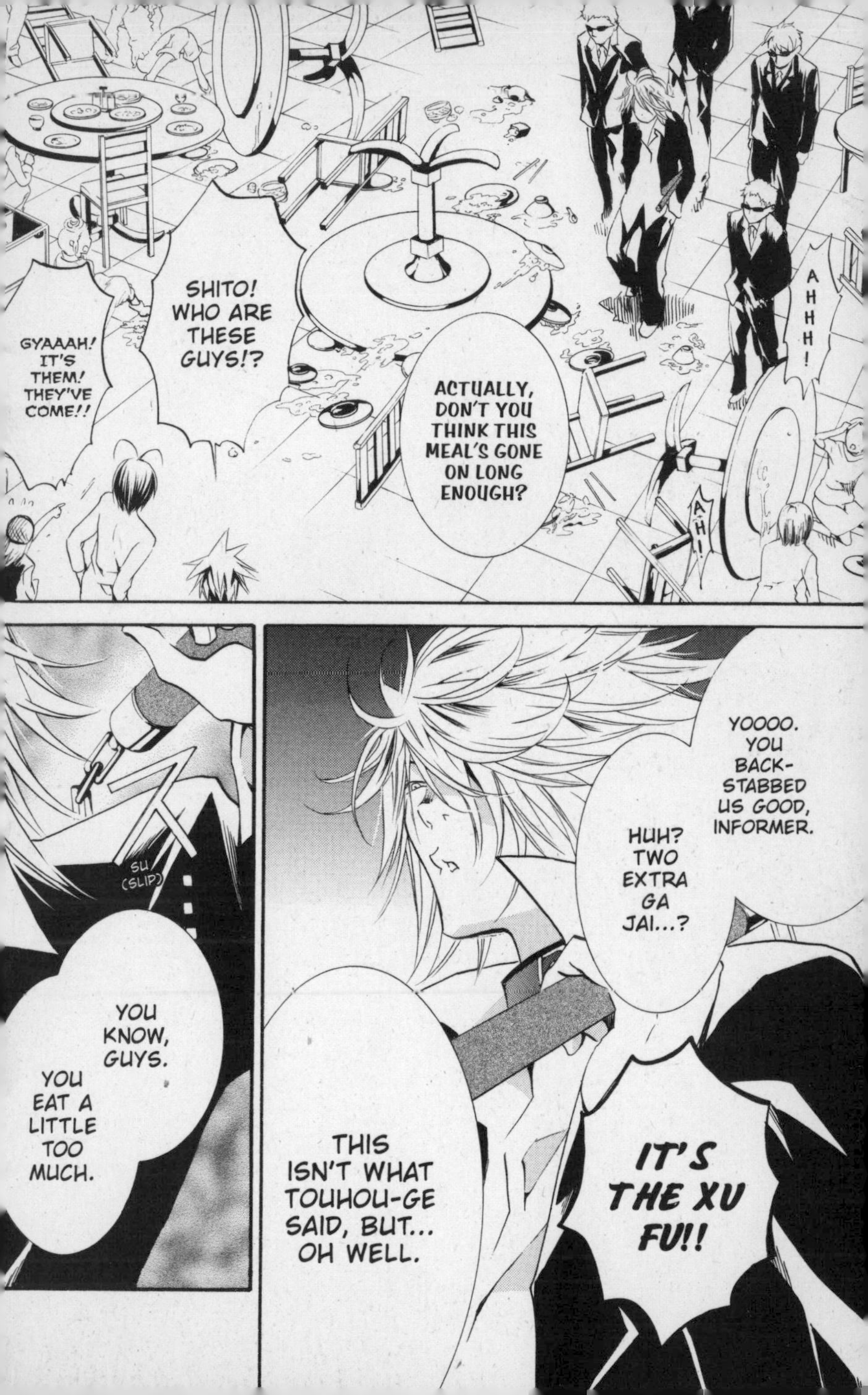

AHHHH!
SHITO! WHO ARE THESE GUYS!?
GYAAAH! IT'S THEM! THEY'VE COME!!
ACTUALLY, DON'T YOU THINK THIS MEAL'S GONE ON LONG ENOUGH?
AHI!
YOOOO. YOU BACK-STABBED US GOOD, INFORMER.
HUH? TWO EXTRA GA JAI...?
IT'S THE XU FU!!
THIS ISN'T WHAT TOUHOU-GE SAID, BUT... OH WELL.
SU (SLIP)
YOU KNOW, GUYS.
YOU EAT A LITTLE TOO MUCH.

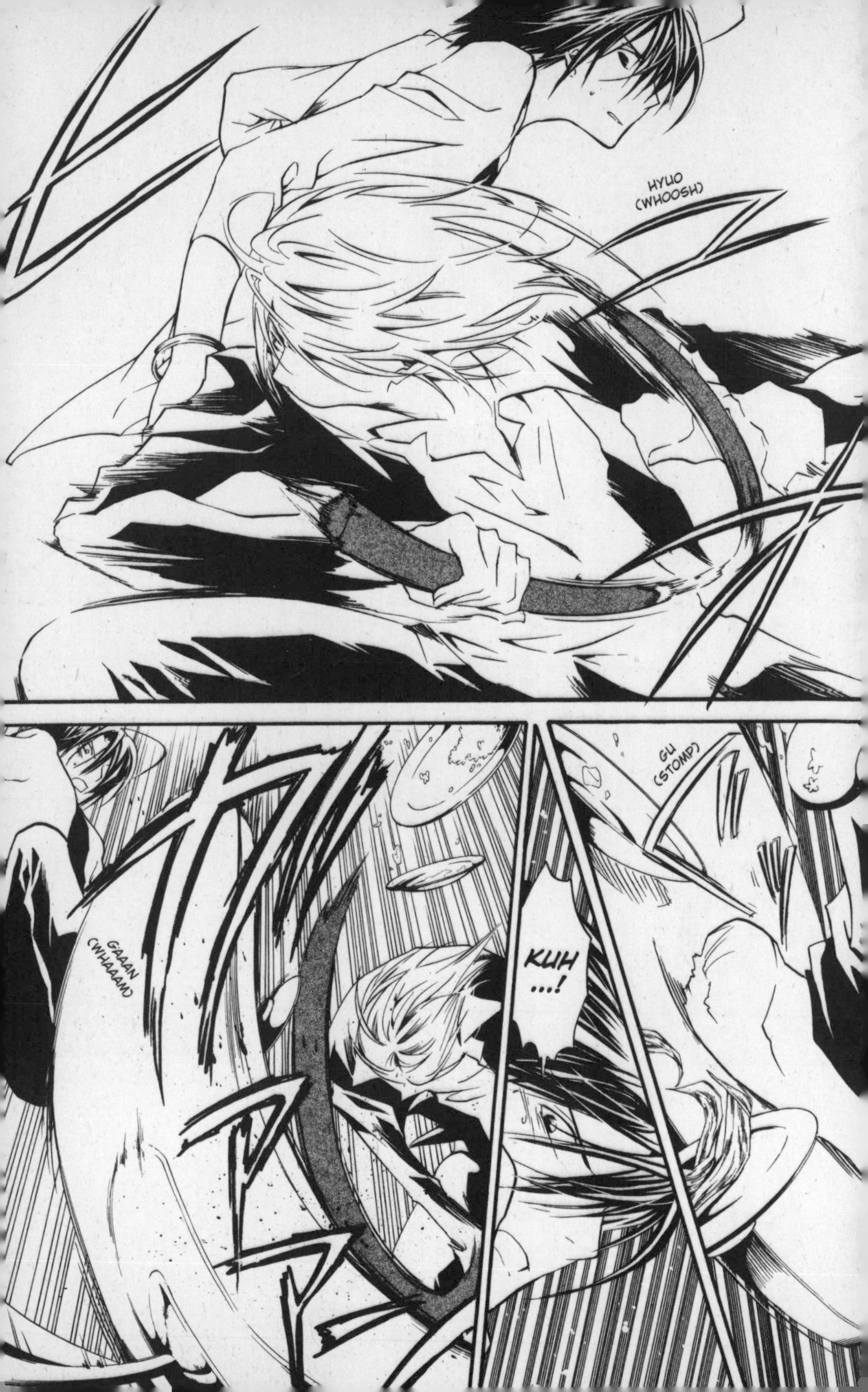
HYUO
(WHOOSH)
GU
(STOMP)
KUH
...!
GAAAN
(WHAAAM)

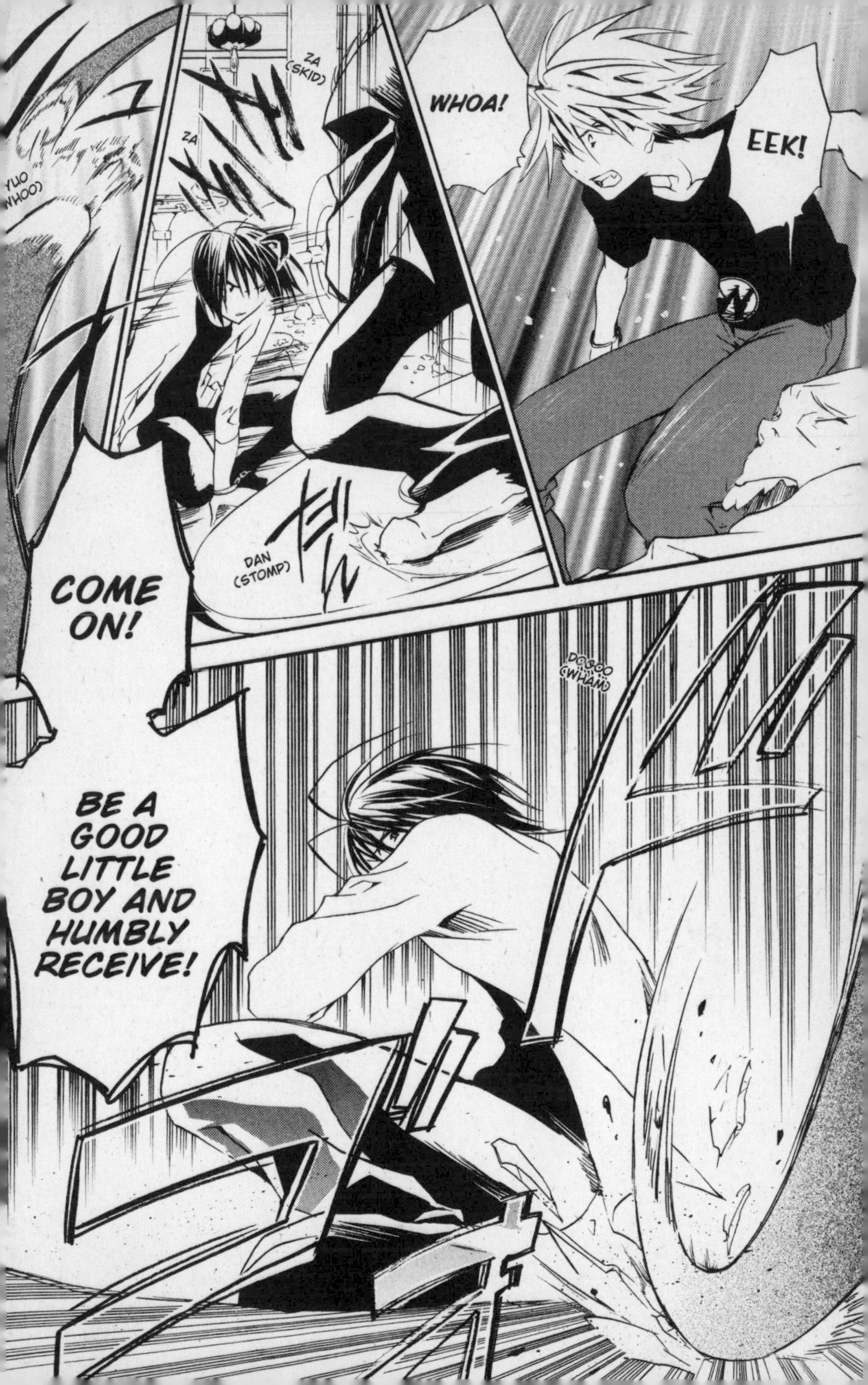
EEK!
WHOA!
ZA (SKID)
ZA
DAN (STOMP)
YUO (WHOO)
COME ON!
DOGOO (WHAM)
BE A GOOD LITTLE BOY AND HUMBLY RECEIVE!

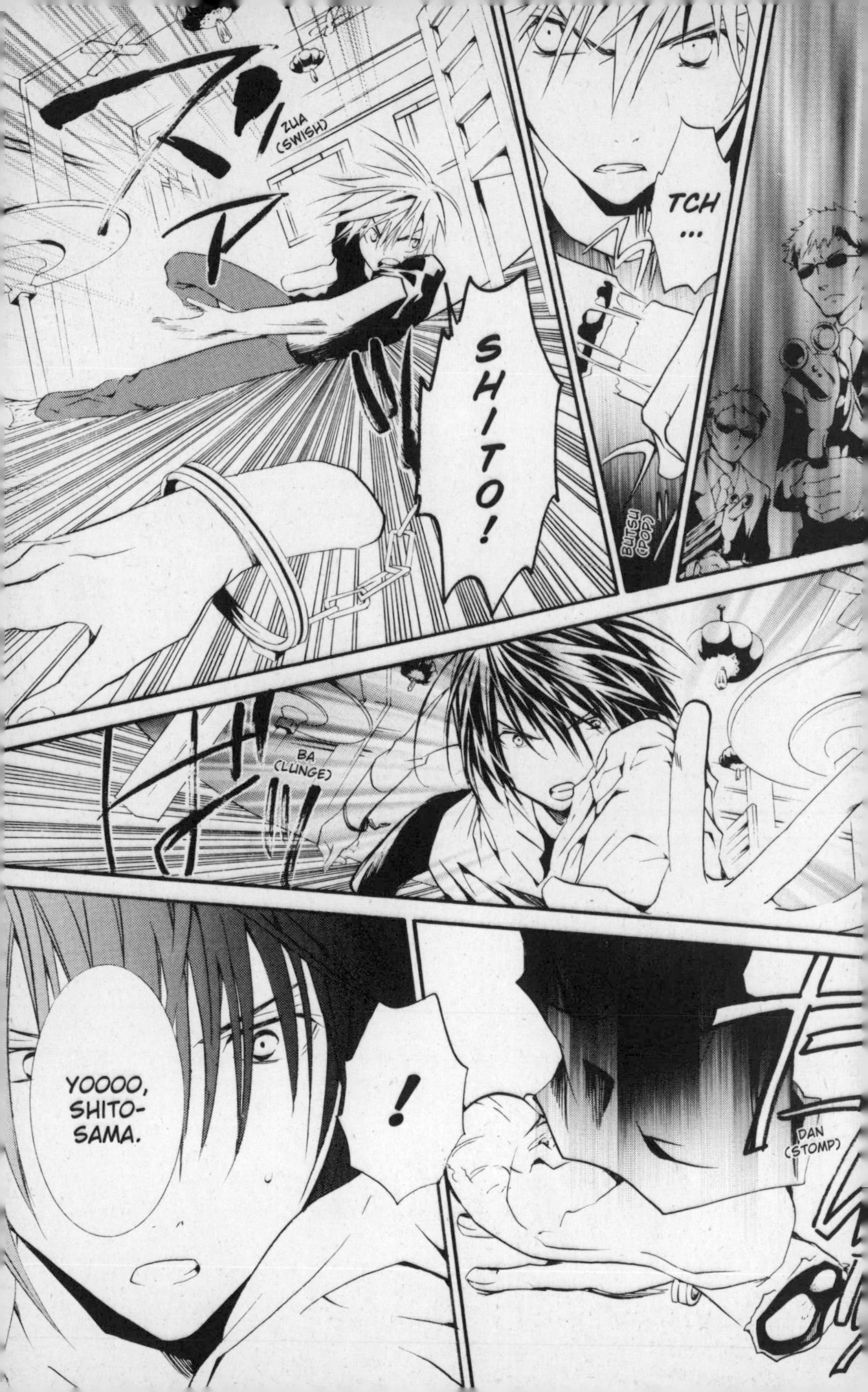
TCH ...
BUTSU (POP)
ZUA (SWISH)
SHITO!
BA (LUNGE)
DAN (STOMP)
!
YOOOO, SHITO-SAMA.

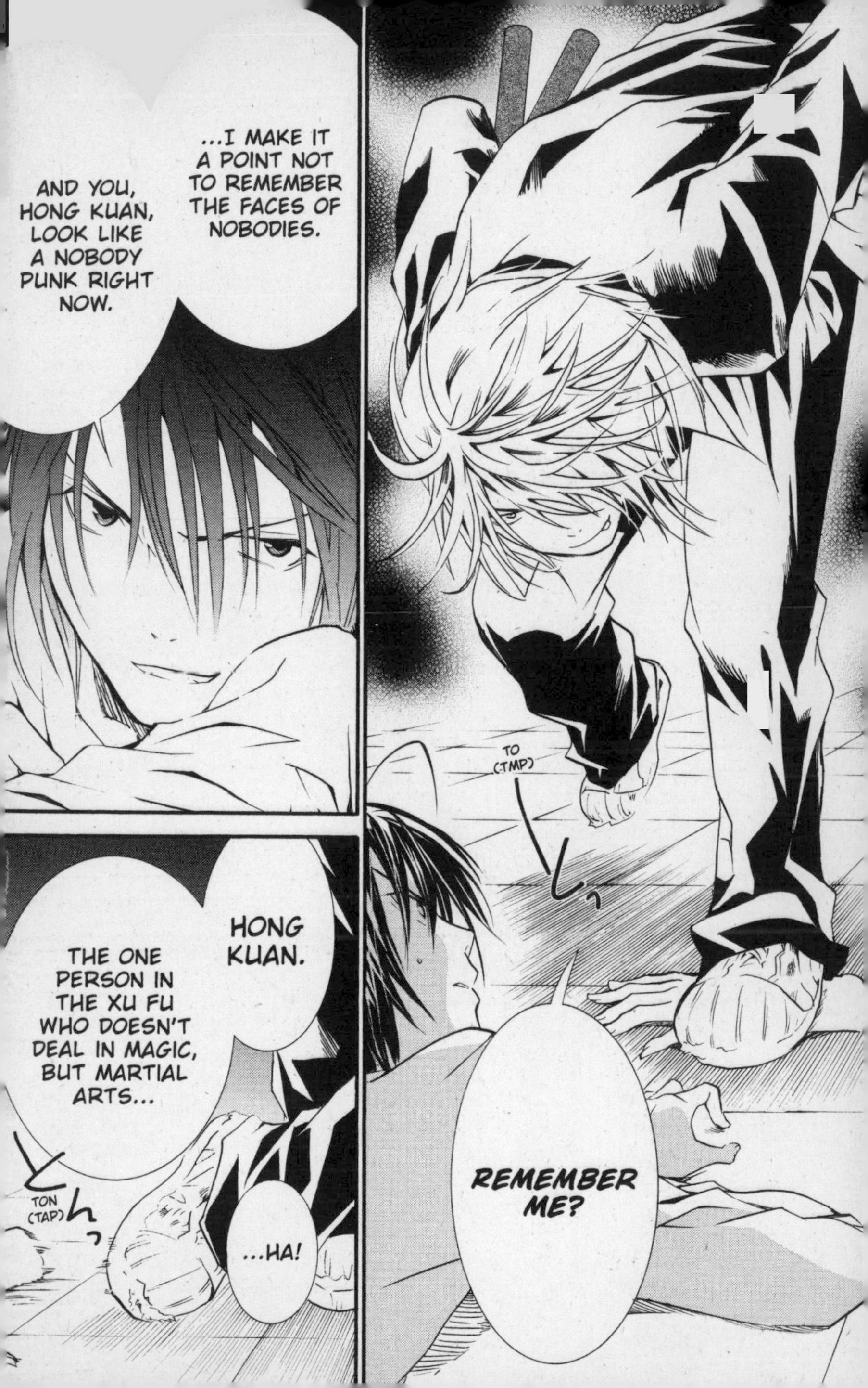

TO (TMP)
REMEMBER ME?
...I MAKE IT A POINT NOT TO REMEMBER THE FACES OF NOBODIES.
AND YOU, HONG KUAN, LOOK LIKE A NOBODY PUNK RIGHT NOW.
HONG KUAN.
THE ONE PERSON IN THE XU FU WHO DOESN'T DEAL IN MAGIC, BUT MARTIAL ARTS...
...HA!
TON (TAP)

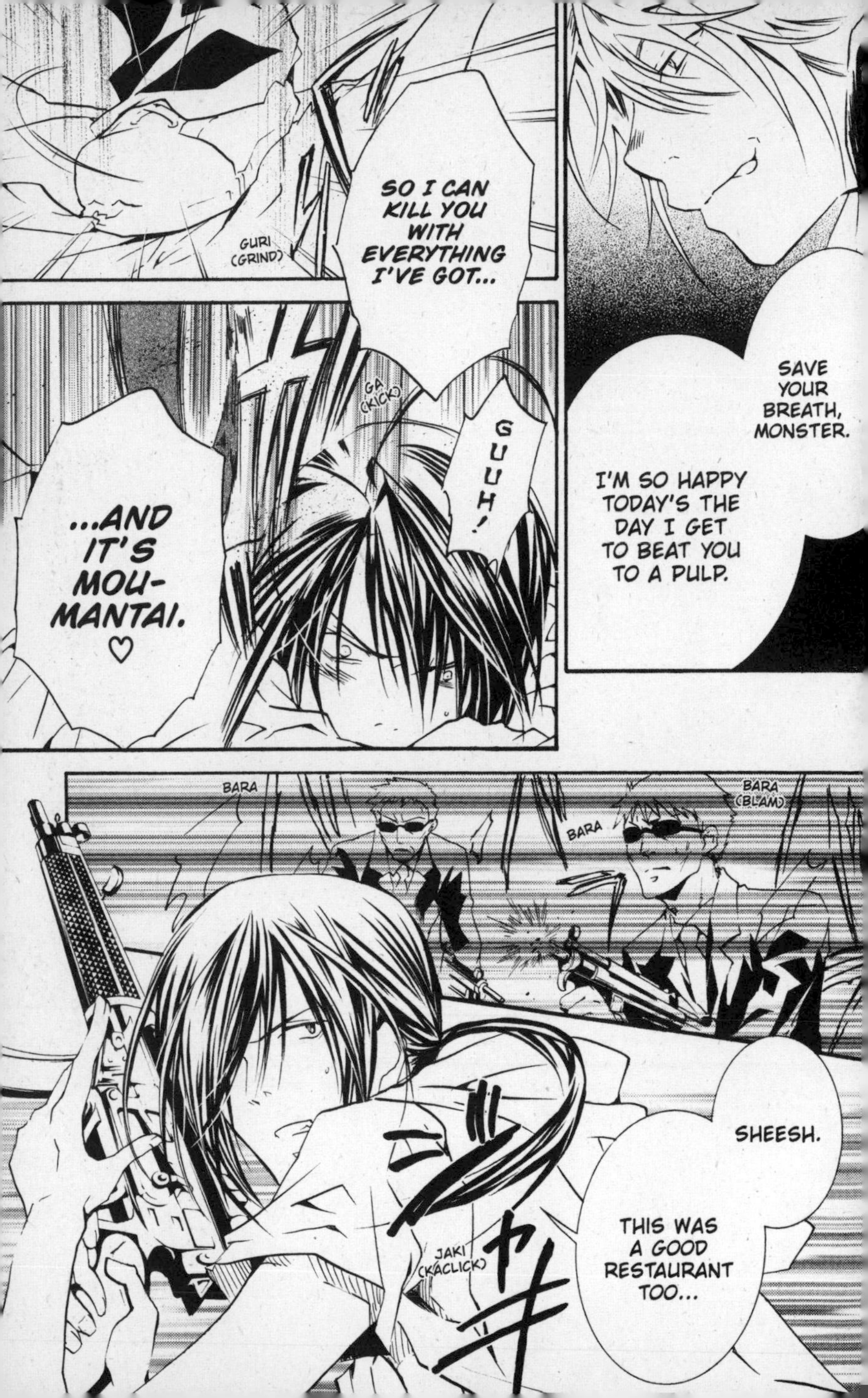
SAVE YOUR BREATH, MONSTER.
I'M SO HAPPY TODAY'S THE DAY I GET TO BEAT YOU TO A PULP.
SO I CAN KILL YOU WITH EVERYTHING I'VE GOT...
GURI (GRIND)
GA (KICK)
GUUH!
...AND IT'S MOU-MANTAI. ♡
BARA (BLAM)
BARA
BARA
SHEESH.
THIS WAS A GOOD RESTAURANT TOO...
JAKI (KACLICK)

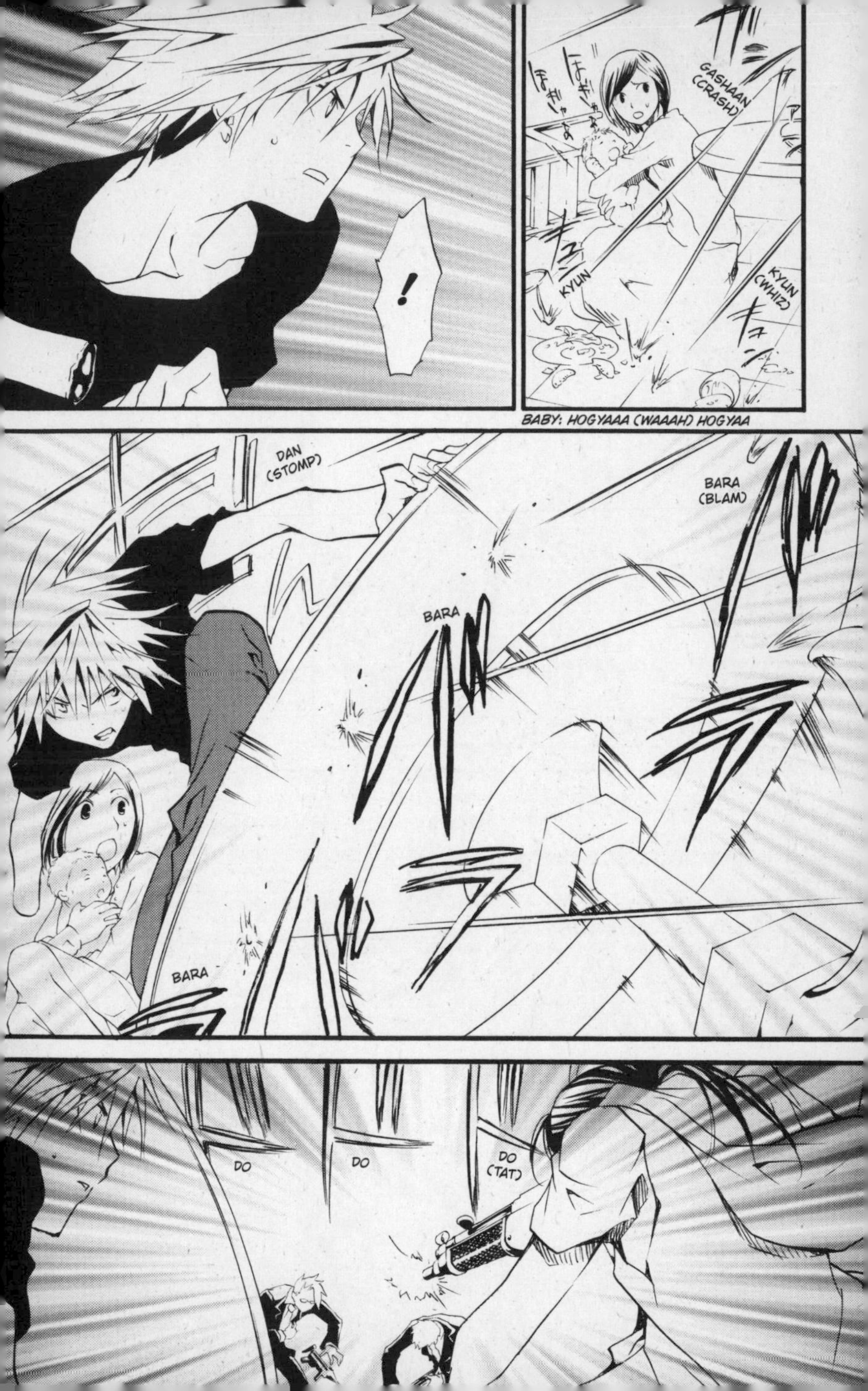
GASHAAN (CRASH)
KYUN (WHIZ)
KYUN
BABY: HOGYAAA (WAAAH) HOGYAA
!
BARA (BLAM)
DAN (STOMP)
BARA
BARA
DO (TAT)
DO
DO

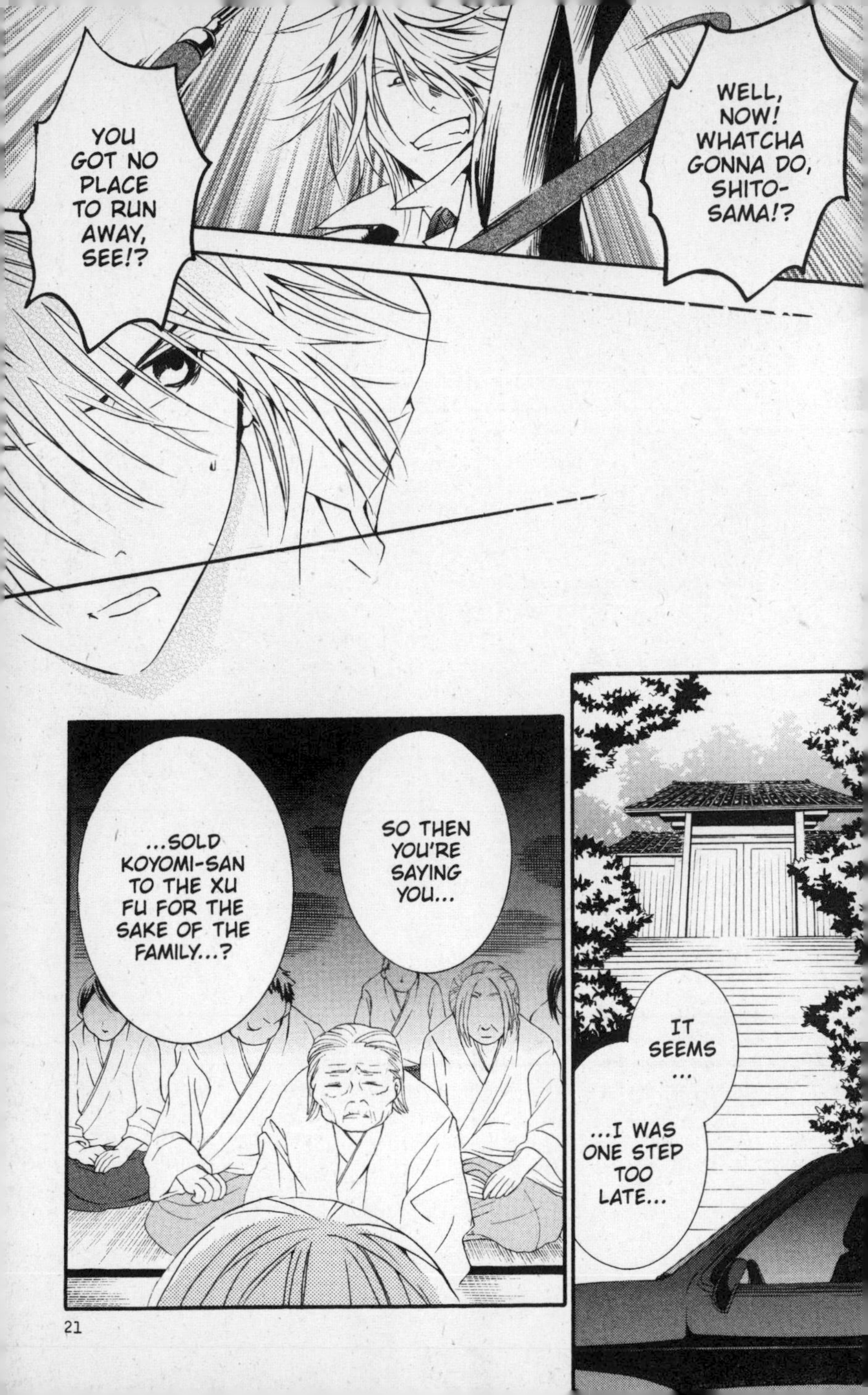
WELL, NOW! WHATCHA GONNA DO, SHITO-SAMA!?
YOU GOT NO PLACE TO RUN AWAY, SEE!?
IT SEEMS...
...I WAS ONE STEP TOO LATE...
SO THEN YOU'RE SAYING YOU...
...SOLD KOYOMI-SAN TO THE XU FU FOR THE SAKE OF THE FAMILY...?

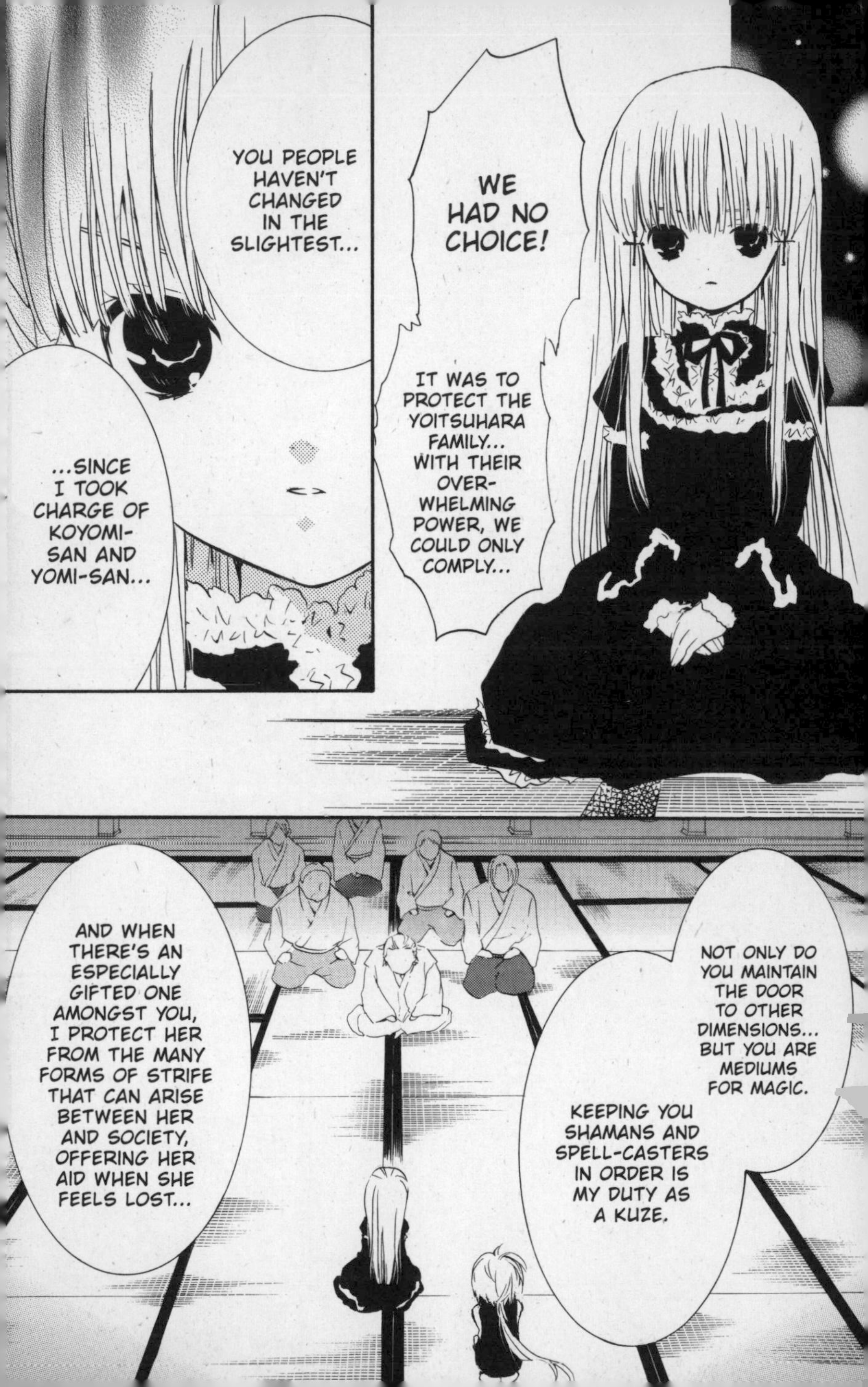
WE HAD NO CHOICE!
IT WAS TO PROTECT THE YOITSUHARA FAMILY... WITH THEIR OVER-WHELMING POWER, WE COULD ONLY COMPLY...
YOU PEOPLE HAVEN'T CHANGED IN THE SLIGHTEST...
...SINCE I TOOK CHARGE OF KOYOMI-SAN AND YOMI-SAN...
NOT ONLY DO YOU MAINTAIN THE DOOR TO OTHER DIMENSIONS... BUT YOU ARE MEDIUMS FOR MAGIC.
KEEPING YOU SHAMANS AND SPELL-CASTERS IN ORDER IS MY DUTY AS A KUZE.
AND WHEN THERE'S AN ESPECIALLY GIFTED ONE AMONGST YOU, I PROTECT HER FROM THE MANY FORMS OF STRIFE THAT CAN ARISE BETWEEN HER AND SOCIETY, OFFERING HER AID WHEN SHE FEELS LOST...

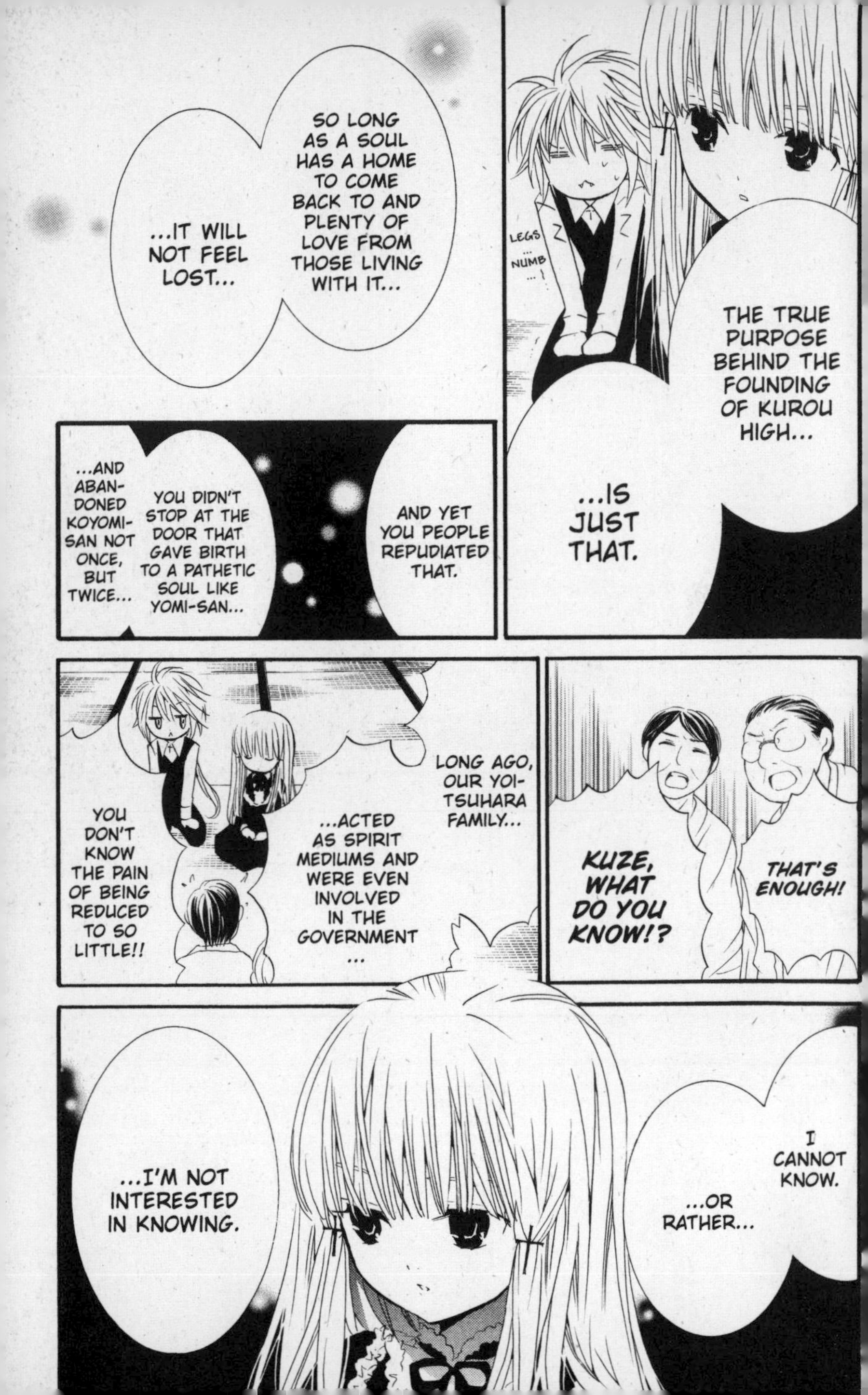
LEGS ... NUMB ... !
THE TRUE PURPOSE BEHIND THE FOUNDING OF KUROU HIGH...
...IS JUST THAT.
SO LONG AS A SOUL HAS A HOME TO COME BACK TO AND PLENTY OF LOVE FROM THOSE LIVING WITH IT...
...IT WILL NOT FEEL LOST...
AND YET YOU PEOPLE REPUDIATED THAT.
YOU DIDN'T STOP AT THE DOOR THAT GAVE BIRTH TO A PATHETIC SOUL LIKE YOMI-SAN...
...AND ABAN-DONED KOYOMI-SAN NOT ONCE, BUT TWICE...
THAT'S ENOUGH!
KUZE, WHAT DO YOU KNOW!?
LONG AGO, OUR YOI-TSUHARA FAMILY...
...ACTED AS SPIRIT MEDIUMS AND WERE EVEN INVOLVED IN THE GOVERNMENT ...
YOU DON'T KNOW THE PAIN OF BEING REDUCED TO SO LITTLE!!
I CANNOT KNOW.
...OR RATHER...
...I'M NOT INTERESTED IN KNOWING.

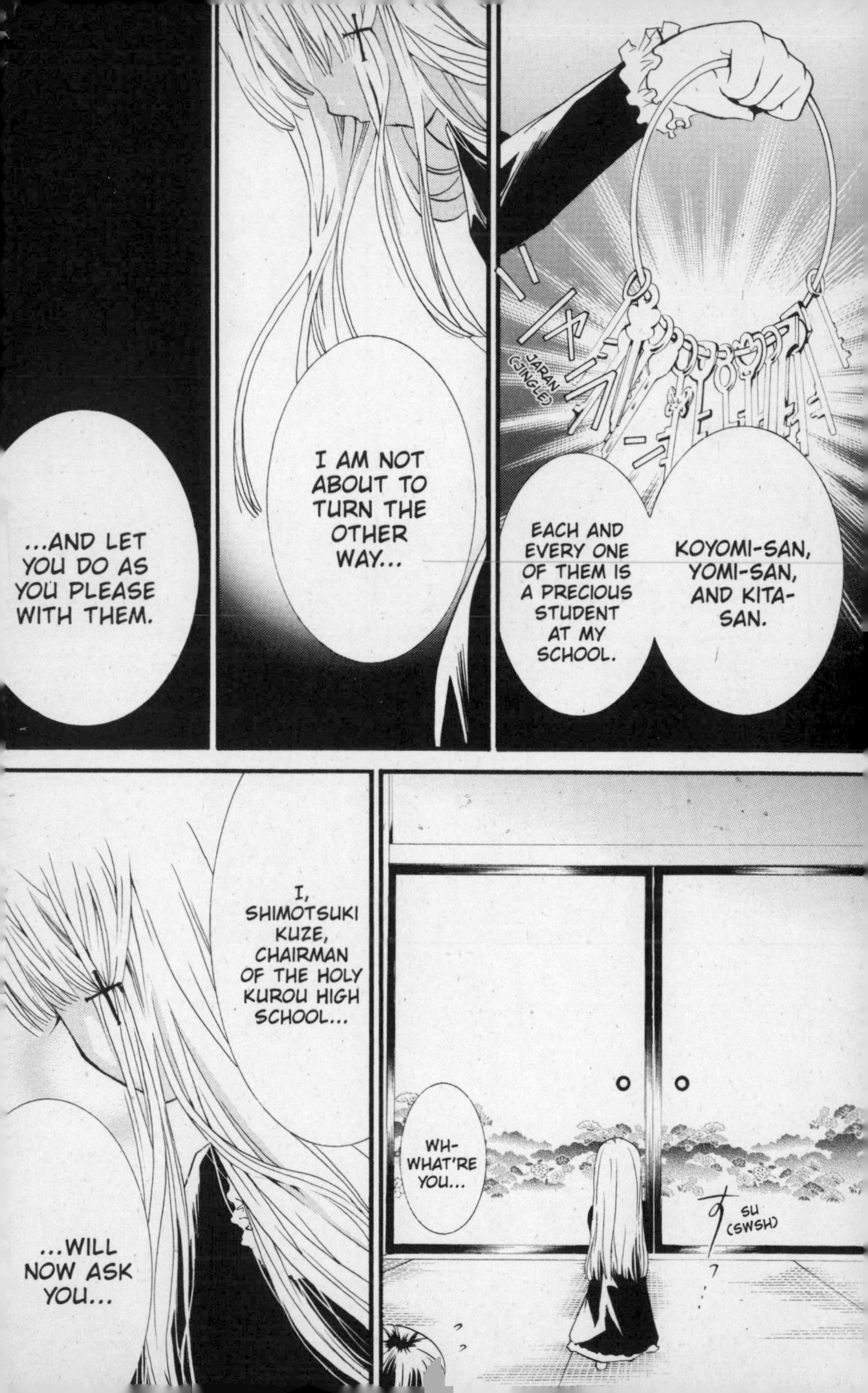

JARAN (JINGLE)
KOYOMI-SAN, YOMI-SAN, AND KITA-SAN.
EACH AND EVERY ONE OF THEM IS A PRECIOUS STUDENT AT MY SCHOOL.
I AM NOT ABOUT TO TURN THE OTHER WAY...
...AND LET YOU DO AS YOU PLEASE WITH THEM.
WH-WHAT'RE YOU...
SU (SWSH)
I, SHIMOTSUKI KUZE, CHAIRMAN OF THE HOLY KUROU HIGH SCHOOL...
...WILL NOW ASK YOU...

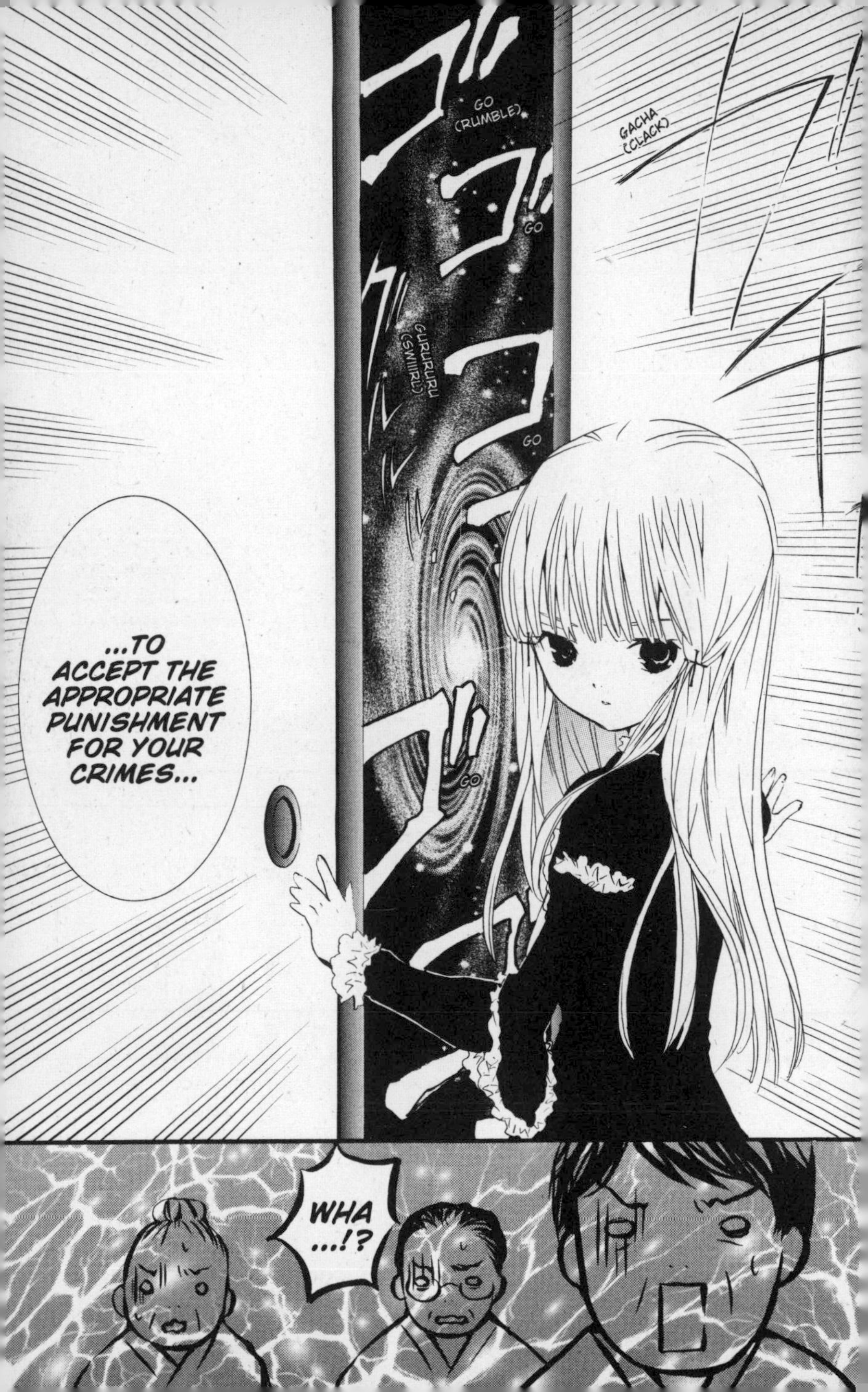
GACHA (CLACK)
GO (RUMBLE)
GO
GURURURU (SWIIRL)
GO
GO
...TO ACCEPT THE APPROPRIATE PUNISHMENT FOR YOUR CRIMES...
WHA ...!?

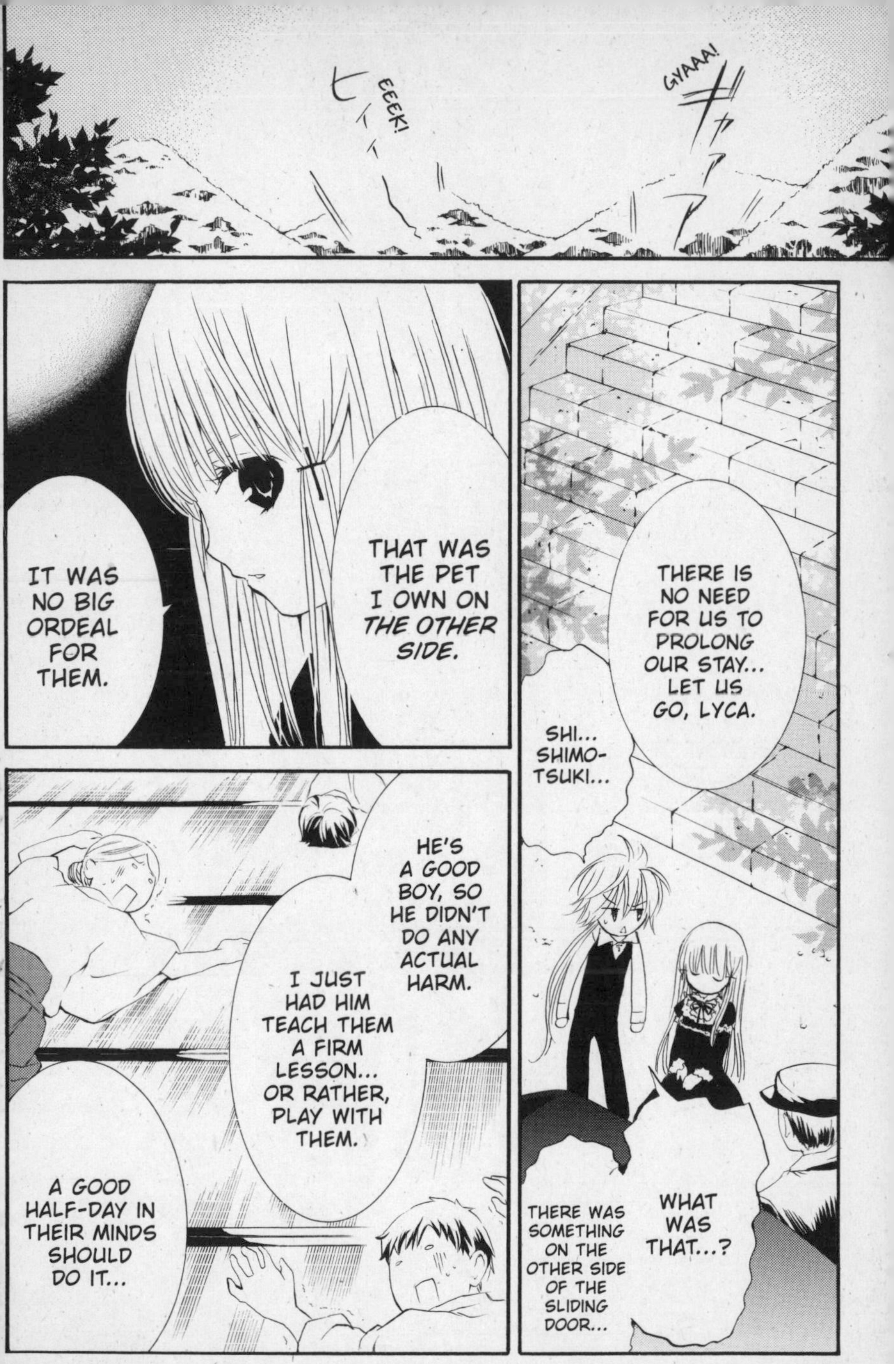
GYAAA!
EEEK!
THERE IS NO NEED FOR US TO PROLONG OUR STAY... LET US GO, LYCA.
SHI... SHIMO-TSUKI...
WHAT WAS THAT...?
THERE WAS SOMETHING ON THE OTHER SIDE OF THE SLIDING DOOR...
THAT WAS THE PET I OWN ON *THE OTHER SIDE.*
IT WAS NO BIG ORDEAL FOR THEM.
HE'S A GOOD BOY, SO HE DIDN'T DO ANY ACTUAL HARM.
I JUST HAD HIM TEACH THEM A FIRM LESSON... OR RATHER, PLAY WITH THEM.
A GOOD HALF-DAY IN THEIR MINDS SHOULD DO IT...

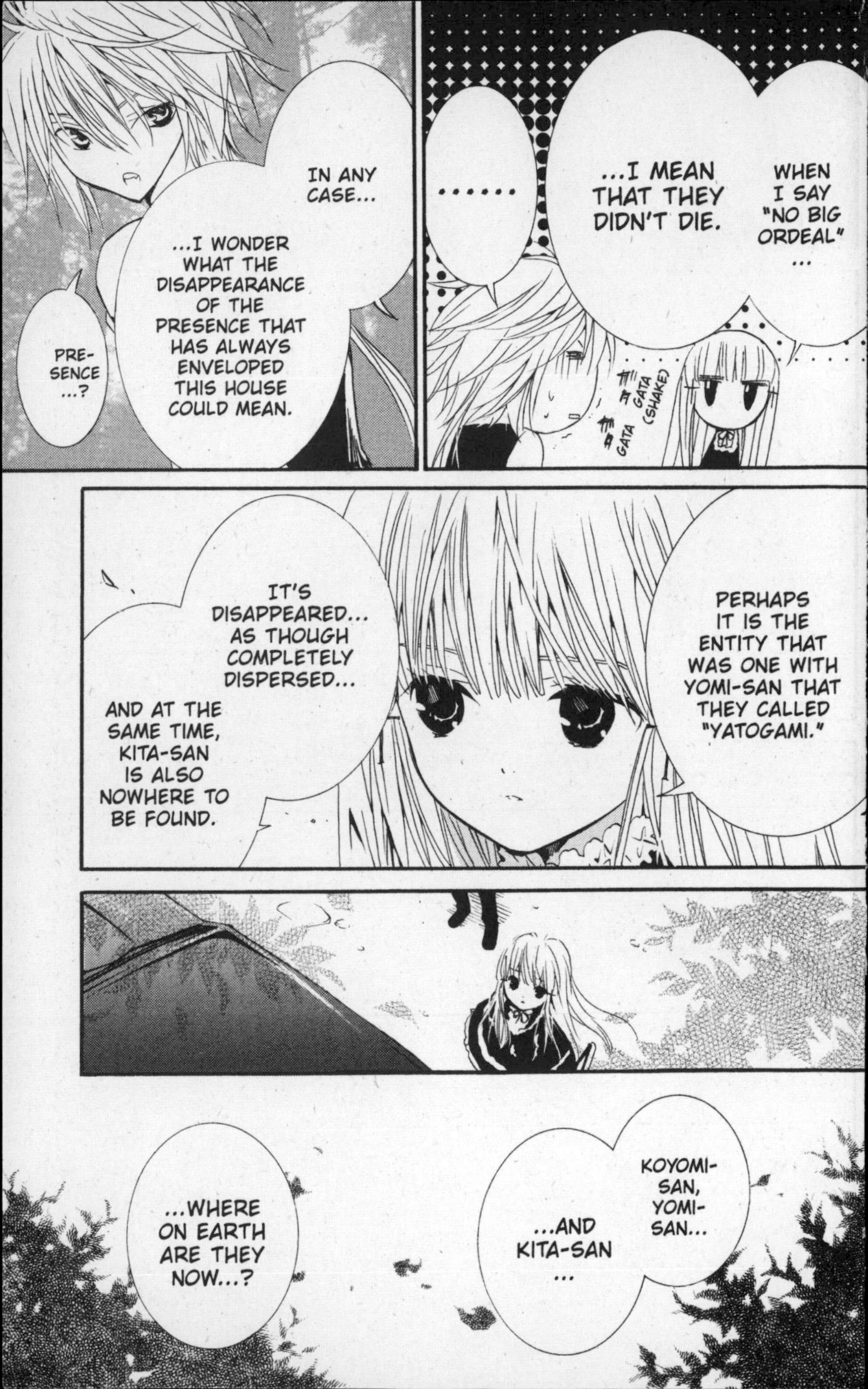
WHEN I SAY "NO BIG ORDEAL" ...
...I MEAN THAT THEY DIDN'T DIE.
......
GATA GATA (SHAKE) GATA
IN ANY CASE...
...I WONDER WHAT THE DISAPPEARANCE OF THE PRESENCE THAT HAS ALWAYS ENVELOPED THIS HOUSE COULD MEAN.
PRE-SENCE ...?
PERHAPS IT IS THE ENTITY THAT WAS ONE WITH YOMI-SAN THAT THEY CALLED "YATOGAMI."
IT'S DISAPPEARED... AS THOUGH COMPLETELY DISPERSED...
AND AT THE SAME TIME, KITA-SAN IS ALSO NOWHERE TO BE FOUND.
KOYOMI-SAN, YOMI-SAN...
...AND KITA-SAN ...
...WHERE ON EARTH ARE THEY NOW...?

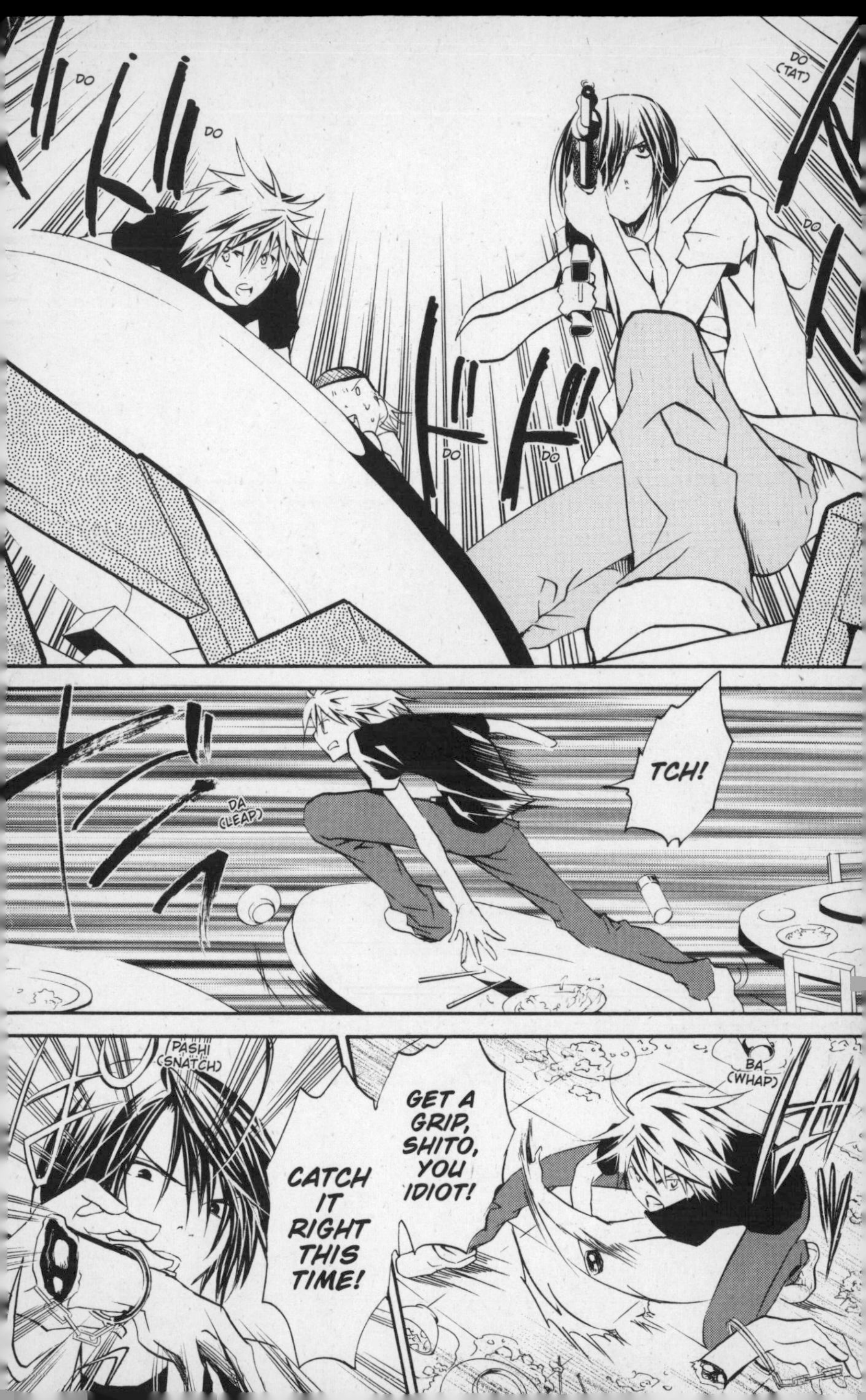
DO (TAT)
DO
DO
DO
DO
DO
TCH!
DA (LEAP)
BA (WHAP)
GET A GRIP, SHITO, YOU IDIOT!
CATCH IT RIGHT THIS TIME!
PASHI (SNATCH)

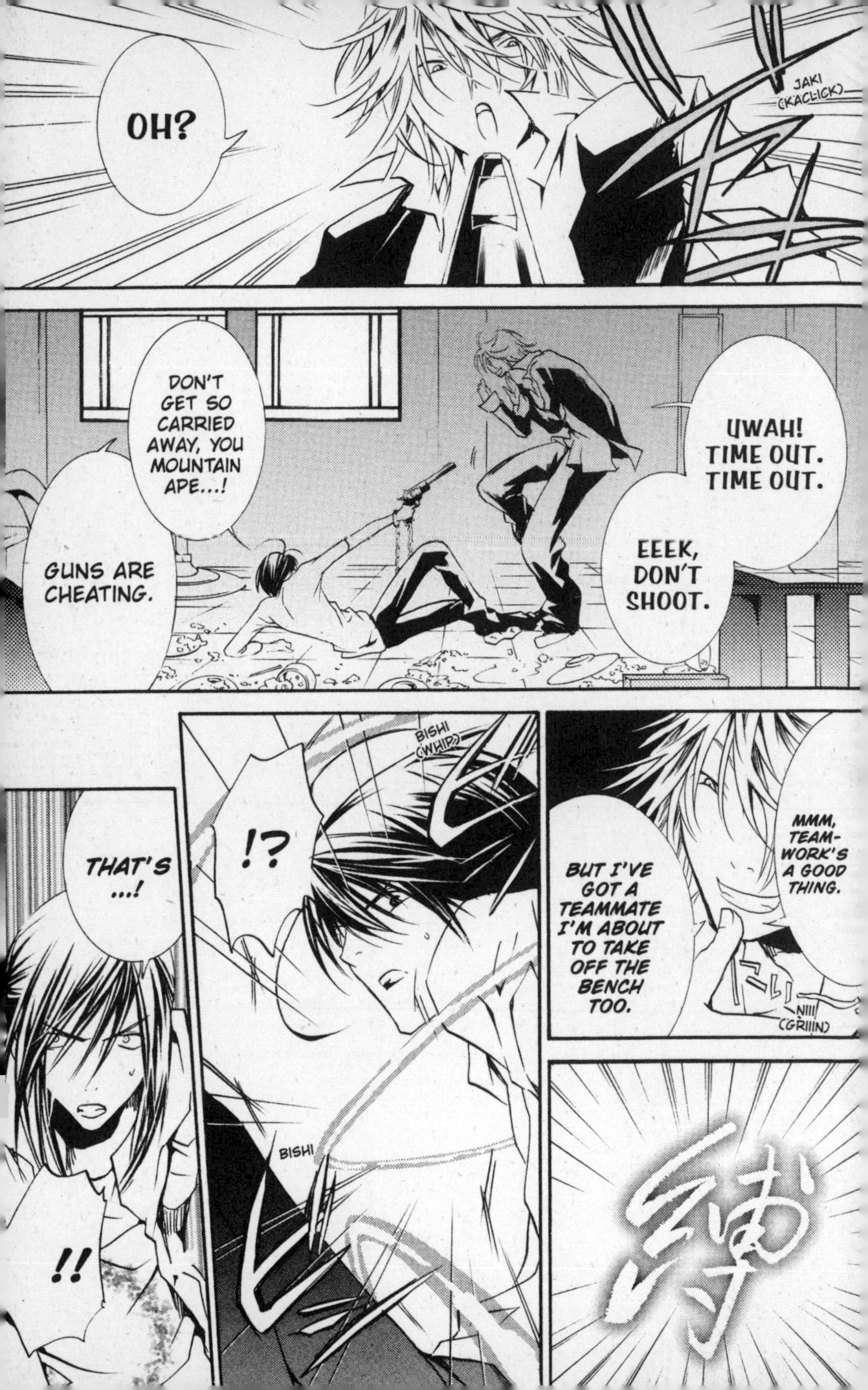
JAKI
(KACLICK)
OH?
UWAH! TIME OUT. TIME OUT.
EEEK, DON'T SHOOT.
DON'T GET SO CARRIED AWAY, YOU MOUNTAIN APE...!
GUNS ARE CHEATING.
MMM, TEAM-WORK'S A GOOD THING.
BUT I'VE GOT A TEAMMATE I'M ABOUT TO TAKE OFF THE BENCH TOO.
NIII
(GRIIIN)
BISHI
(WHIP)
!?
BISHI
THAT'S ...!
!!

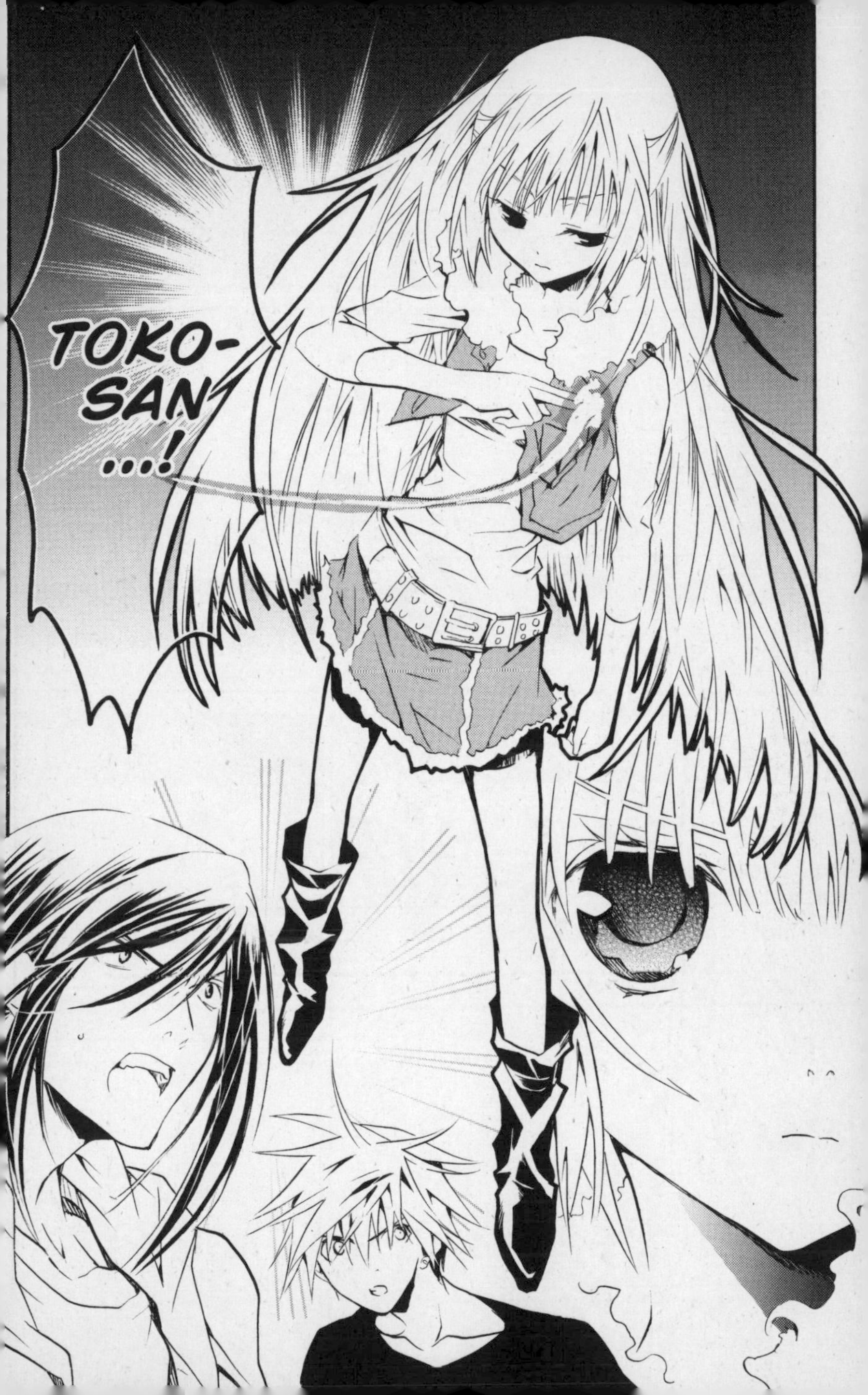
TOKO-SAN ...!

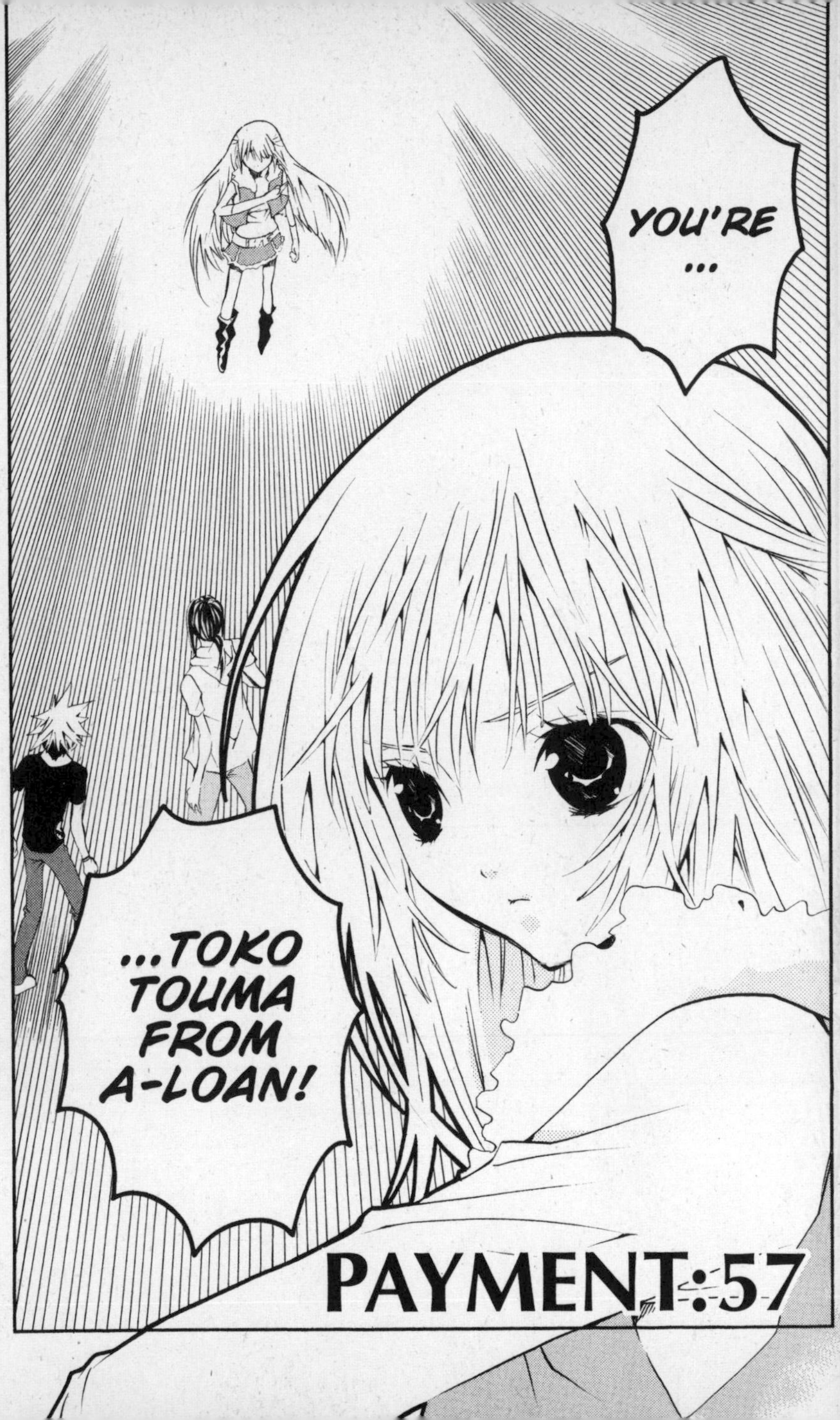
YOU'RE ...
...TOKO TOUMA FROM A-LOAN!
PAYMENT:57

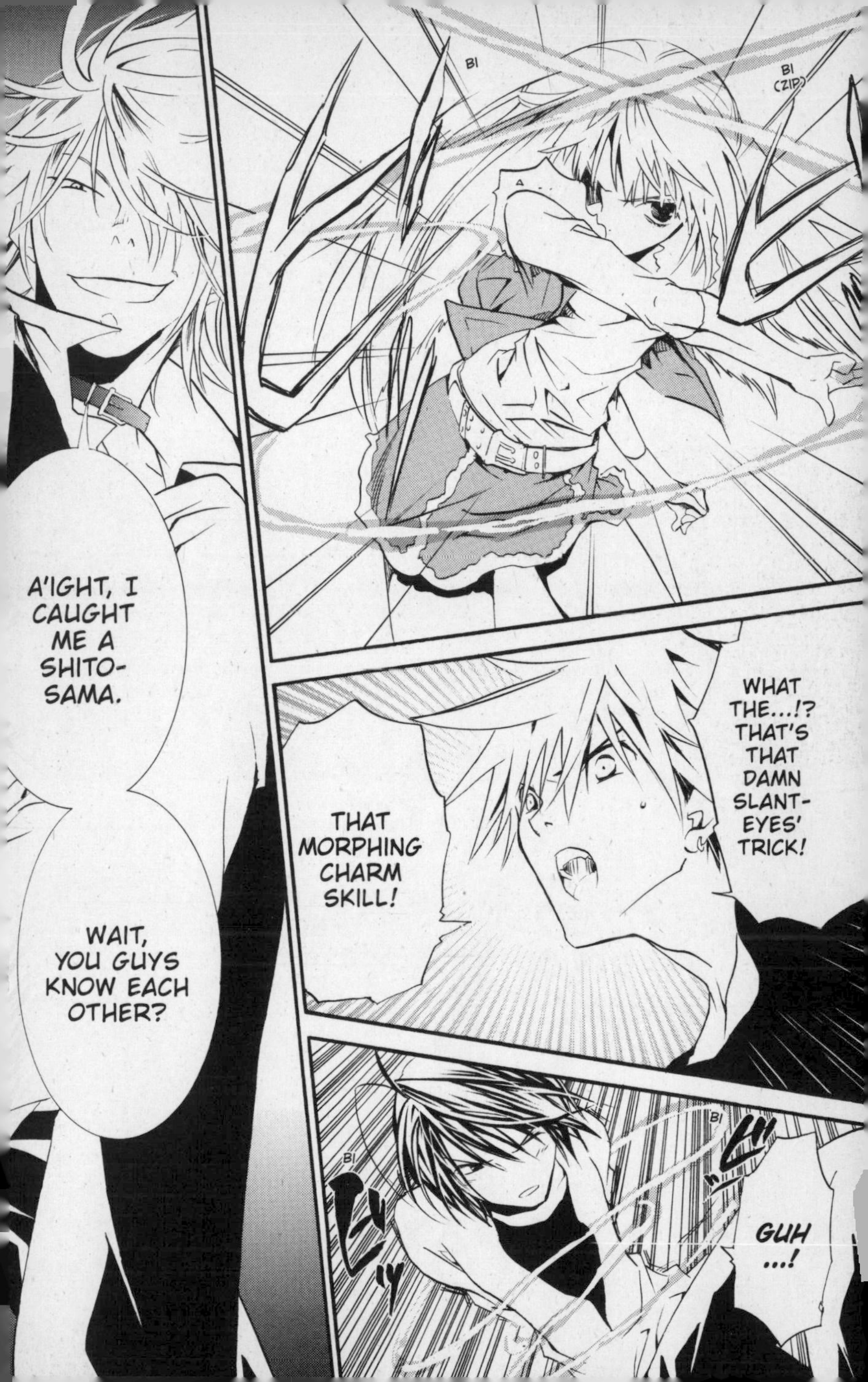
BI
BI (ZIP)
WHAT THE...!? THAT'S THAT DAMN SLANT-EYES' TRICK!
THAT MORPHING CHARM SKILL!
BI
BI
GUH ...!
A'IGHT, I CAUGHT ME A SHITO-SAMA.
WAIT, YOU GUYS KNOW EACH OTHER?

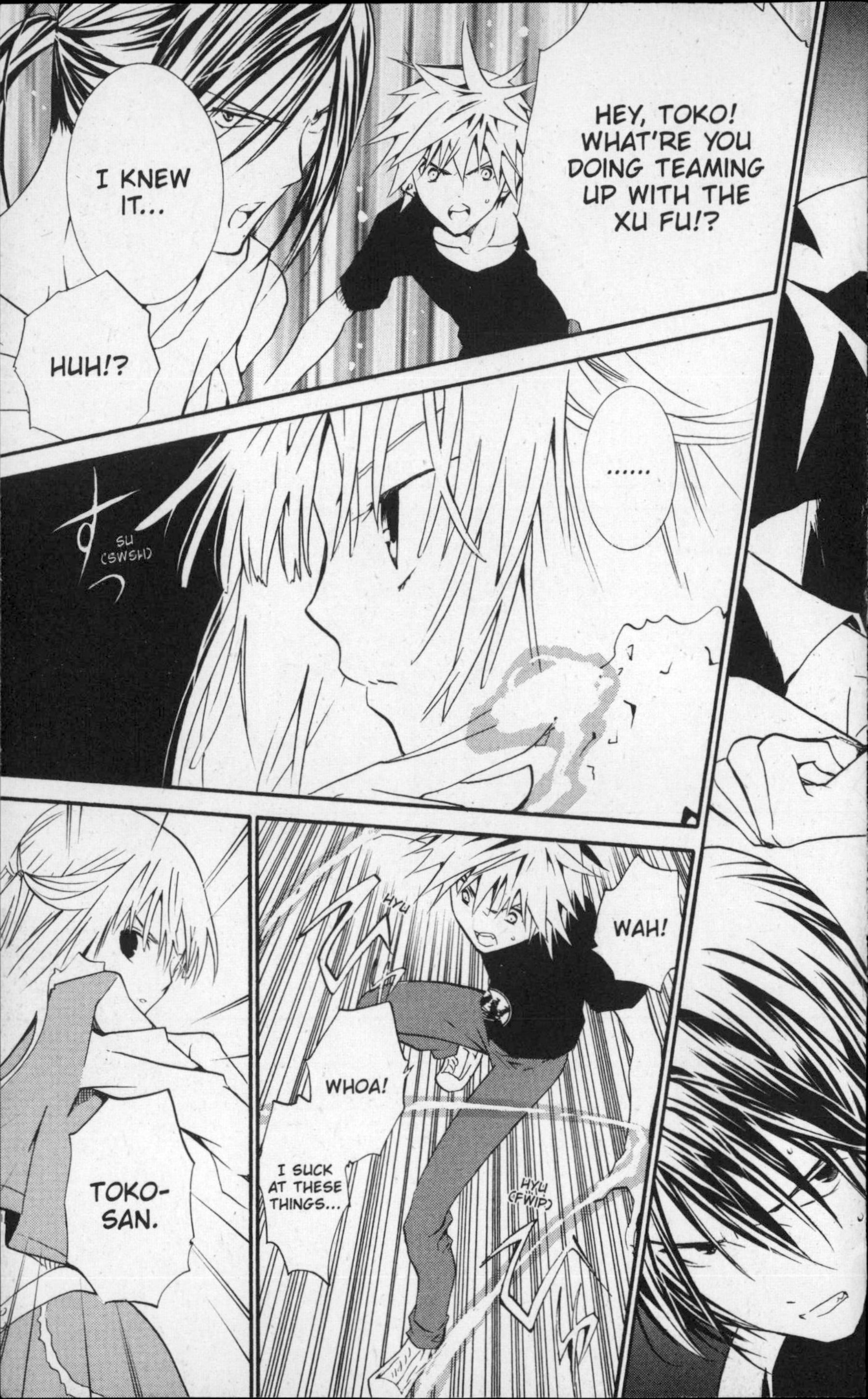
HEY, TOKO! WHAT'RE YOU DOING TEAMING UP WITH THE XU FU!?
I KNEW IT...
HUH!?
......
す SU (SWSH)
HYU
WAH!
WHOA!
I SUCK AT THESE THINGS...
HYU (FWIP)
TOKO-SAN.

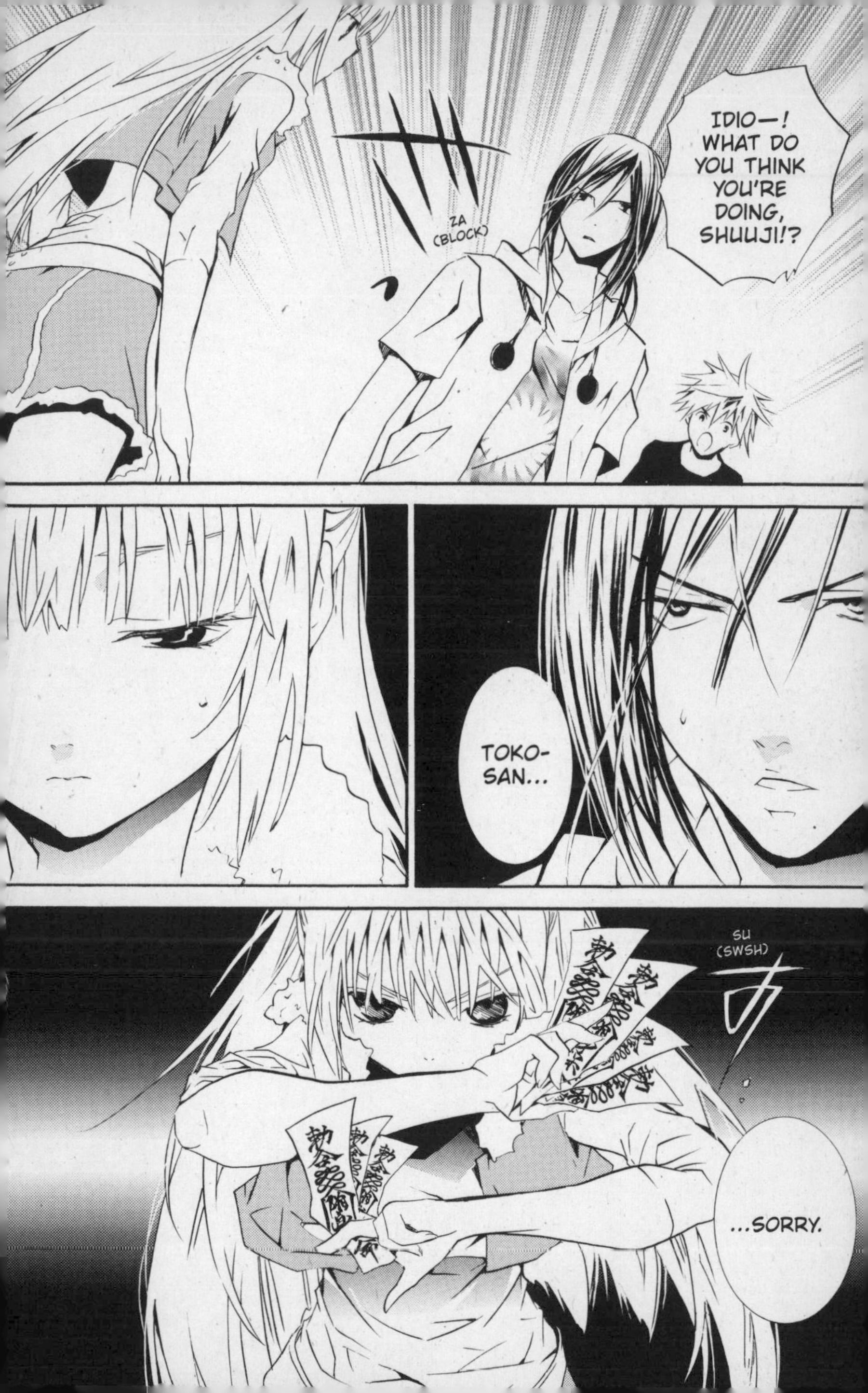
IDIO—! WHAT DO YOU THINK YOU'RE DOING, SHUUJI!?
ZA (BLOCK)
TOKO-SAN...
SU (SWSH)
...SORRY.

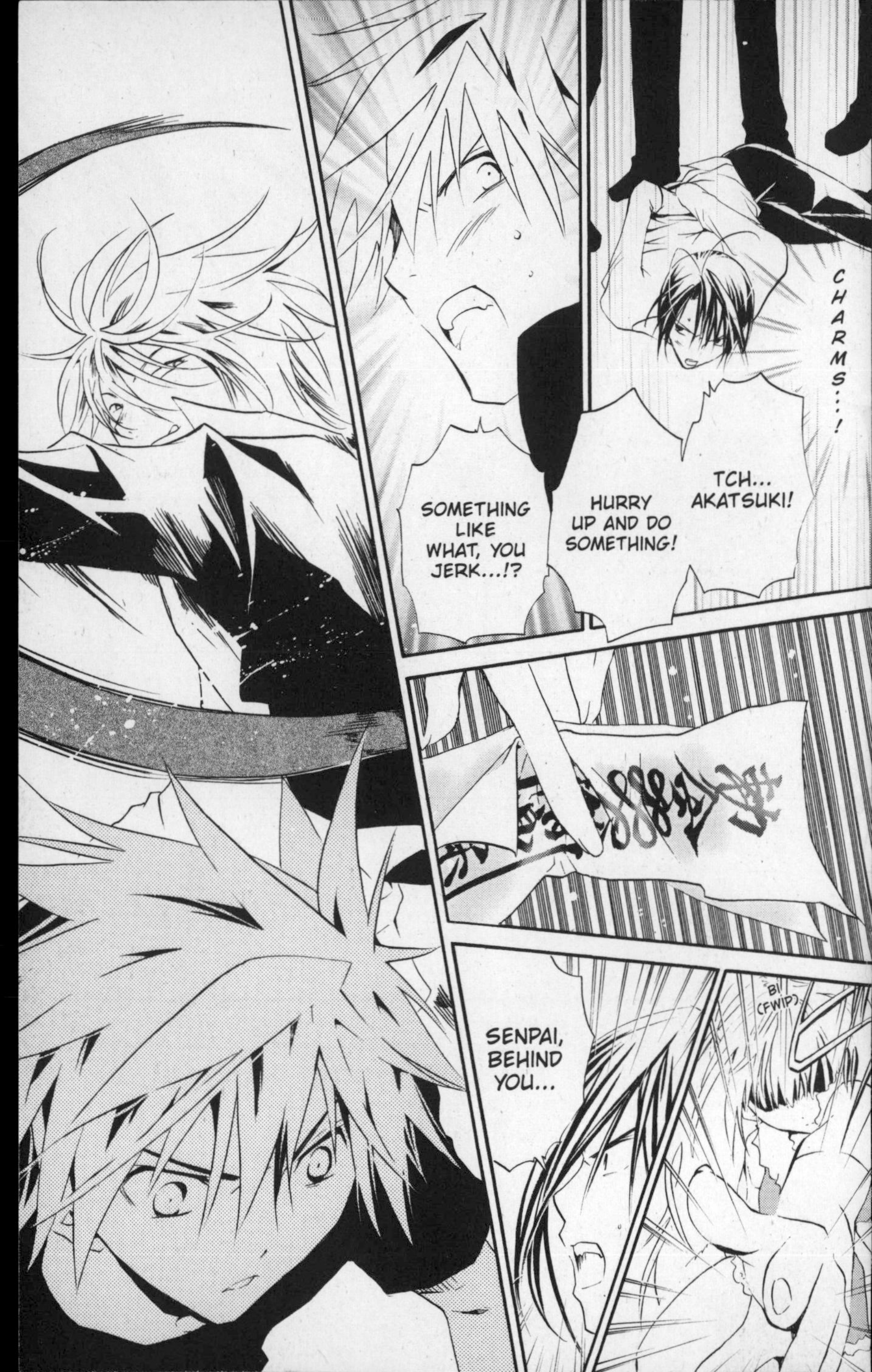
CHARMS...!
TCH... AKATSUKI!
HURRY UP AND DO SOMETHING!
SOMETHING LIKE WHAT, YOU JERK...!?
BI (FWIP)
SENPAI, BEHIND YOU...

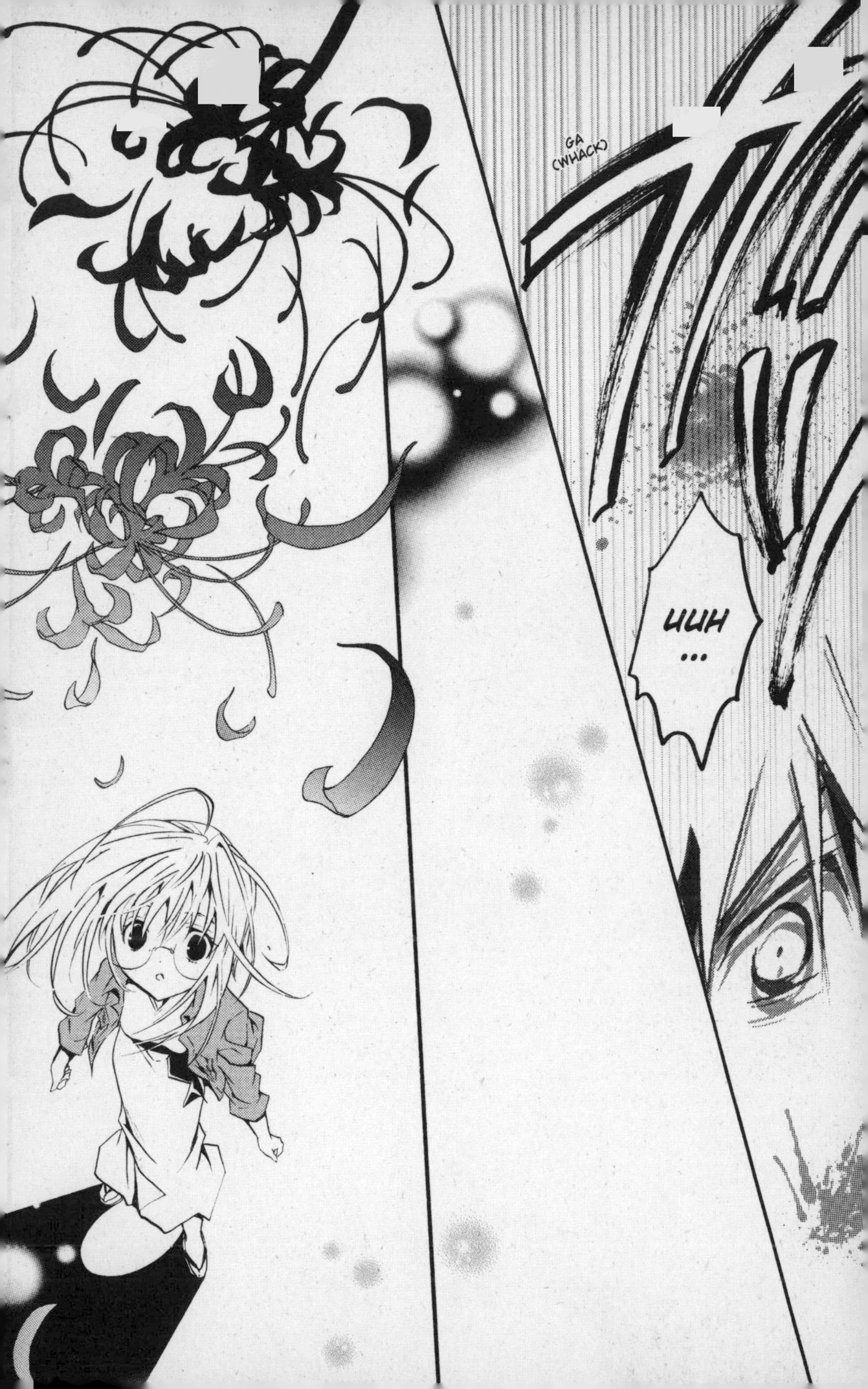
GA (WHACK)
UUH ...

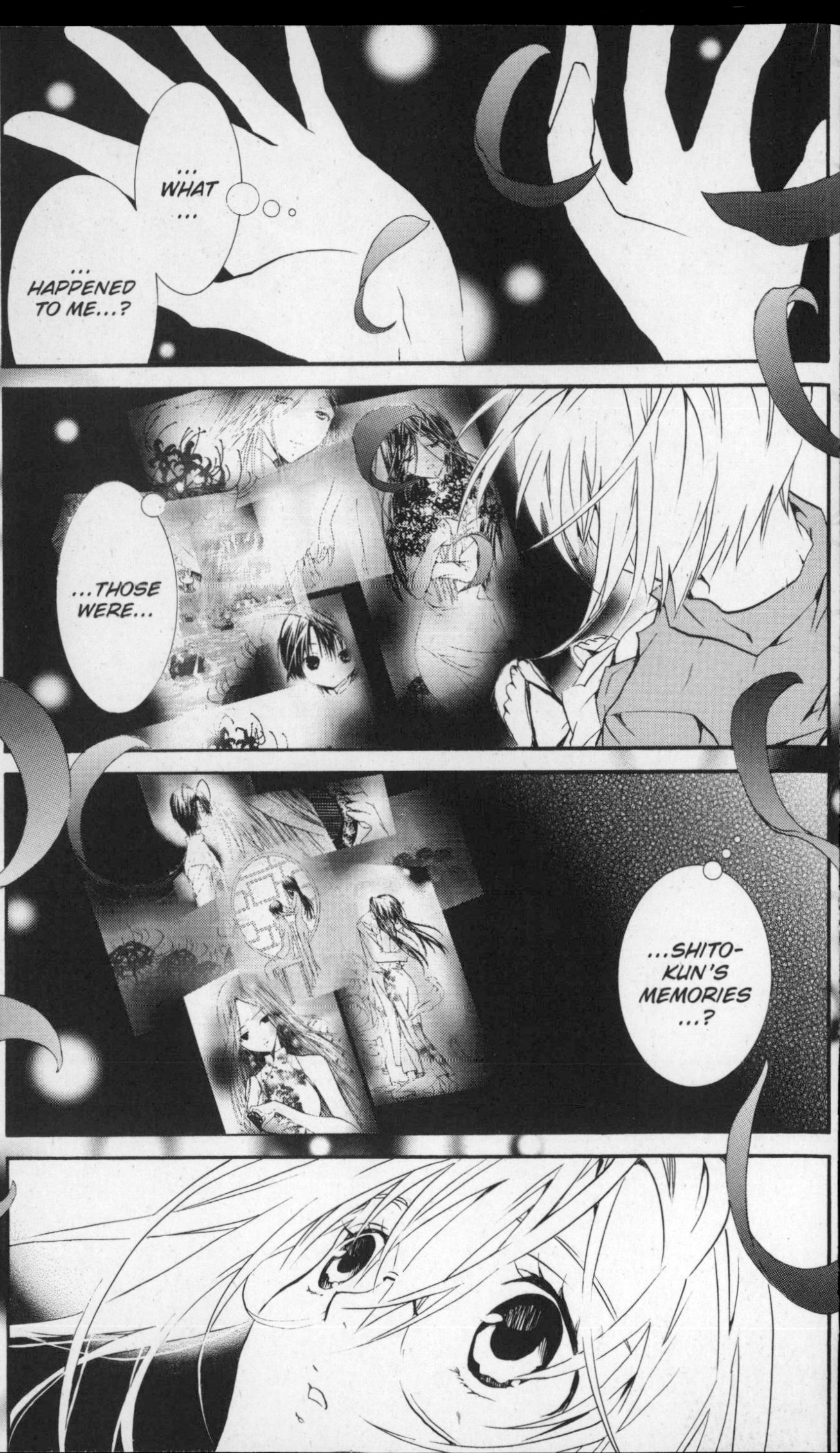
...WHAT...
...HAPPENED TO ME...?
...THOSE WERE...
...SHITO-KUN'S MEMORIES...?

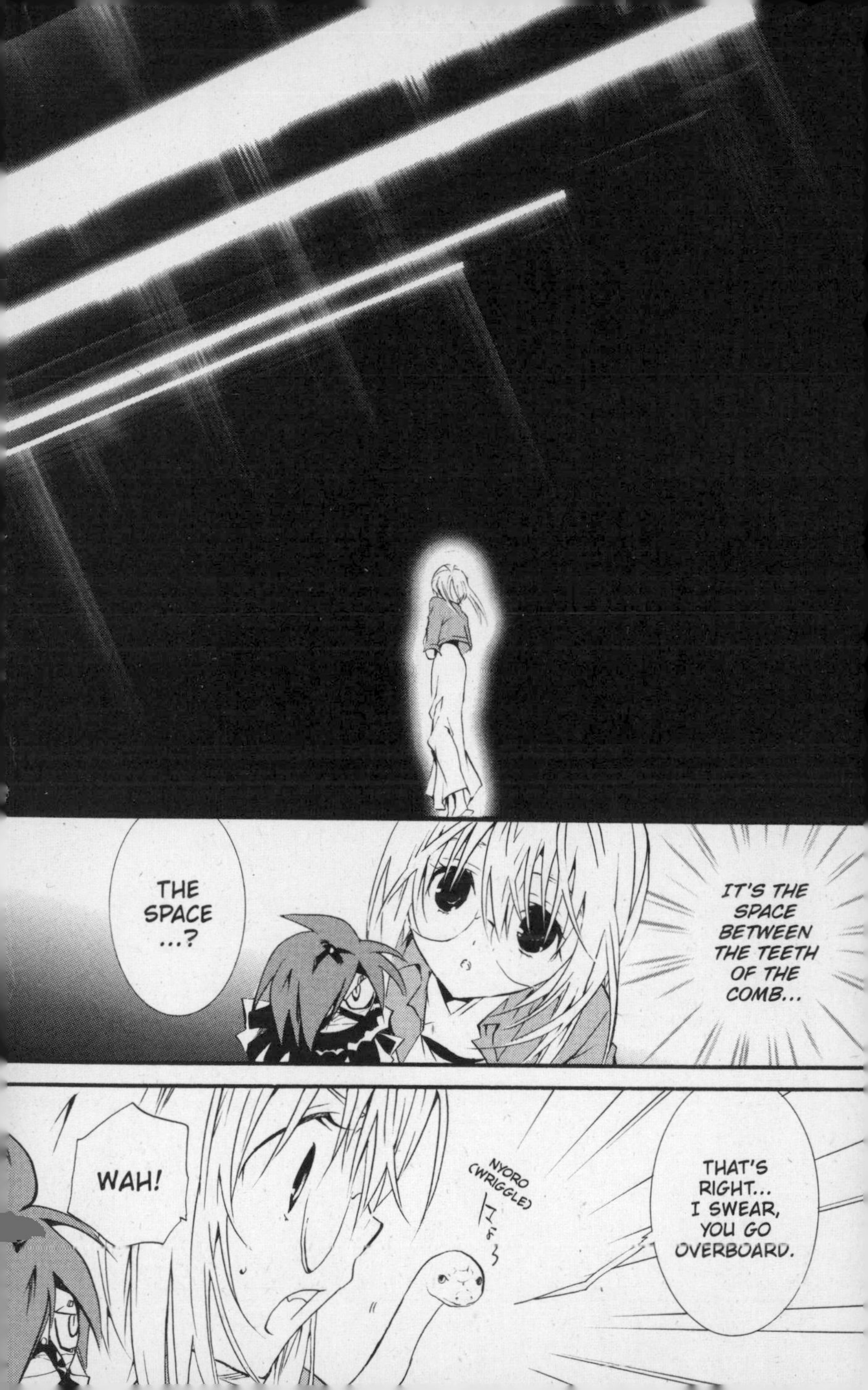
IT'S THE SPACE BETWEEN THE TEETH OF THE COMB...
THE SPACE ...?
THAT'S RIGHT... I SWEAR, YOU GO OVERBOARD.
NYORO (WRIGGLE)
WAH!

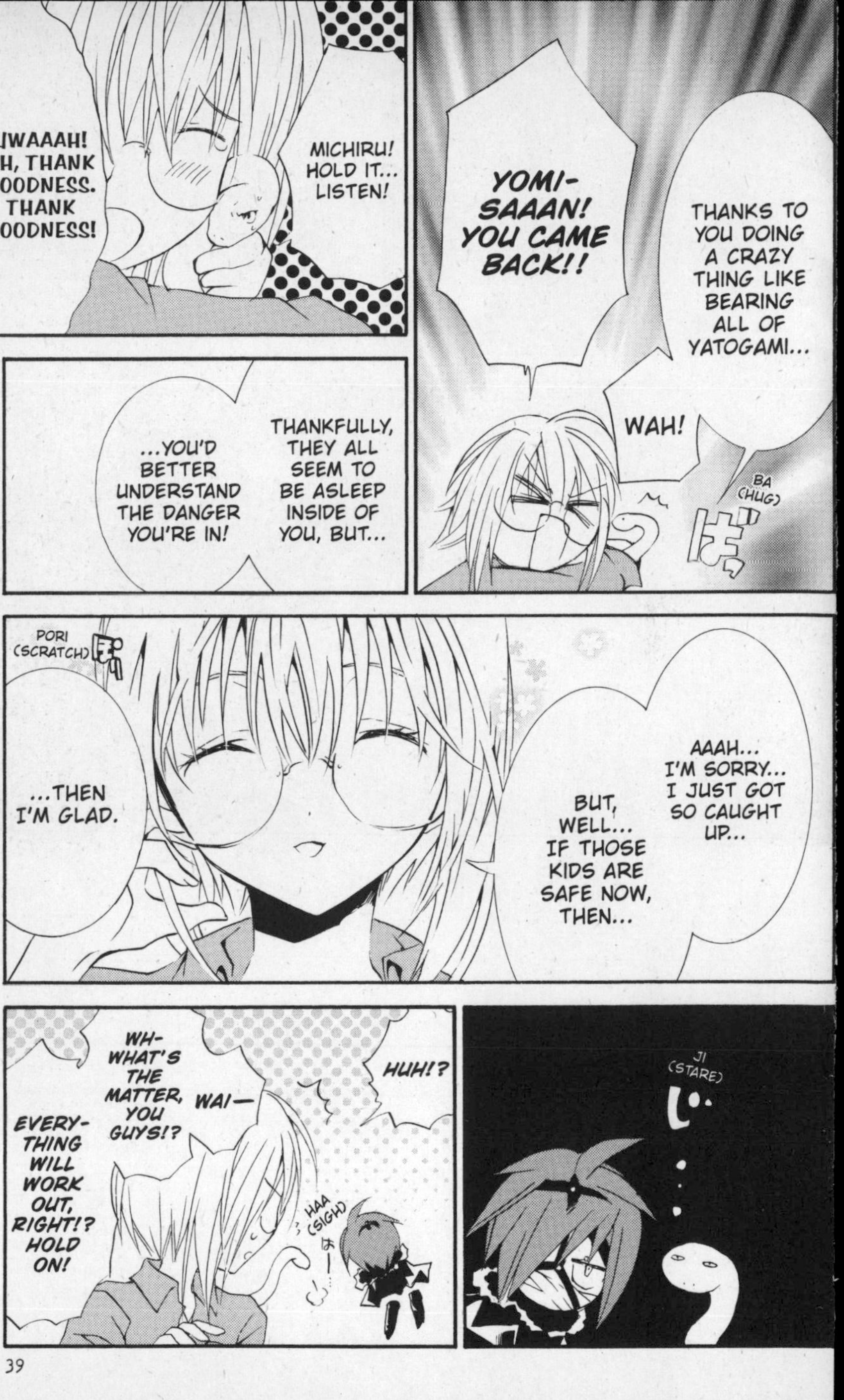
YOMI-SAAAN! YOU CAME BACK!!
THANKS TO YOU DOING A CRAZY THING LIKE BEARING ALL OF YATOGAMI...
WAH!
BA (HUG)
MICHIRU! HOLD IT... LISTEN!
UWAAAH! OH, THANK GOODNESS. THANK GOODNESS!
THANKFULLY, THEY ALL SEEM TO BE ASLEEP INSIDE OF YOU, BUT...
...YOU'D BETTER UNDERSTAND THE DANGER YOU'RE IN!
AAAH... I'M SORRY... I JUST GOT SO CAUGHT UP...
BUT, WELL... IF THOSE KIDS ARE SAFE NOW, THEN...
PORI (SCRATCH)
...THEN I'M GLAD.
JI (STARE)
HUH!?
WH-WHAT'S THE MATTER, YOU GUYS!?
WAI—
EVERY-THING WILL WORK OUT, RIGHT!? HOLD ON!
HAA (SIGH)

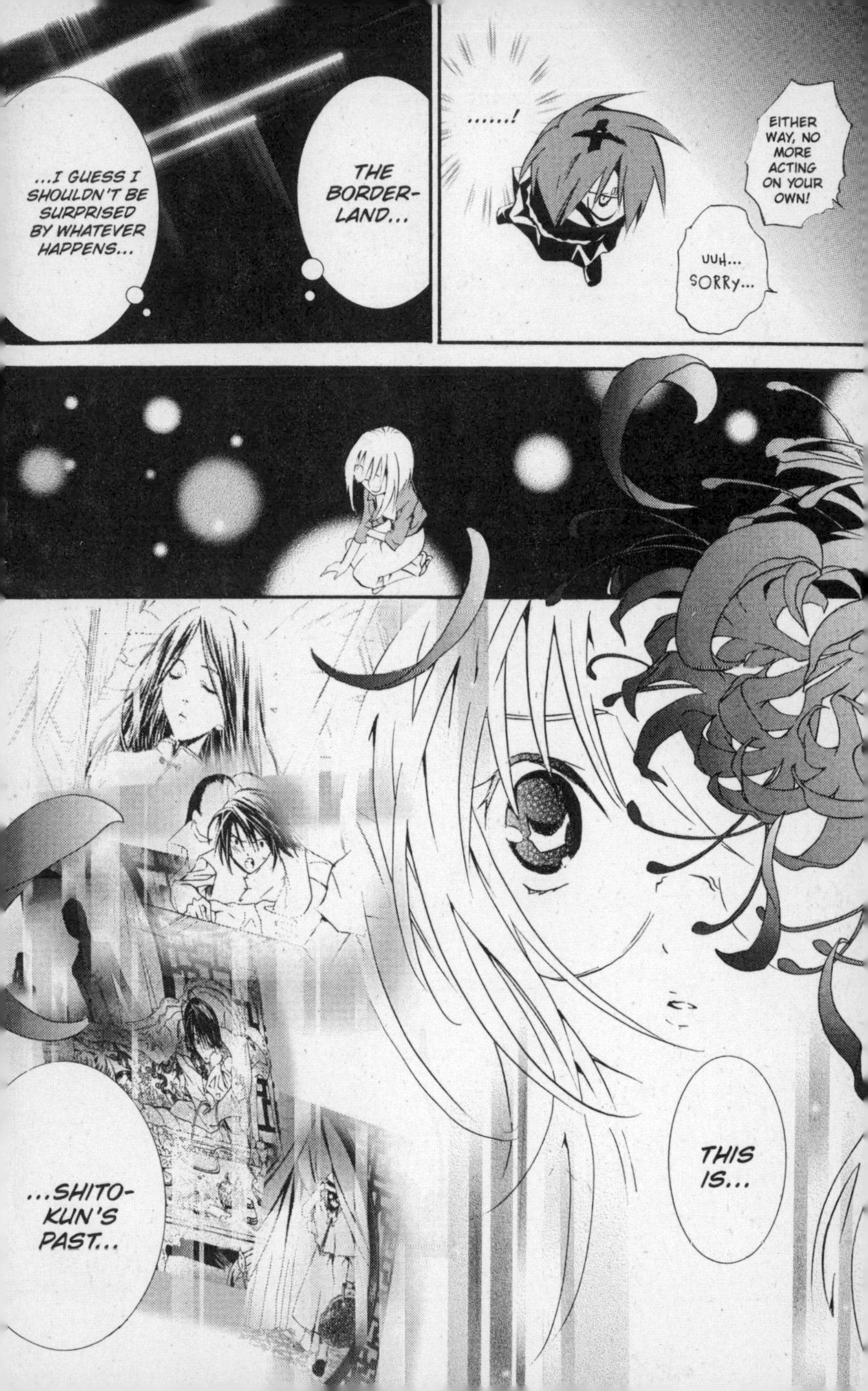
EITHER WAY, NO MORE ACTING ON YOUR OWN!
......!
UUH... SORRY...
THE BORDERLAND...
...I GUESS I SHOULDN'T BE SURPRISED BY WHATEVER HAPPENS...
THIS IS...
...SHITO-KUN'S PAST...

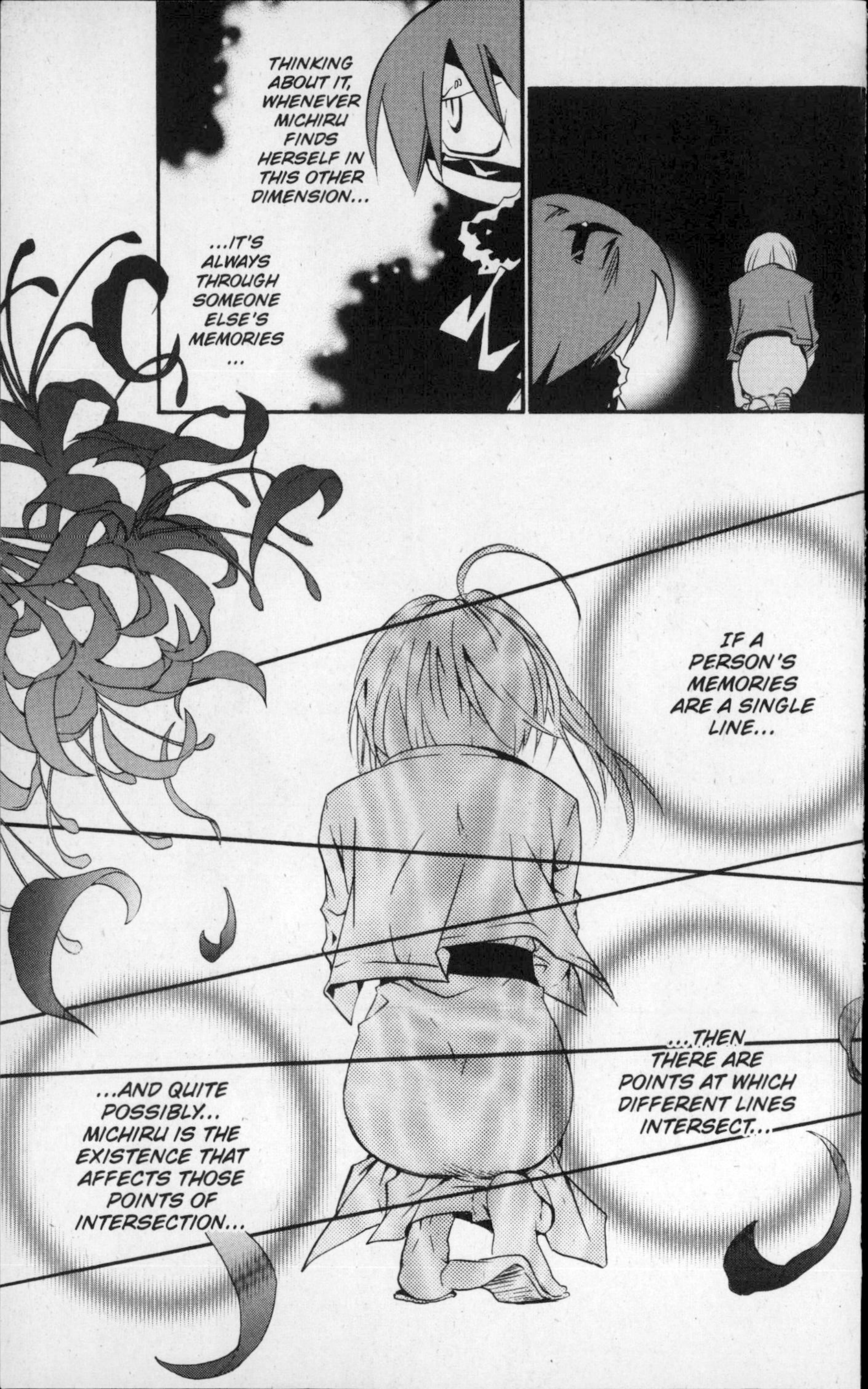
THINKING ABOUT IT, WHENEVER MICHIRU FINDS HERSELF IN THIS OTHER DIMENSION...
...IT'S ALWAYS THROUGH SOMEONE ELSE'S MEMORIES...
IF A PERSON'S MEMORIES ARE A SINGLE LINE...
...THEN THERE ARE POINTS AT WHICH DIFFERENT LINES INTERSECT...
...AND QUITE POSSIBLY... MICHIRU IS THE EXISTENCE THAT AFFECTS THOSE POINTS OF INTERSECTION...

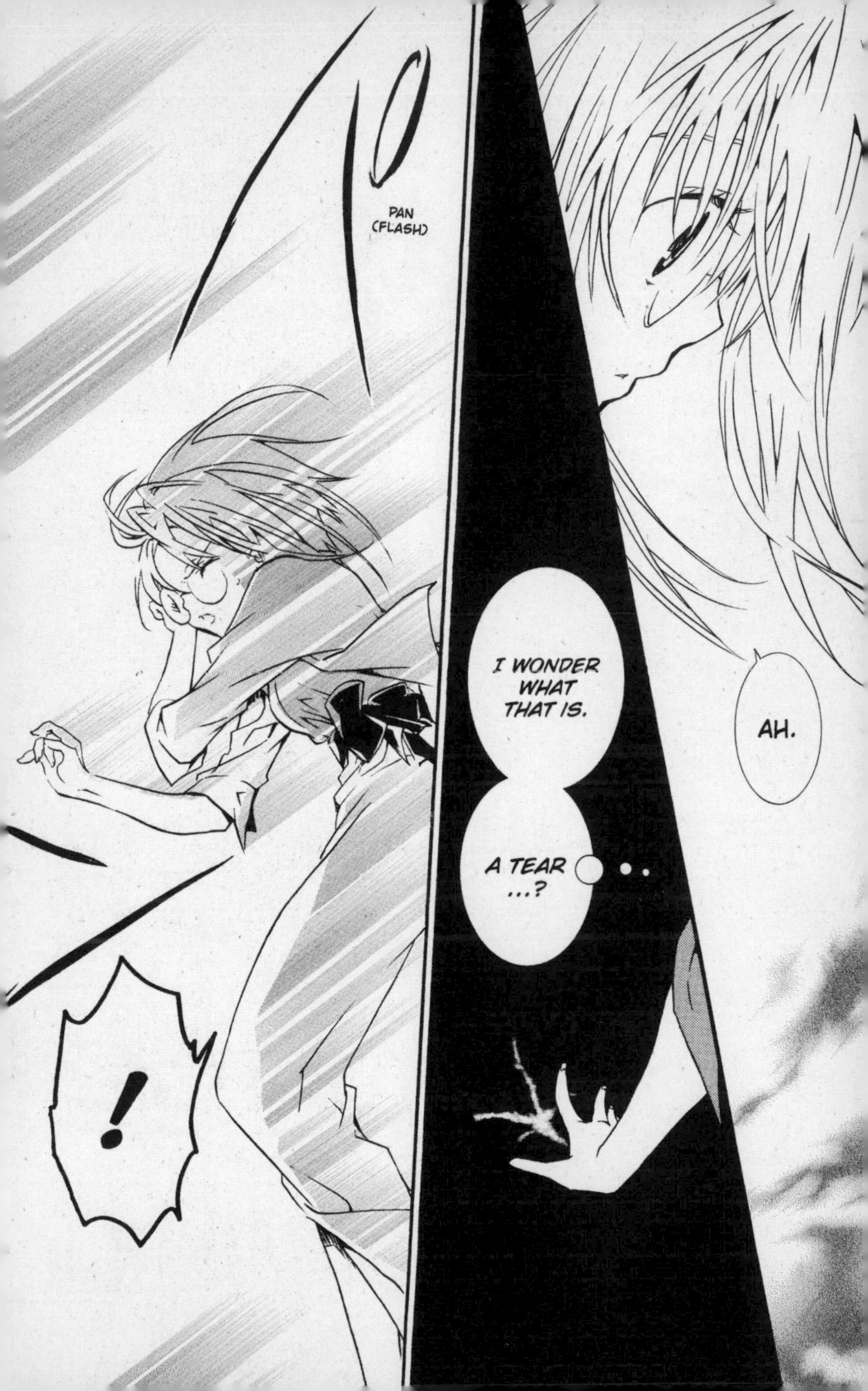
AH.
I WONDER WHAT THAT IS.
A TEAR ...?
PAN (FLASH)
!

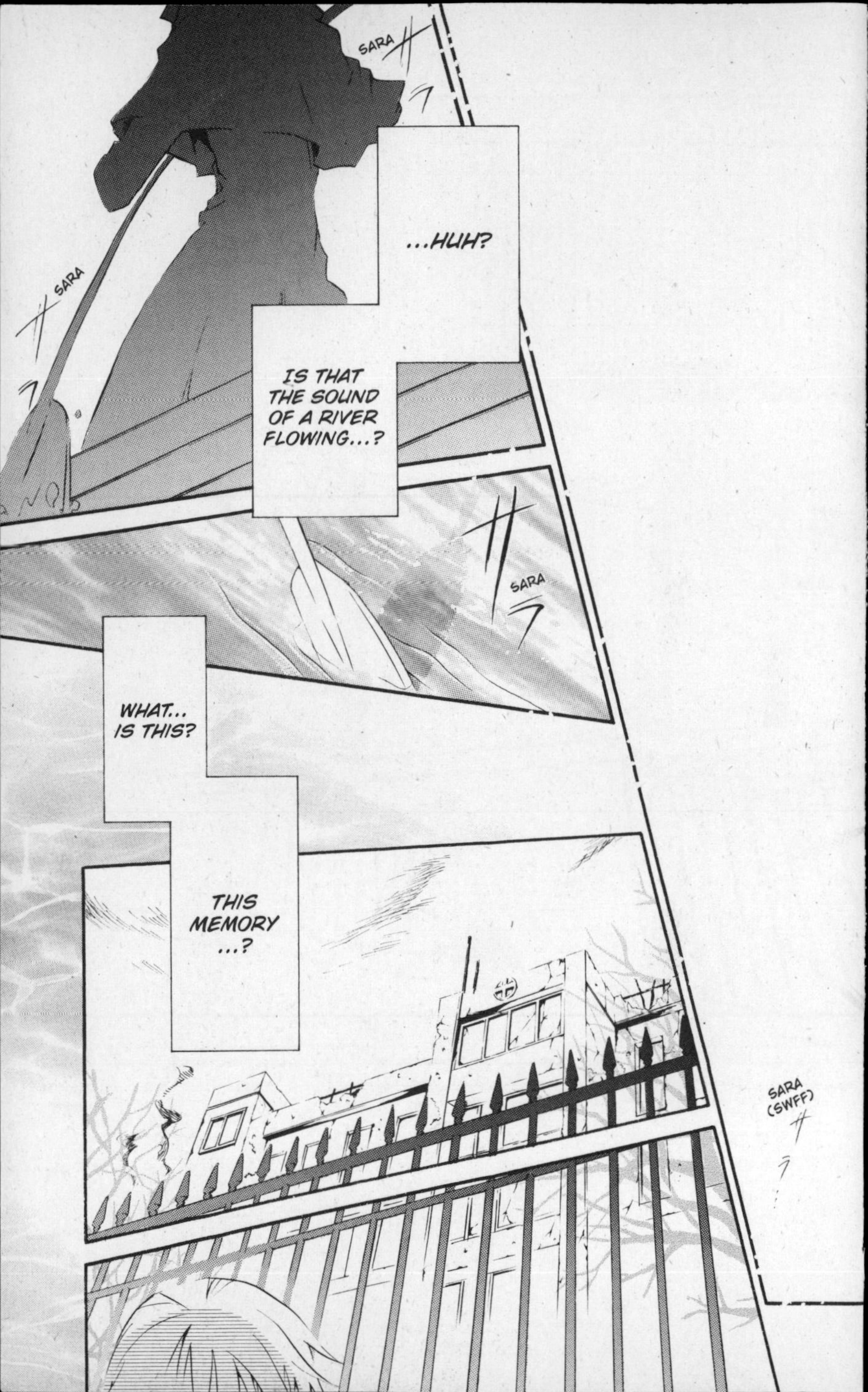
SARA
SARA
...HUH?
IS THAT THE SOUND OF A RIVER FLOWING...?
SARA
WHAT... IS THIS?
THIS MEMORY ...?
SARA (SWFF)

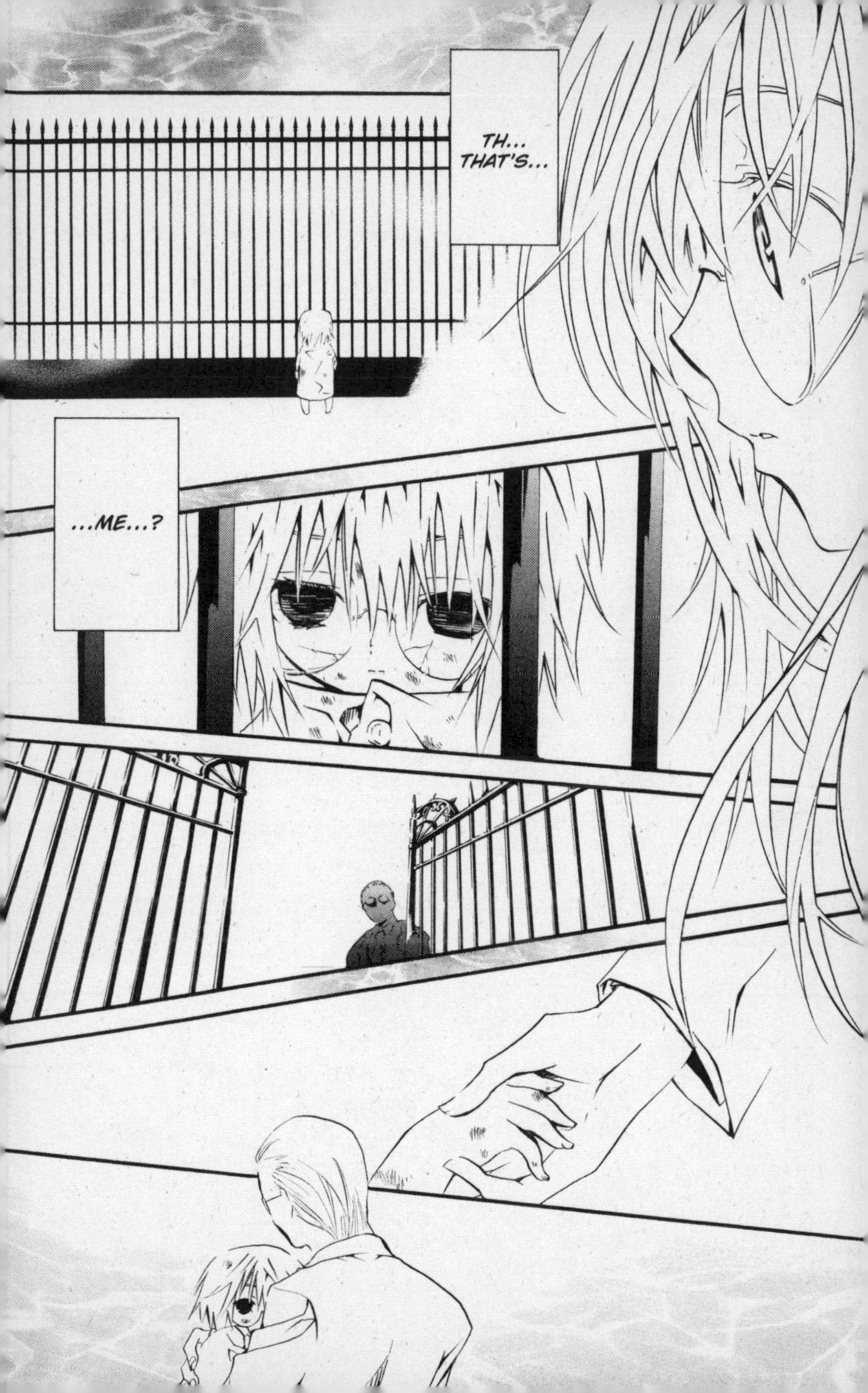
TH... THAT'S...
...ME...?

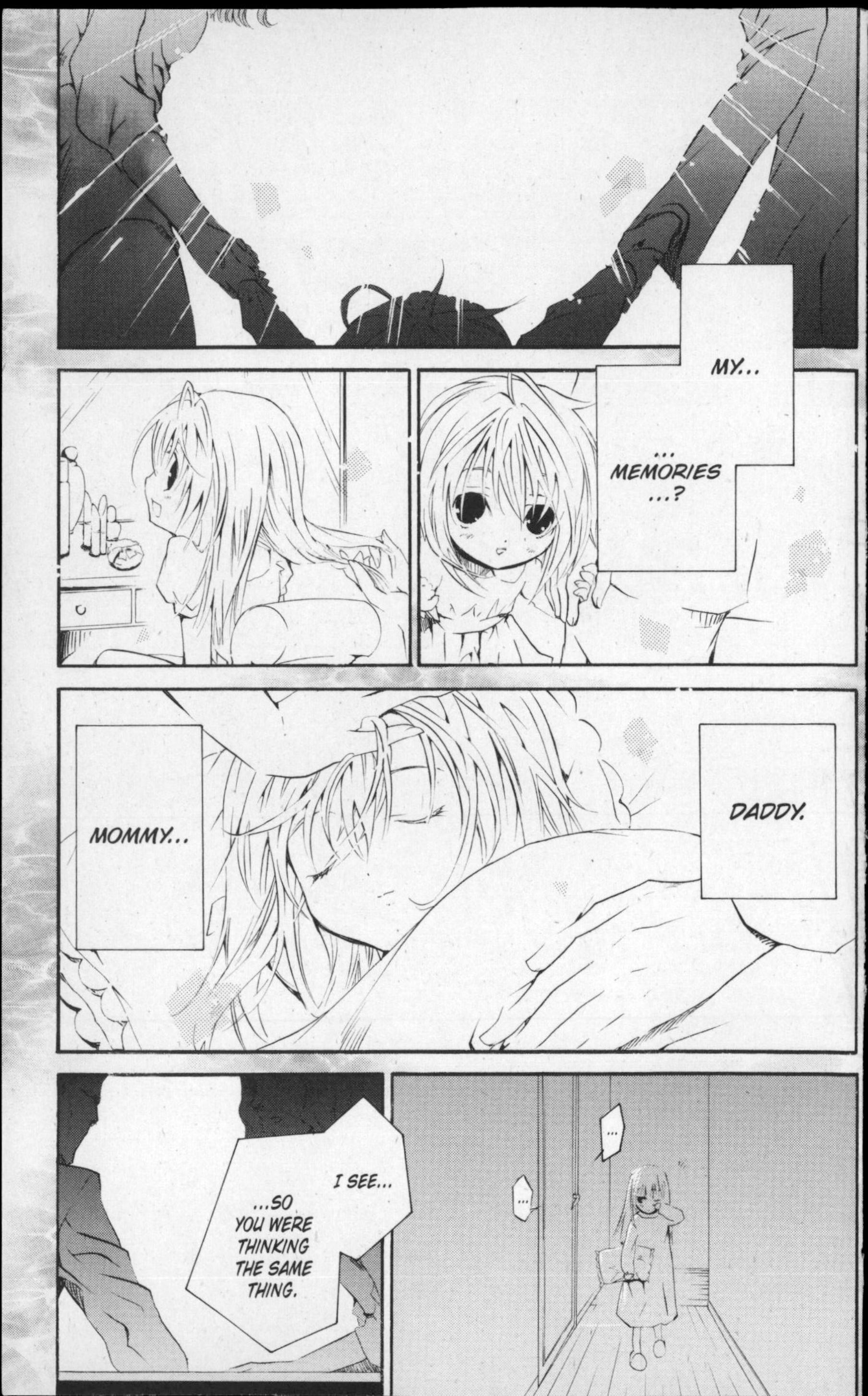
MY...
...MEMORIES...?
DADDY.
MOMMY...
...
...
I SEE...
...SO YOU WERE THINKING THE SAME THING.

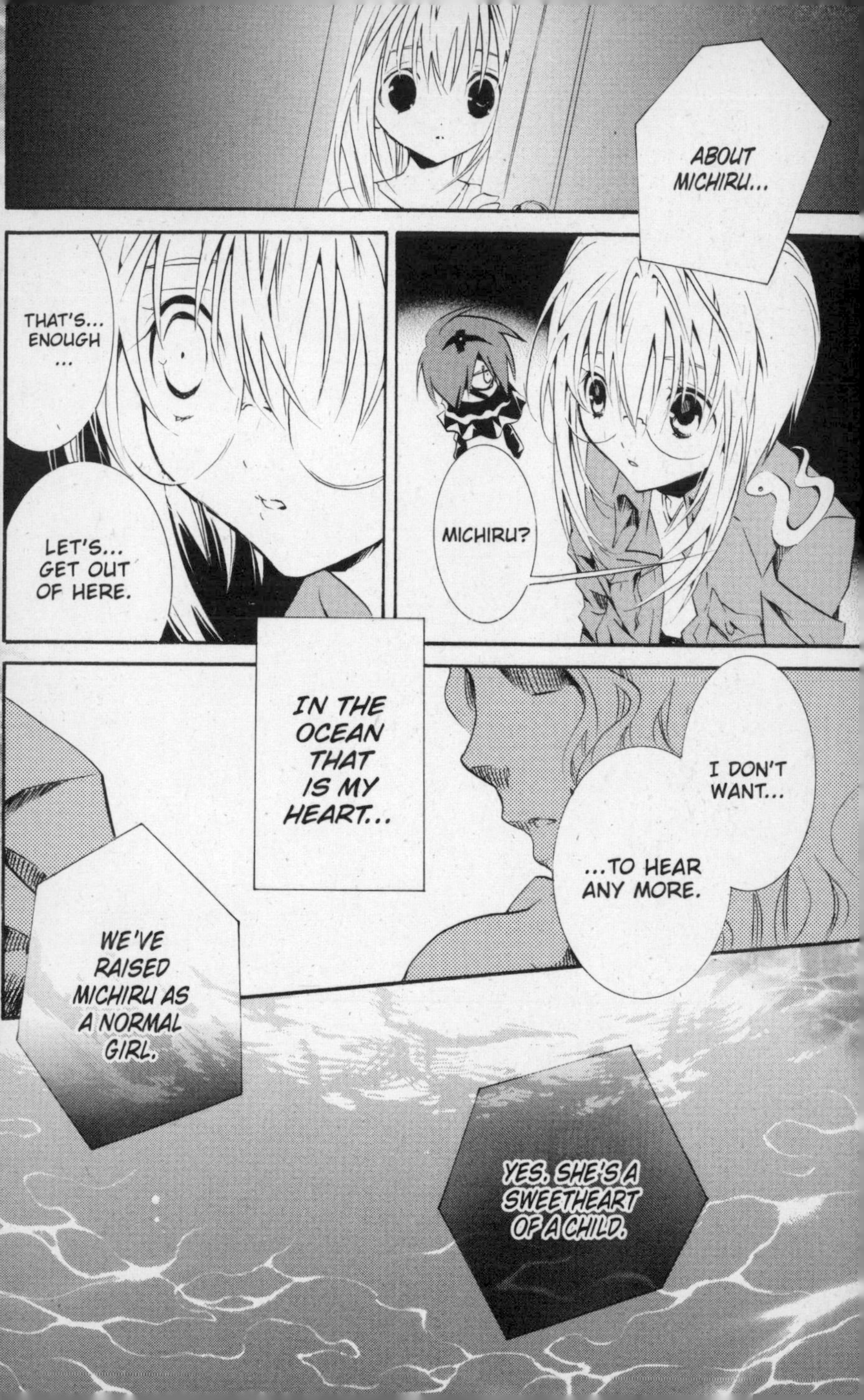
ABOUT MICHIRU...
MICHIRU?
THAT'S... ENOUGH ...
LET'S... GET OUT OF HERE.
I DON'T WANT...
...TO HEAR ANY MORE.
IN THE OCEAN THAT IS MY HEART...
WE'VE RAISED MICHIRU AS A NORMAL GIRL.
YES. SHE'S A SWEETHEART OF A CHILD.

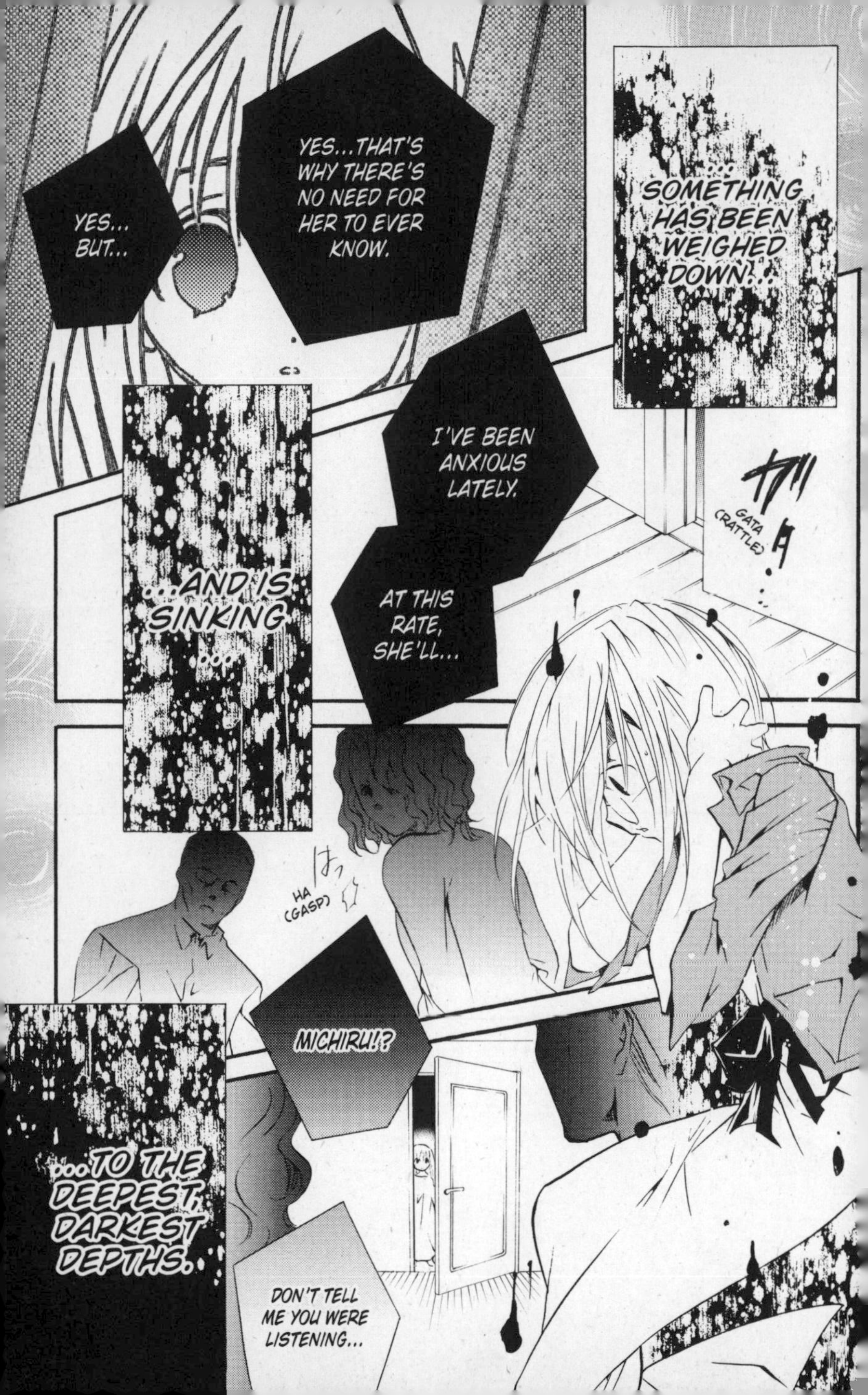
...SOMETHING HAS BEEN WEIGHED DOWN...
YES...THAT'S WHY THERE'S NO NEED FOR HER TO EVER KNOW.
YES... BUT...
I'VE BEEN ANXIOUS LATELY.
GATA (RATTLE)
AT THIS RATE, SHE'LL...
...AND IS SINKING...
HA (GASP)
MICHIRU!?
DON'T TELL ME YOU WERE LISTENING...
...TO THE DEEPEST, DARKEST DEPTHS.

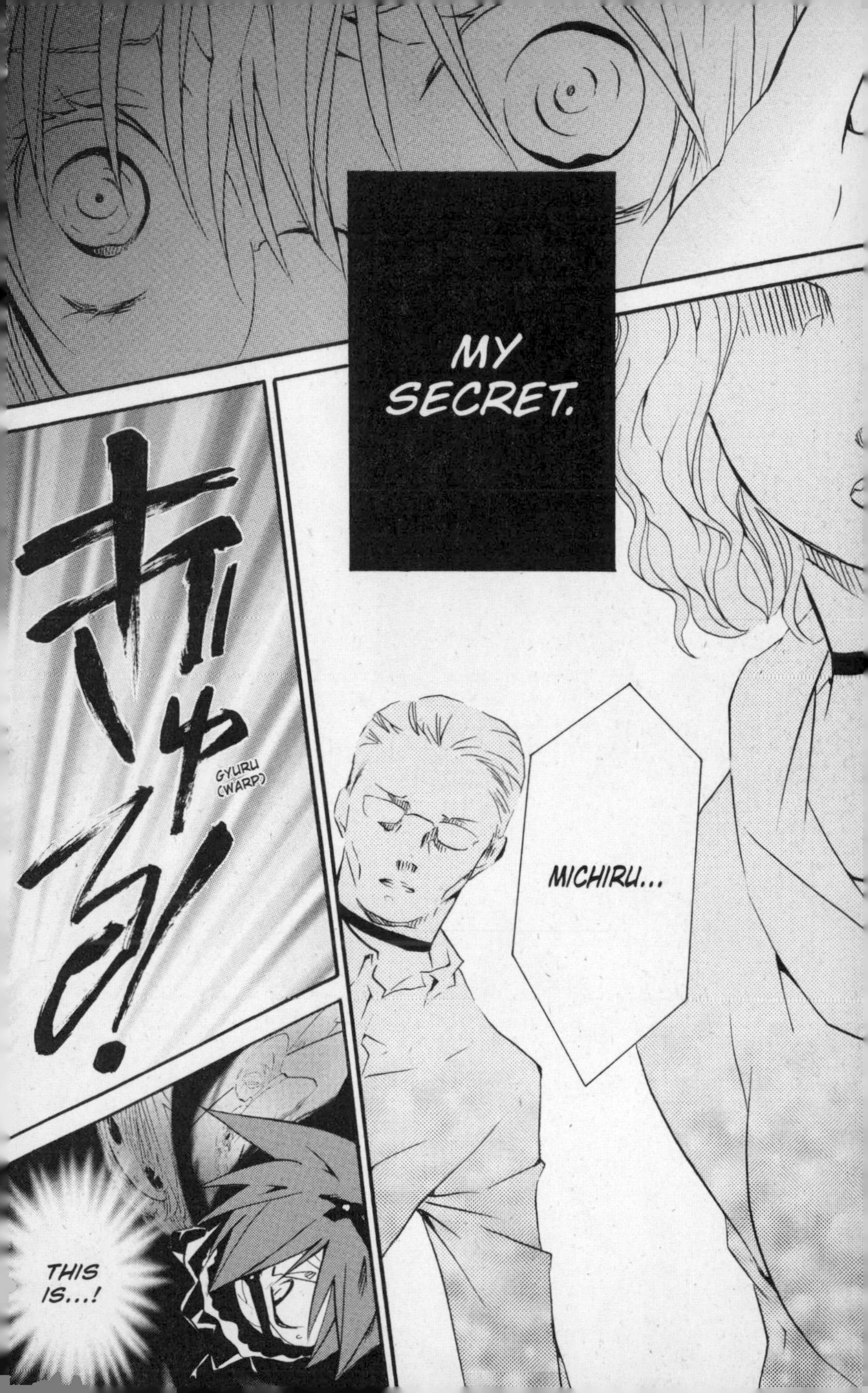
MY SECRET.
MICHIRU...
GYURU (WARP)
THIS IS...!

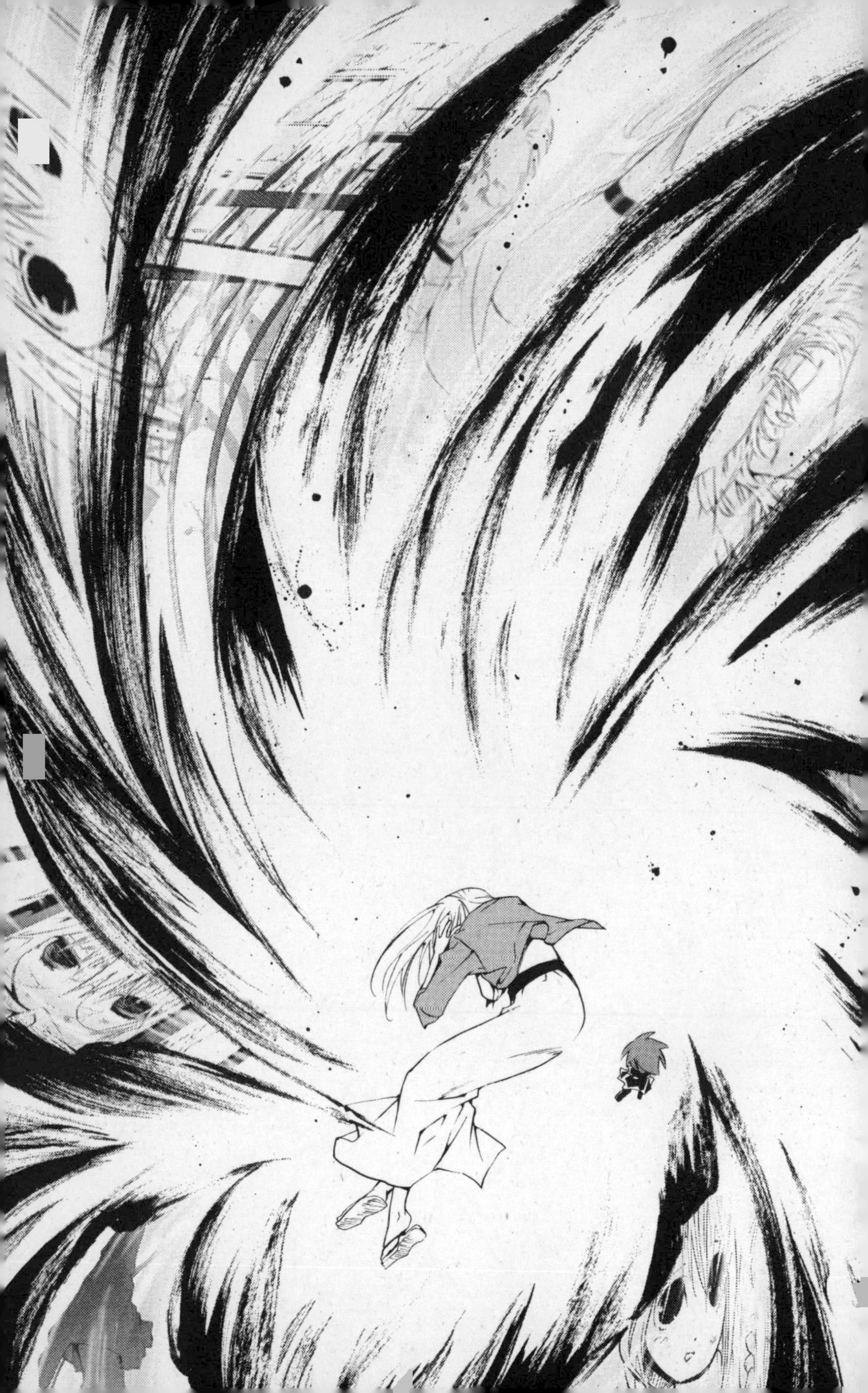

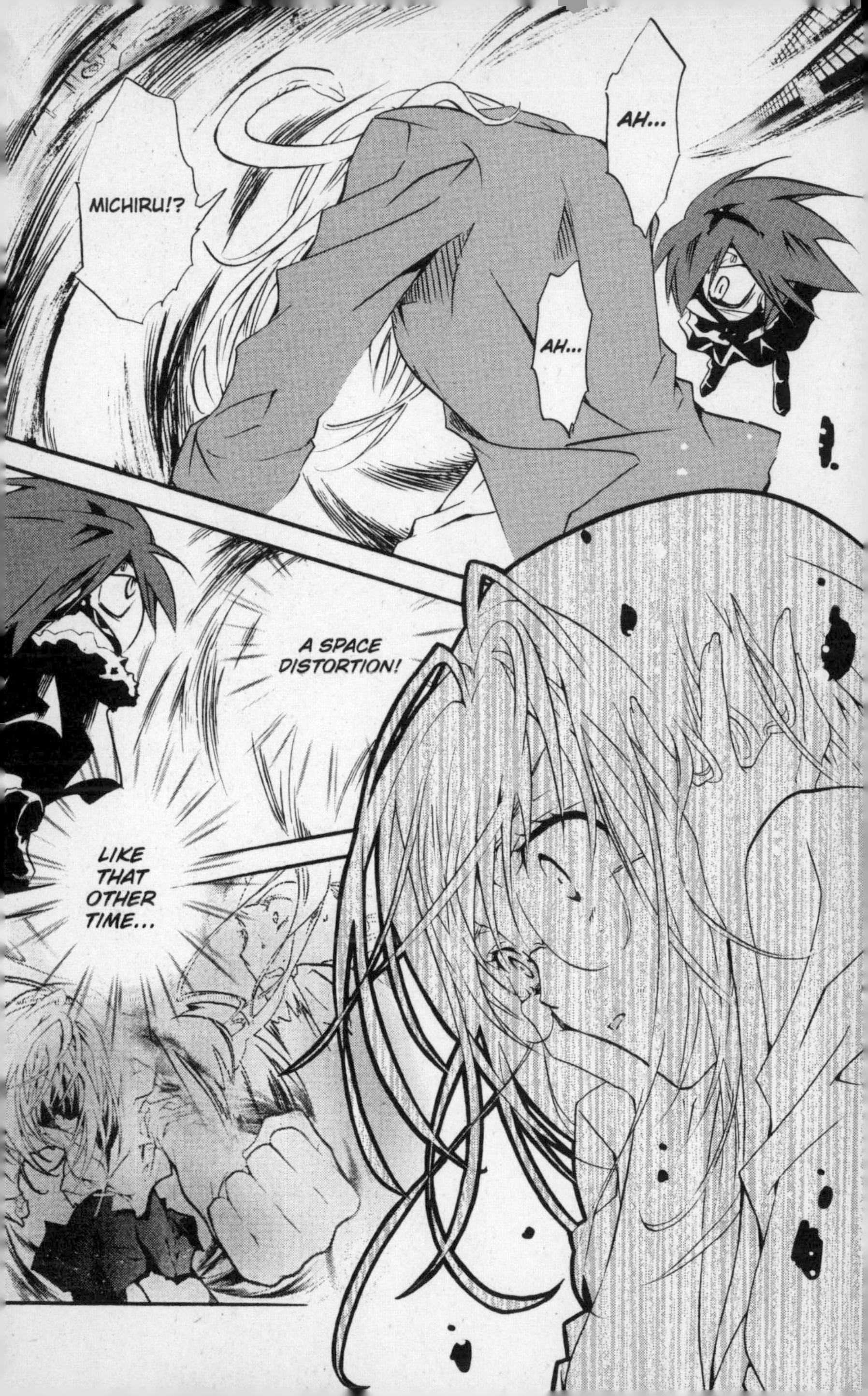
AH...
AH...
MICHIRU!?
A SPACE DISTORTION!
LIKE THAT OTHER TIME...

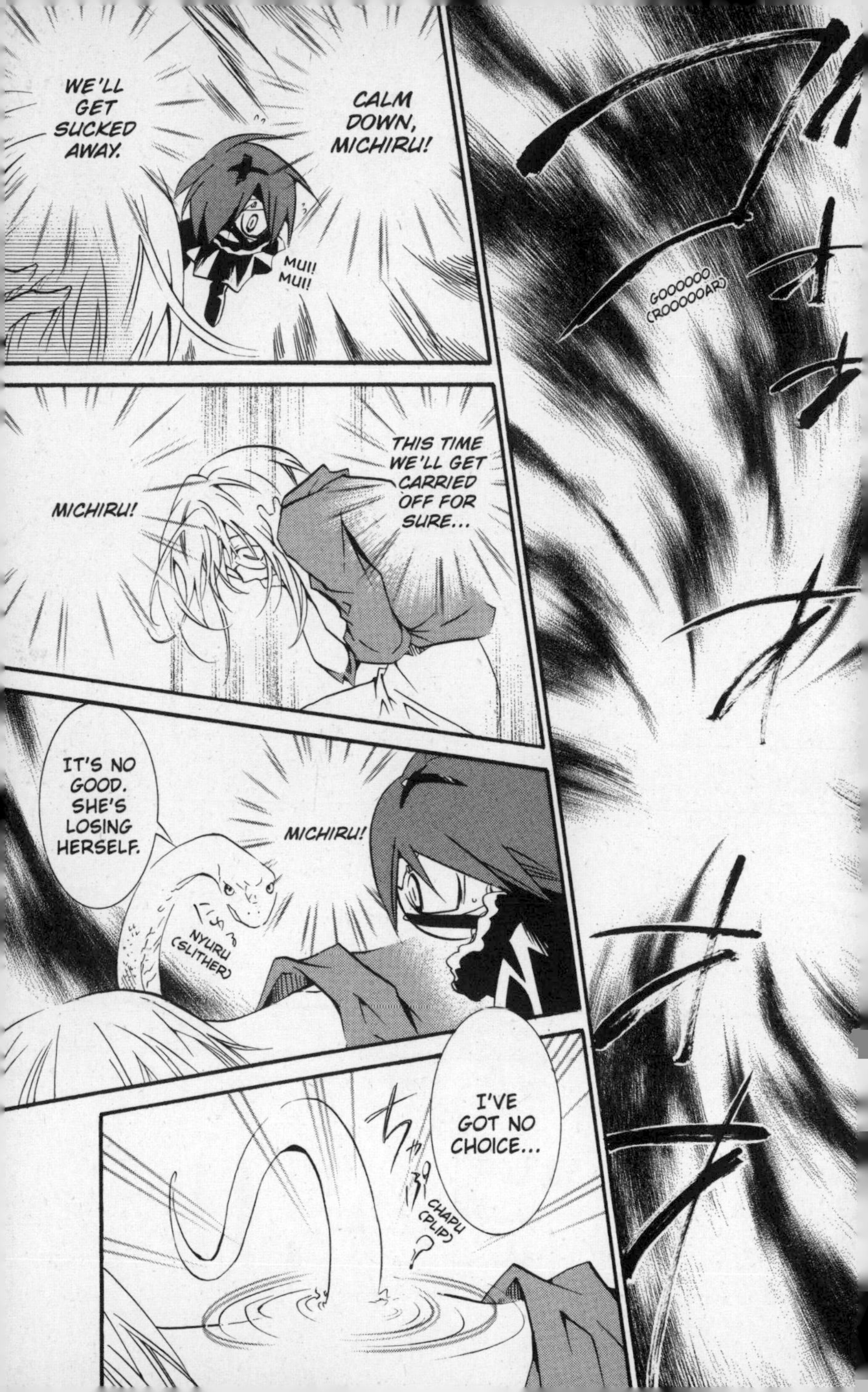
GOOOOOO (ROOOOOAR)
CALM DOWN, MICHIRU!
WE'LL GET SUCKED AWAY.
MUI! MUI!
THIS TIME WE'LL GET CARRIED OFF FOR SURE...
MICHIRU!
MICHIRU!
IT'S NO GOOD. SHE'S LOSING HERSELF.
NYURU (SLITHER)
I'VE GOT NO CHOICE...
CHAPU (PLIP)

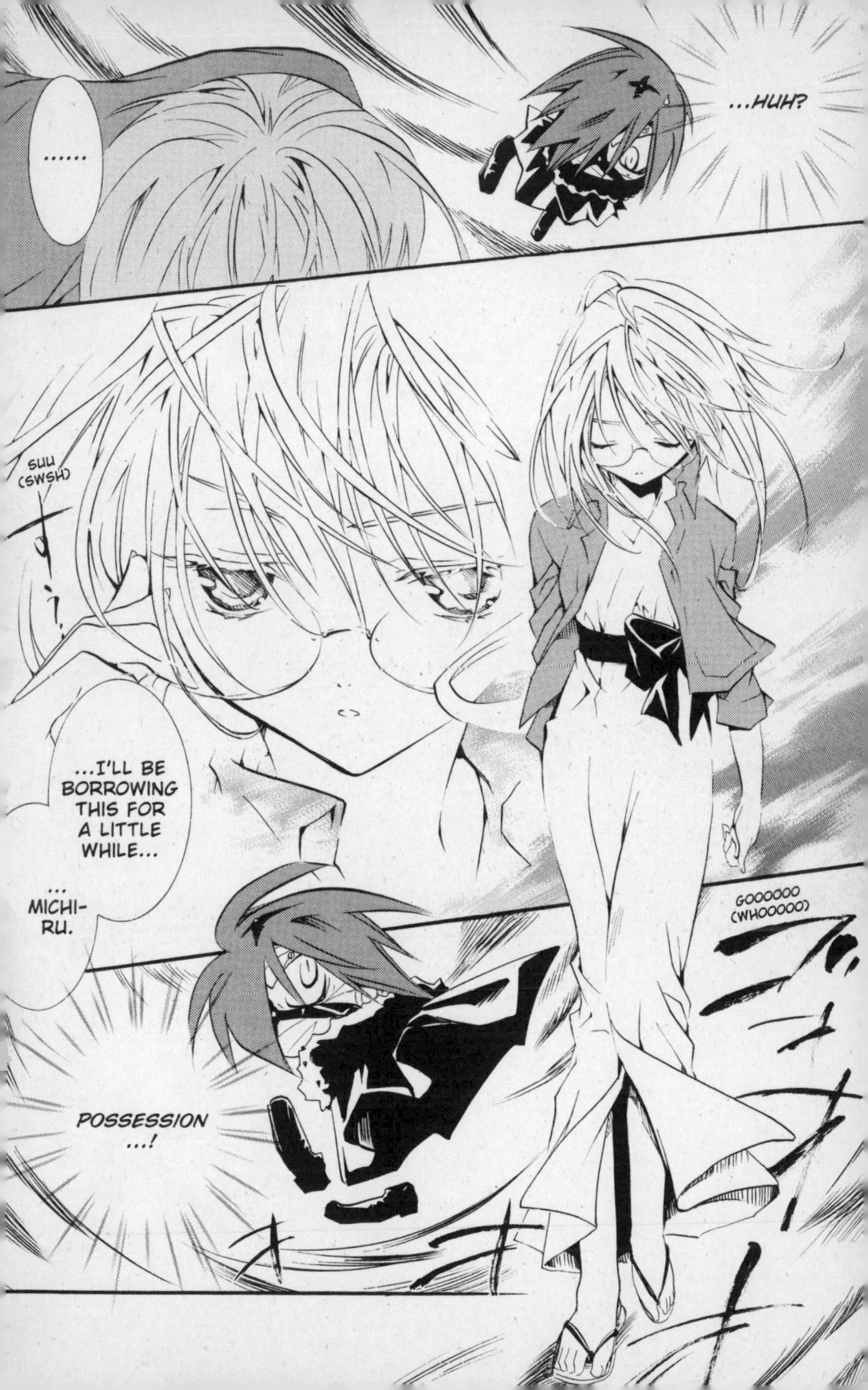
...HUH?
......
SUU (SWSH)
...I'LL BE BORROWING THIS FOR A LITTLE WHILE... ... MICHI-RU.
GOOOOOO (WHOOOOO)
POSSESSION ...!

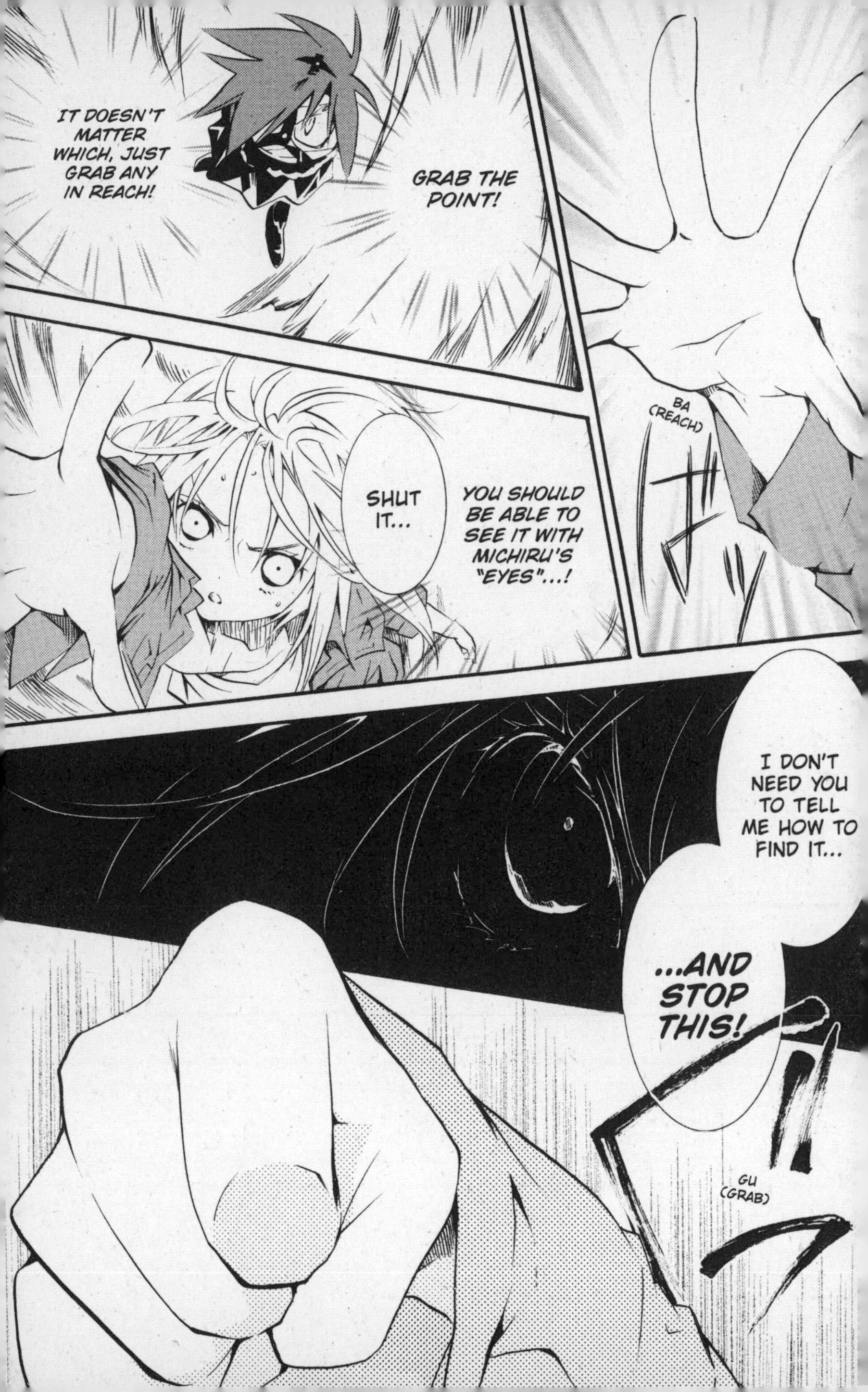
BA (REACH)
GRAB THE POINT!
IT DOESN'T MATTER WHICH, JUST GRAB ANY IN REACH!
YOU SHOULD BE ABLE TO SEE IT WITH MICHIRU'S "EYES"...!
SHUT IT...
I DON'T NEED YOU TO TELL ME HOW TO FIND IT...
...AND STOP THIS!
GU (GRAB)

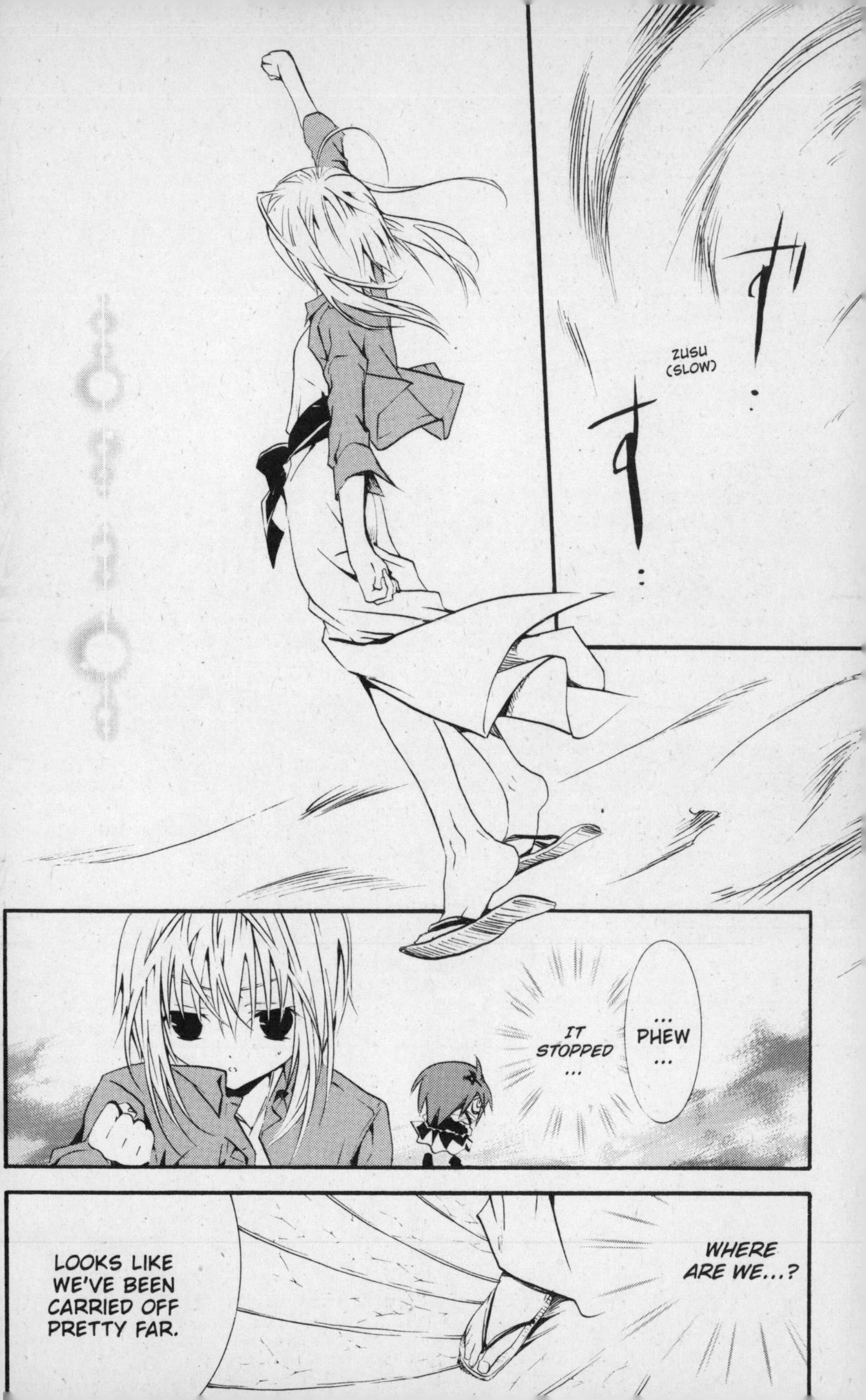

ずず…
ZUSU (SLOW)
... PHEW ...
IT STOPPED ...
WHERE ARE WE...?
LOOKS LIKE WE'VE BEEN CARRIED OFF PRETTY FAR.

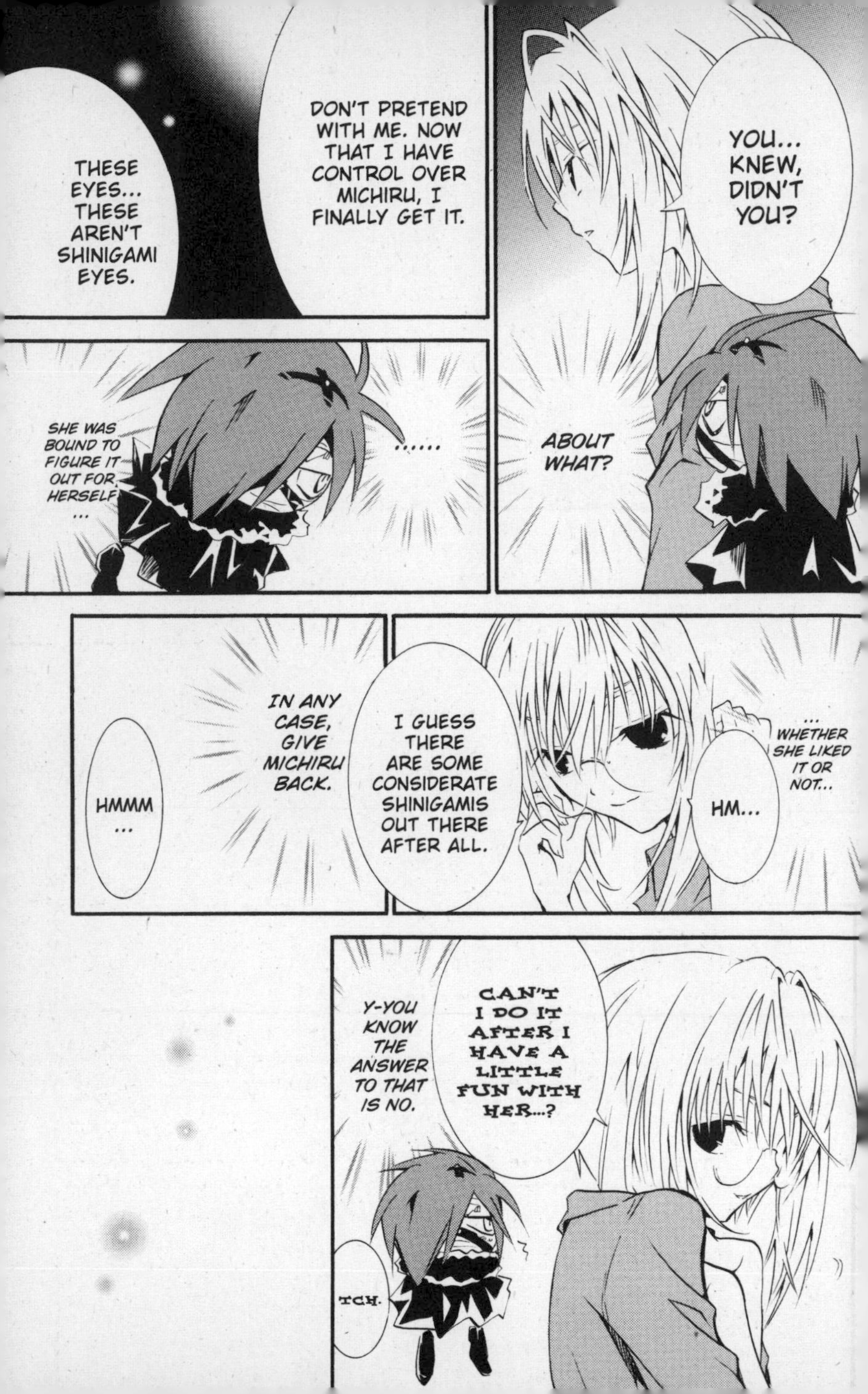
YOU... KNEW, DIDN'T YOU?
ABOUT WHAT?
DON'T PRETEND WITH ME. NOW THAT I HAVE CONTROL OVER MICHIRU, I FINALLY GET IT.
THESE EYES... THESE AREN'T SHINIGAMI EYES.
......
SHE WAS BOUND TO FIGURE IT OUT FOR HERSELF...
... WHETHER SHE LIKED IT OR NOT...
HM...
I GUESS THERE ARE SOME CONSIDERATE SHINIGAMIS OUT THERE AFTER ALL.
IN ANY CASE, GIVE MICHIRU BACK.
HMMM...
CAN'T I DO IT AFTER I HAVE A LITTLE FUN WITH HER...?
Y-YOU KNOW THE ANSWER TO THAT IS NO.
TCH.

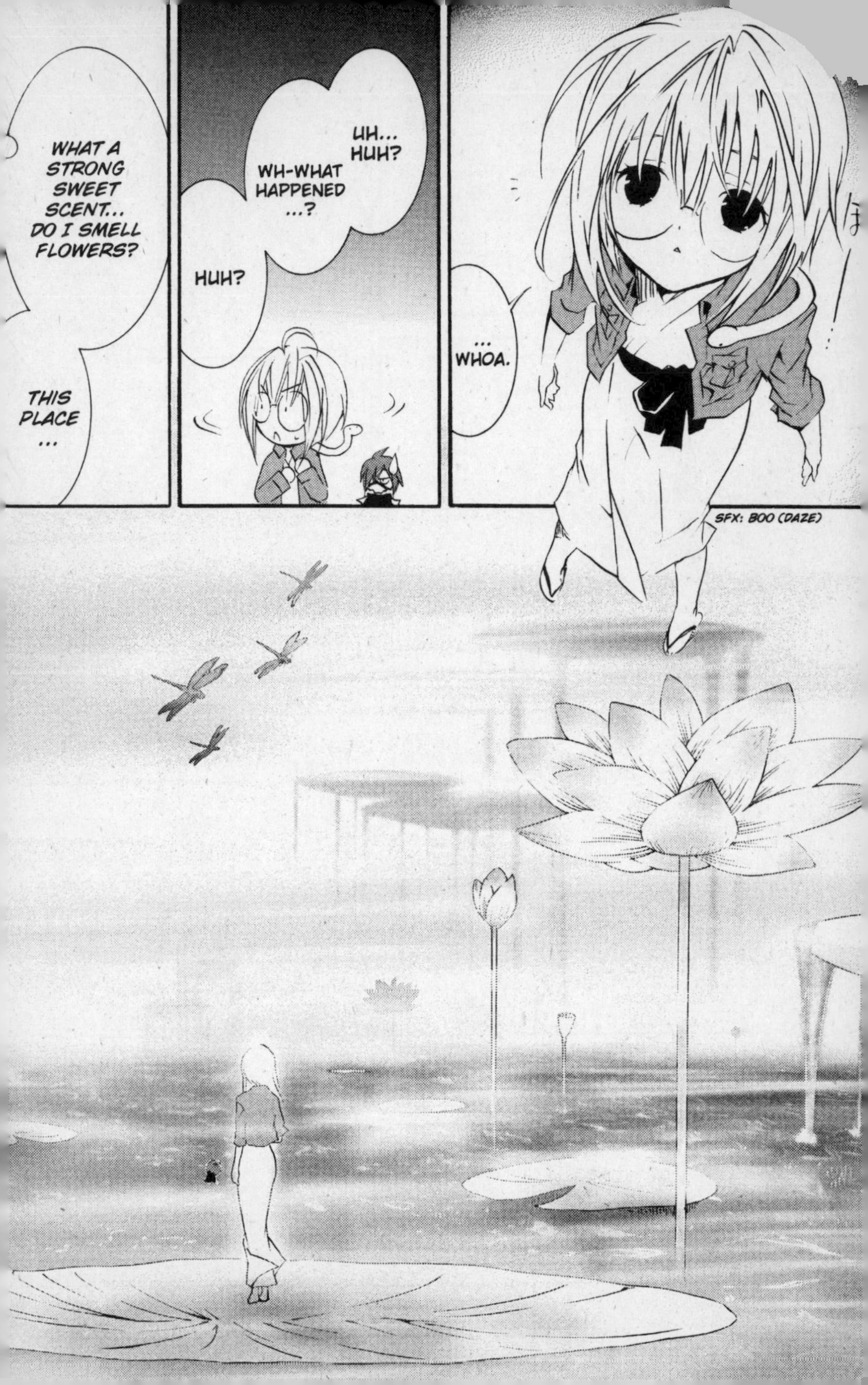
... WHOA.
SFX: BOO (DAZE)
UH... HUH?
WH-WHAT HAPPENED ...?
HUH?
WHAT A STRONG SWEET SCENT... DO I SMELL FLOWERS?
THIS PLACE ...

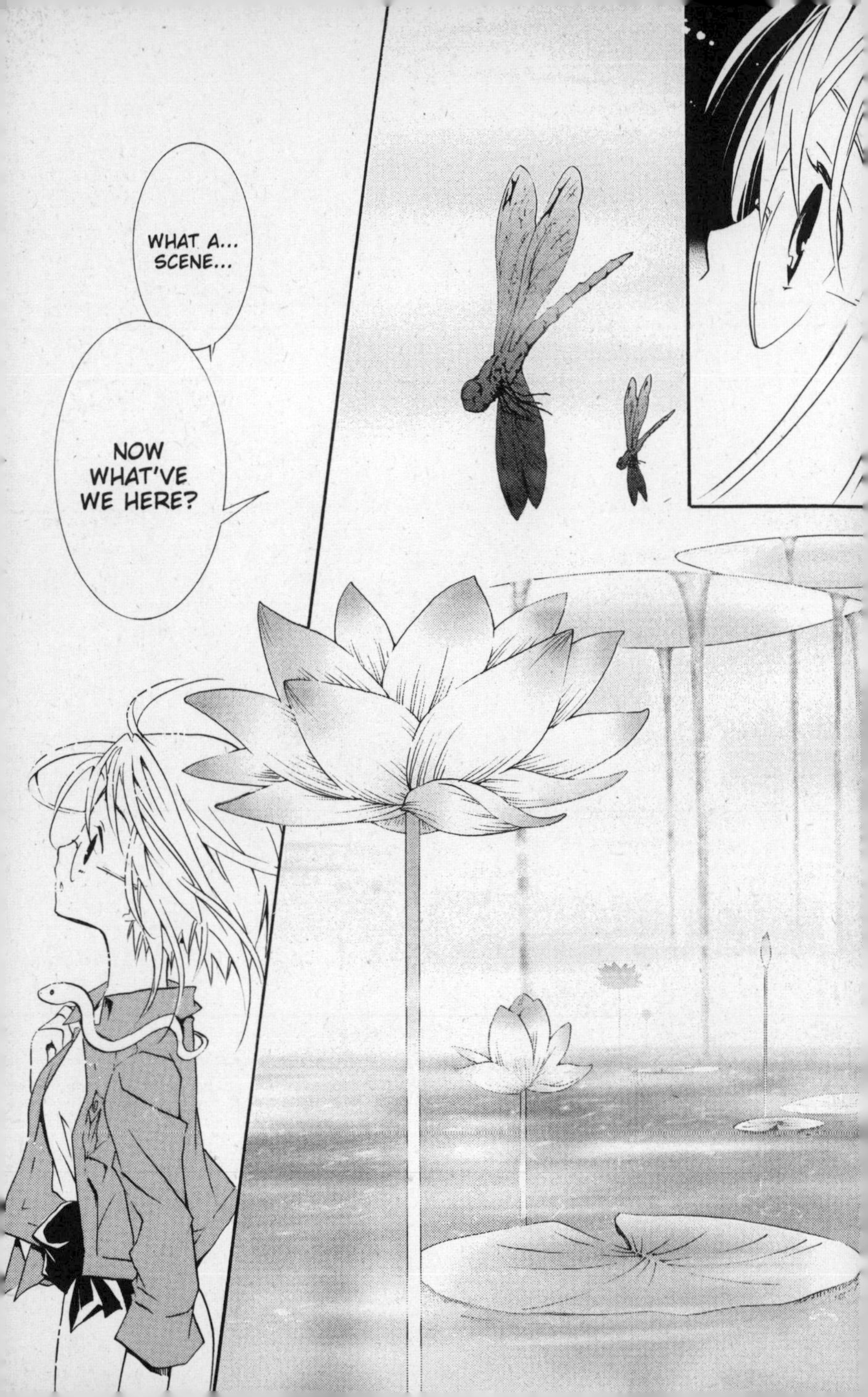
WHAT A... SCENE...
NOW WHAT'VE WE HERE?

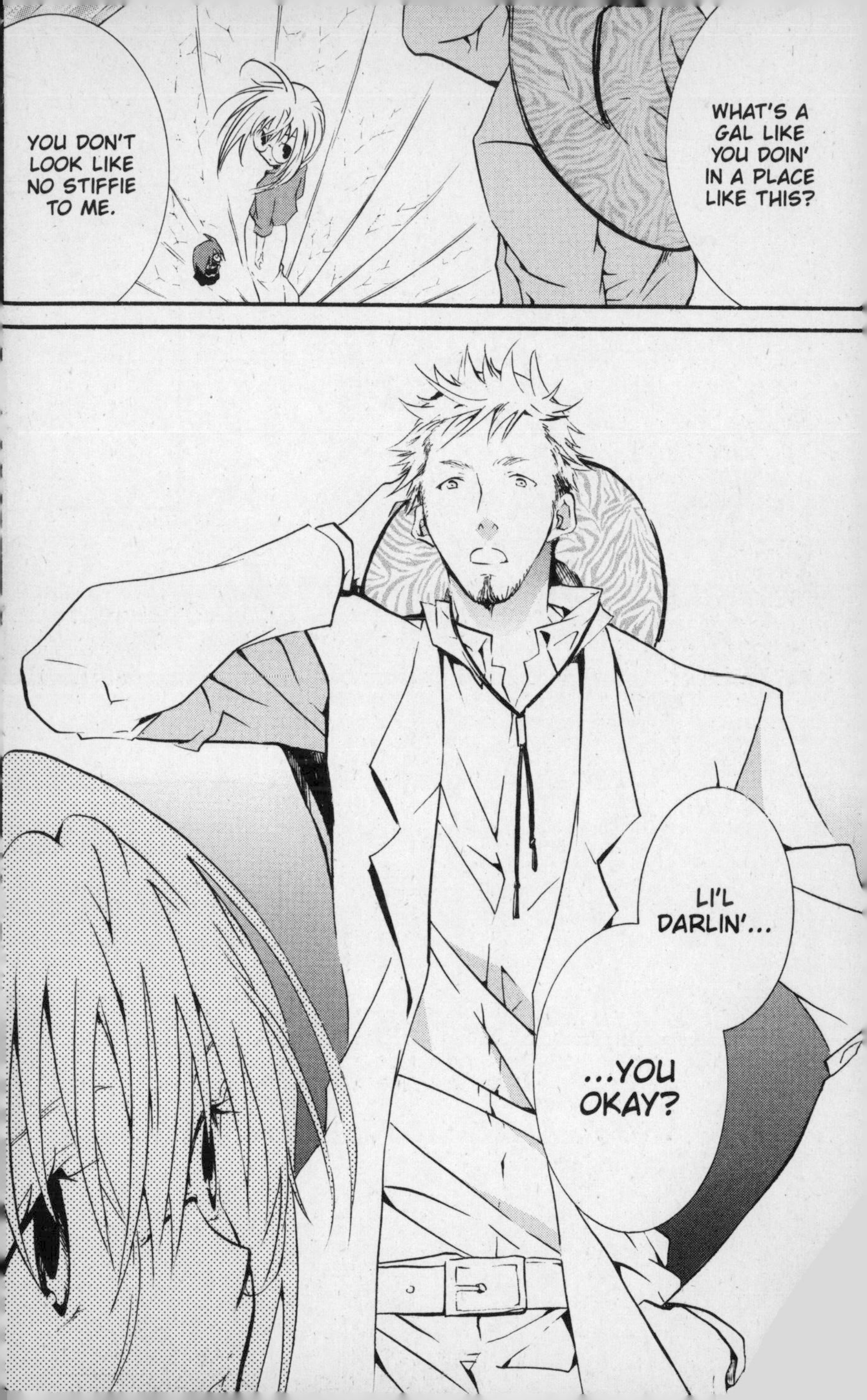
WHAT'S A GAL LIKE YOU DOIN' IN A PLACE LIKE THIS?
YOU DON'T LOOK LIKE NO STIFFIE TO ME.
LI'L DARLIN'...
...YOU OKAY?

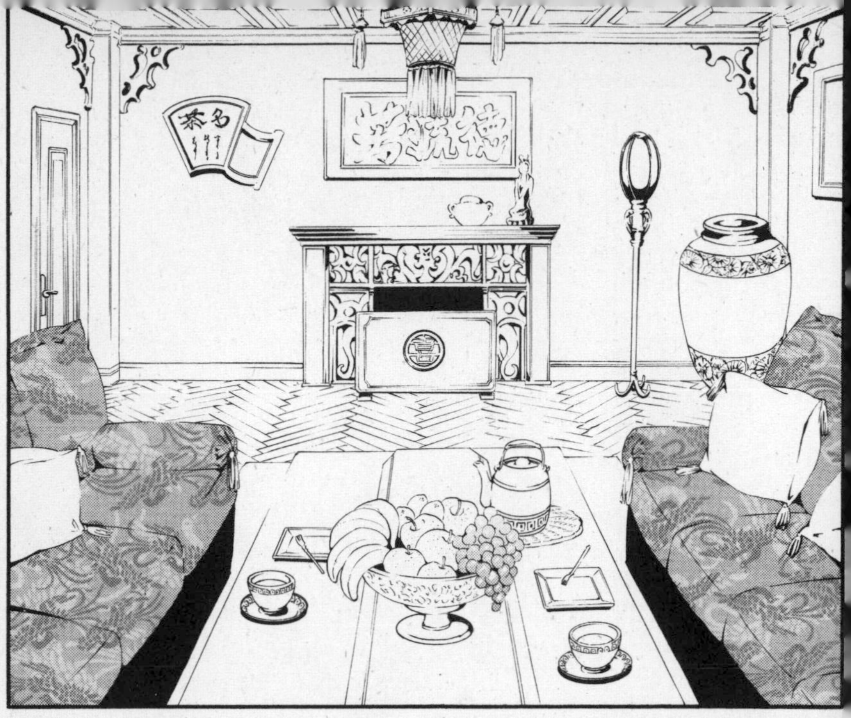

PAYMENT:58

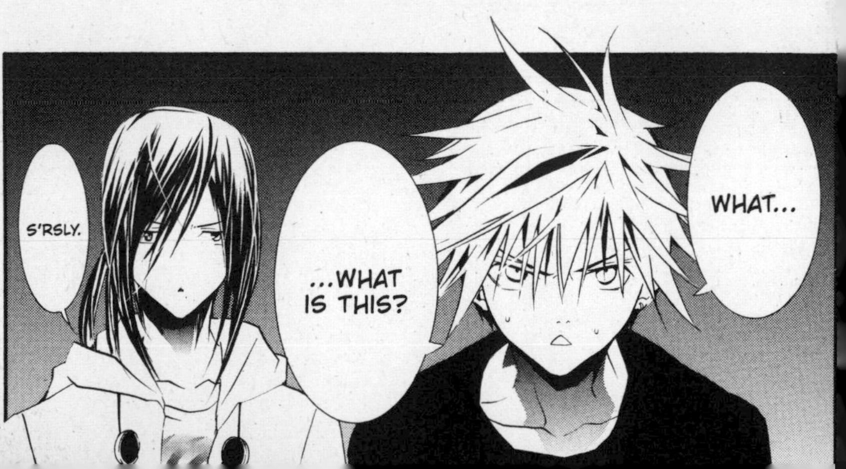
WHAT...
...WHAT IS THIS?
S'RSLY.

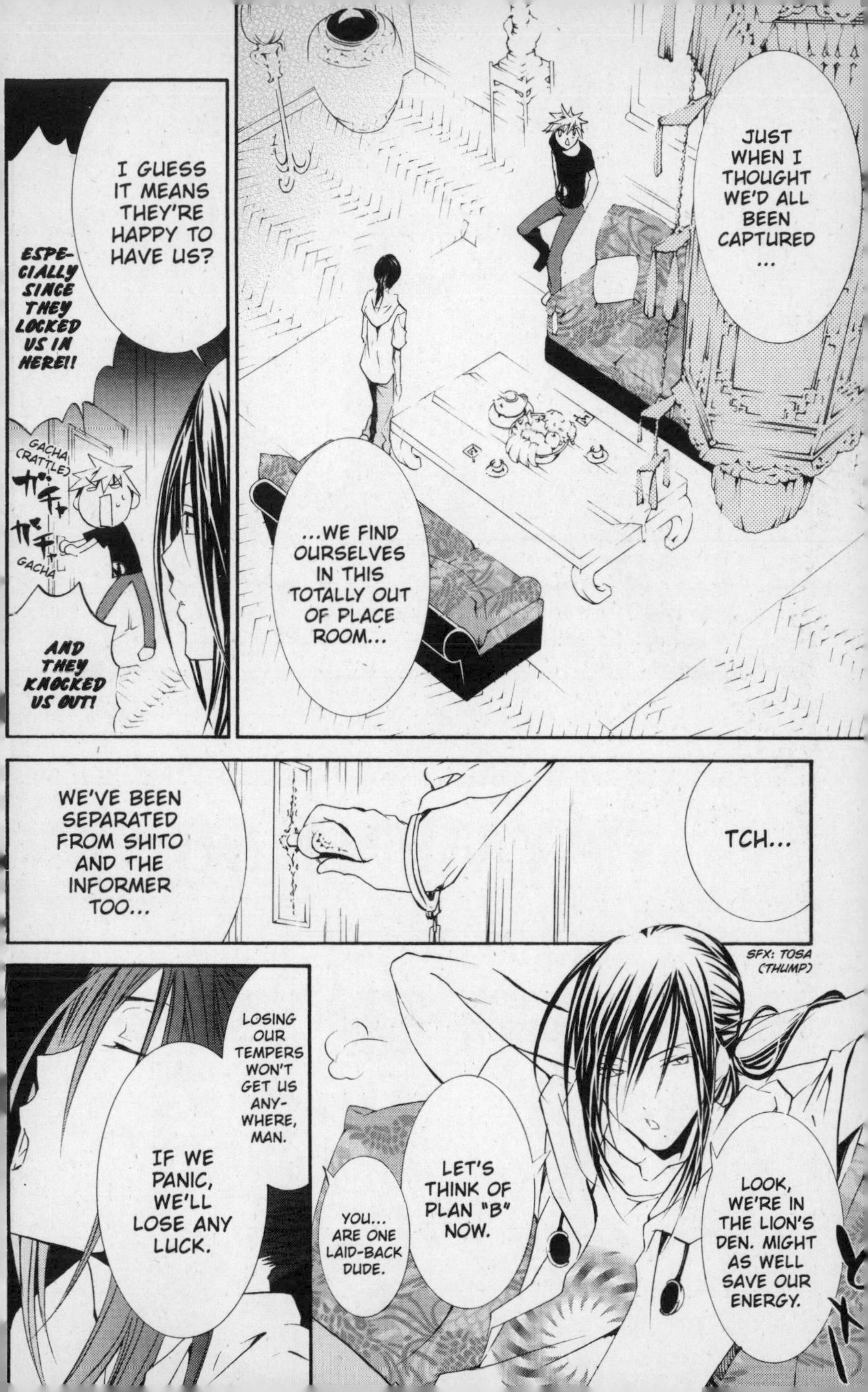
JUST WHEN I THOUGHT WE'D ALL BEEN CAPTURED ...
...WE FIND OURSELVES IN THIS TOTALLY OUT OF PLACE ROOM...
I GUESS IT MEANS THEY'RE HAPPY TO HAVE US?
ESPECIALLY SINCE THEY LOCKED US IN HERE!!
GACHA (RATTLE)
GACHA
AND THEY KNOCKED US OUT!
TCH...
WE'VE BEEN SEPARATED FROM SHITO AND THE INFORMER TOO...
SFX: TOSA (THUMP)
LOOK, WE'RE IN THE LION'S DEN. MIGHT AS WELL SAVE OUR ENERGY.
LET'S THINK OF PLAN "B" NOW.
YOU... ARE ONE LAID-BACK DUDE.
LOSING OUR TEMPERS WON'T GET US ANYWHERE, MAN.
IF WE PANIC, WE'LL LOSE ANY LUCK.

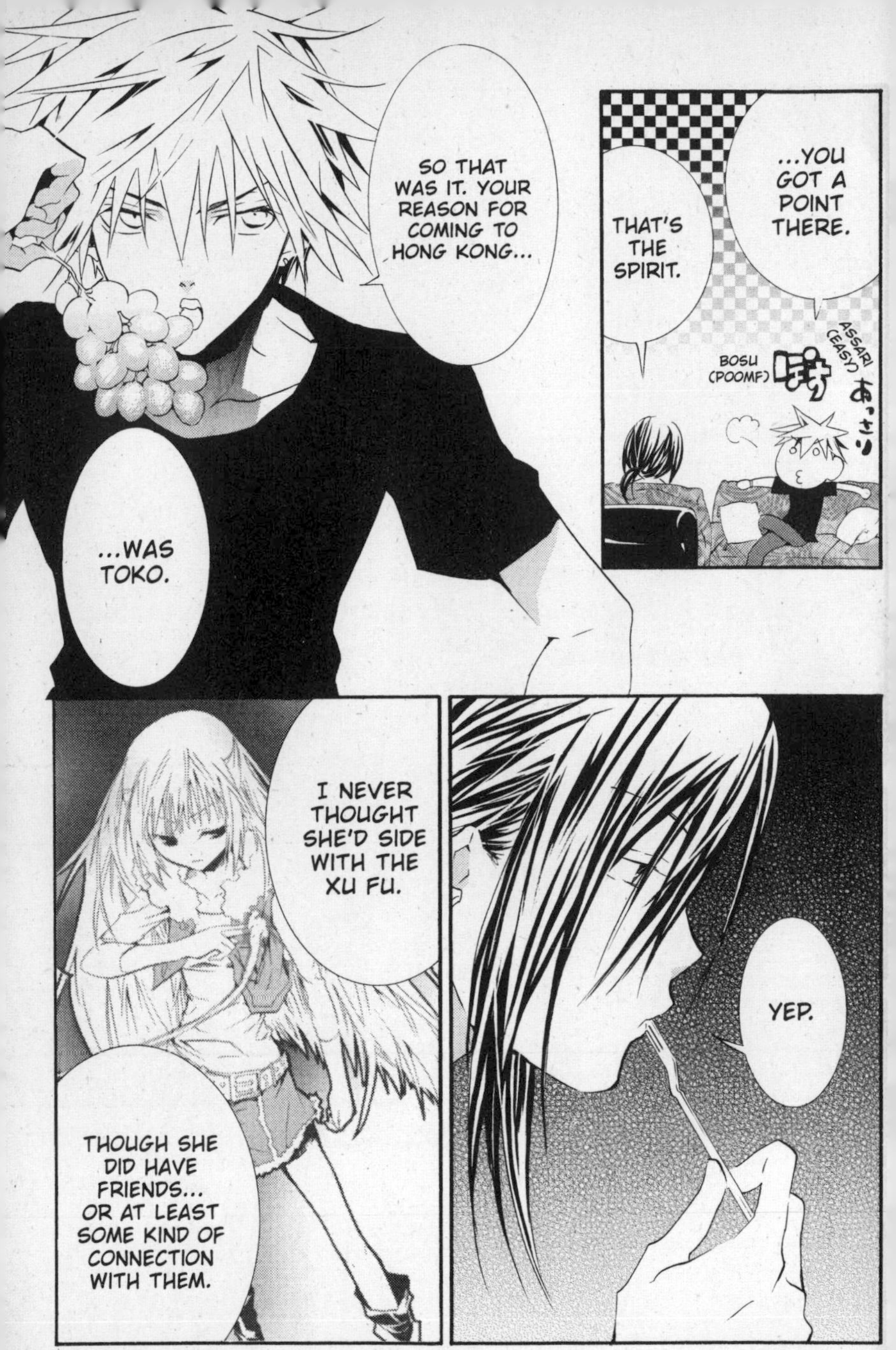
...YOU GOT A POINT THERE.
THAT'S THE SPIRIT.
ASSARI (EASY)
あっさり
BOSU (POOMF)
ぼす
SO THAT WAS IT. YOUR REASON FOR COMING TO HONG KONG...
...WAS TOKO.
YEP.
I NEVER THOUGHT SHE'D SIDE WITH THE XU FU.
THOUGH SHE DID HAVE FRIENDS... OR AT LEAST SOME KIND OF CONNECTION WITH THEM.

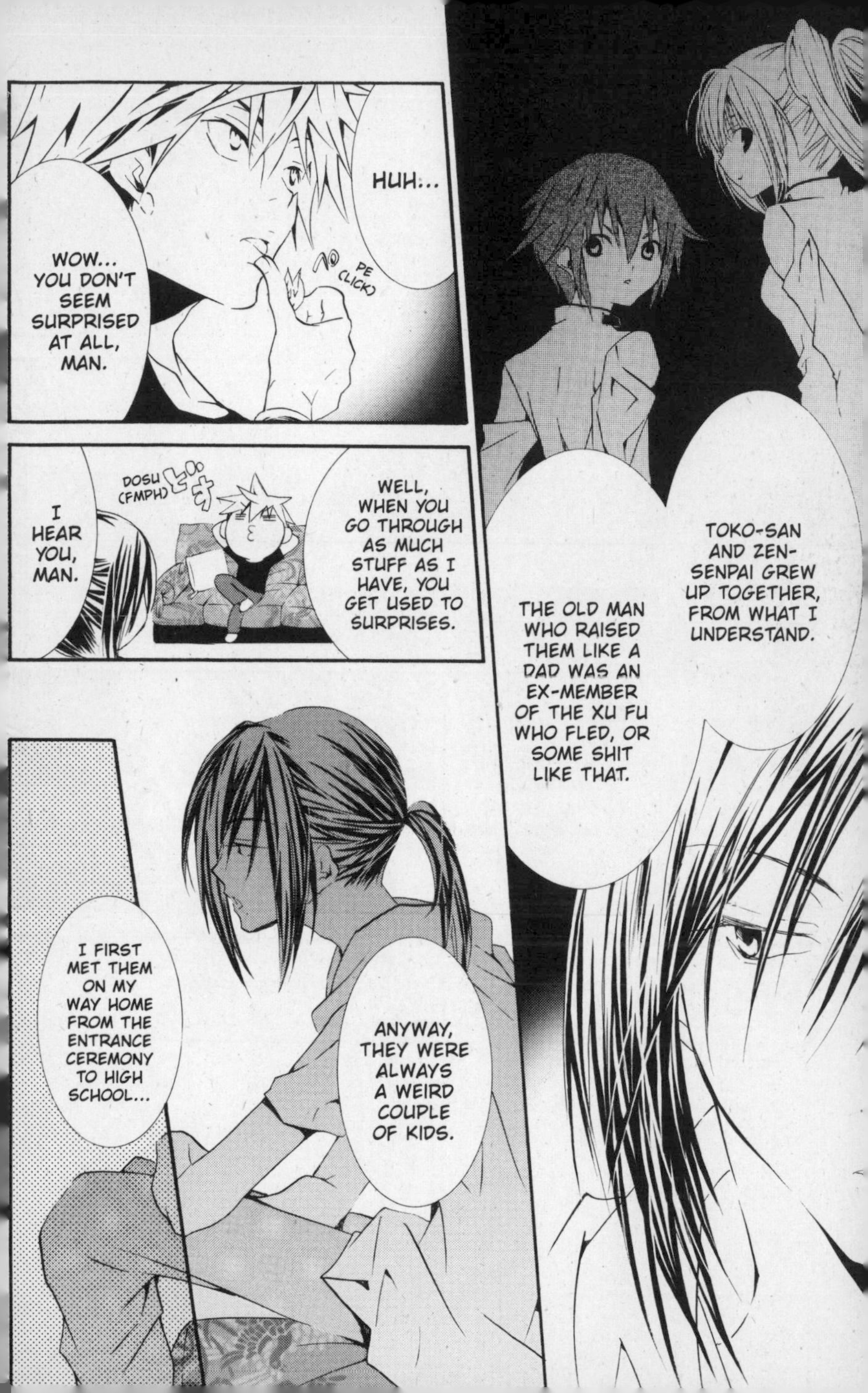
TOKO-SAN AND ZEN-SENPAI GREW UP TOGETHER, FROM WHAT I UNDERSTAND.
THE OLD MAN WHO RAISED THEM LIKE A DAD WAS AN EX-MEMBER OF THE XU FU WHO FLED, OR SOME SHIT LIKE THAT.
HUH...
PE (LICK)
WOW... YOU DON'T SEEM SURPRISED AT ALL, MAN.
WELL, WHEN YOU GO THROUGH AS MUCH STUFF AS I HAVE, YOU GET USED TO SURPRISES.
DOSU (FMPH)
I HEAR YOU, MAN.
I FIRST MET THEM ON MY WAY HOME FROM THE ENTRANCE CEREMONY TO HIGH SCHOOL...
ANYWAY, THEY WERE ALWAYS A WEIRD COUPLE OF KIDS.

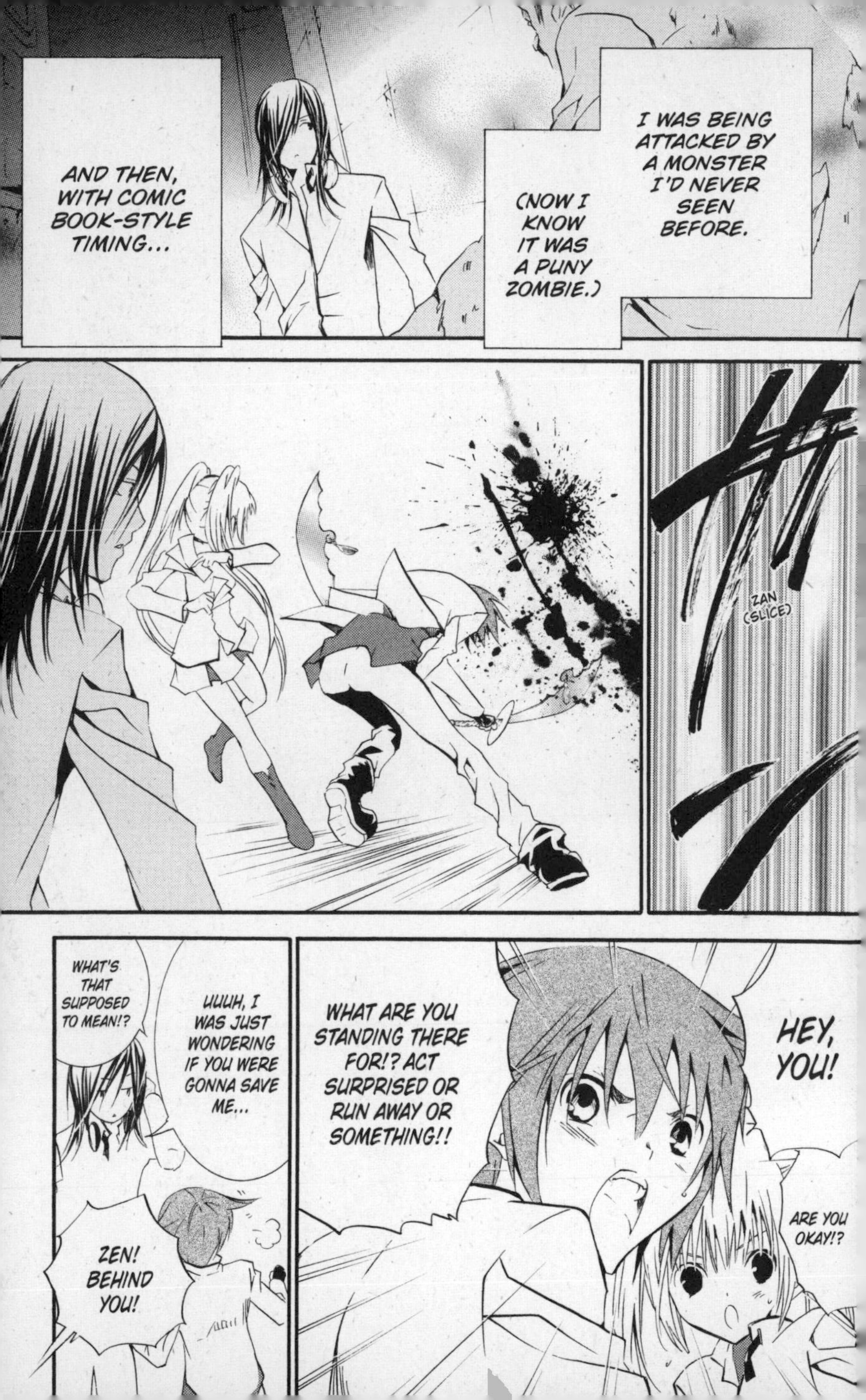
I WAS BEING ATTACKED BY A MONSTER I'D NEVER SEEN BEFORE.
(NOW I KNOW IT WAS A PUNY ZOMBIE.)
AND THEN, WITH COMIC BOOK-STYLE TIMING...
ZAN (SLICE)
HEY, YOU!
WHAT ARE YOU STANDING THERE FOR!? ACT SURPRISED OR RUN AWAY OR SOMETHING!!
ARE YOU OKAY!?
UUUH, I WAS JUST WONDERING IF YOU WERE GONNA SAVE ME...
WHAT'S THAT SUPPOSED TO MEAN!?
ZEN! BEHIND YOU!

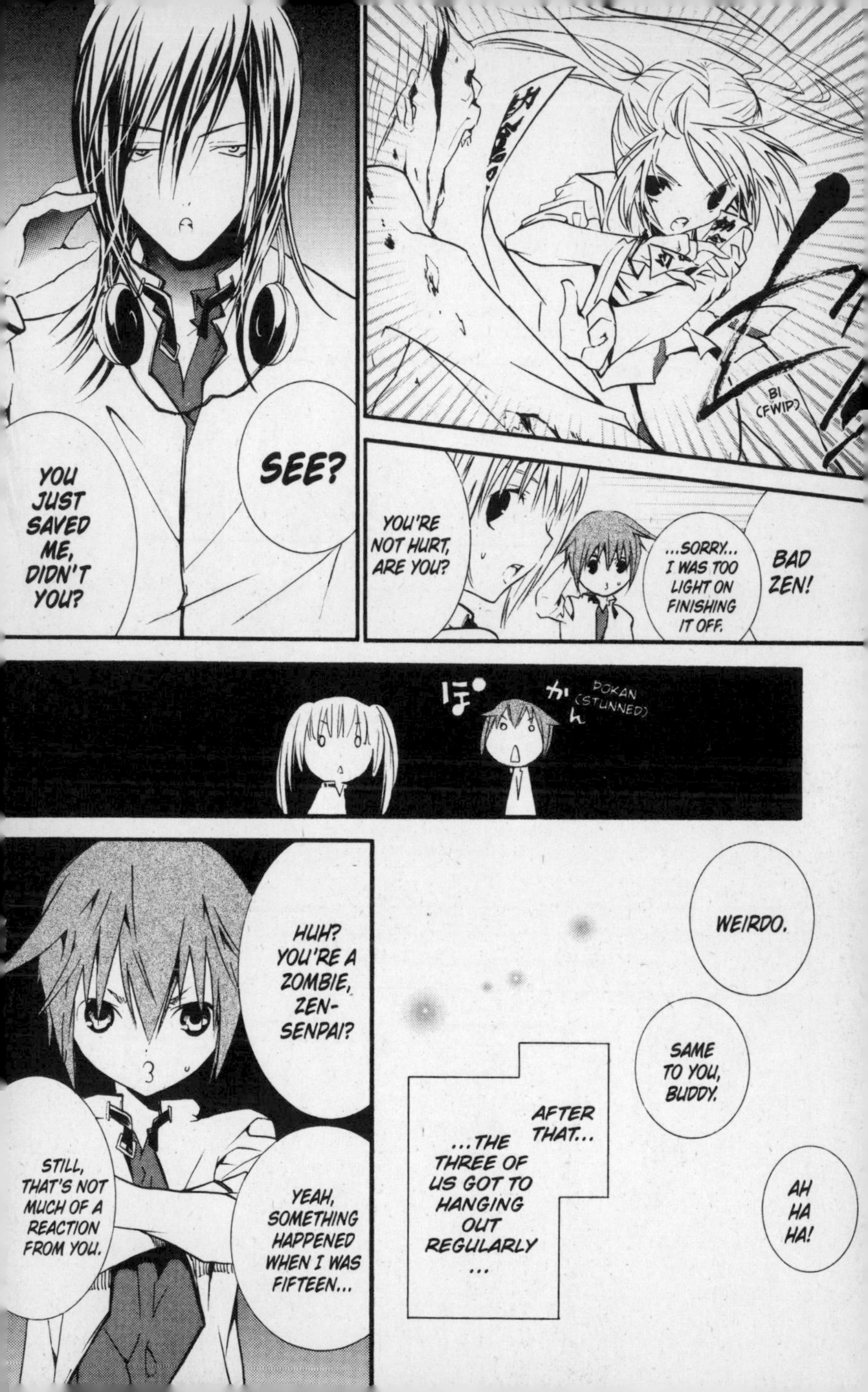
BI (FWIP)
BAD ZEN!
...SORRY... I WAS TOO LIGHT ON FINISHING IT OFF.
YOU'RE NOT HURT, ARE YOU?
SEE?
YOU JUST SAVED ME, DIDN'T YOU?
ぽかん
POKAN (STUNNED)
WEIRDO.
SAME TO YOU, BUDDY.
AH HA HA!
AFTER THAT...
...THE THREE OF US GOT TO HANGING OUT REGULARLY...
HUH? YOU'RE A ZOMBIE, ZEN-SENPAI?
YEAH, SOMETHING HAPPENED WHEN I WAS FIFTEEN...
STILL, THAT'S NOT MUCH OF A REACTION FROM YOU.

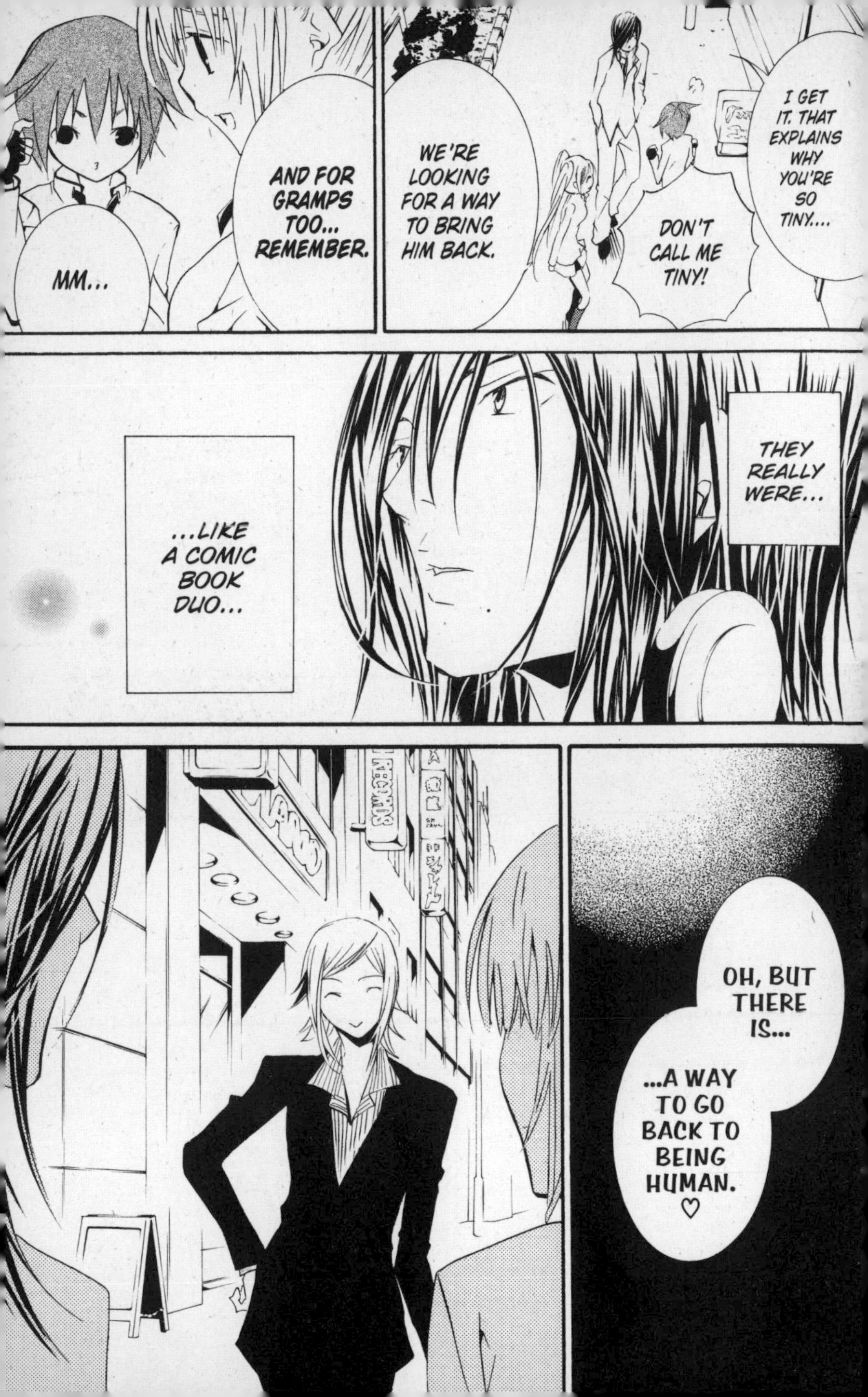
I GET IT. THAT EXPLAINS WHY YOU'RE SO TINY....
DON'T CALL ME TINY!
WE'RE LOOKING FOR A WAY TO BRING HIM BACK.
AND FOR GRAMPS TOO... REMEMBER.
MM...
THEY REALLY WERE...
...LIKE A COMIC BOOK DUO...
OH, BUT THERE IS...
...A WAY TO GO BACK TO BEING HUMAN. ♡

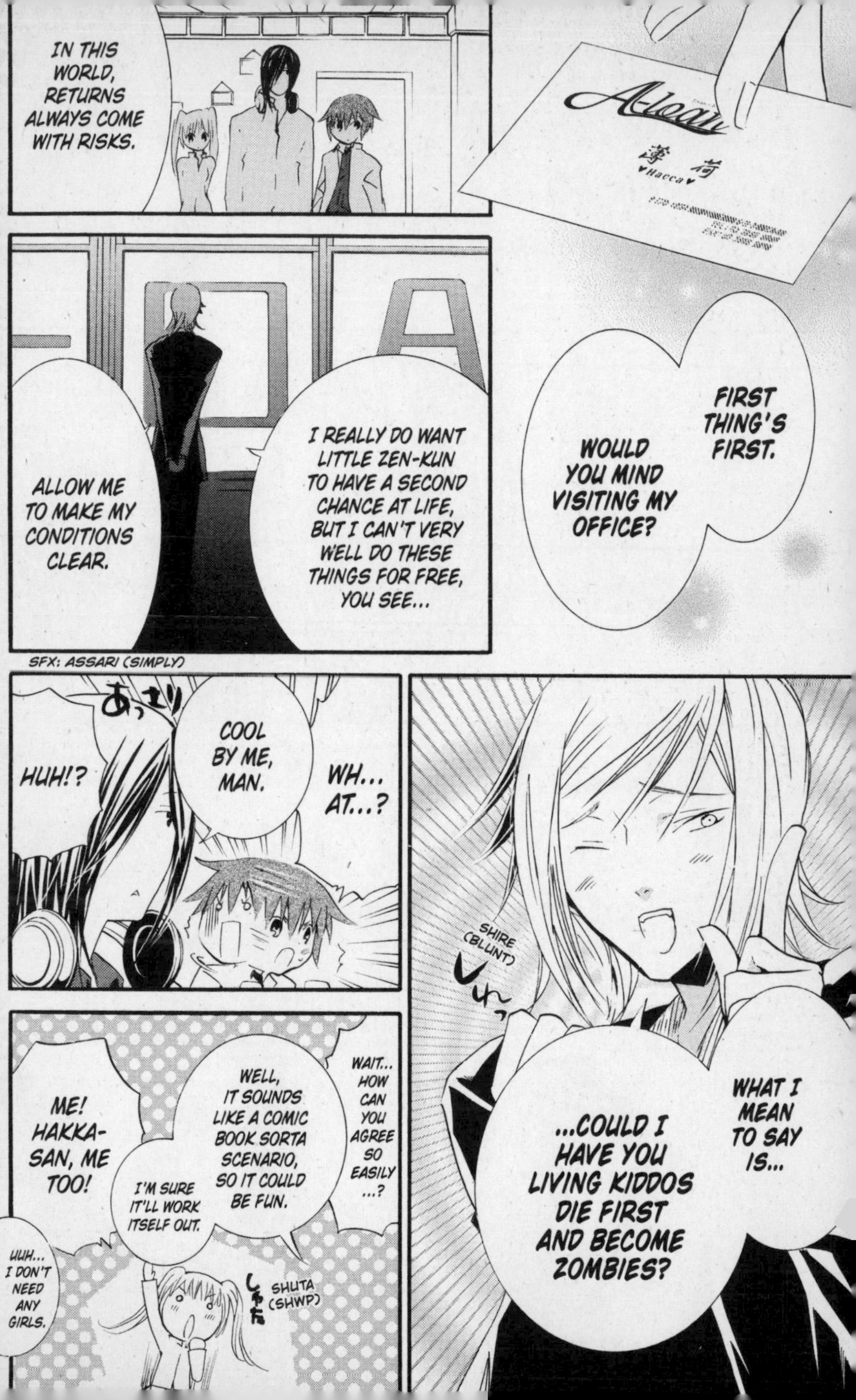

薄荷
Hacca
FIRST THING'S FIRST.
WOULD YOU MIND VISITING MY OFFICE?
IN THIS WORLD, RETURNS ALWAYS COME WITH RISKS.
I REALLY DO WANT LITTLE ZEN-KUN TO HAVE A SECOND CHANCE AT LIFE, BUT I CAN'T VERY WELL DO THESE THINGS FOR FREE, YOU SEE...
ALLOW ME TO MAKE MY CONDITIONS CLEAR.
SFX: ASSARI (SIMPLY)
WHAT I MEAN TO SAY IS...
...COULD I HAVE YOU LIVING KIDDOS DIE FIRST AND BECOME ZOMBIES?
SHIRE (BLUNT)
あっさり
WH... AT...?
COOL BY ME, MAN.
HUH!?
WAIT... HOW CAN YOU AGREE SO EASILY...?
WELL, IT SOUNDS LIKE A COMIC BOOK SORTA SCENARIO, SO IT COULD BE FUN.
I'M SURE IT'LL WORK ITSELF OUT.
ME! HAKKA-SAN, ME TOO!
SHUTA (SHWP)
UUH... I DON'T NEED ANY GIRLS.

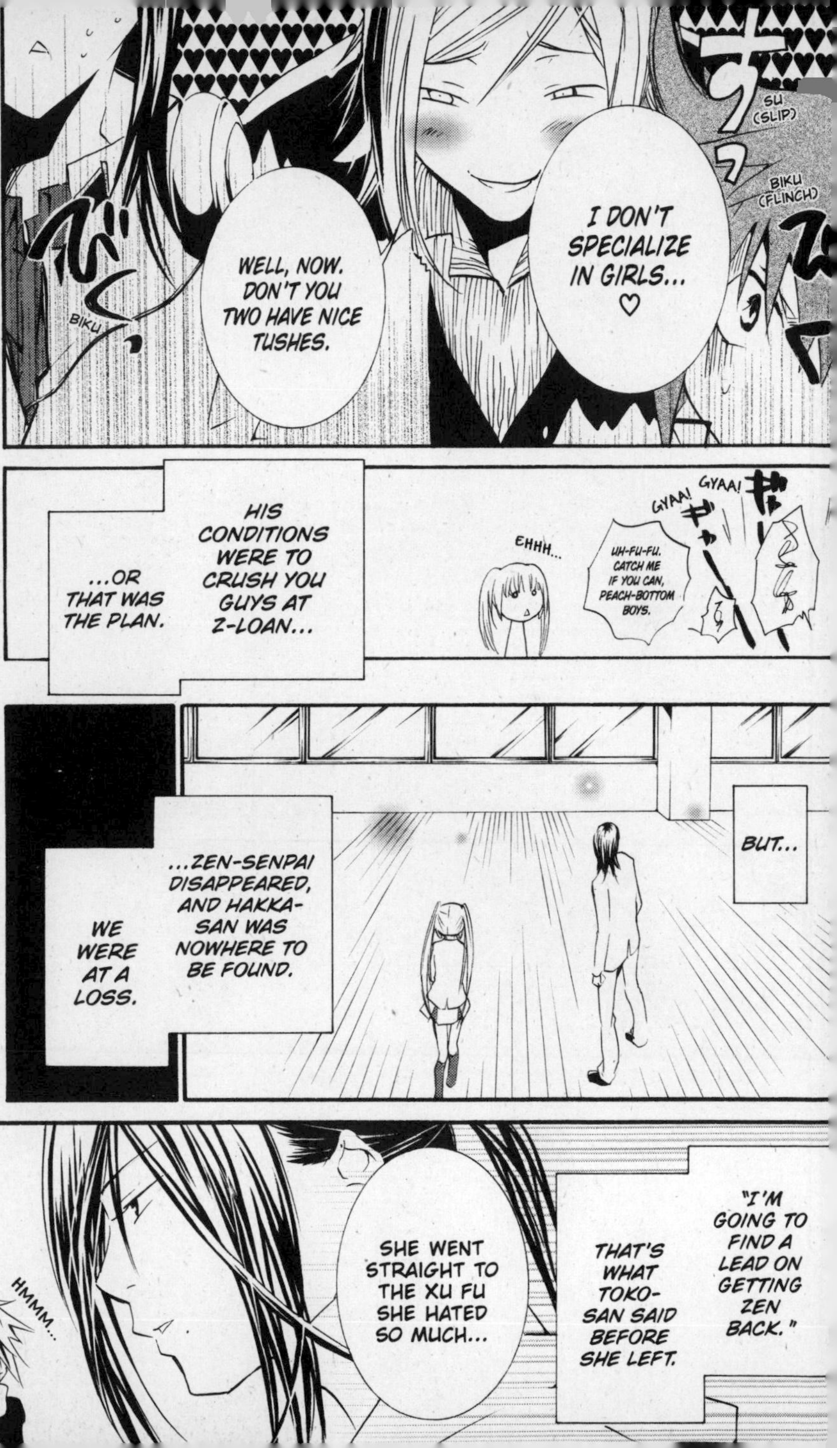
SU (SLIP)
BIKU (FLINCH)
I DON'T SPECIALIZE IN GIRLS... ♡
WELL, NOW. DON'T YOU TWO HAVE NICE TUSHES.
BIKU
GYAA! GYAA!
UH-FU-FU. CATCH ME IF YOU CAN, PEACH-BOTTOM BOYS.
EHHH...
HIS CONDITIONS WERE TO CRUSH YOU GUYS AT Z-LOAN...
...OR THAT WAS THE PLAN.
BUT...
...ZEN-SENPAI DISAPPEARED, AND HAKKA-SAN WAS NOWHERE TO BE FOUND.
WE WERE AT A LOSS.
"I'M GOING TO FIND A LEAD ON GETTING ZEN BACK."
THAT'S WHAT TOKO-SAN SAID BEFORE SHE LEFT.
SHE WENT STRAIGHT TO THE XU FU SHE HATED SO MUCH...
HMMM...

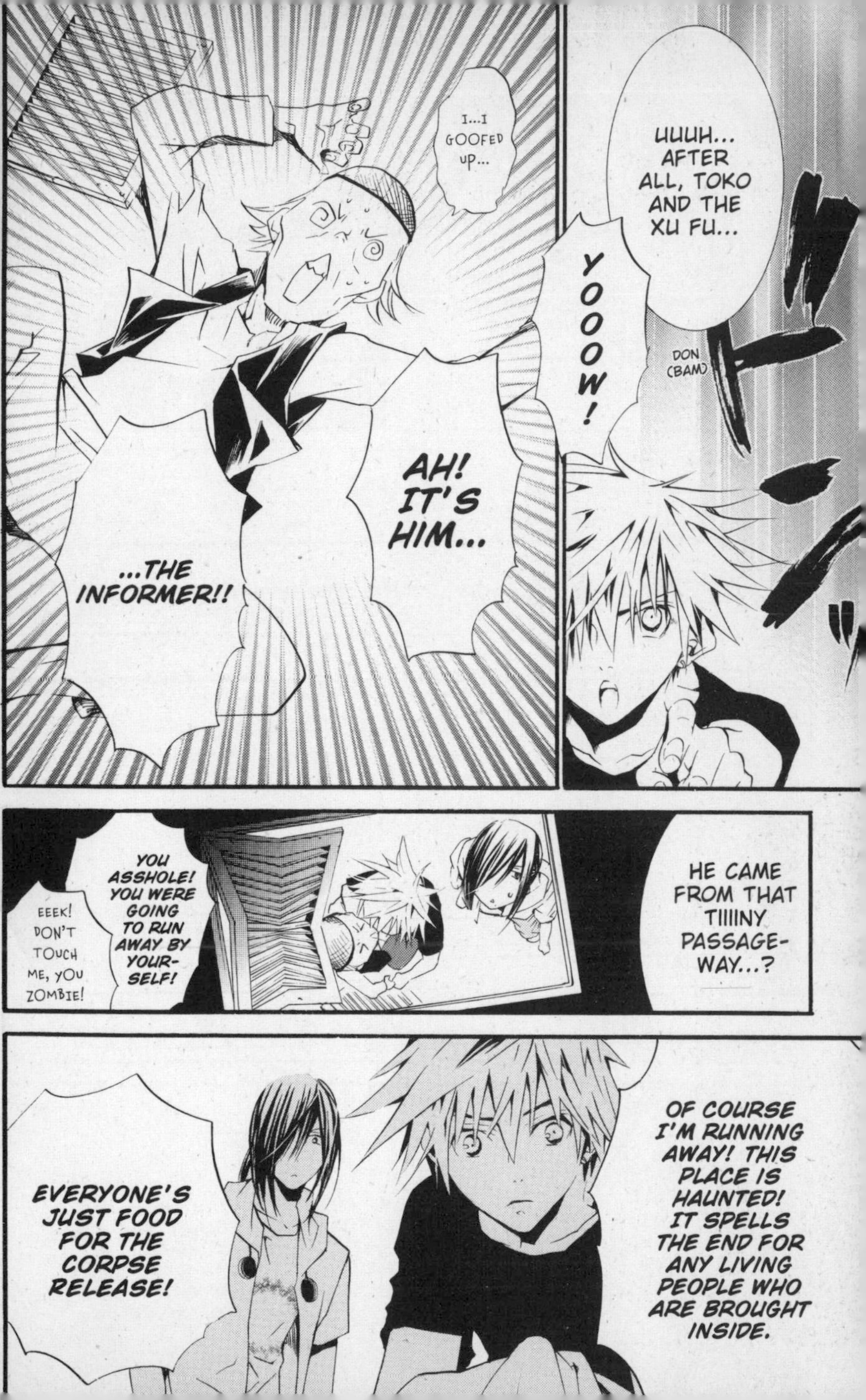
UUUH... AFTER ALL, TOKO AND THE XU FU...
YOOOW!
DON (BAM)
I...I GOOFED UP...
AH! IT'S HIM...
...THE INFORMER!!
HE CAME FROM THAT TIIIINY PASSAGE-WAY...?
YOU ASSHOLE! YOU WERE GOING TO RUN AWAY BY YOUR-SELF!
EEEK! DON'T TOUCH ME, YOU ZOMBIE!
OF COURSE I'M RUNNING AWAY! THIS PLACE IS HAUNTED! IT SPELLS THE END FOR ANY LIVING PEOPLE WHO ARE BROUGHT INSIDE.
EVERYONE'S JUST FOOD FOR THE CORPSE RELEASE!

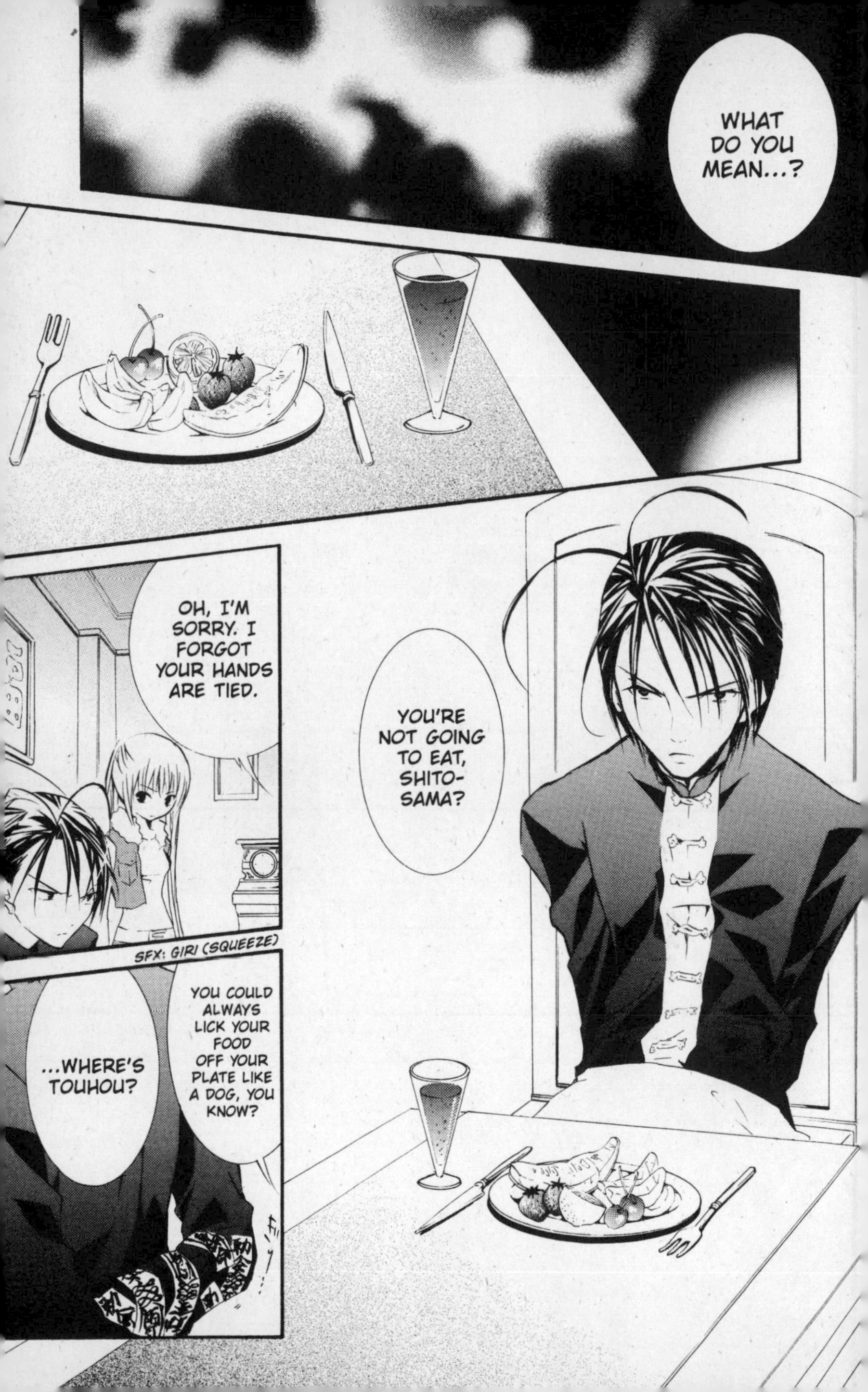
WHAT DO YOU MEAN...?
YOU'RE NOT GOING TO EAT, SHITO-SAMA?
OH, I'M SORRY. I FORGOT YOUR HANDS ARE TIED.
SFX: GIRI (SQUEEZE)
YOU COULD ALWAYS LICK YOUR FOOD OFF YOUR PLATE LIKE A DOG, YOU KNOW?
...WHERE'S TOUHOU?

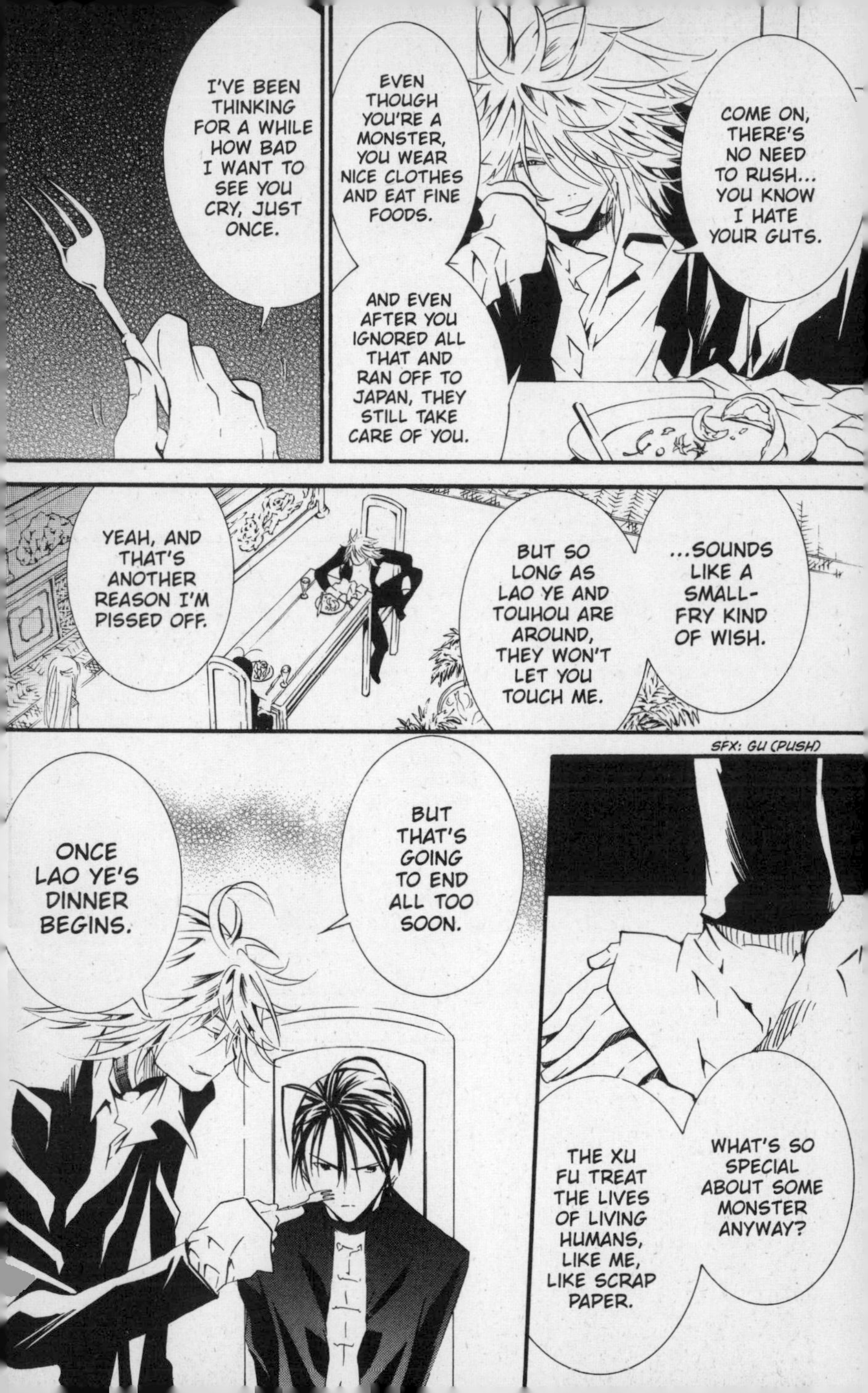
COME ON, THERE'S NO NEED TO RUSH... YOU KNOW I HATE YOUR GUTS.
EVEN THOUGH YOU'RE A MONSTER, YOU WEAR NICE CLOTHES AND EAT FINE FOODS.
AND EVEN AFTER YOU IGNORED ALL THAT AND RAN OFF TO JAPAN, THEY STILL TAKE CARE OF YOU.
I'VE BEEN THINKING FOR A WHILE HOW BAD I WANT TO SEE YOU CRY, JUST ONCE.
...SOUNDS LIKE A SMALL-FRY KIND OF WISH.
BUT SO LONG AS LAO YE AND TOUHOU ARE AROUND, THEY WON'T LET YOU TOUCH ME.
YEAH, AND THAT'S ANOTHER REASON I'M PISSED OFF.
SFX: GU (PUSH)
WHAT'S SO SPECIAL ABOUT SOME MONSTER ANYWAY?
THE XU FU TREAT THE LIVES OF LIVING HUMANS, LIKE ME, LIKE SCRAP PAPER.
BUT THAT'S GOING TO END ALL TOO SOON.
ONCE LAO YE'S DINNER BEGINS.

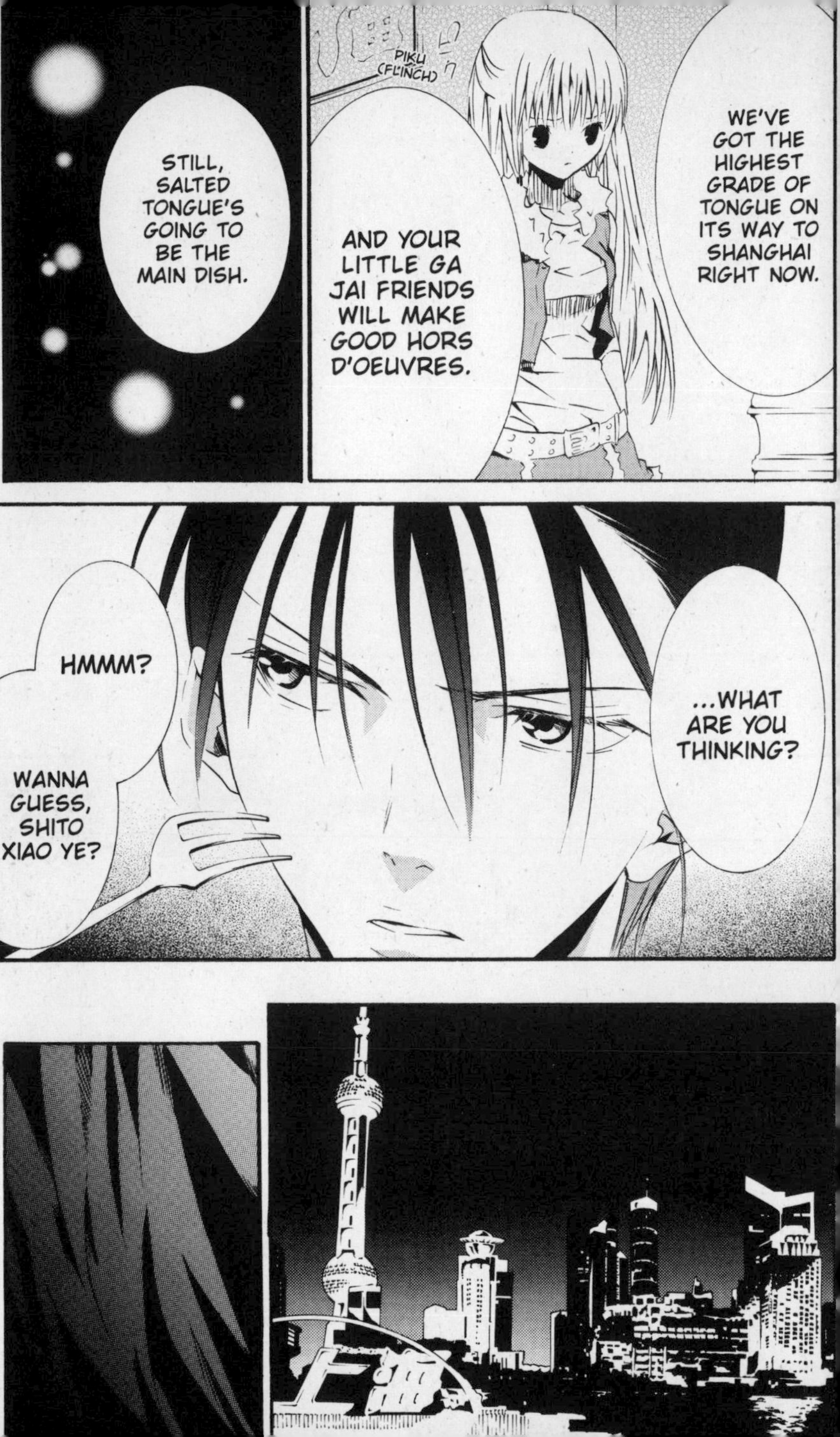
WE'VE GOT THE HIGHEST GRADE OF TONGUE ON ITS WAY TO SHANGHAI RIGHT NOW.
PIKU (FLINCH)
AND YOUR LITTLE GA JAI FRIENDS WILL MAKE GOOD HORS D'OEUVRES.
STILL, SALTED TONGUE'S GOING TO BE THE MAIN DISH.
...WHAT ARE YOU THINKING?
HMMM?
WANNA GUESS, SHITO XIAO YE?

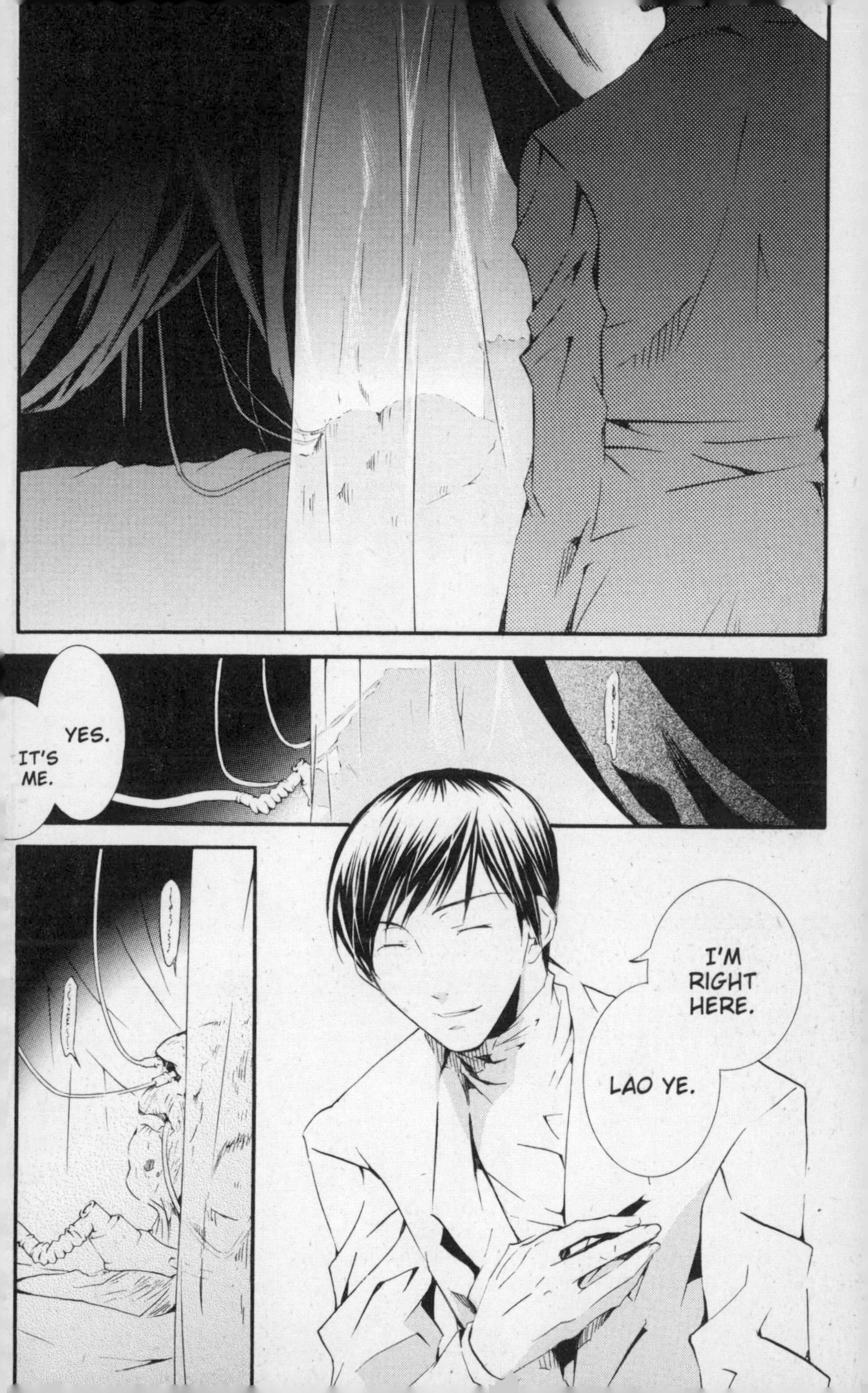
YES. IT'S ME.
I'M RIGHT HERE.
LAO YE.

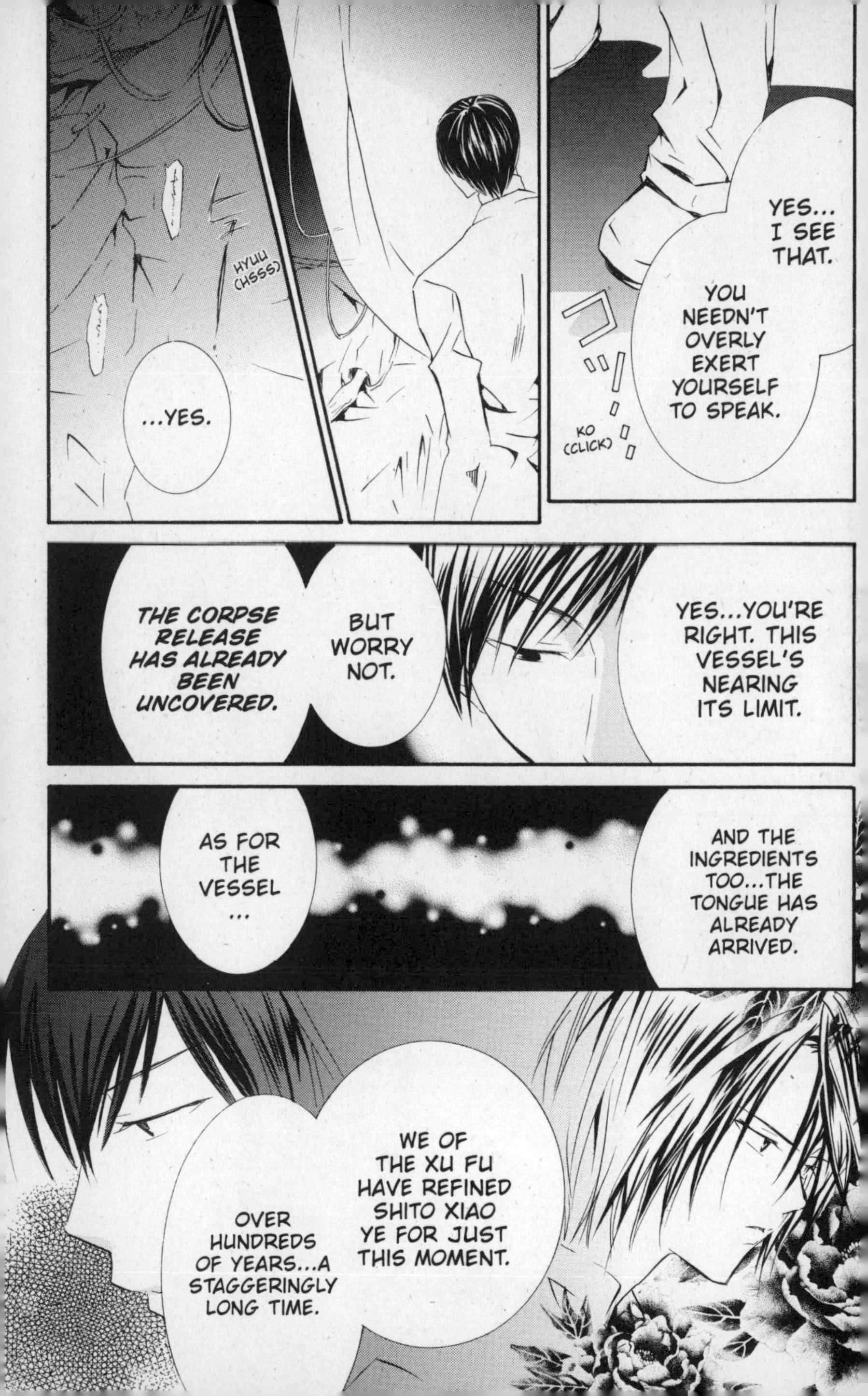
YES... I SEE THAT.
YOU NEEDN'T OVERLY EXERT YOURSELF TO SPEAK.
KO (CLICK)
HYUU (HSSS)
...YES.
YES...YOU'RE RIGHT. THIS VESSEL'S NEARING ITS LIMIT.
BUT WORRY NOT.
THE CORPSE RELEASE HAS ALREADY BEEN UNCOVERED.
AND THE INGREDIENTS TOO...THE TONGUE HAS ALREADY ARRIVED.
AS FOR THE VESSEL ...
WE OF THE XU FU HAVE REFINED SHITO XIAO YE FOR JUST THIS MOMENT.
OVER HUNDREDS OF YEARS...A STAGGERINGLY LONG TIME.

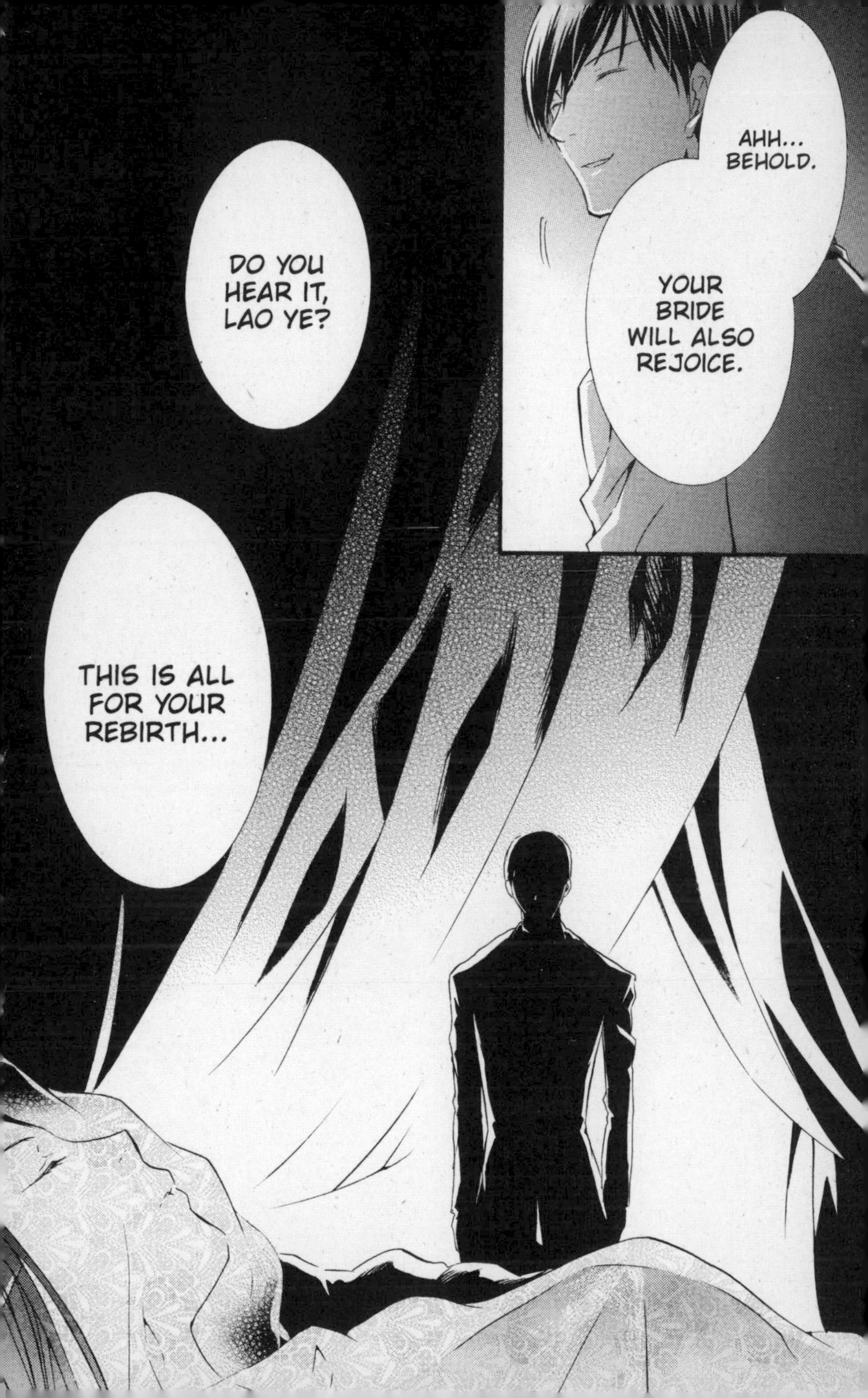
AHH... BEHOLD.
YOUR BRIDE WILL ALSO REJOICE.
DO YOU HEAR IT, LAO YE?
THIS IS ALL FOR YOUR REBIRTH...

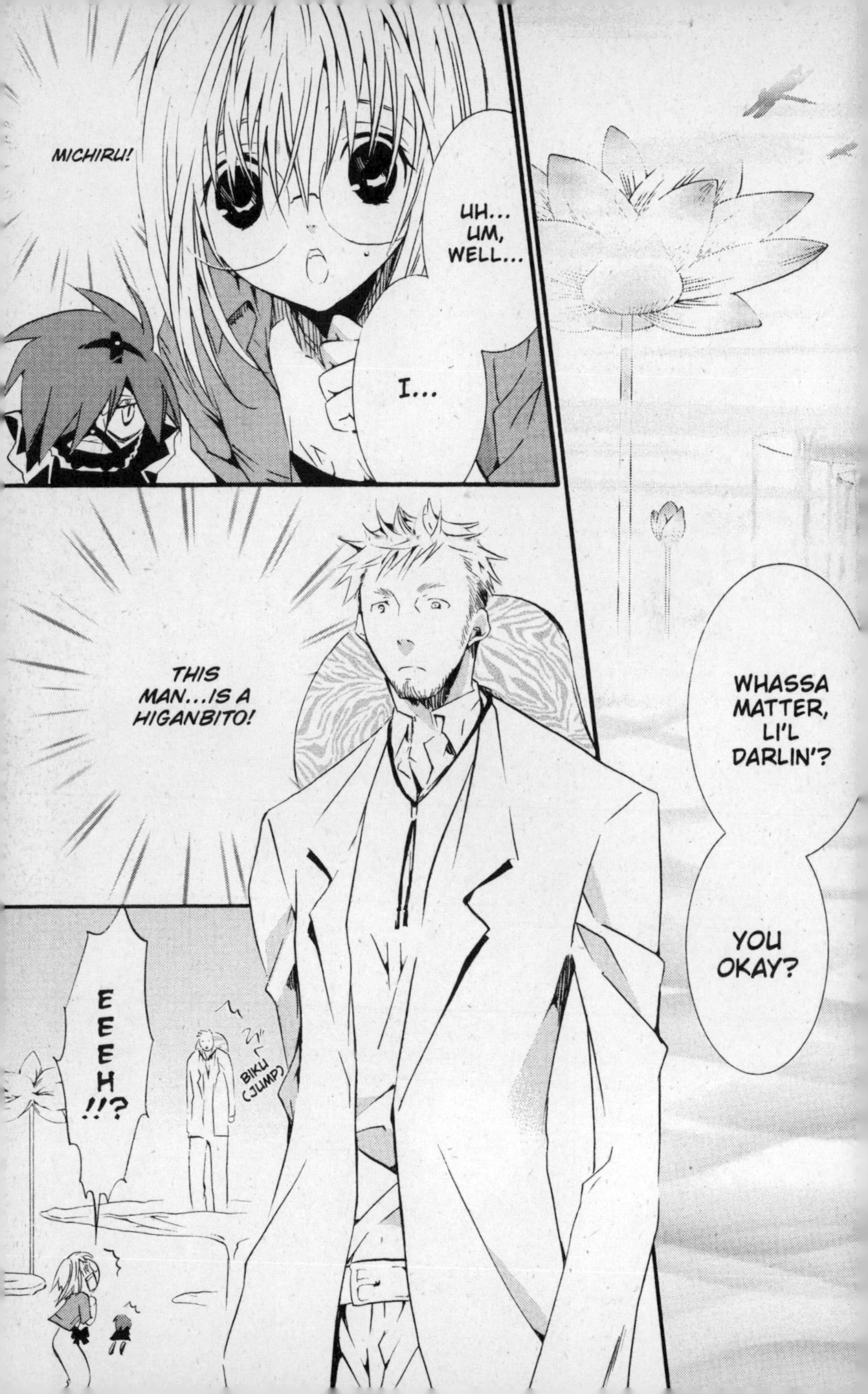
WHASSA MATTER, LI'L DARLIN'?
YOU OKAY?
UH... UM, WELL...
I...
MICHIRU!
THIS MAN...IS A HIGANBITO!
EEEEH!!?
BIKU (JUMP)

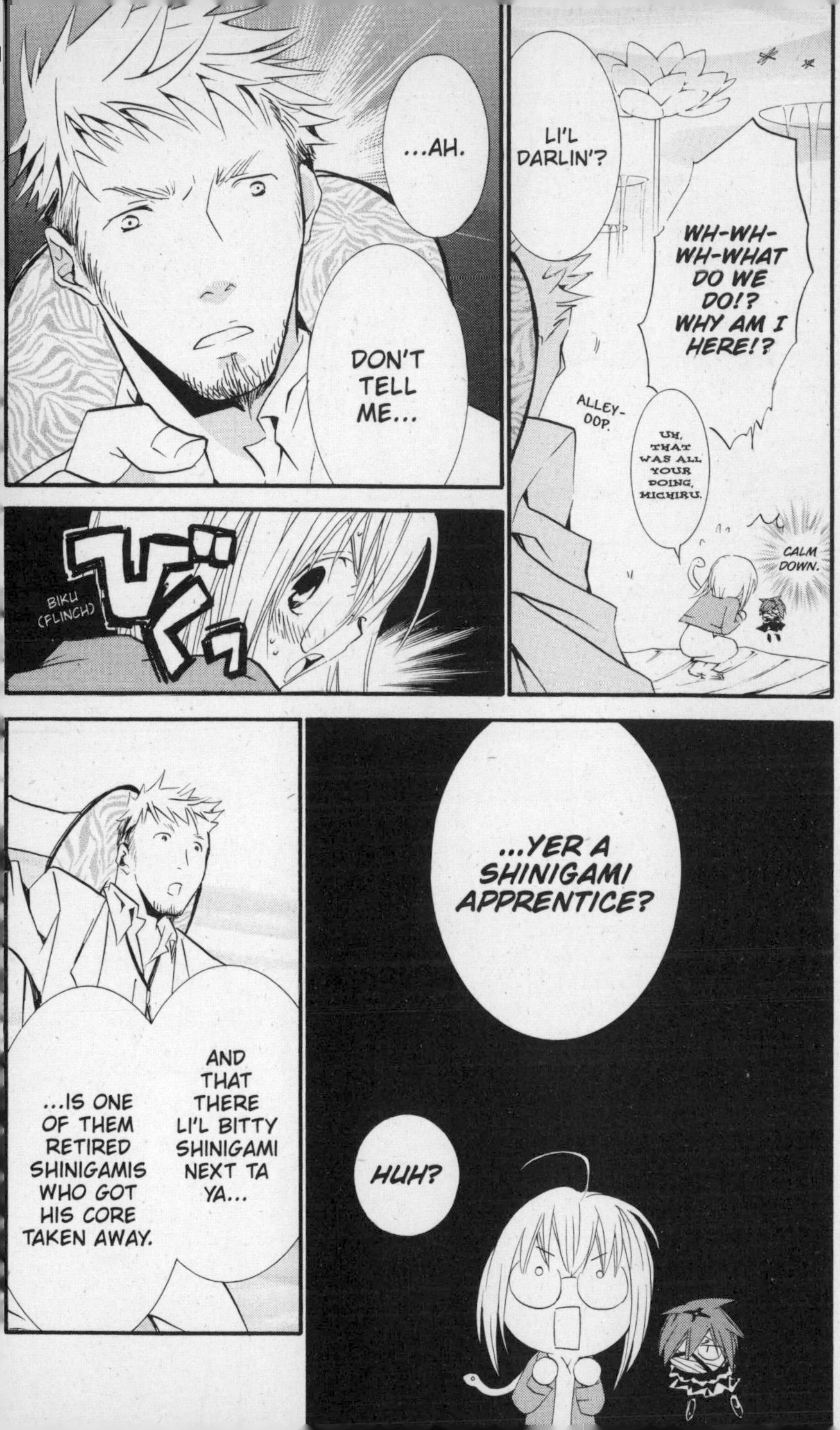
LI'L DARLIN'?
WH-WH-WH-WHAT DO WE DO!? WHY AM I HERE!?
ALLEY-OOP.
UH, THAT WAS ALL YOUR DOING, MICHIRU.
CALM DOWN.
...AH.
DON'T TELL ME...
BIKU (FLINCH)
...YER A SHINIGAMI APPRENTICE?
HUH?
AND THAT THERE LI'L BITTY SHINIGAMI NEXT TA YA...
...IS ONE OF THEM RETIRED SHINIGAMIS WHO GOT HIS CORE TAKEN AWAY.

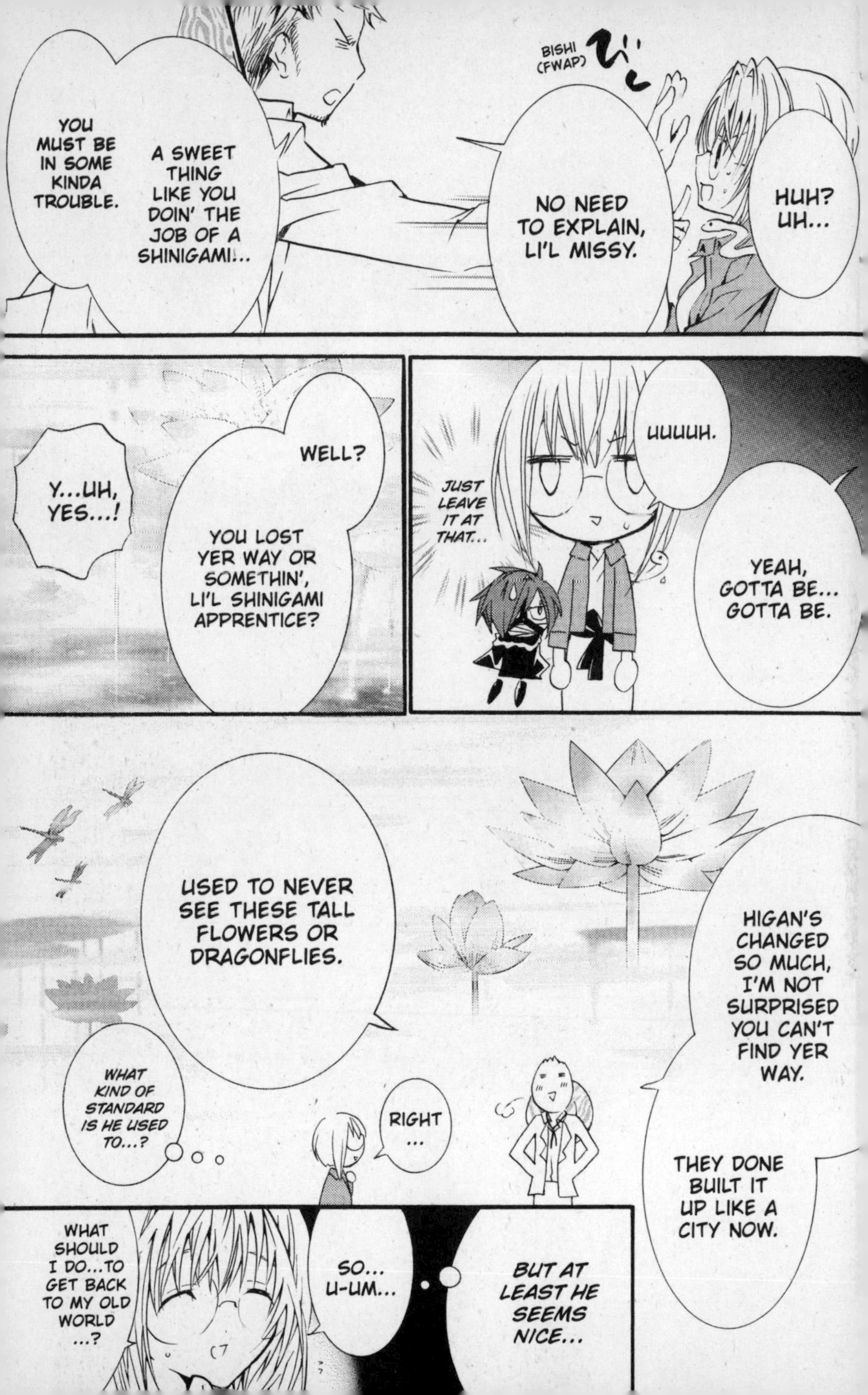
HUH? UH...
BISHI (FWAP)
NO NEED TO EXPLAIN, LI'L MISSY.
A SWEET THING LIKE YOU DOIN' THE JOB OF A SHINIGAMI...
YOU MUST BE IN SOME KINDA TROUBLE.
UUUUH.
YEAH, GOTTA BE... GOTTA BE.
JUST LEAVE IT AT THAT...
WELL?
YOU LOST YER WAY OR SOMETHIN', LI'L SHINIGAMI APPRENTICE?
Y...UH, YES...!
HIGAN'S CHANGED SO MUCH, I'M NOT SURPRISED YOU CAN'T FIND YER WAY.
THEY DONE BUILT IT UP LIKE A CITY NOW.
USED TO NEVER SEE THESE TALL FLOWERS OR DRAGONFLIES.
RIGHT...
WHAT KIND OF STANDARD IS HE USED TO...?
BUT AT LEAST HE SEEMS NICE...
SO... U-UM...
WHAT SHOULD I DO...TO GET BACK TO MY OLD WORLD...?

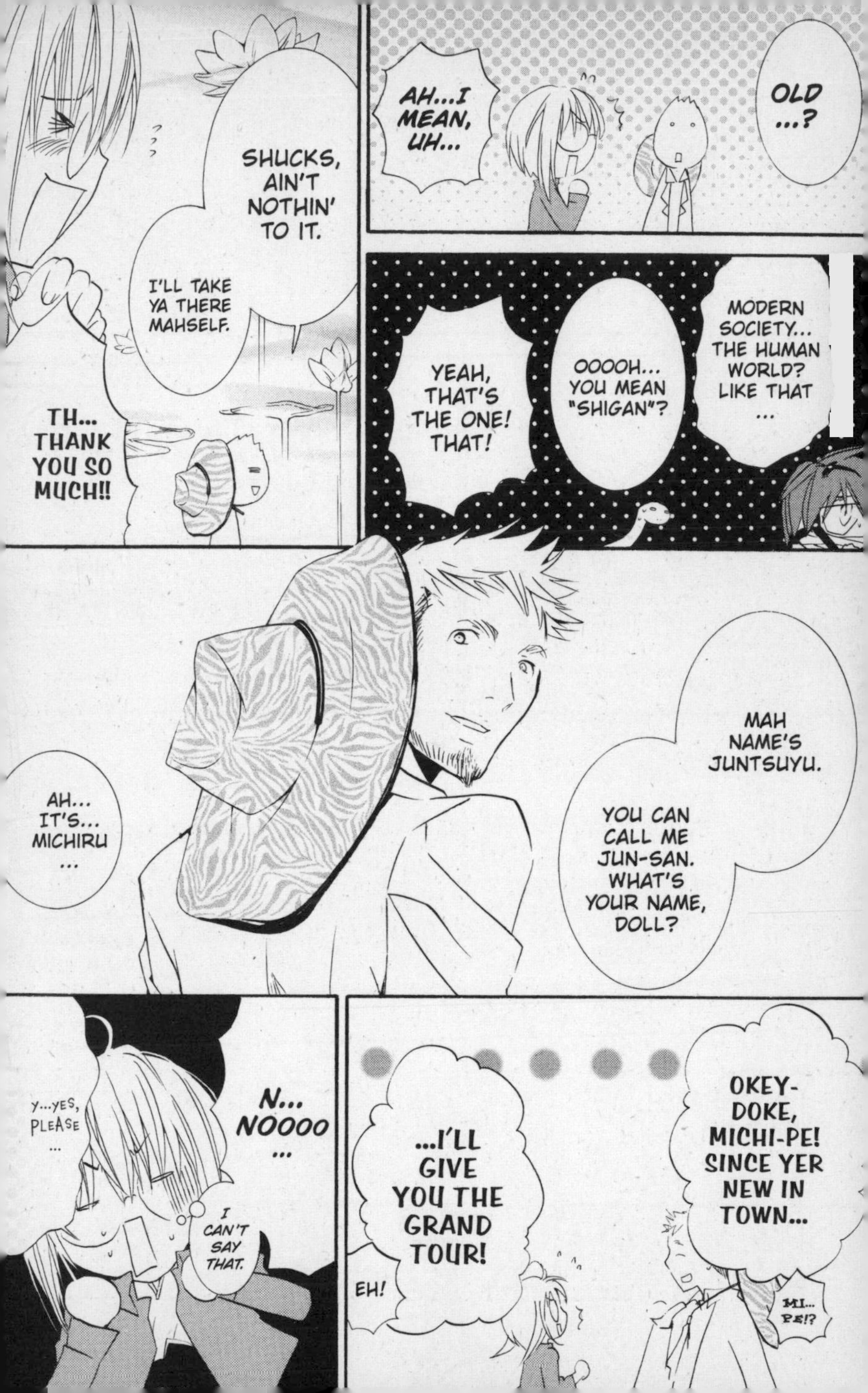
OLD ...?
AH...I MEAN, UH...
MODERN SOCIETY... THE HUMAN WORLD? LIKE THAT ...
OOOOH... YOU MEAN "SHIGAN"?
YEAH, THAT'S THE ONE! THAT!
SHUCKS, AIN'T NOTHIN' TO IT.
I'LL TAKE YA THERE MAHSELF.
TH... THANK YOU SO MUCH!!
MAH NAME'S JUNTSUYU.
YOU CAN CALL ME JUN-SAN. WHAT'S YOUR NAME, DOLL?
AH... IT'S... MICHIRU ...
OKEY-DOKE, MICHI-PE! SINCE YER NEW IN TOWN...
MI... PE!?
...I'LL GIVE YOU THE GRAND TOUR!
EH!
N... NOOOO ...
I CAN'T SAY THAT.
Y...YES, PLEASE ...

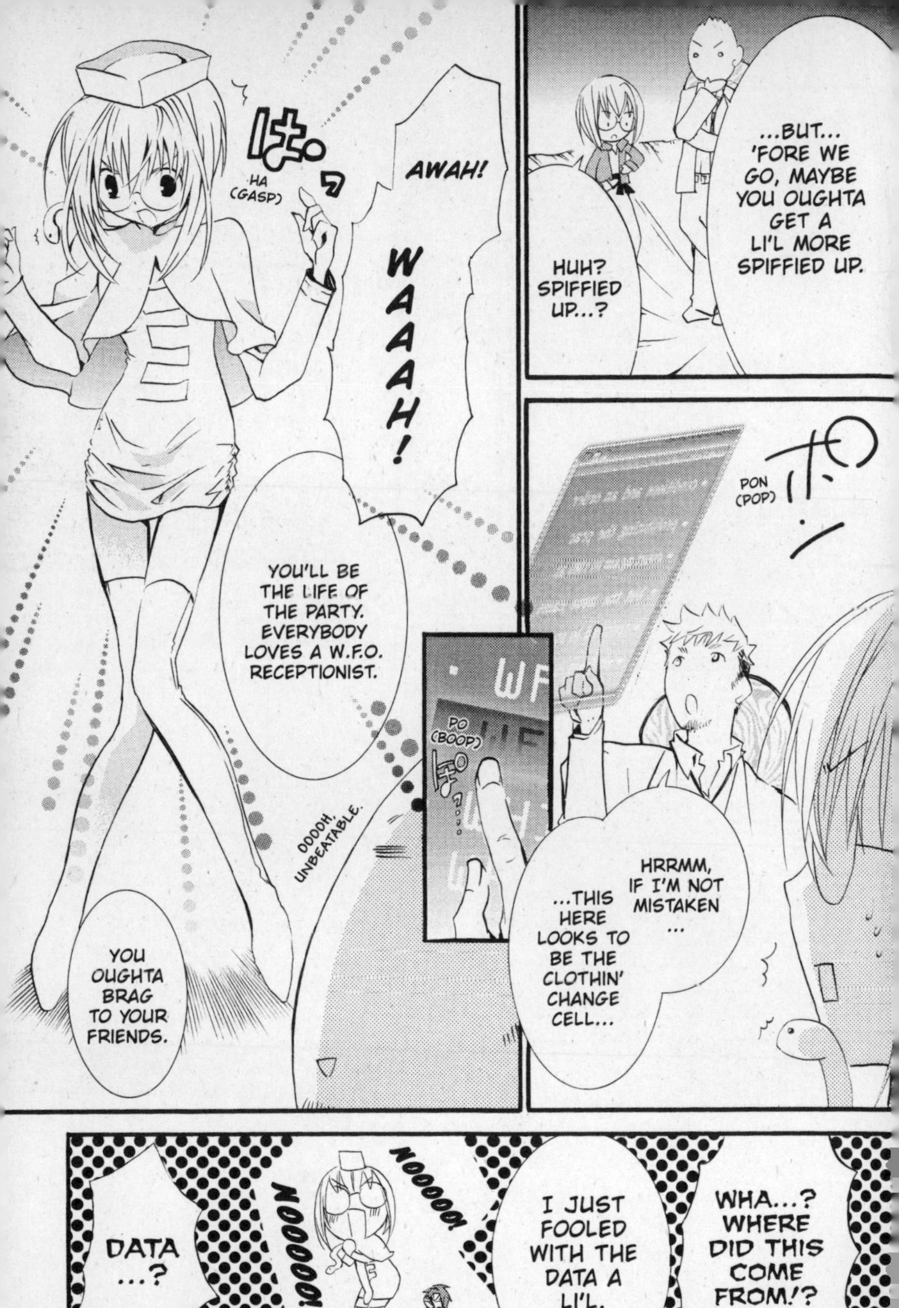
...BUT... 'FORE WE GO, MAYBE YOU OUGHTA GET A LI'L MORE SPIFFIED UP.
HUH? SPIFFIED UP...?
PON (POP)
HRRMM, IF I'M NOT MISTAKEN ...
...THIS HERE LOOKS TO BE THE CLOTHIN' CHANGE CELL...
PO (BOOP)
OOOOH, UNBEATABLE.
HA (GASP)
AWAH!
WAAAAH!
YOU'LL BE THE LIFE OF THE PARTY. EVERYBODY LOVES A W.F.O. RECEPTIONIST.
YOU OUGHTA BRAG TO YOUR FRIENDS.
WHA...? WHERE DID THIS COME FROM!?
I JUST FOOLED WITH THE DATA A LI'L.
NOOOOOO!
DATA ...?

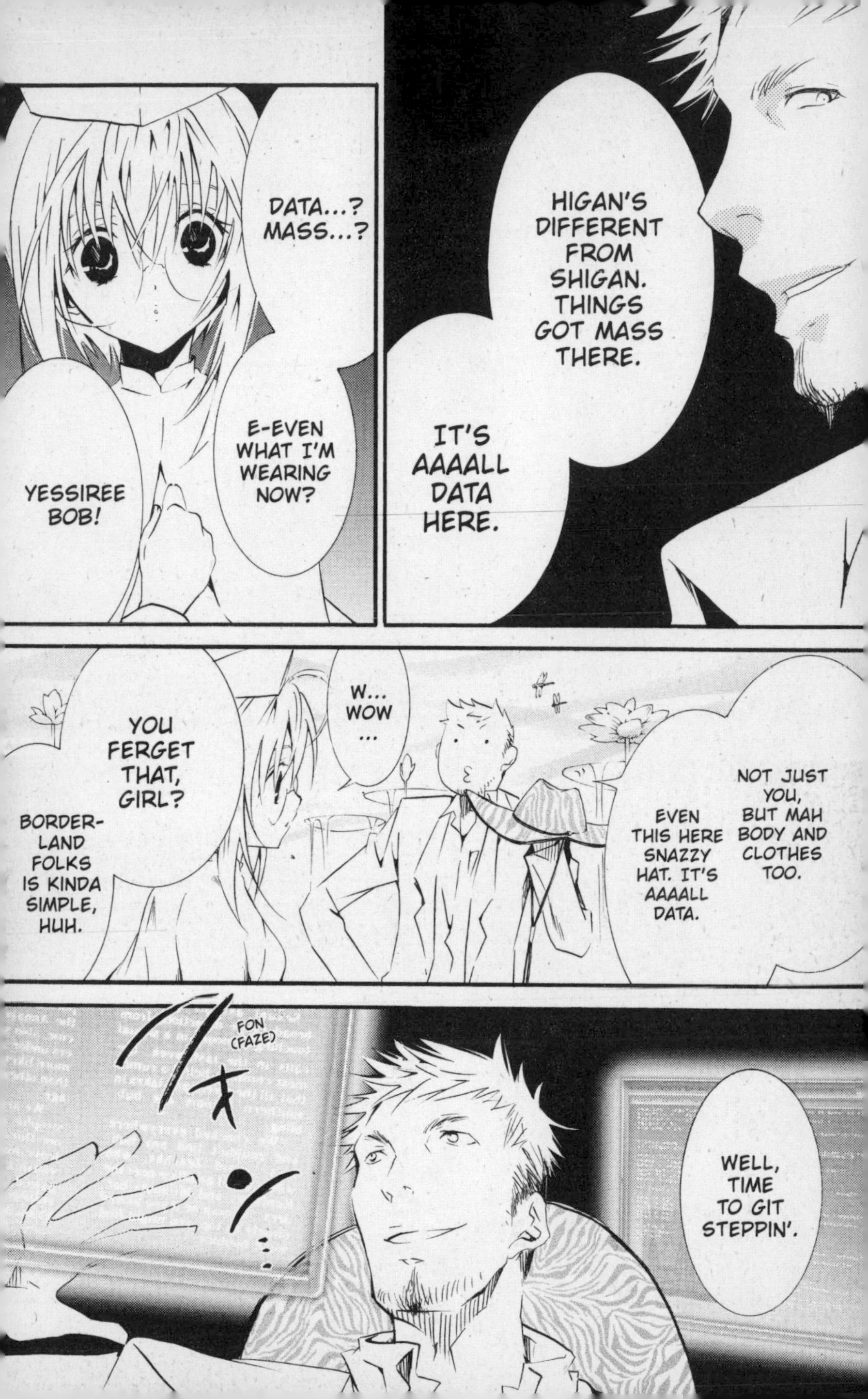
HIGAN'S DIFFERENT FROM SHIGAN. THINGS GOT MASS THERE.
IT'S AAAALL DATA HERE.
DATA...? MASS...?
E-EVEN WHAT I'M WEARING NOW?
YESSIREE BOB!
NOT JUST YOU, BUT MAH BODY AND CLOTHES TOO.
EVEN THIS HERE SNAZZY HAT. IT'S AAAALL DATA.
W... WOW ...
YOU FERGET THAT, GIRL?
BORDERLAND FOLKS IS KINDA SIMPLE, HUH.
WELL, TIME TO GIT STEPPIN'.
FON (FAZE)

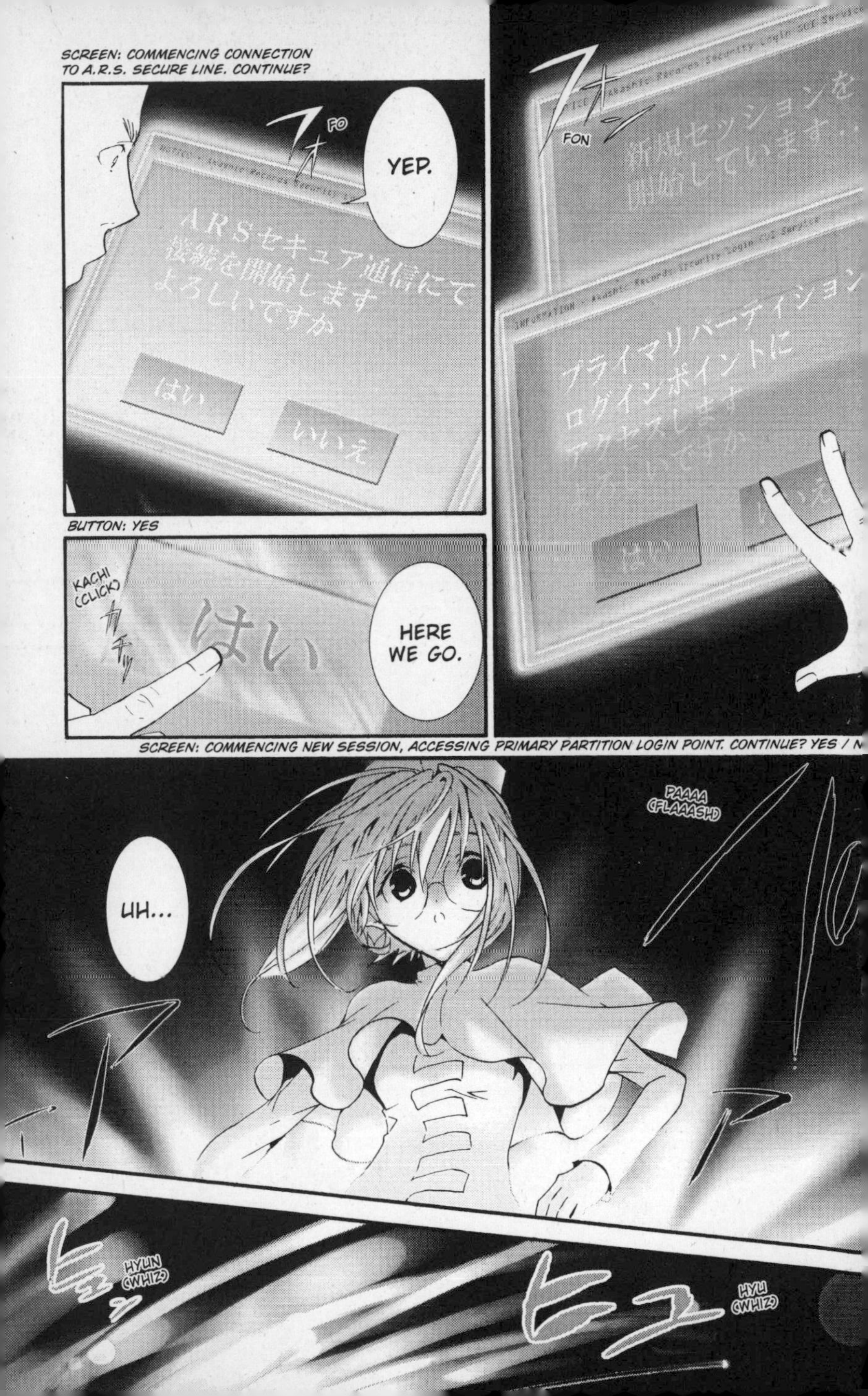
FON
SCREEN: COMMENCING NEW SESSION, ACCESSING PRIMARY PARTITION LOGIN POINT. CONTINUE? YES / N
SCREEN: COMMENCING CONNECTION TO A.R.S. SECURE LINE. CONTINUE?
FO
YEP.
ARSセキュア通信にて接続を開始します よろしいですか
はい
いいえ
BUTTON: YES
KACHI (CLICK)
はい
HERE WE GO.
PAAAA (FLAAASH)
UH...
HYU (WHIZ)
HYUN (WHIZ)

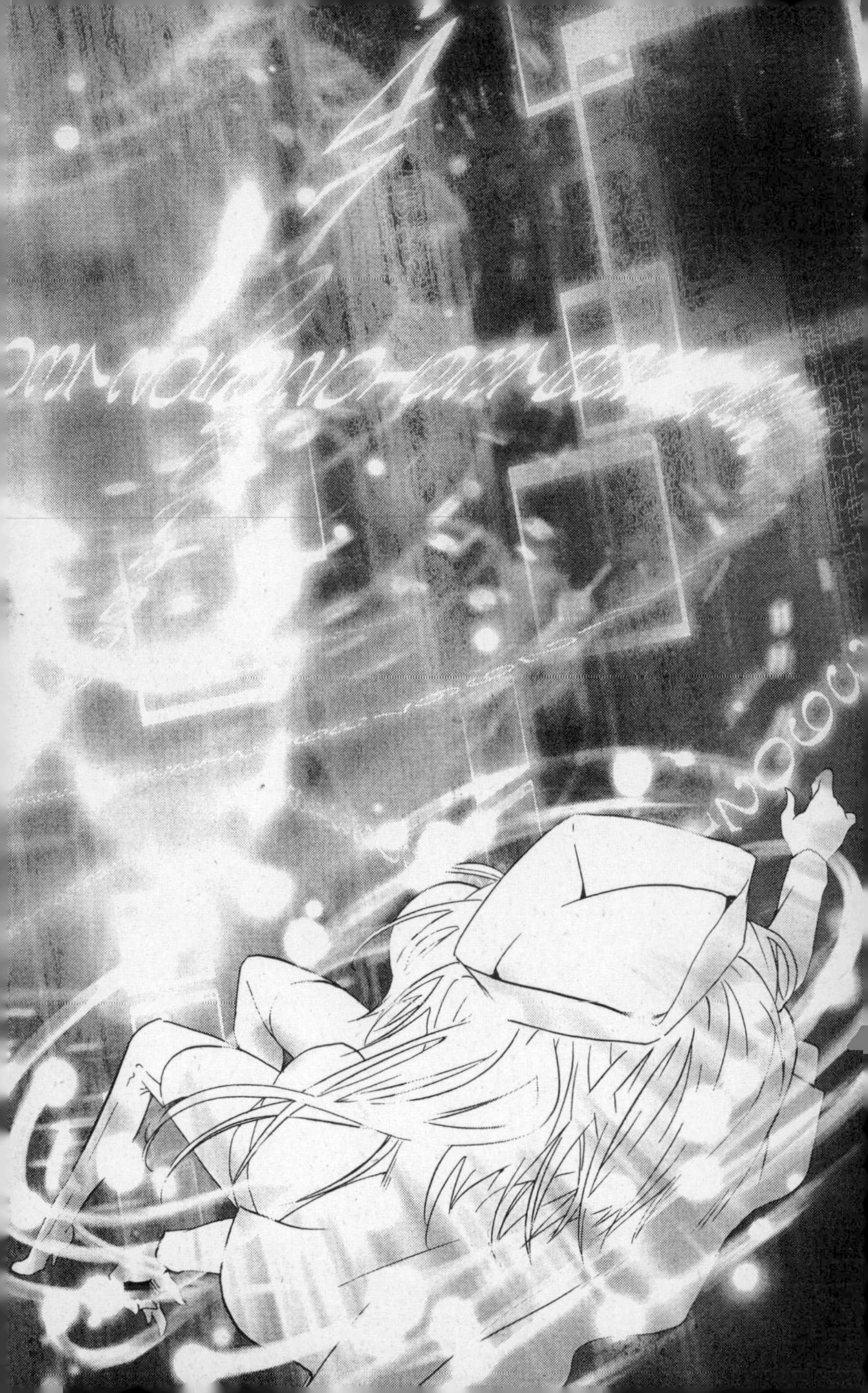

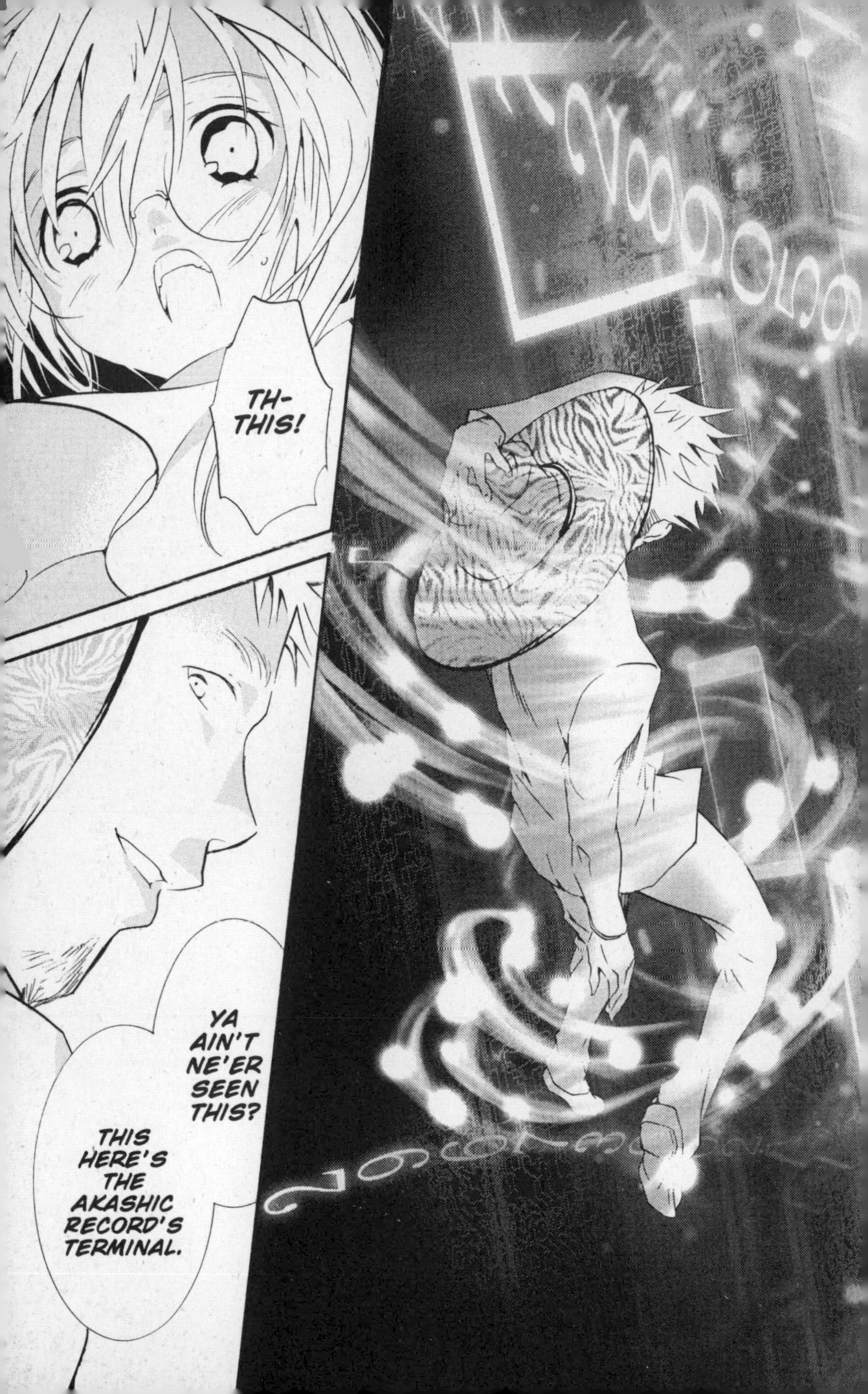
TH- THIS!
YA AIN'T NE'ER SEEN THIS?
THIS HERE'S THE AKASHIC RECORD'S TERMINAL.

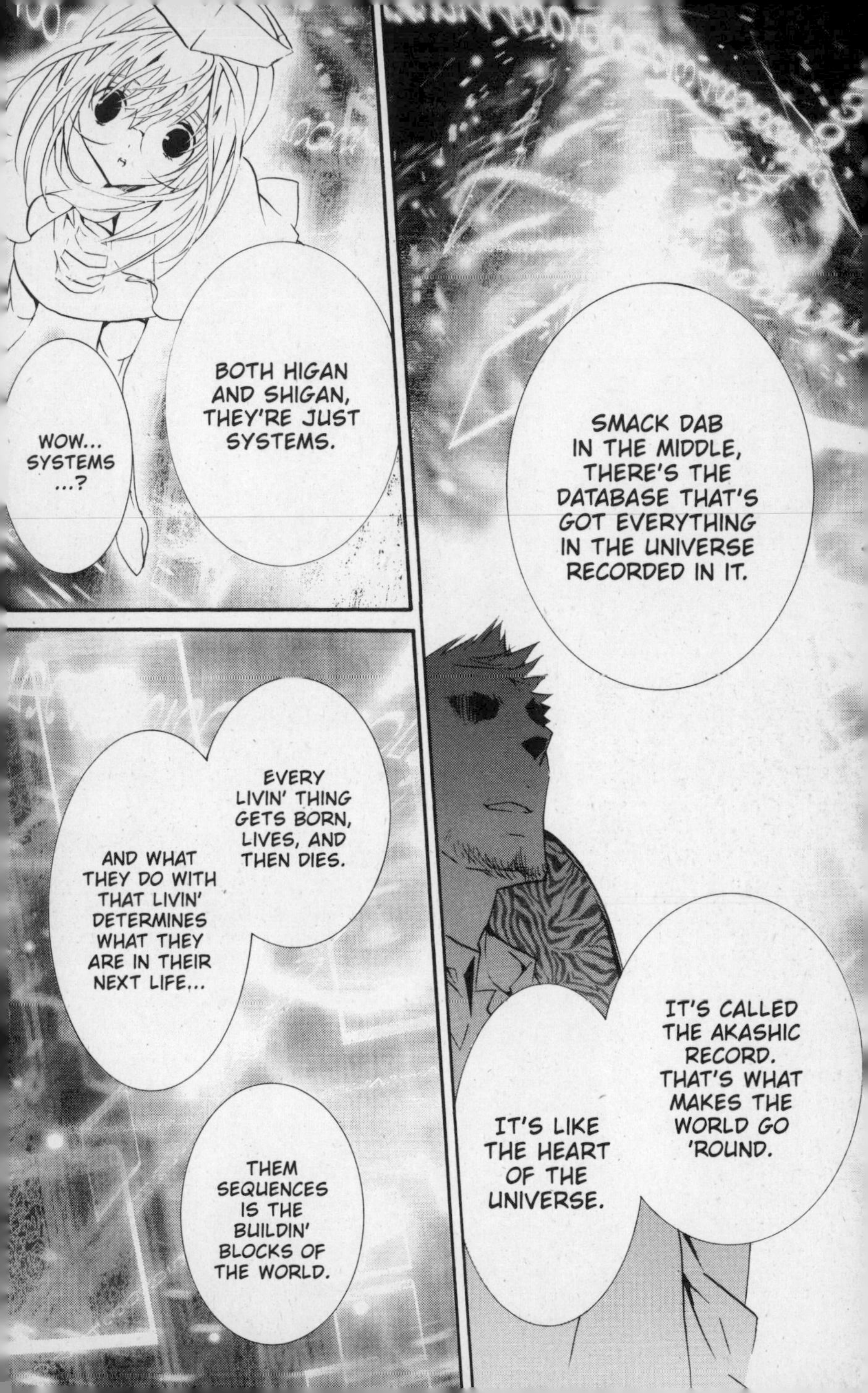
SMACK DAB IN THE MIDDLE, THERE'S THE DATABASE THAT'S GOT EVERYTHING IN THE UNIVERSE RECORDED IN IT.
IT'S CALLED THE AKASHIC RECORD. THAT'S WHAT MAKES THE WORLD GO 'ROUND.
IT'S LIKE THE HEART OF THE UNIVERSE.
BOTH HIGAN AND SHIGAN, THEY'RE JUST SYSTEMS.
WOW... SYSTEMS ...?
EVERY LIVIN' THING GETS BORN, LIVES, AND THEN DIES.
AND WHAT THEY DO WITH THAT LIVIN' DETERMINES WHAT THEY ARE IN THEIR NEXT LIFE...
THEM SEQUENCES IS THE BUILDIN' BLOCKS OF THE WORLD.

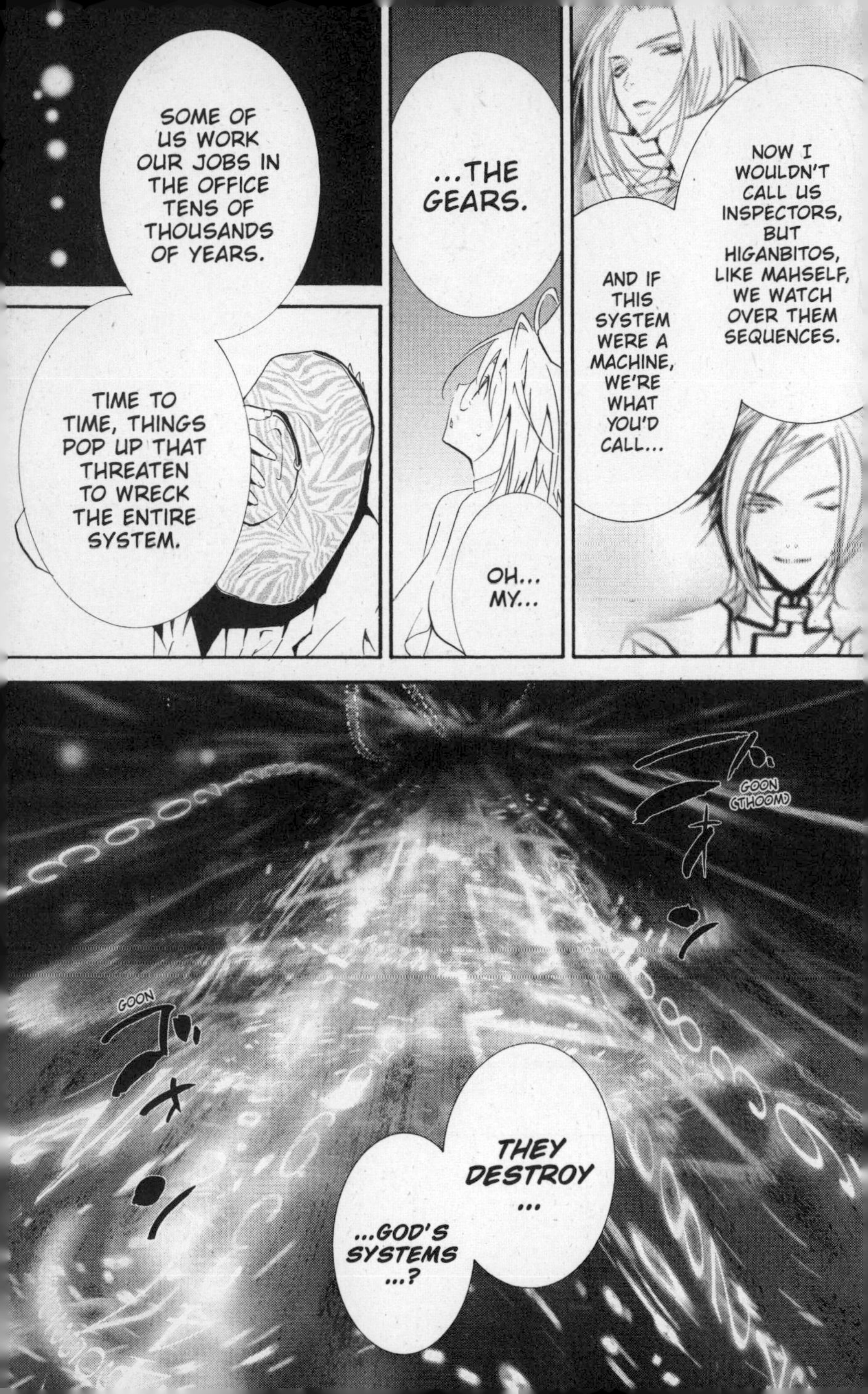
NOW I WOULDN'T CALL US INSPECTORS, BUT HIGANBITOS, LIKE MAHSELF, WE WATCH OVER THEM SEQUENCES.
AND IF THIS SYSTEM WERE A MACHINE, WE'RE WHAT YOU'D CALL...
...THE GEARS.
OH... MY...
SOME OF US WORK OUR JOBS IN THE OFFICE TENS OF THOUSANDS OF YEARS.
TIME TO TIME, THINGS POP UP THAT THREATEN TO WRECK THE ENTIRE SYSTEM.
GOON (THOOM)
GOON
THEY DESTROY ...
...GOD'S SYSTEMS ...?

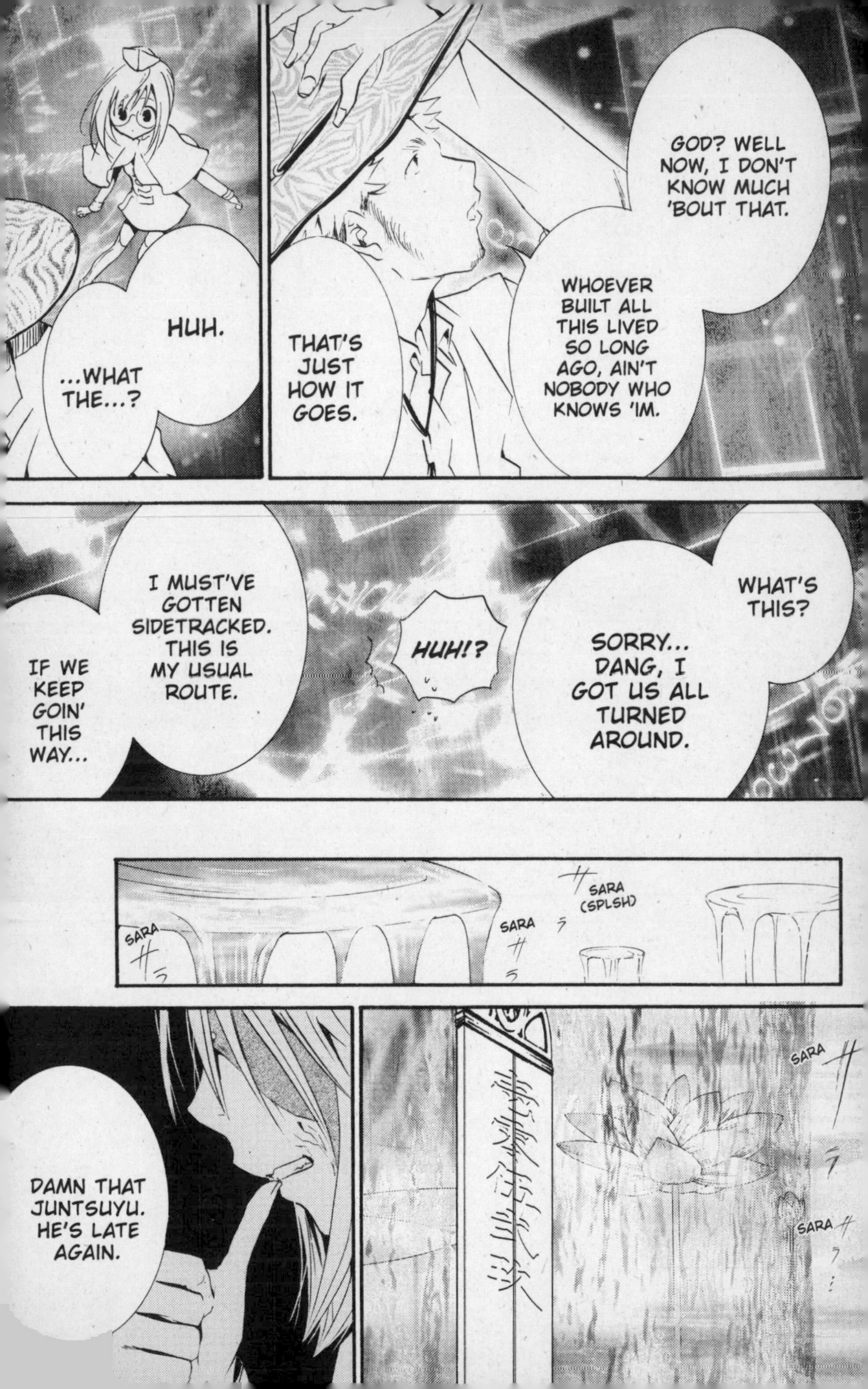
GOD? WELL NOW, I DON'T KNOW MUCH 'BOUT THAT.
WHOEVER BUILT ALL THIS LIVED SO LONG AGO, AIN'T NOBODY WHO KNOWS 'IM.
THAT'S JUST HOW IT GOES.
HUH.
...WHAT THE...?
WHAT'S THIS?
SORRY... DANG, I GOT US ALL TURNED AROUND.
HUH!?
I MUST'VE GOTTEN SIDETRACKED. THIS IS MY USUAL ROUTE.
IF WE KEEP GOIN' THIS WAY...
SARA (SPLSH)
SARA
SARA
SARA
SARA
DAMN THAT JUNTSUYU. HE'S LATE AGAIN.

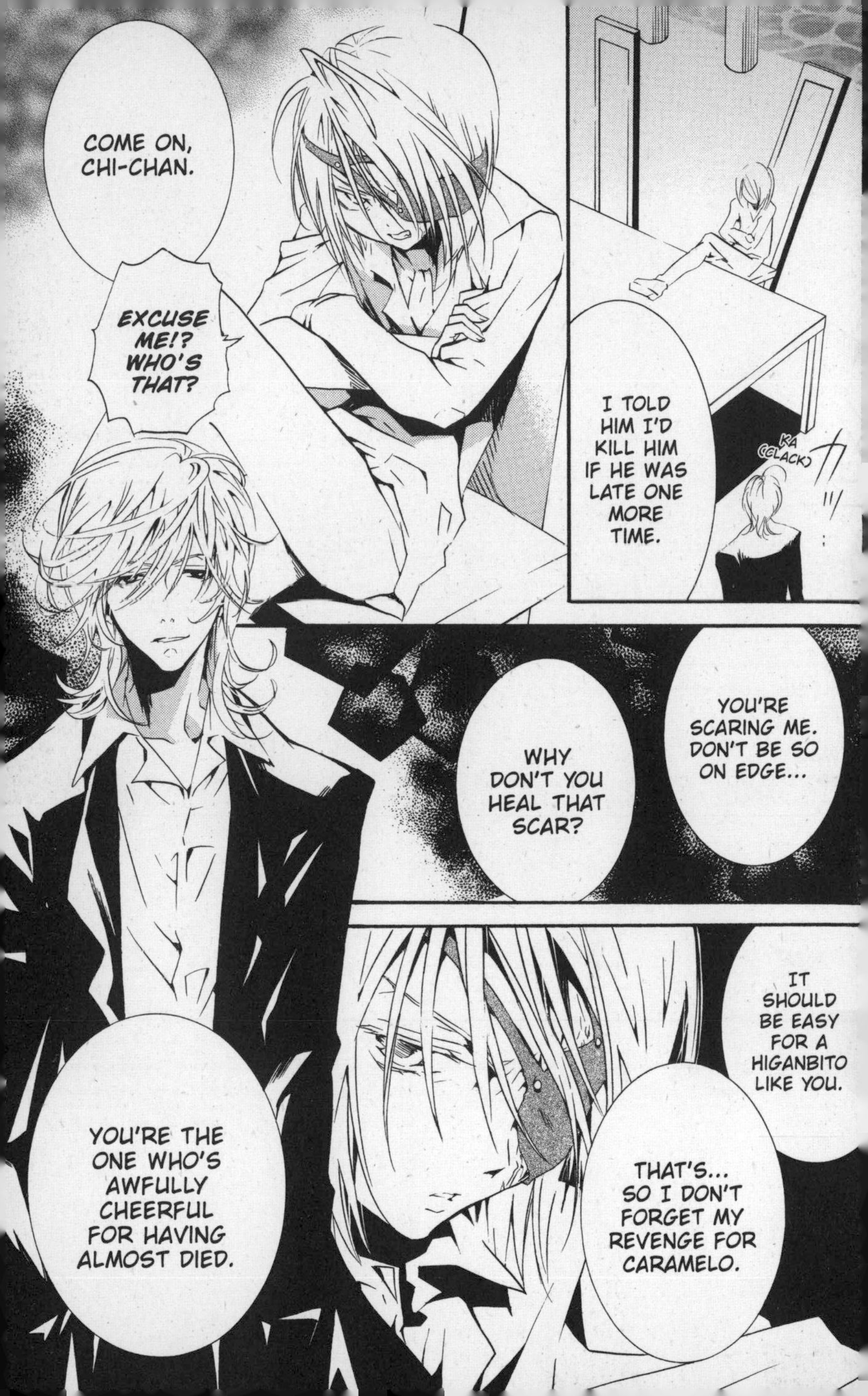
I TOLD HIM I'D KILL HIM IF HE WAS LATE ONE MORE TIME.
KA (CLACK)
COME ON, CHI-CHAN.
EXCUSE ME!? WHO'S THAT?
YOU'RE SCARING ME. DON'T BE SO ON EDGE...
WHY DON'T YOU HEAL THAT SCAR?
IT SHOULD BE EASY FOR A HIGANBITO LIKE YOU.
THAT'S... SO I DON'T FORGET MY REVENGE FOR CARAMELO.
YOU'RE THE ONE WHO'S AWFULLY CHEERFUL FOR HAVING ALMOST DIED.

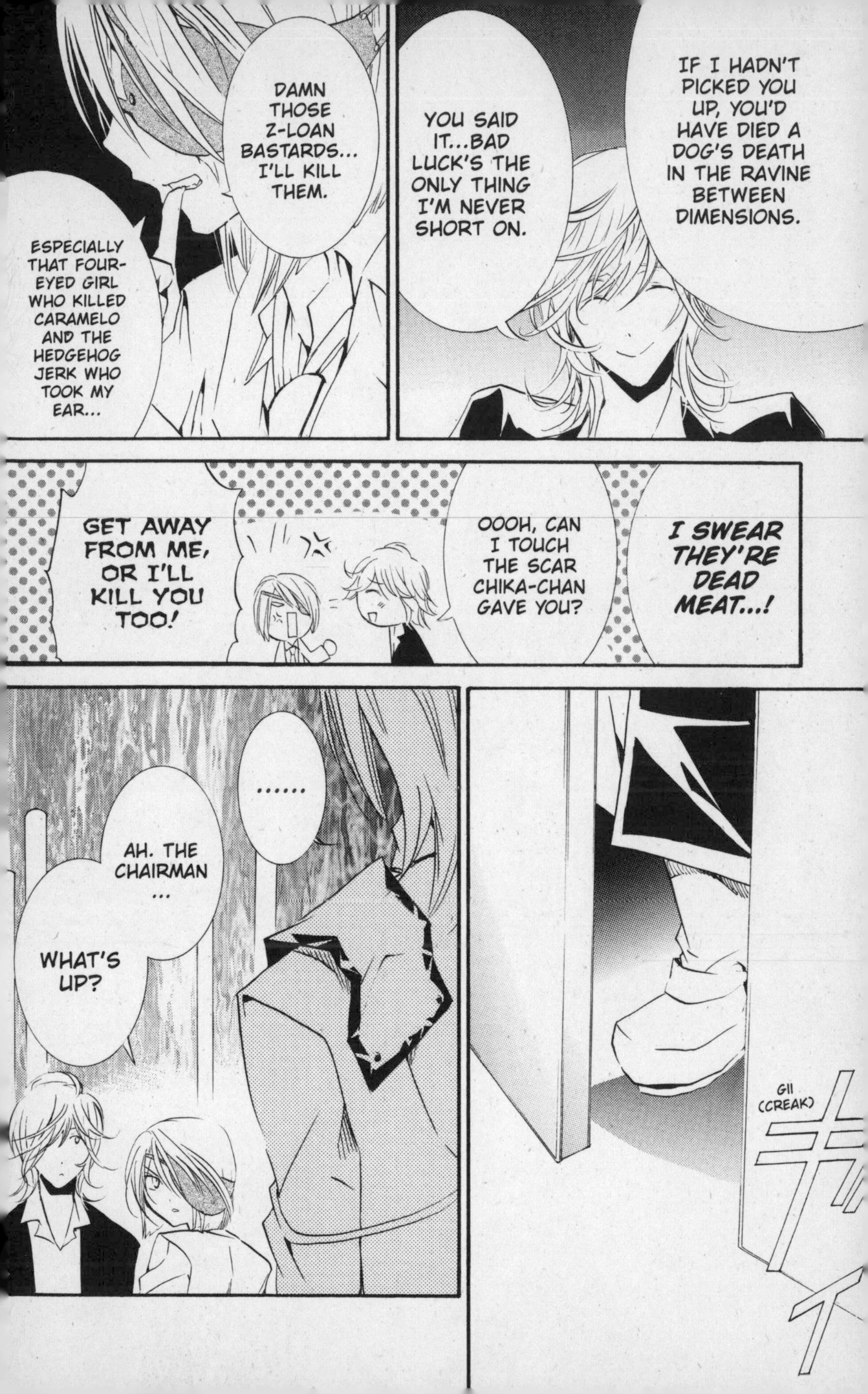
IF I HADN'T PICKED YOU UP, YOU'D HAVE DIED A DOG'S DEATH IN THE RAVINE BETWEEN DIMENSIONS.
YOU SAID IT...BAD LUCK'S THE ONLY THING I'M NEVER SHORT ON.
DAMN THOSE Z-LOAN BASTARDS... I'LL KILL THEM.
ESPECIALLY THAT FOUR-EYED GIRL WHO KILLED CARAMELO AND THE HEDGEHOG JERK WHO TOOK MY EAR...
I SWEAR THEY'RE DEAD MEAT...!
OOOH, CAN I TOUCH THE SCAR CHIKA-CHAN GAVE YOU?
GET AWAY FROM ME, OR I'LL KILL YOU TOO!
GII (CREAK)
......
AH. THE CHAIRMAN ...
WHAT'S UP?

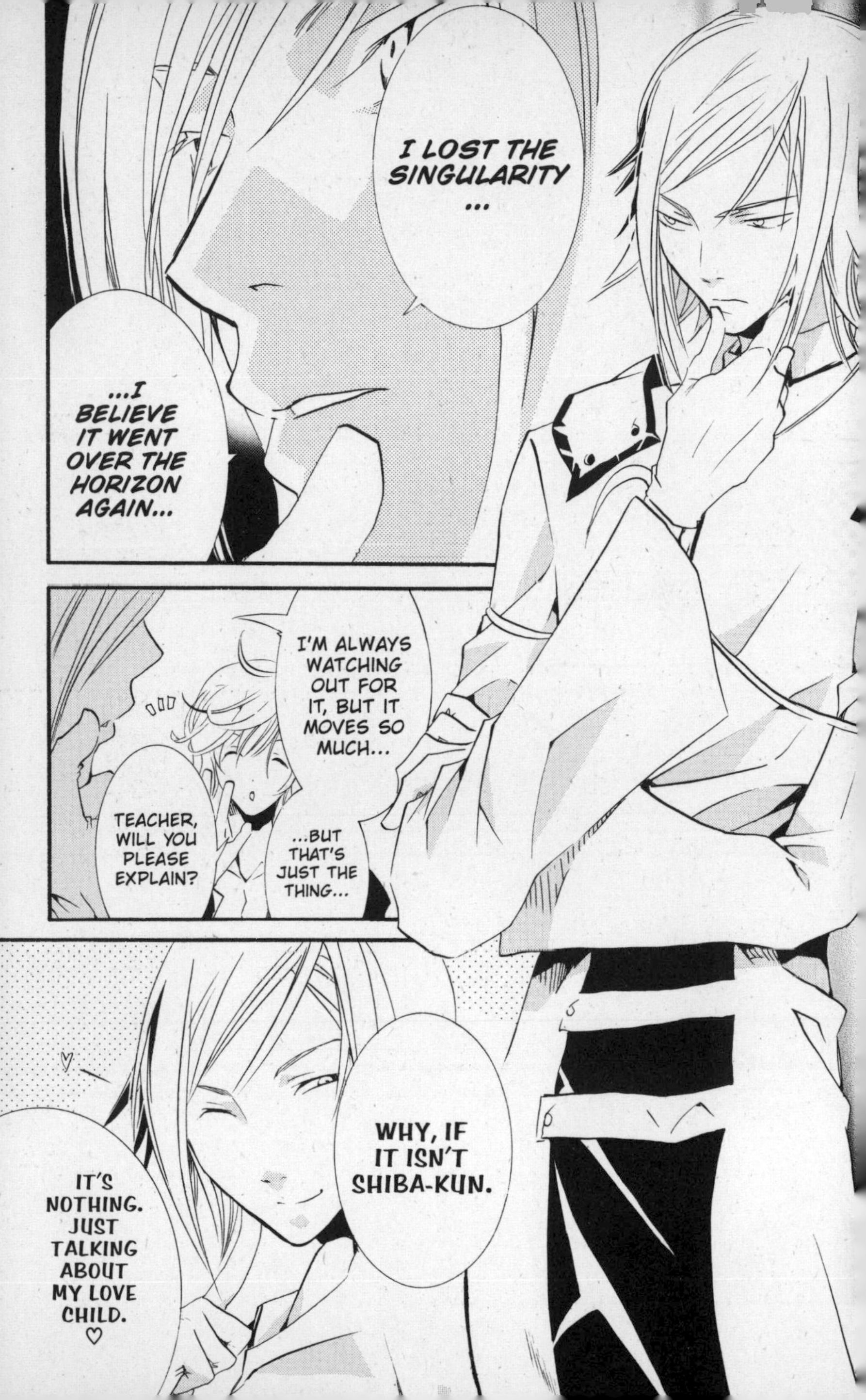
I LOST THE SINGULARITY ...
...I BELIEVE IT WENT OVER THE HORIZON AGAIN...
I'M ALWAYS WATCHING OUT FOR IT, BUT IT MOVES SO MUCH...
...BUT THAT'S JUST THE THING...
TEACHER, WILL YOU PLEASE EXPLAIN?
WHY, IF IT ISN'T SHIBA-KUN.
IT'S NOTHING. JUST TALKING ABOUT MY LOVE CHILD. ♡

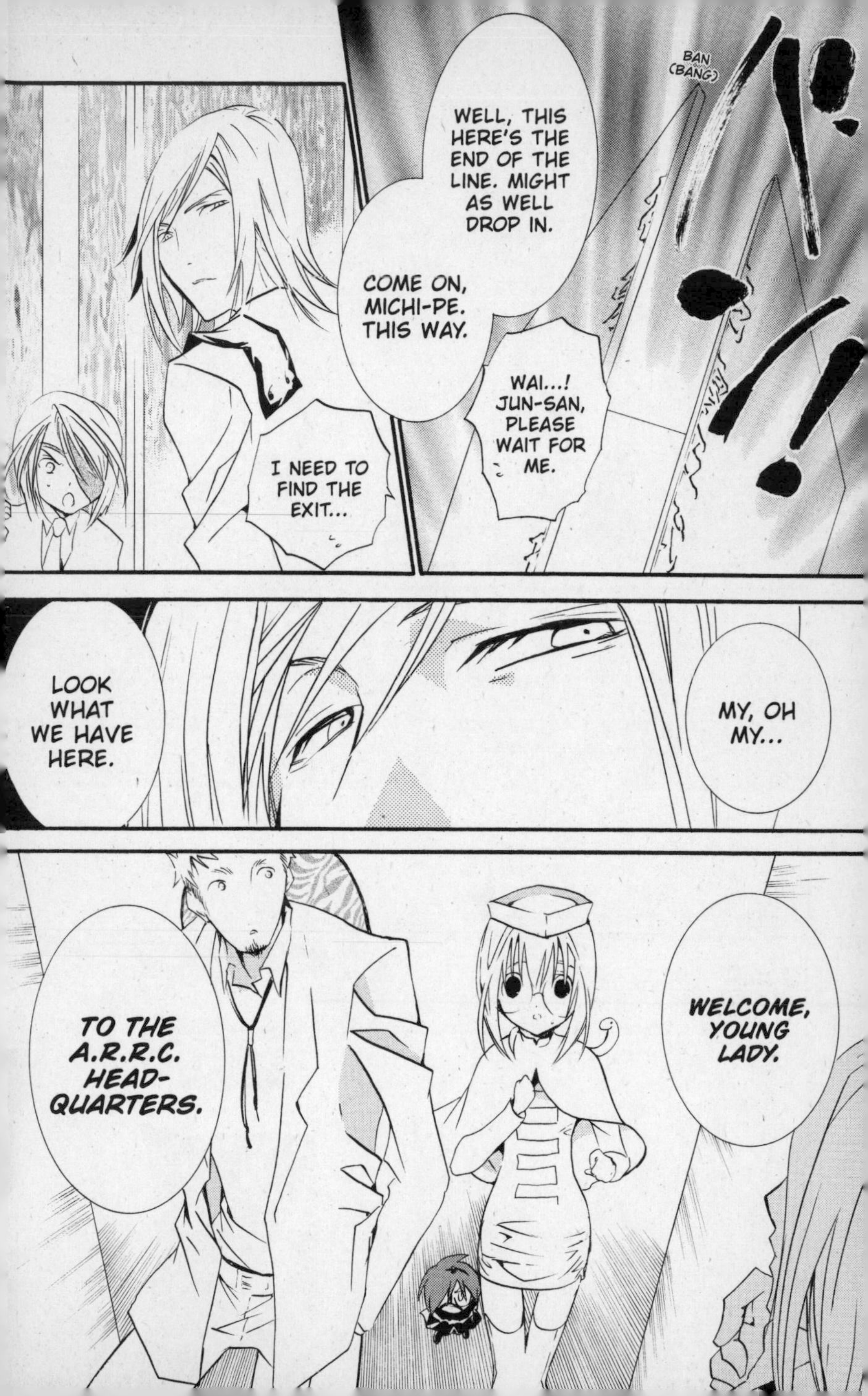
BAN
(BANG)
WELL, THIS HERE'S THE END OF THE LINE. MIGHT AS WELL DROP IN.
COME ON, MICHI-PE. THIS WAY.
WAI...! JUN-SAN, PLEASE WAIT FOR ME.
I NEED TO FIND THE EXIT...
MY, OH MY...
LOOK WHAT WE HAVE HERE.
WELCOME, YOUNG LADY.
TO THE A.R.R.C. HEAD-QUARTERS.

PAYMENT:59

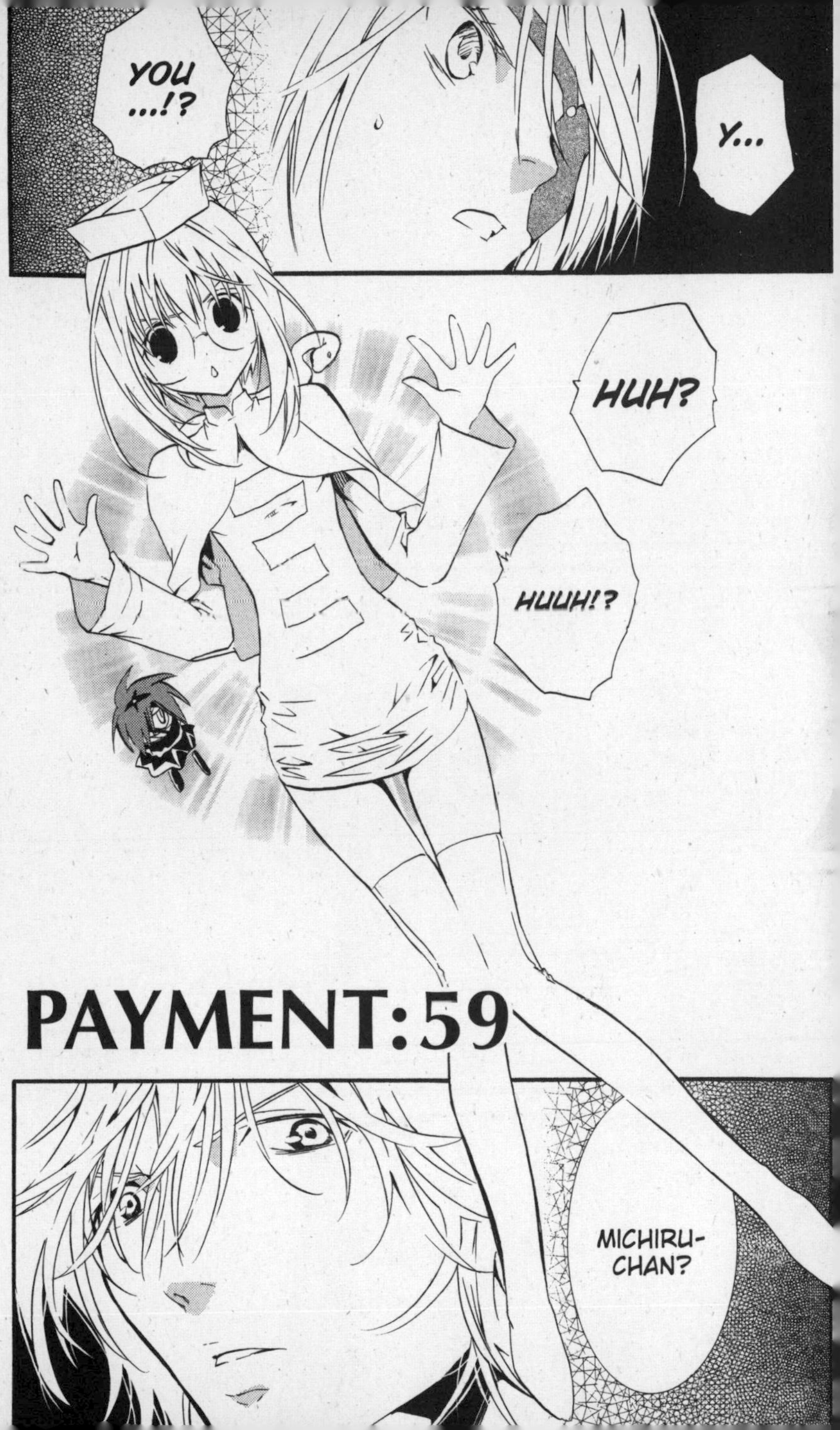
Y...
YOU ...!?
HUH?
HUUH!?
MICHIRU-CHAN?

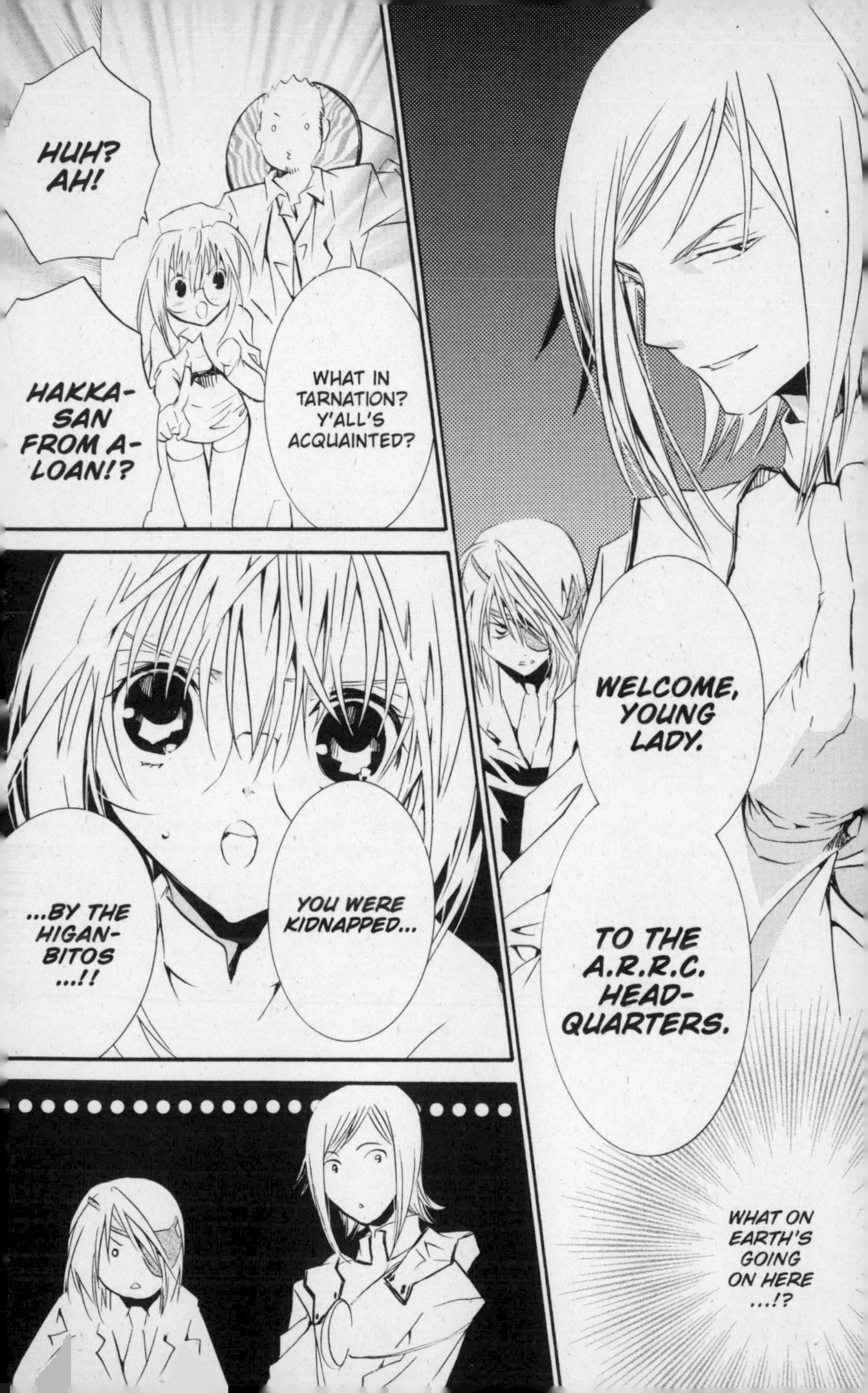
WELCOME, YOUNG LADY.
TO THE A.R.R.C. HEAD-QUARTERS.
WHAT ON EARTH'S GOING ON HERE ...!?
HUH? AH!
HAKKA-SAN FROM A-LOAN!?
WHAT IN TARNATION? Y'ALL'S ACQUAINTED?
YOU WERE KIDNAPPED...
...BY THE HIGAN-BITOS ...!!
....

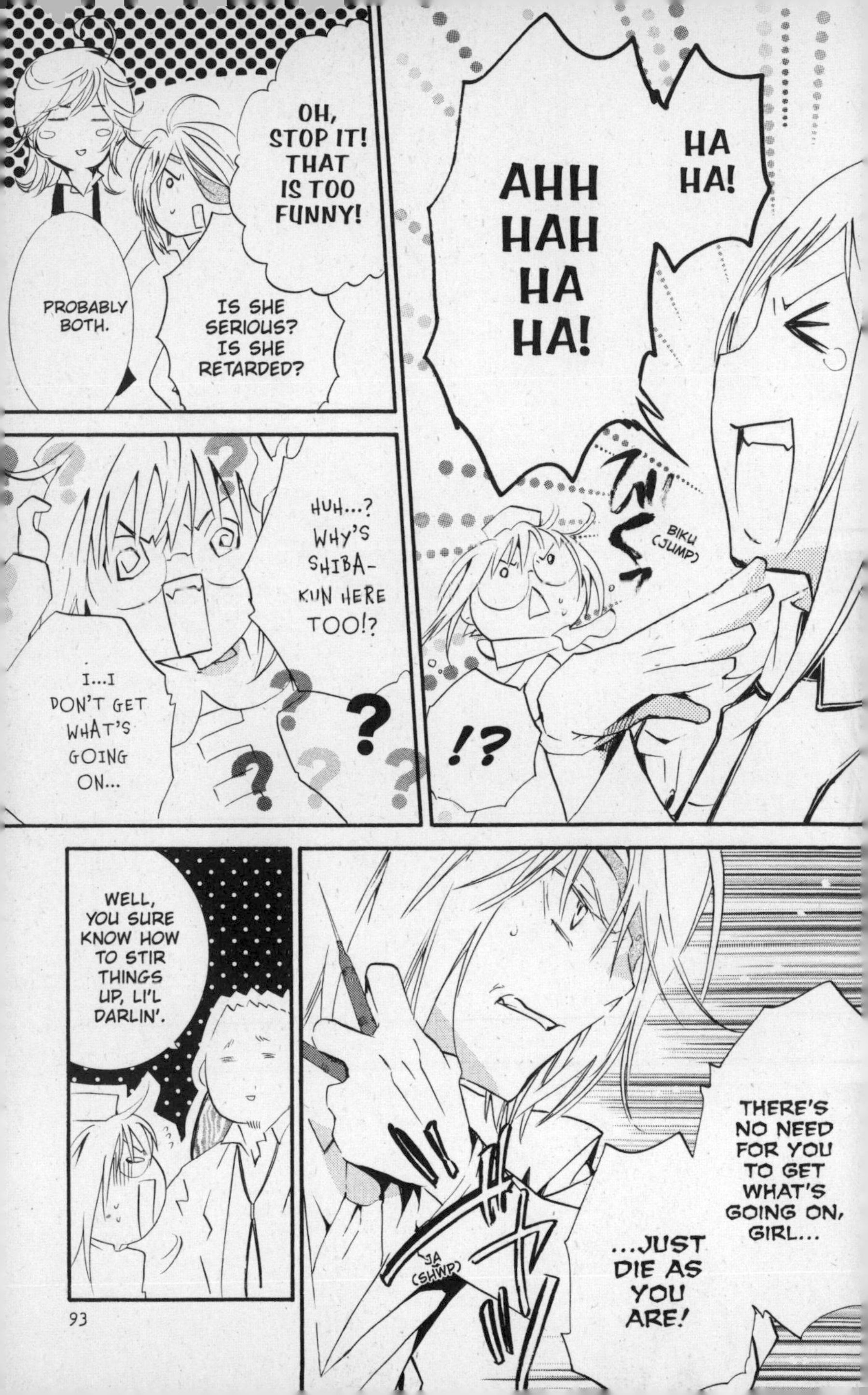
HA HA!
AHH HAH HA HA!
BIKU (JUMP)
!?
OH, STOP IT! THAT IS TOO FUNNY!
IS SHE SERIOUS? IS SHE RETARDED?
PROBABLY BOTH.
HUH...? WHY'S SHIBA-KUN HERE TOO!?
I...I DON'T GET WHAT'S GOING ON...
?
THERE'S NO NEED FOR YOU TO GET WHAT'S GOING ON, GIRL...
...JUST DIE AS YOU ARE!
JA (SHWP)
WELL, YOU SURE KNOW HOW TO STIR THINGS UP, LI'L DARLIN'.

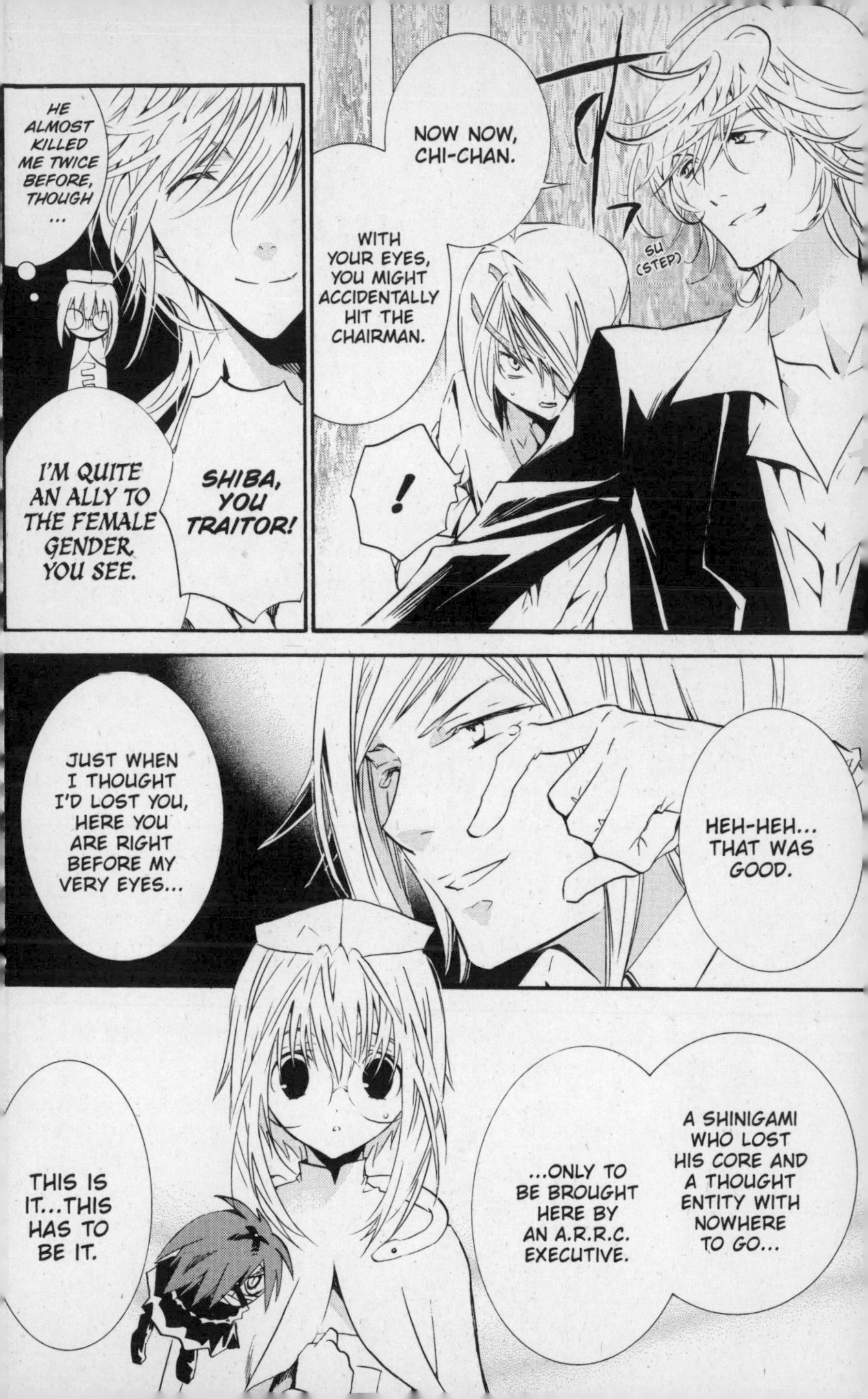
NOW NOW, CHI-CHAN.
SU (STEP)
WITH YOUR EYES, YOU MIGHT ACCIDENTALLY HIT THE CHAIRMAN.
!
HE ALMOST KILLED ME TWICE BEFORE, THOUGH ...
SHIBA, YOU TRAITOR!
I'M QUITE AN ALLY TO THE FEMALE GENDER, YOU SEE.
HEH-HEH... THAT WAS GOOD.
JUST WHEN I THOUGHT I'D LOST YOU, HERE YOU ARE RIGHT BEFORE MY VERY EYES...
A SHINIGAMI WHO LOST HIS CORE AND A THOUGHT ENTITY WITH NOWHERE TO GO...
...ONLY TO BE BROUGHT HERE BY AN A.R.R.C. EXECUTIVE.
THIS IS IT...THIS HAS TO BE IT.

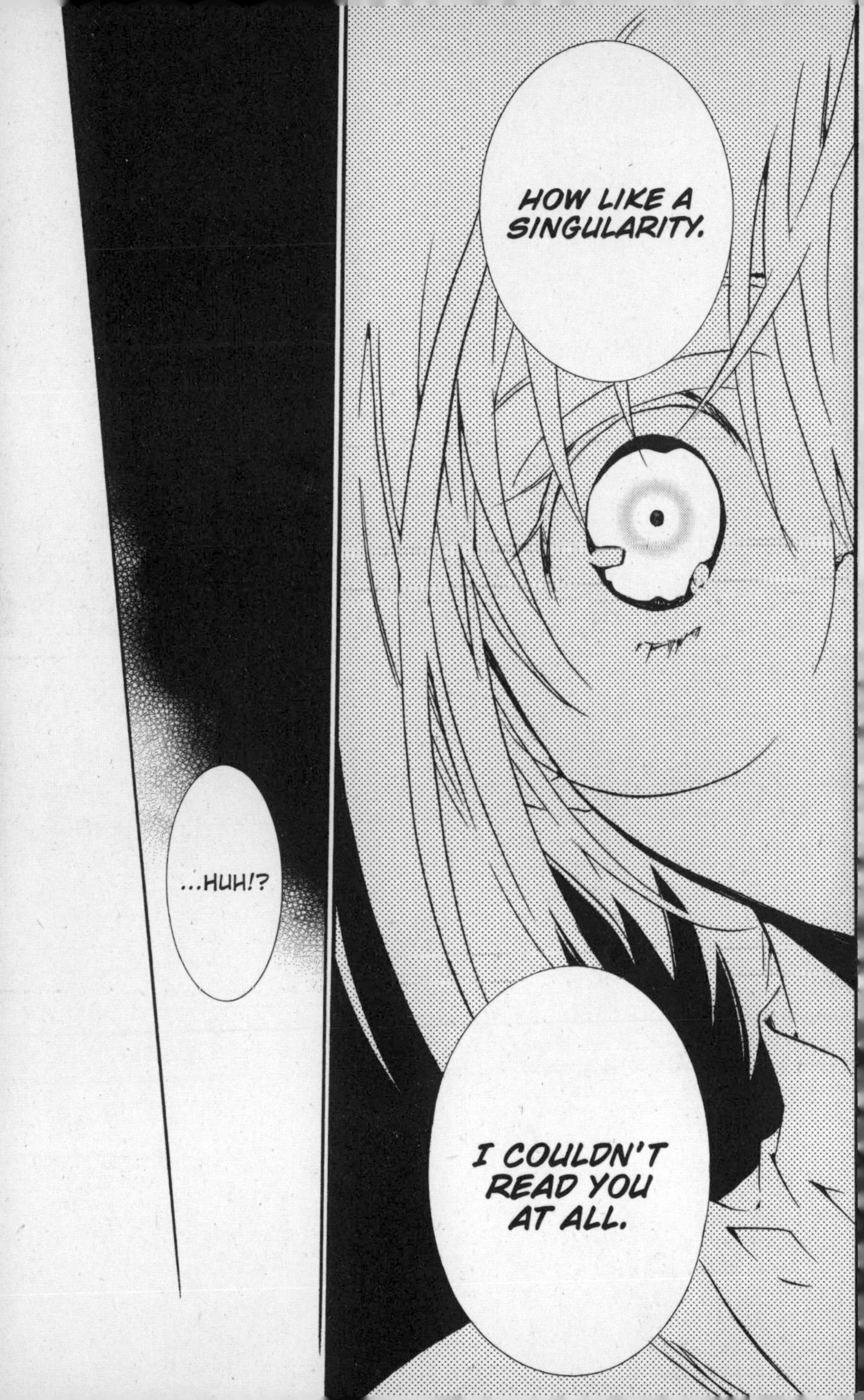
HOW LIKE A SINGULARITY.
I COULDN'T READ YOU AT ALL.
...HUH!?

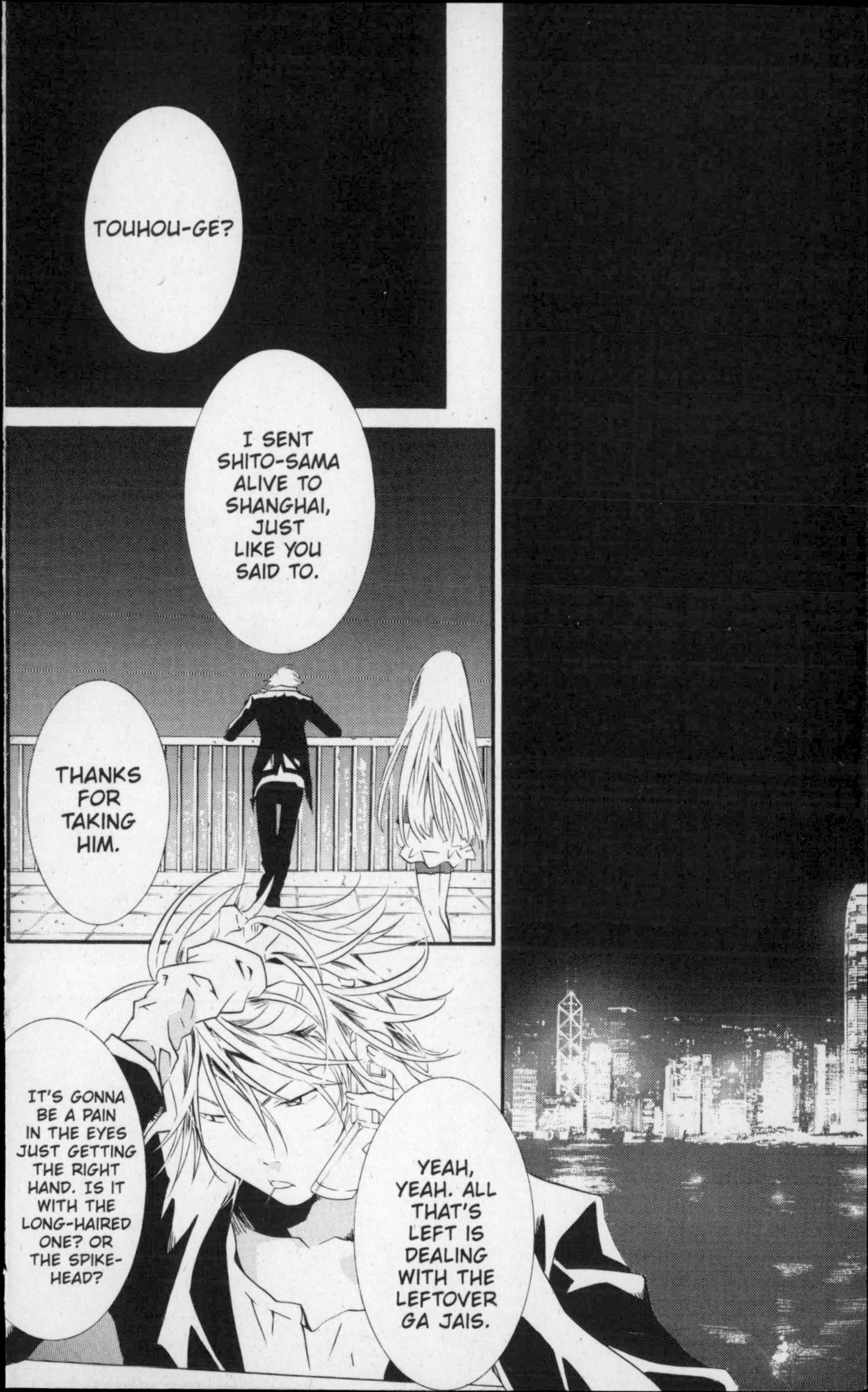
TOUHOU-GE?
I SENT SHITO-SAMA ALIVE TO SHANGHAI, JUST LIKE YOU SAID TO.
THANKS FOR TAKING HIM.
YEAH, YEAH. ALL THAT'S LEFT IS DEALING WITH THE LEFTOVER GA JAIS.
IT'S GONNA BE A PAIN IN THE EYES JUST GETTING THE RIGHT HAND. IS IT WITH THE LONG-HAIRED ONE? OR THE SPIKE-HEAD?

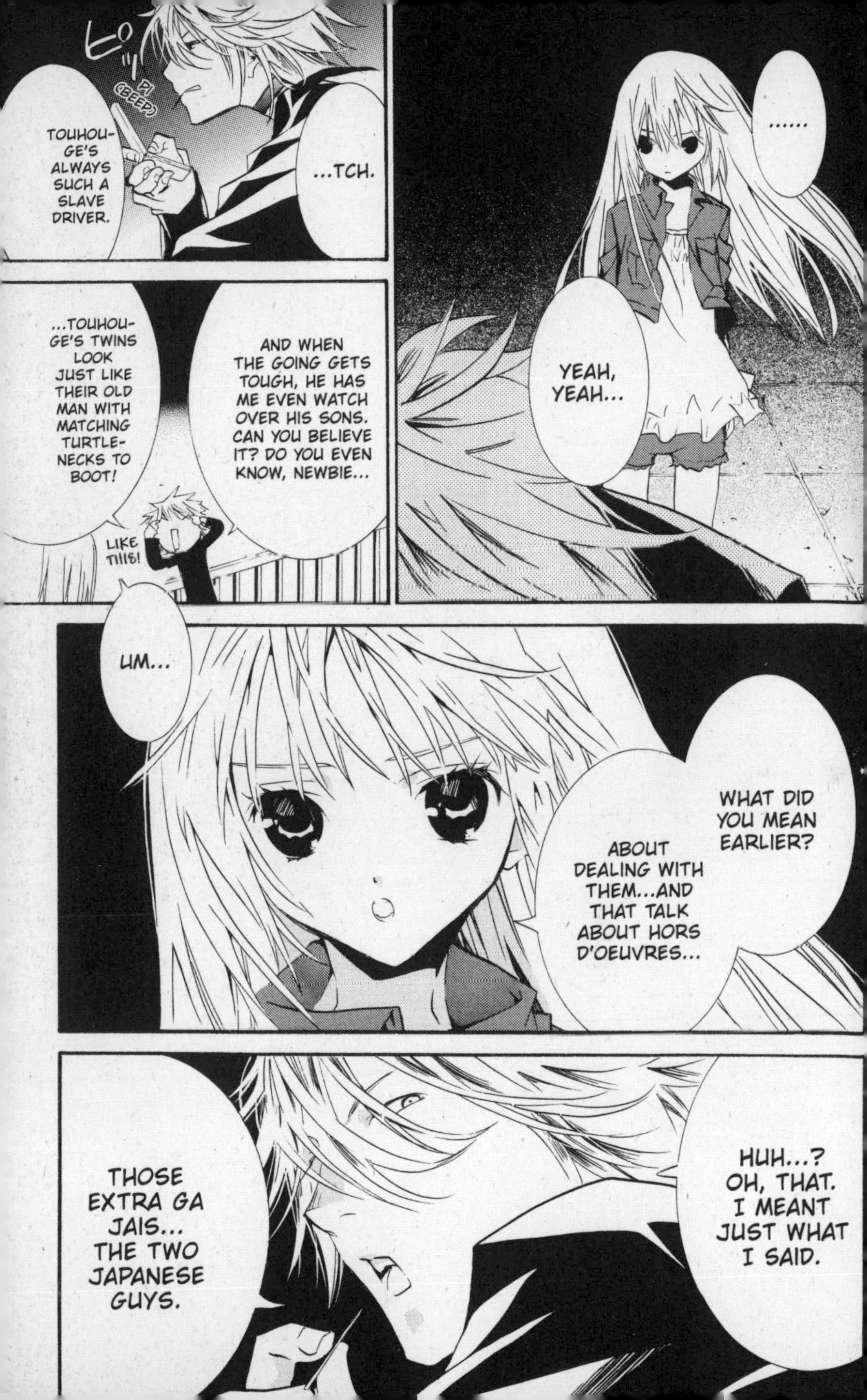
......
YEAH, YEAH...
ピッ
PI (BEEP)
...TCH.
TOUHOUGE'S ALWAYS SUCH A SLAVE DRIVER.
AND WHEN THE GOING GETS TOUGH, HE HAS ME EVEN WATCH OVER HIS SONS. CAN YOU BELIEVE IT? DO YOU EVEN KNOW, NEWBIE...
...TOUHOUGE'S TWINS LOOK JUST LIKE THEIR OLD MAN WITH MATCHING TURTLENECKS TO BOOT!
LIKE THIIS!
UM...
WHAT DID YOU MEAN EARLIER?
ABOUT DEALING WITH THEM...AND THAT TALK ABOUT HORS D'OEUVRES...
HUH...? OH, THAT. I MEANT JUST WHAT I SAID.
THOSE EXTRA GA JAIS... THE TWO JAPANESE GUYS.

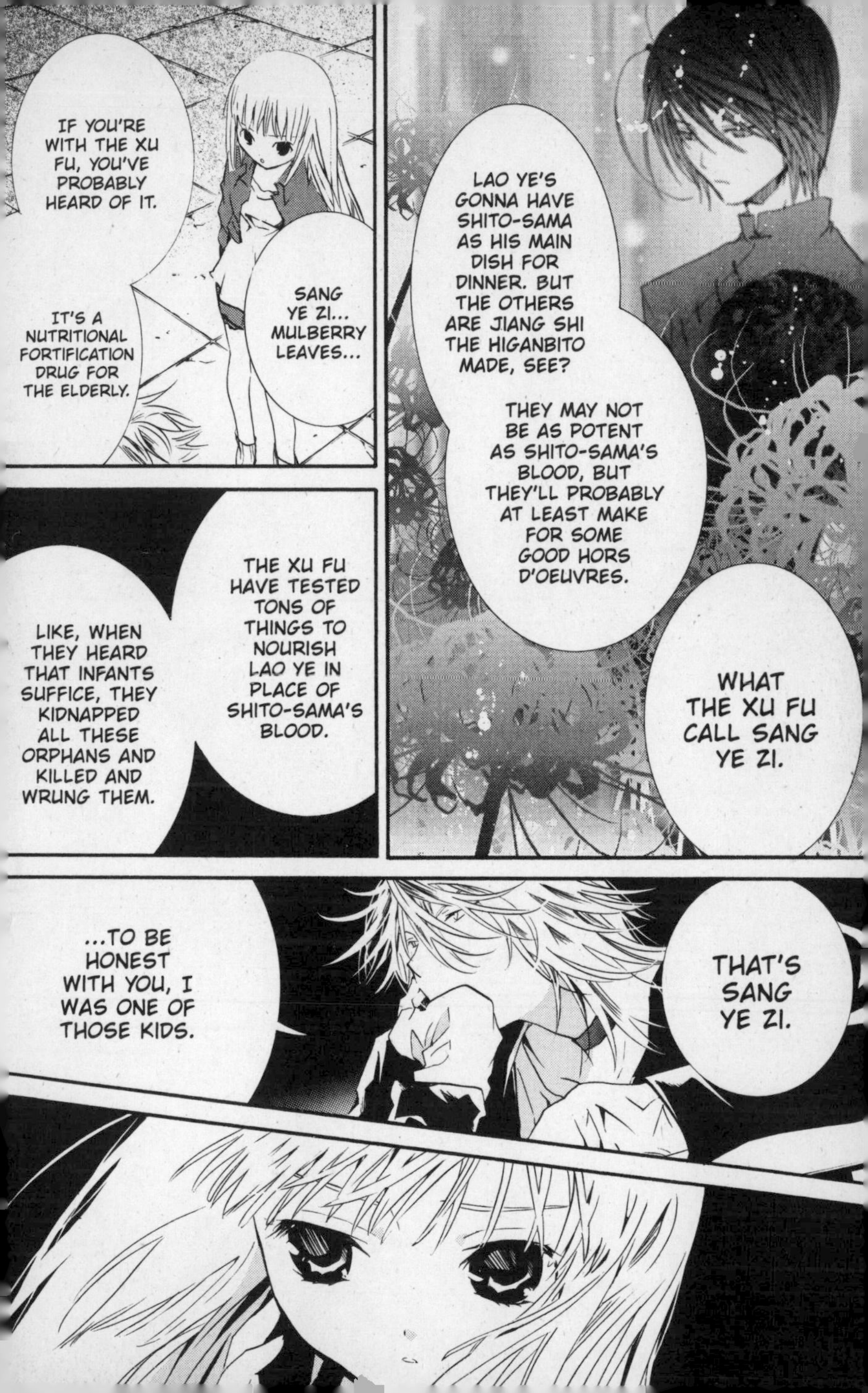
LAO YE'S GONNA HAVE SHITO-SAMA AS HIS MAIN DISH FOR DINNER. BUT THE OTHERS ARE JIANG SHI THE HIGANBITO MADE, SEE?
THEY MAY NOT BE AS POTENT AS SHITO-SAMA'S BLOOD, BUT THEY'LL PROBABLY AT LEAST MAKE FOR SOME GOOD HORS D'OEUVRES.
WHAT THE XU FU CALL SANG YE ZI.
SANG YE ZI... MULBERRY LEAVES...
IF YOU'RE WITH THE XU FU, YOU'VE PROBABLY HEARD OF IT.
IT'S A NUTRITIONAL FORTIFICATION DRUG FOR THE ELDERLY.
THE XU FU HAVE TESTED TONS OF THINGS TO NOURISH LAO YE IN PLACE OF SHITO-SAMA'S BLOOD.
LIKE, WHEN THEY HEARD THAT INFANTS SUFFICE, THEY KIDNAPPED ALL THESE ORPHANS AND KILLED AND WRUNG THEM.
THAT'S SANG YE ZI.
...TO BE HONEST WITH YOU, I WAS ONE OF THOSE KIDS.

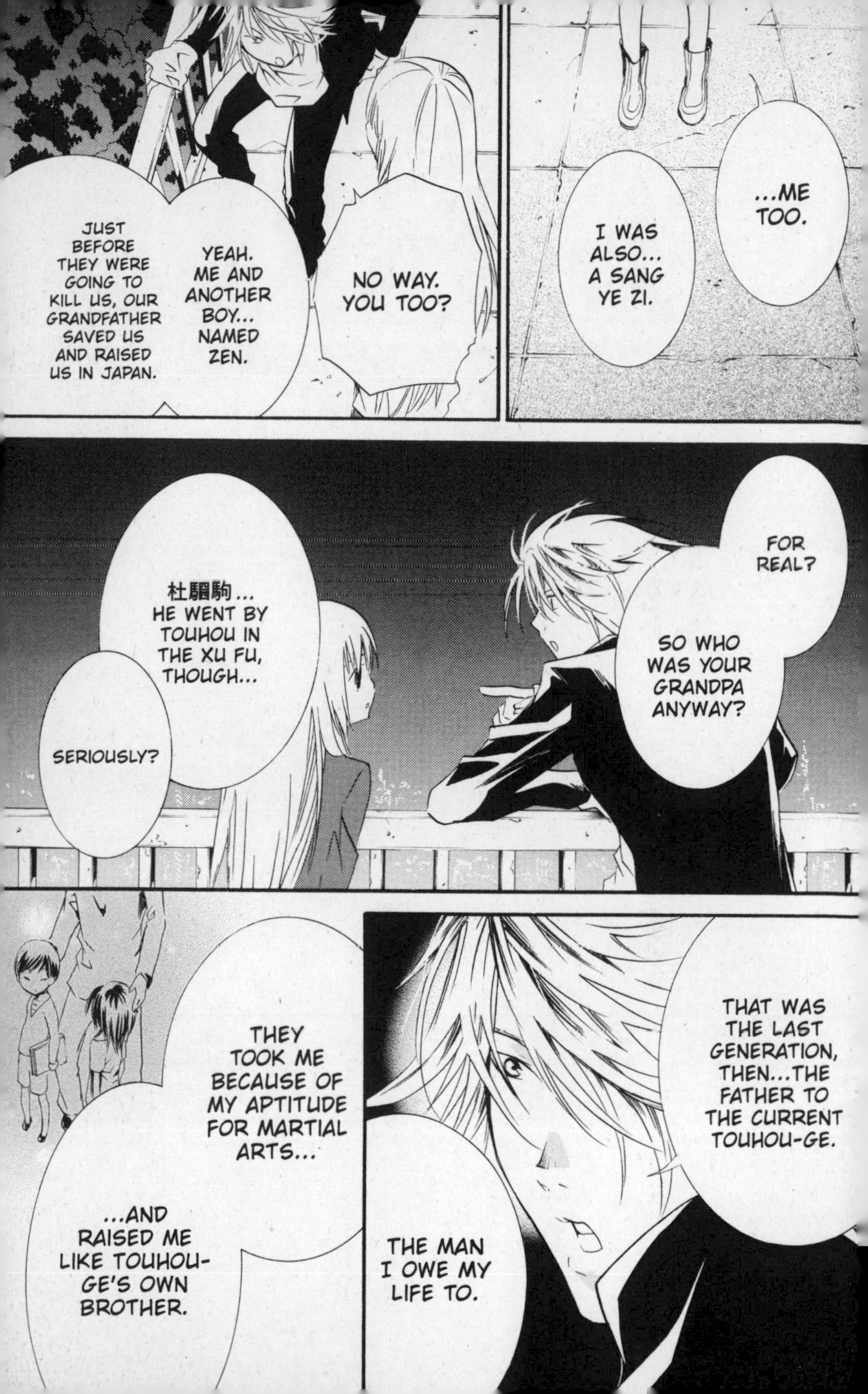
...ME TOO.
I WAS ALSO... A SANG YE ZI.
NO WAY. YOU TOO?
YEAH. ME AND ANOTHER BOY... NAMED ZEN.
JUST BEFORE THEY WERE GOING TO KILL US, OUR GRANDFATHER SAVED US AND RAISED US IN JAPAN.
FOR REAL?
SO WHO WAS YOUR GRANDPA ANYWAY?
杜騮駒... HE WENT BY TOUHOU IN THE XU FU, THOUGH...
SERIOUSLY?
THAT WAS THE LAST GENERATION, THEN...THE FATHER TO THE CURRENT TOUHOU-GE.
THE MAN I OWE MY LIFE TO.
THEY TOOK ME BECAUSE OF MY APTITUDE FOR MARTIAL ARTS...
...AND RAISED ME LIKE TOUHOU-GE'S OWN BROTHER.

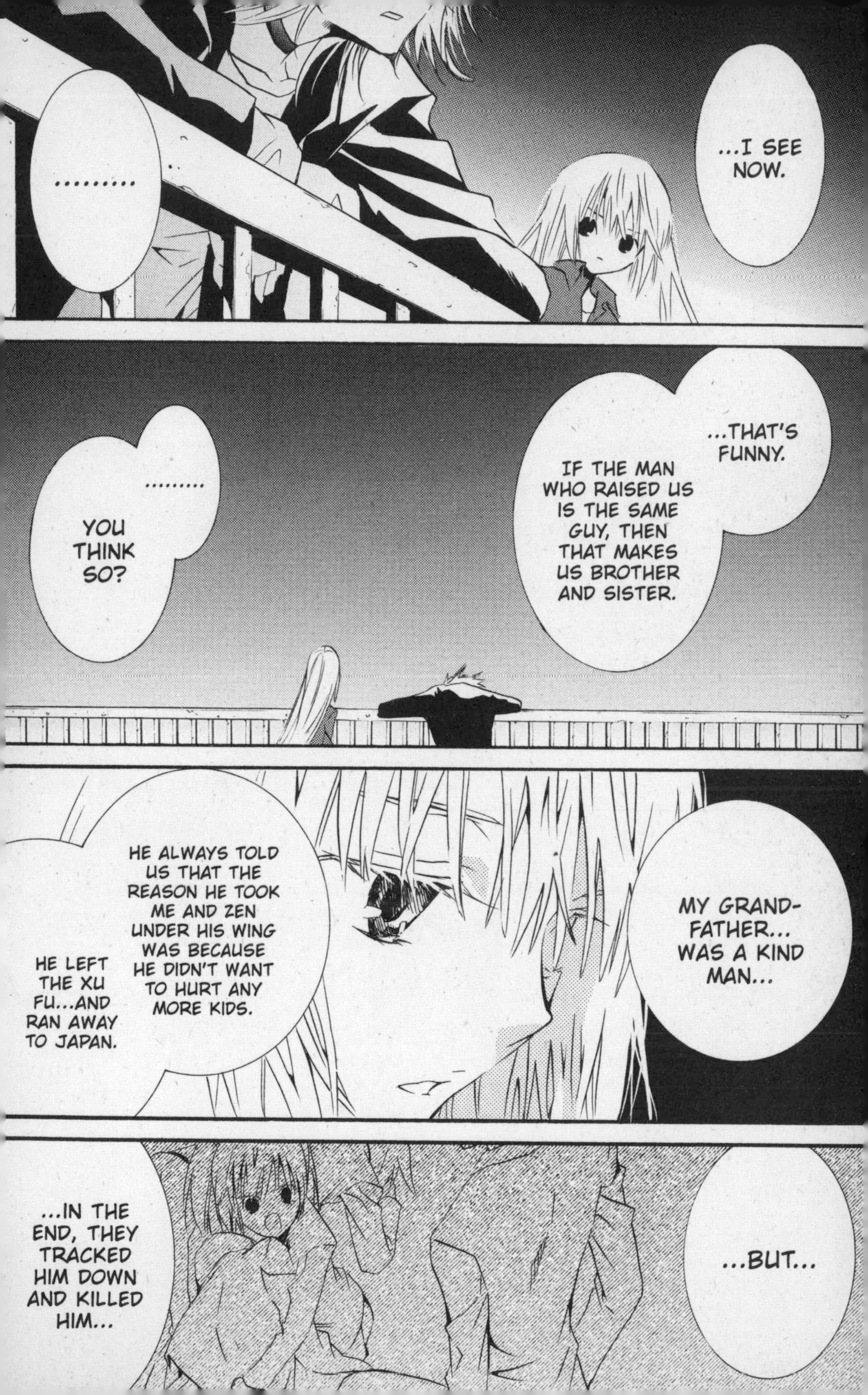
...I SEE NOW.
....
...THAT'S FUNNY.
IF THE MAN WHO RAISED US IS THE SAME GUY, THEN THAT MAKES US BROTHER AND SISTER.
....
YOU THINK SO?
MY GRAND-FATHER... WAS A KIND MAN...
HE ALWAYS TOLD US THAT THE REASON HE TOOK ME AND ZEN UNDER HIS WING WAS BECAUSE HE DIDN'T WANT TO HURT ANY MORE KIDS.
HE LEFT THE XU FU...AND RAN AWAY TO JAPAN.
...BUT...
...IN THE END, THEY TRACKED HIM DOWN AND KILLED HIM...

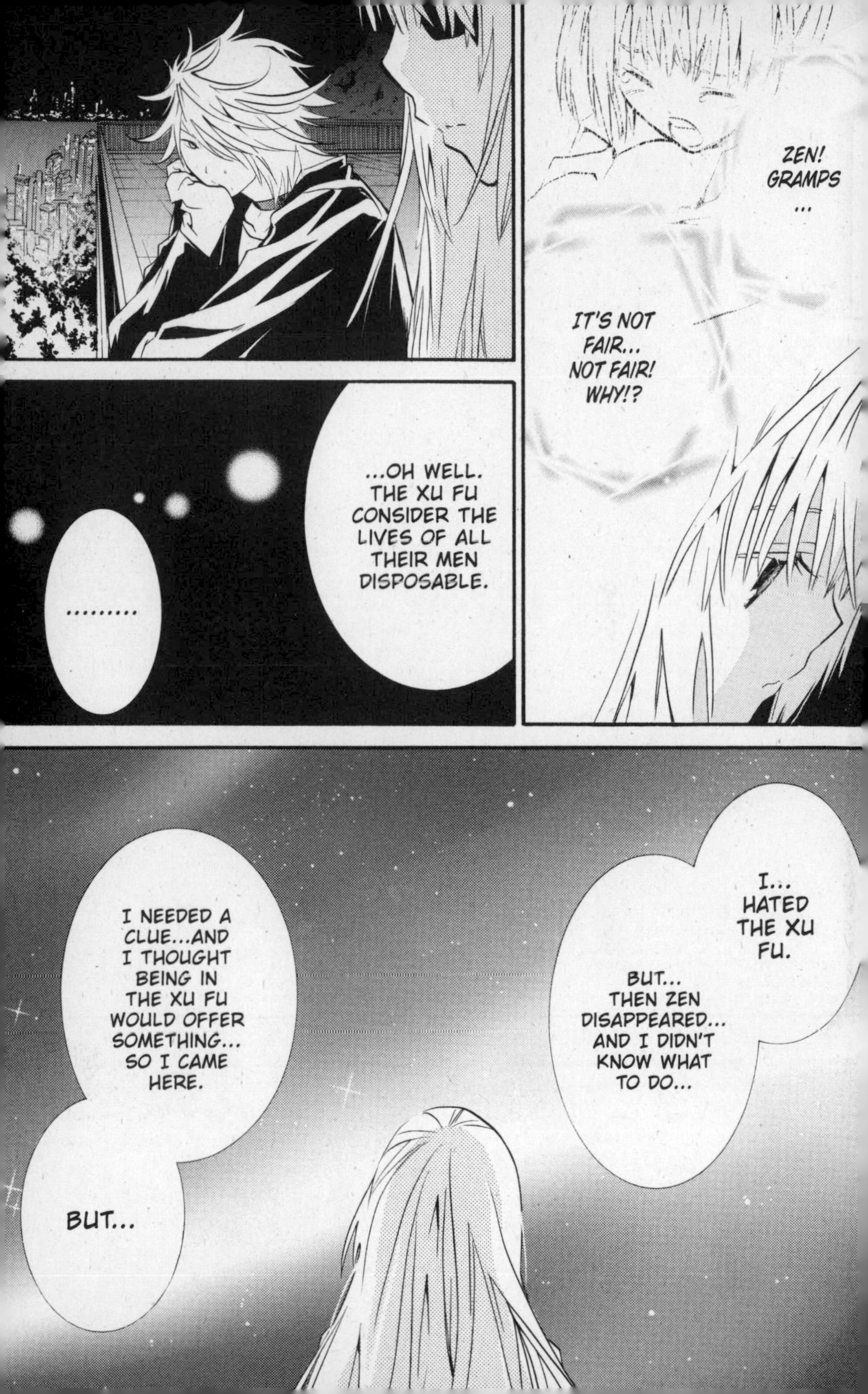
ZEN! GRAMPS ...
IT'S NOT FAIR... NOT FAIR! WHY!?
...OH WELL. THE XU FU CONSIDER THE LIVES OF ALL THEIR MEN DISPOSABLE.
....
I... HATED THE XU FU.
BUT... THEN ZEN DISAPPEARED... AND I DIDN'T KNOW WHAT TO DO...
I NEEDED A CLUE...AND I THOUGHT BEING IN THE XU FU WOULD OFFER SOMETHING... SO I CAME HERE.
BUT...

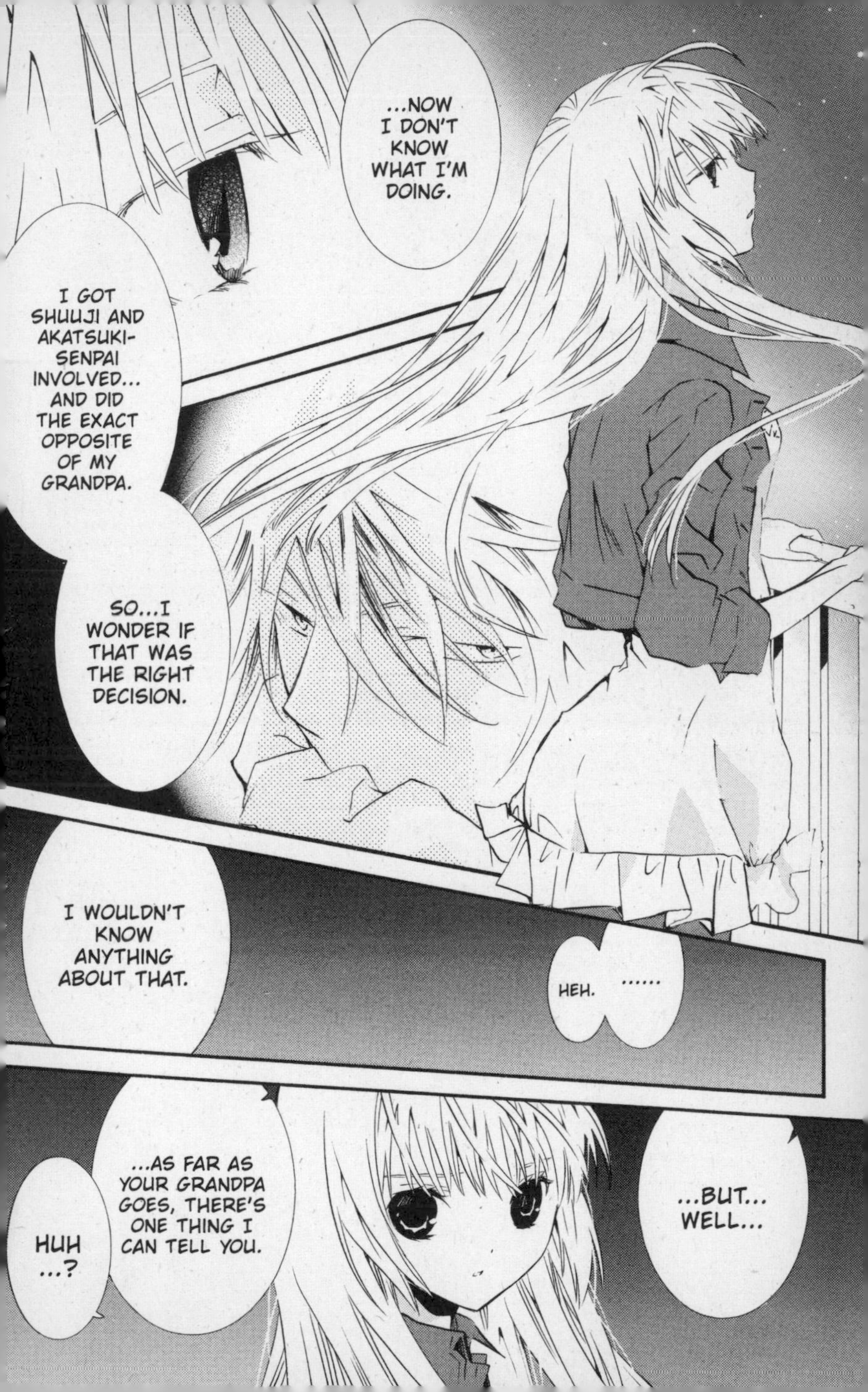
...NOW I DON'T KNOW WHAT I'M DOING.
I GOT SHUUJI AND AKATSUKI-SENPAI INVOLVED... AND DID THE EXACT OPPOSITE OF MY GRANDPA.
SO...I WONDER IF THAT WAS THE RIGHT DECISION.
......
HEH.
I WOULDN'T KNOW ANYTHING ABOUT THAT.
...BUT... WELL...
...AS FAR AS YOUR GRANDPA GOES, THERE'S ONE THING I CAN TELL YOU.
HUH ...?

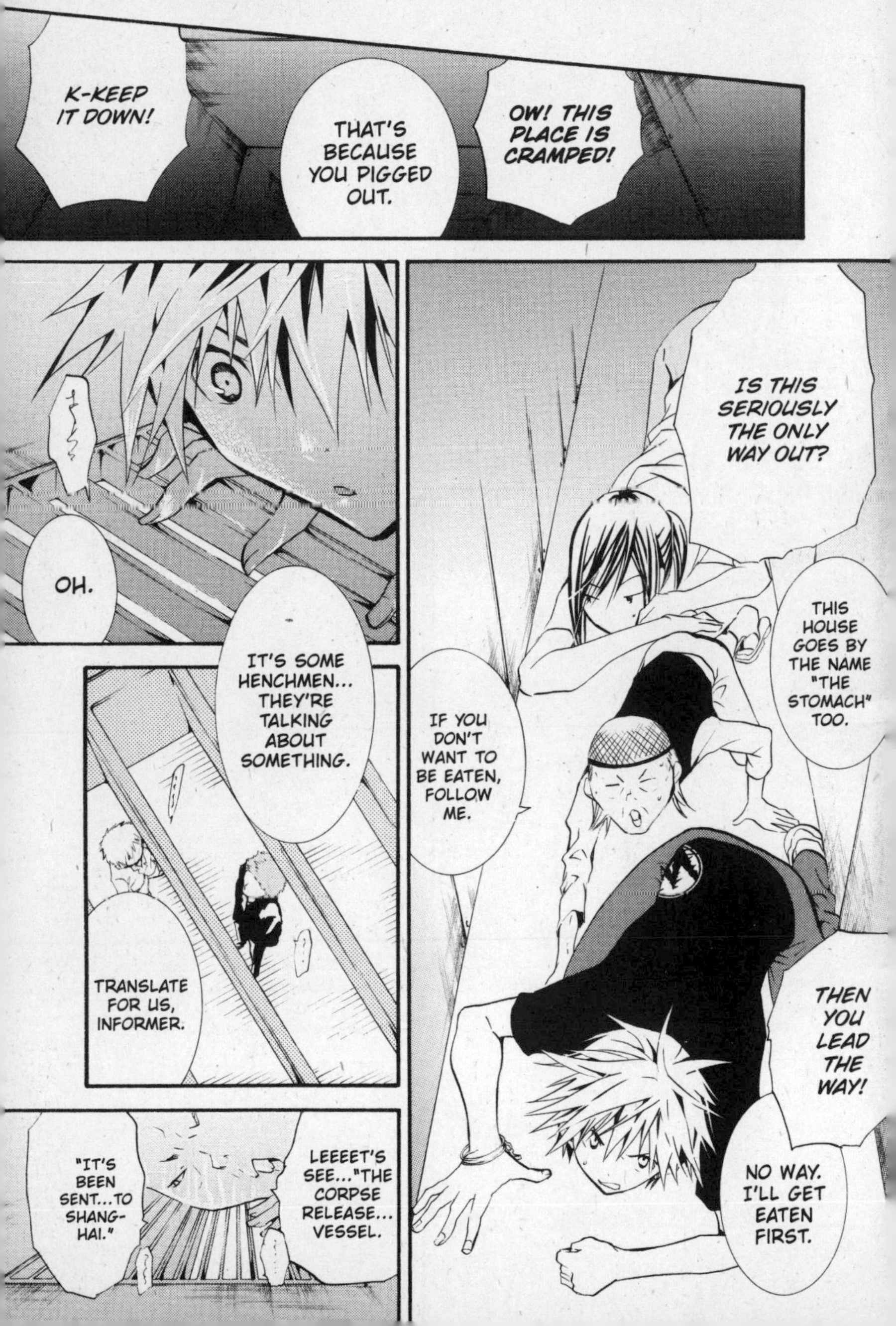
OW! THIS PLACE IS CRAMPED!
THAT'S BECAUSE YOU PIGGED OUT.
K-KEEP IT DOWN!
IS THIS SERIOUSLY THE ONLY WAY OUT?
THIS HOUSE GOES BY THE NAME "THE STOMACH" TOO.
IF YOU DON'T WANT TO BE EATEN, FOLLOW ME.
THEN YOU LEAD THE WAY!
NO WAY. I'LL GET EATEN FIRST.
OH.
IT'S SOME HENCHMEN... THEY'RE TALKING ABOUT SOMETHING.
TRANSLATE FOR US, INFORMER.
LEEEET'S SEE..."THE CORPSE RELEASE... VESSEL.
"IT'S BEEN SENT...TO SHANG-HAI."

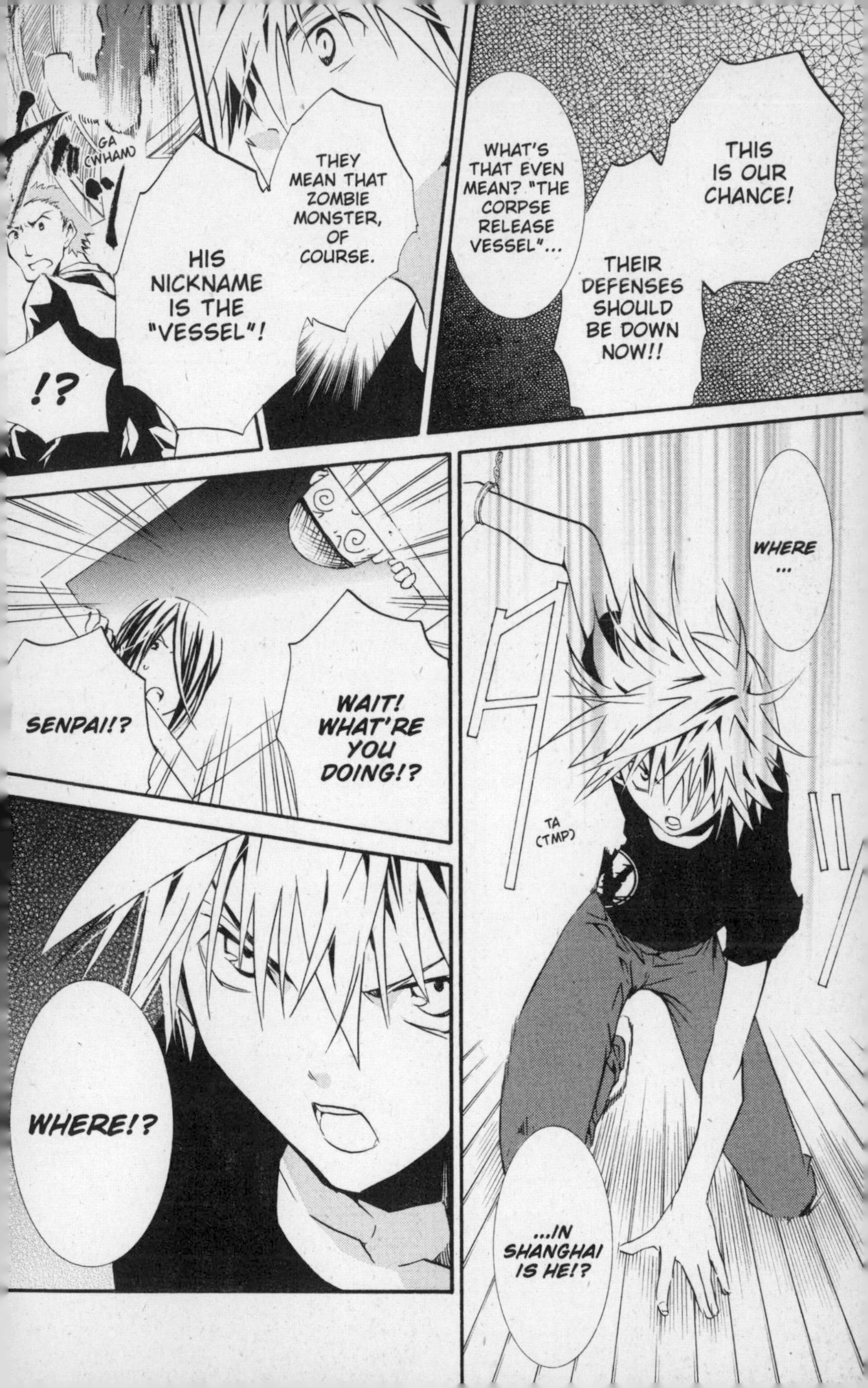

THIS IS OUR CHANCE!
THEIR DEFENSES SHOULD BE DOWN NOW!!
WHAT'S THAT EVEN MEAN? "THE CORPSE RELEASE VESSEL"...
THEY MEAN THAT ZOMBIE MONSTER, OF COURSE.
HIS NICKNAME IS THE "VESSEL"!
GA (WHAM)
!?
WHERE ...
TA (TMP)
...IN SHANGHAI IS HE!?
WAIT! WHAT'RE YOU DOING!?
SENPAI!?
WHERE!?

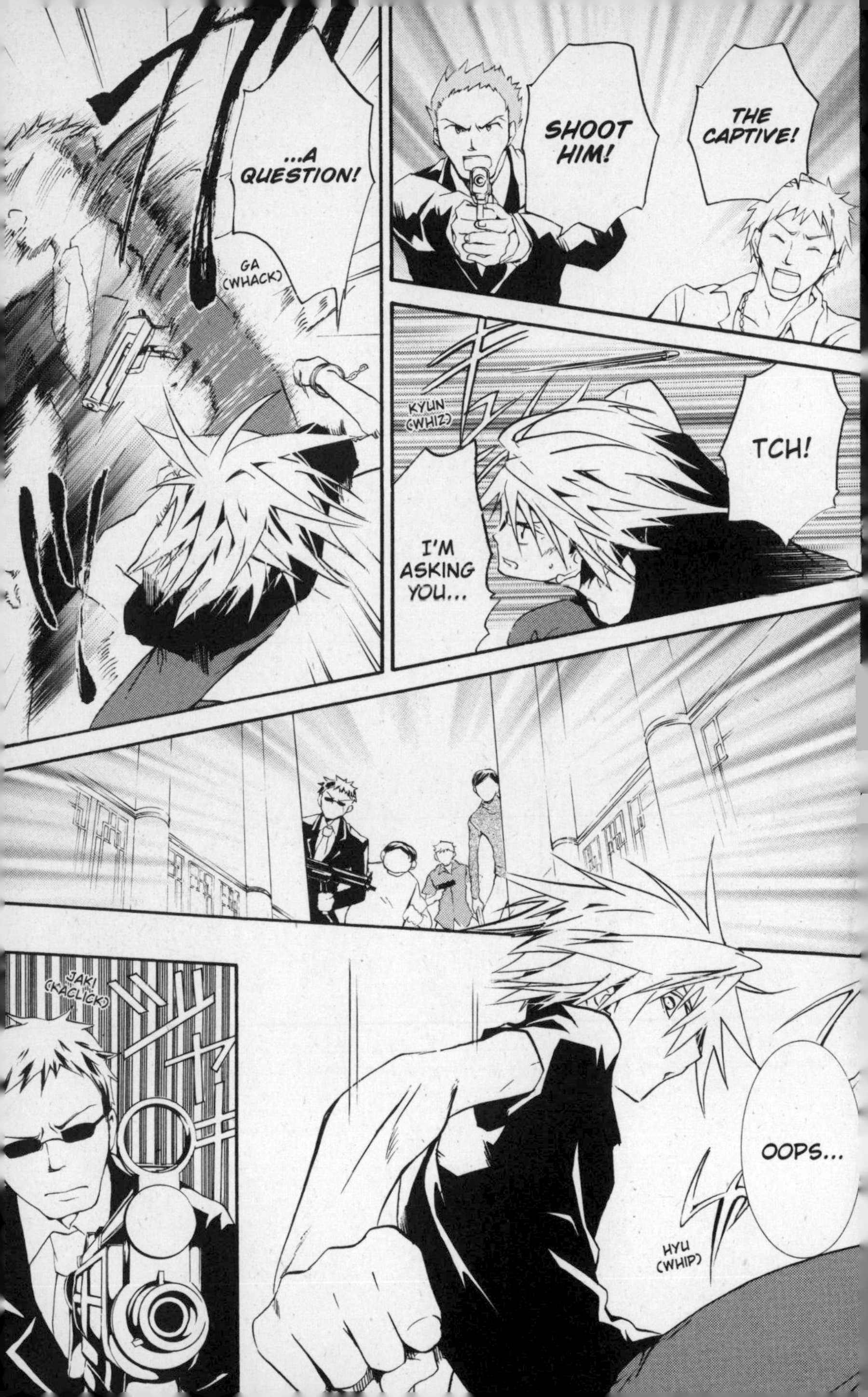
THE CAPTIVE!
SHOOT HIM!
TCH!
KYUN (WHIZ)
I'M ASKING YOU...
...A QUESTION!
GA (WHACK)
OOPS...
HYU (WHIP)
JAKI (KACLICK)

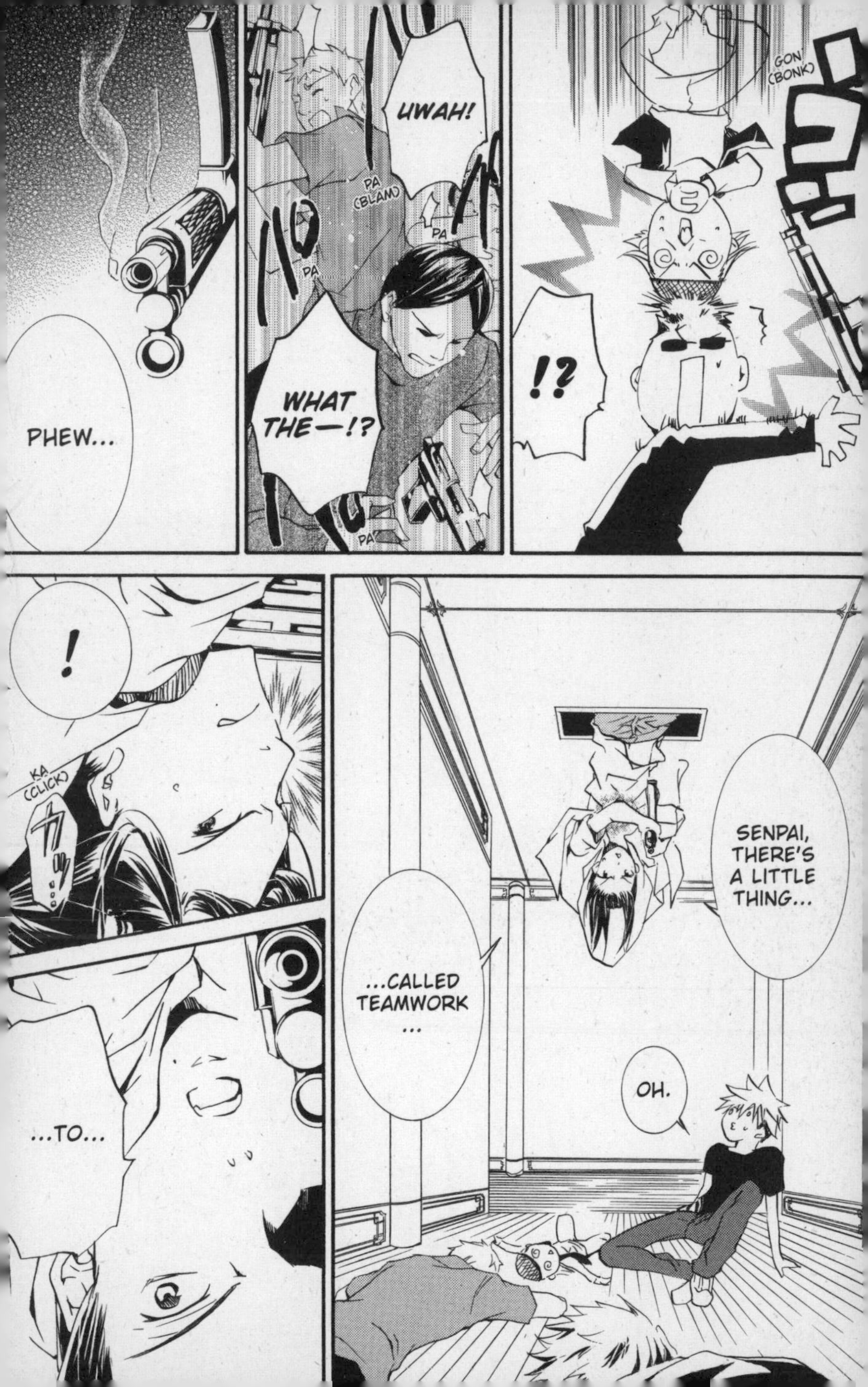
GON (BONK)
!?
UWAH!
PA (BLAM)
PA
PA
WHAT THE—!?
PA
PHEW...
SENPAI, THERE'S A LITTLE THING...
...CALLED TEAMWORK ...
OH.
!
KA (CLICK)
...TO...

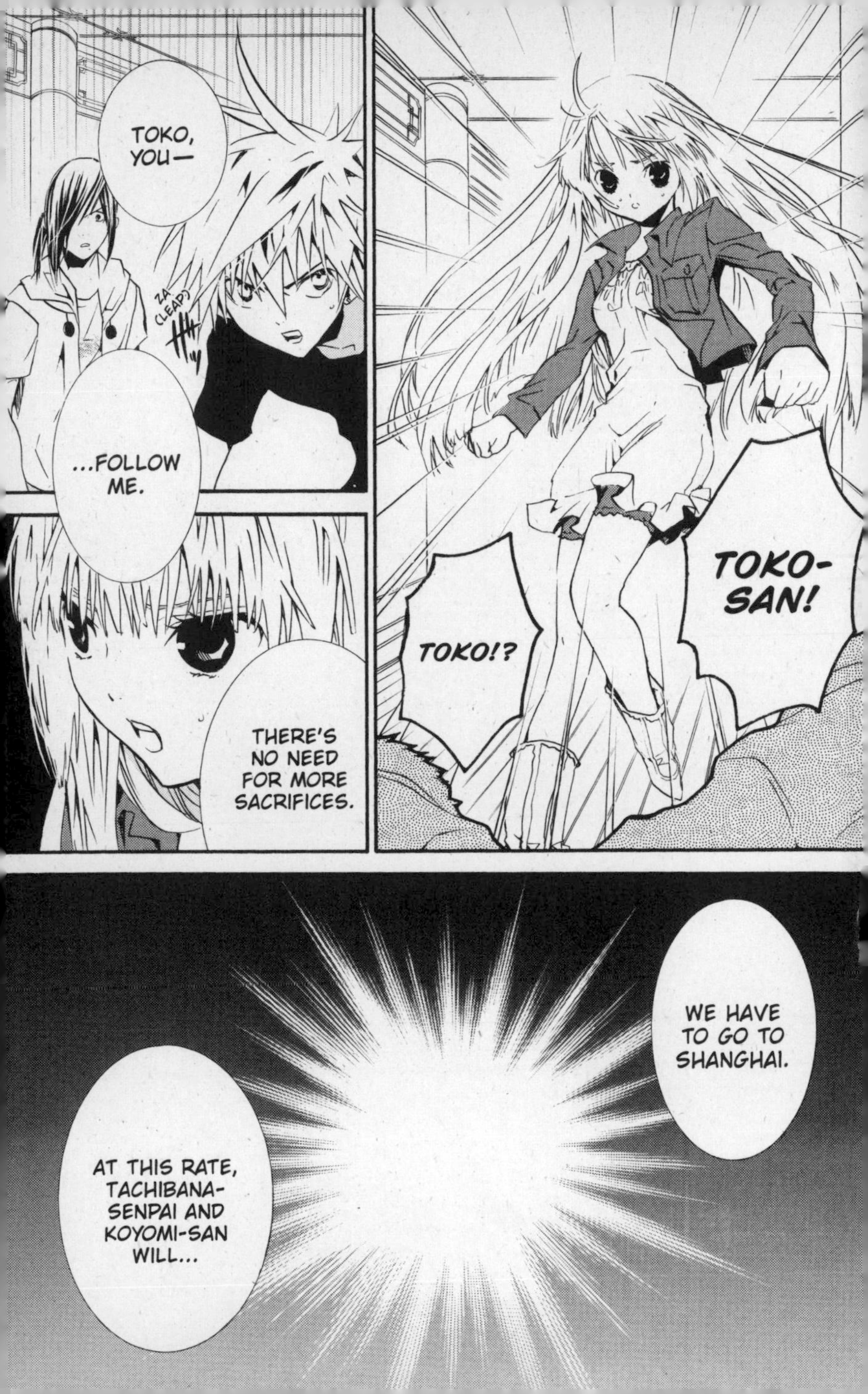
TOKO-SAN!
TOKO!?
TOKO, YOU—
ZA (LEAP)
...FOLLOW ME.
THERE'S NO NEED FOR MORE SACRIFICES.
WE HAVE TO GO TO SHANGHAI.
AT THIS RATE, TACHIBANA-SENPAI AND KOYOMI-SAN WILL...

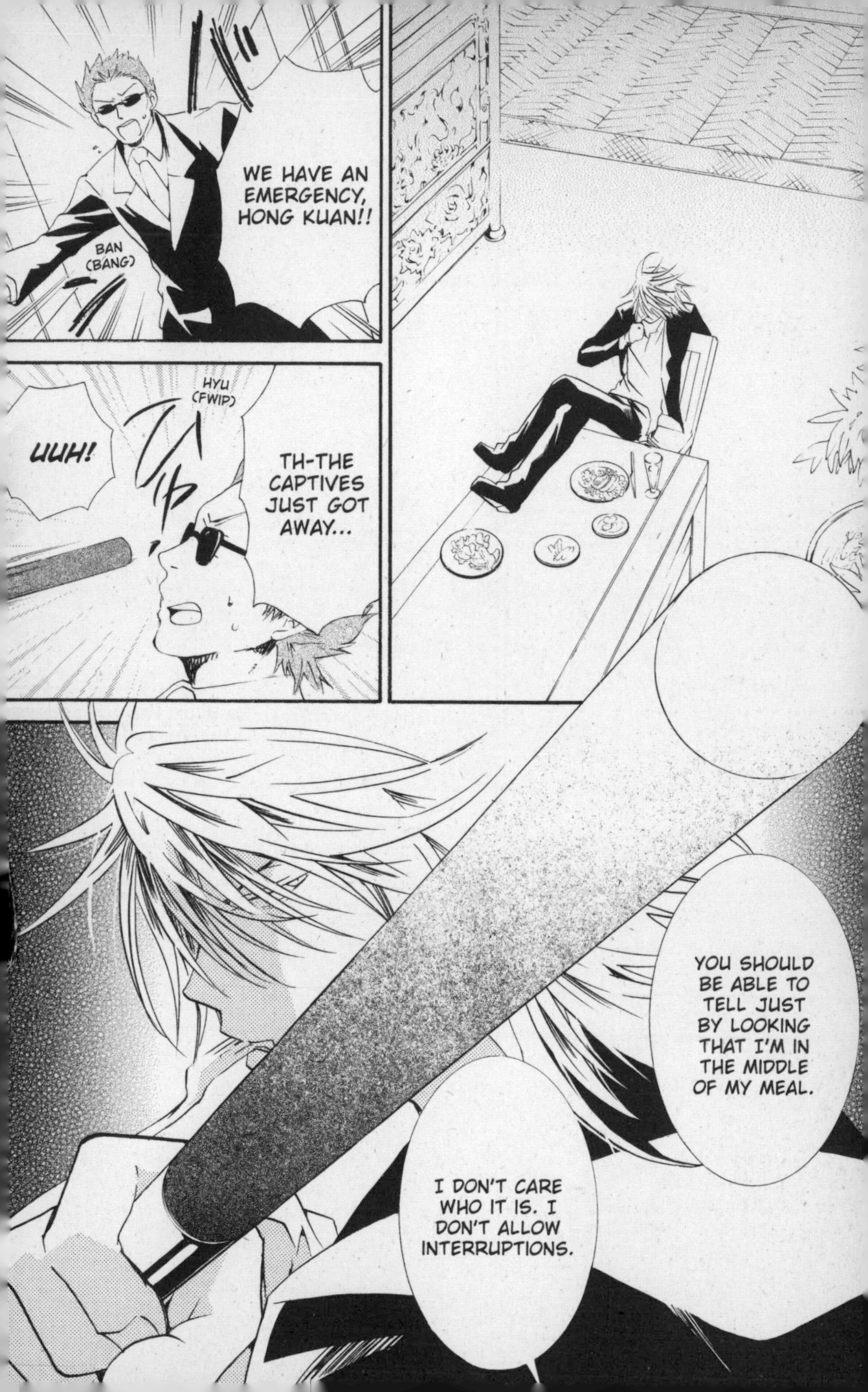
WE HAVE AN EMERGENCY, HONG KUAN!!
BAN (BANG)
HYU (FWIP)
TH-THE CAPTIVES JUST GOT AWAY...
UUH!
YOU SHOULD BE ABLE TO TELL JUST BY LOOKING THAT I'M IN THE MIDDLE OF MY MEAL.
I DON'T CARE WHO IT IS. I DON'T ALLOW INTERRUPTIONS.

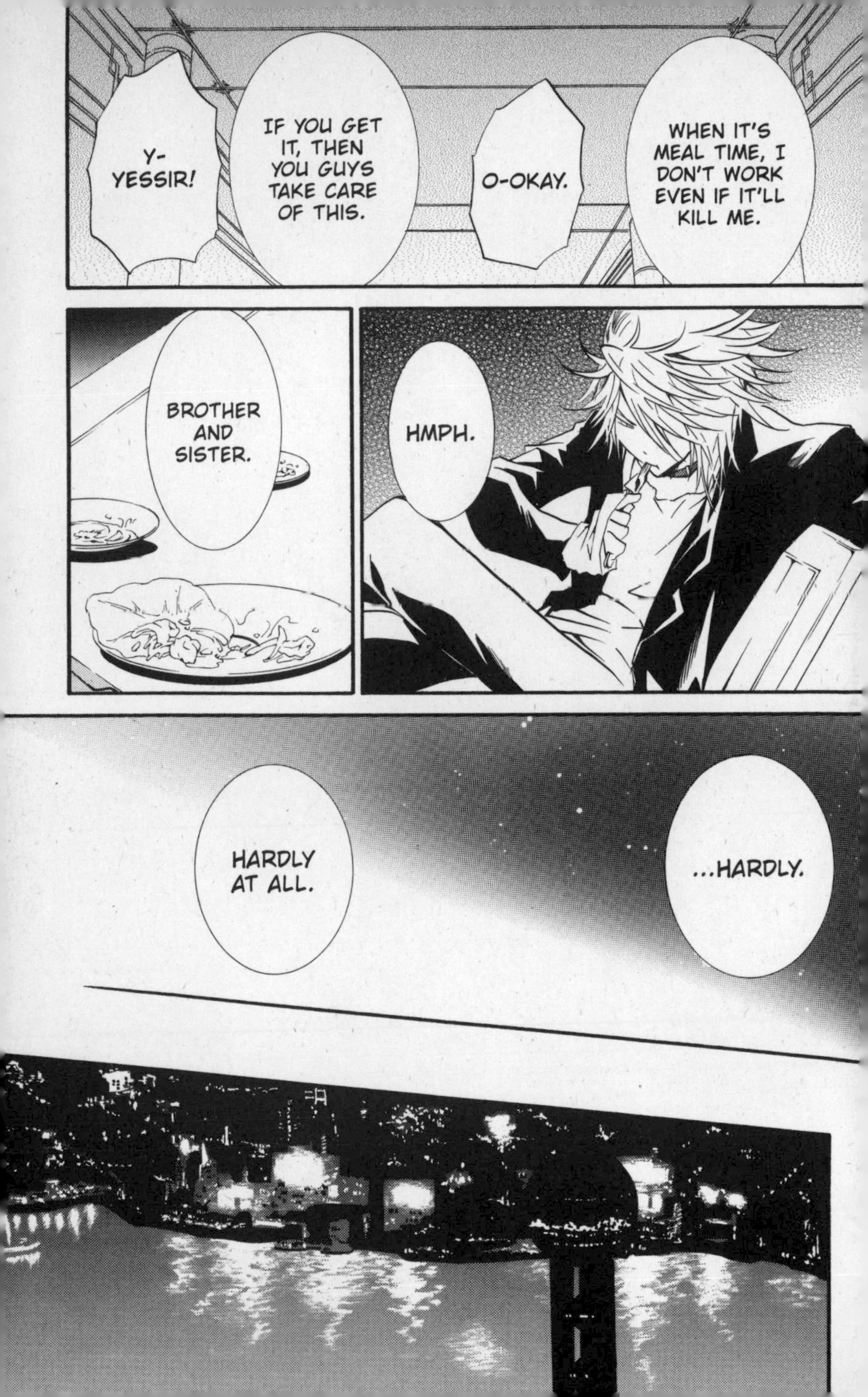
WHEN IT'S MEAL TIME, I DON'T WORK EVEN IF IT'LL KILL ME.
O-OKAY.
IF YOU GET IT, THEN YOU GUYS TAKE CARE OF THIS.
Y-YESSIR!
HMPH.
BROTHER AND SISTER.
...HARDLY.
HARDLY AT ALL.

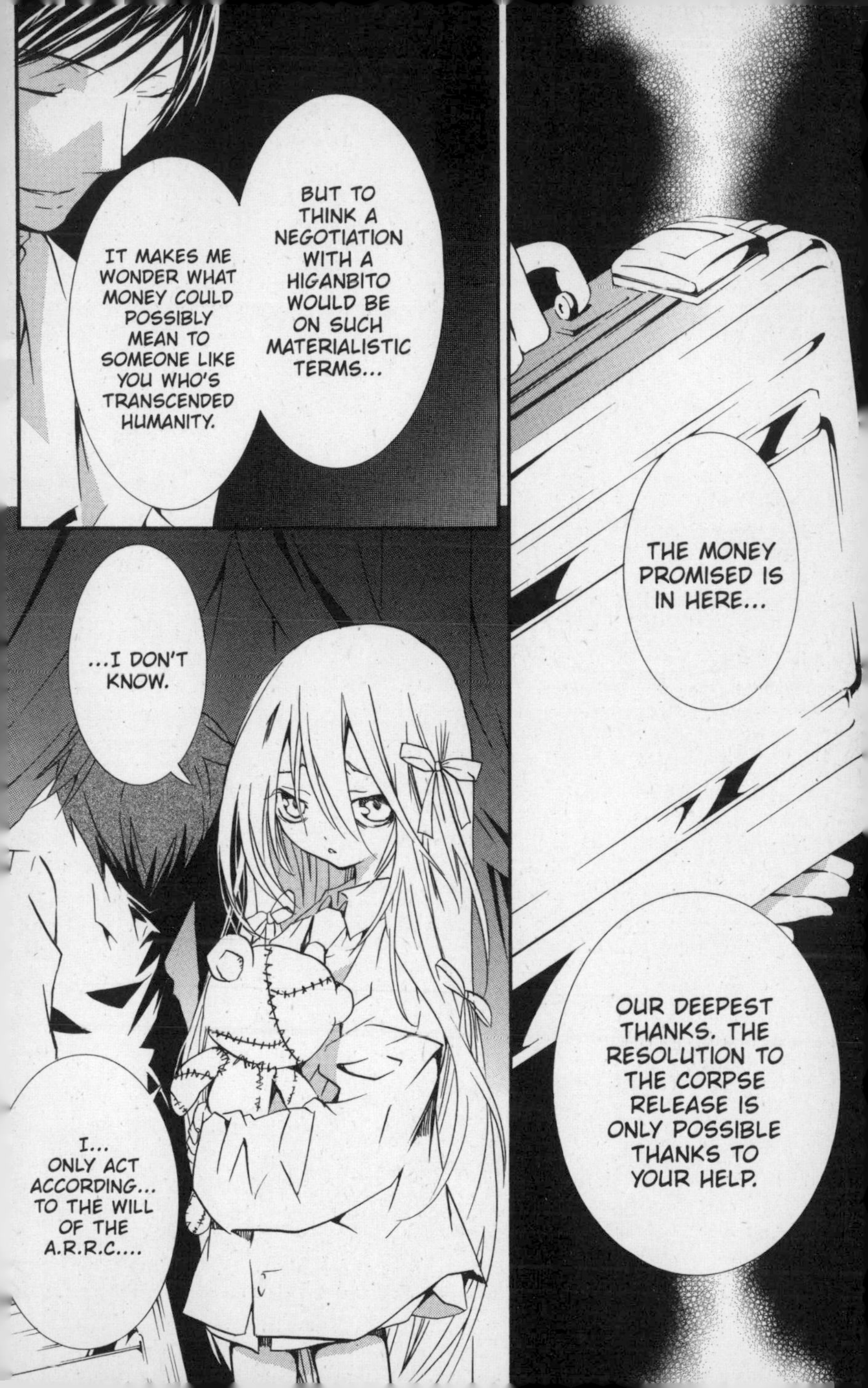
THE MONEY PROMISED IS IN HERE...
OUR DEEPEST THANKS. THE RESOLUTION TO THE CORPSE RELEASE IS ONLY POSSIBLE THANKS TO YOUR HELP.
BUT TO THINK A NEGOTIATION WITH A HIGANBITO WOULD BE ON SUCH MATERIALISTIC TERMS...
IT MAKES ME WONDER WHAT MONEY COULD POSSIBLY MEAN TO SOMEONE LIKE YOU WHO'S TRANSCENDED HUMANITY.
...I DON'T KNOW.
I... ONLY ACT ACCORDING... TO THE WILL OF THE A.R.R.C....

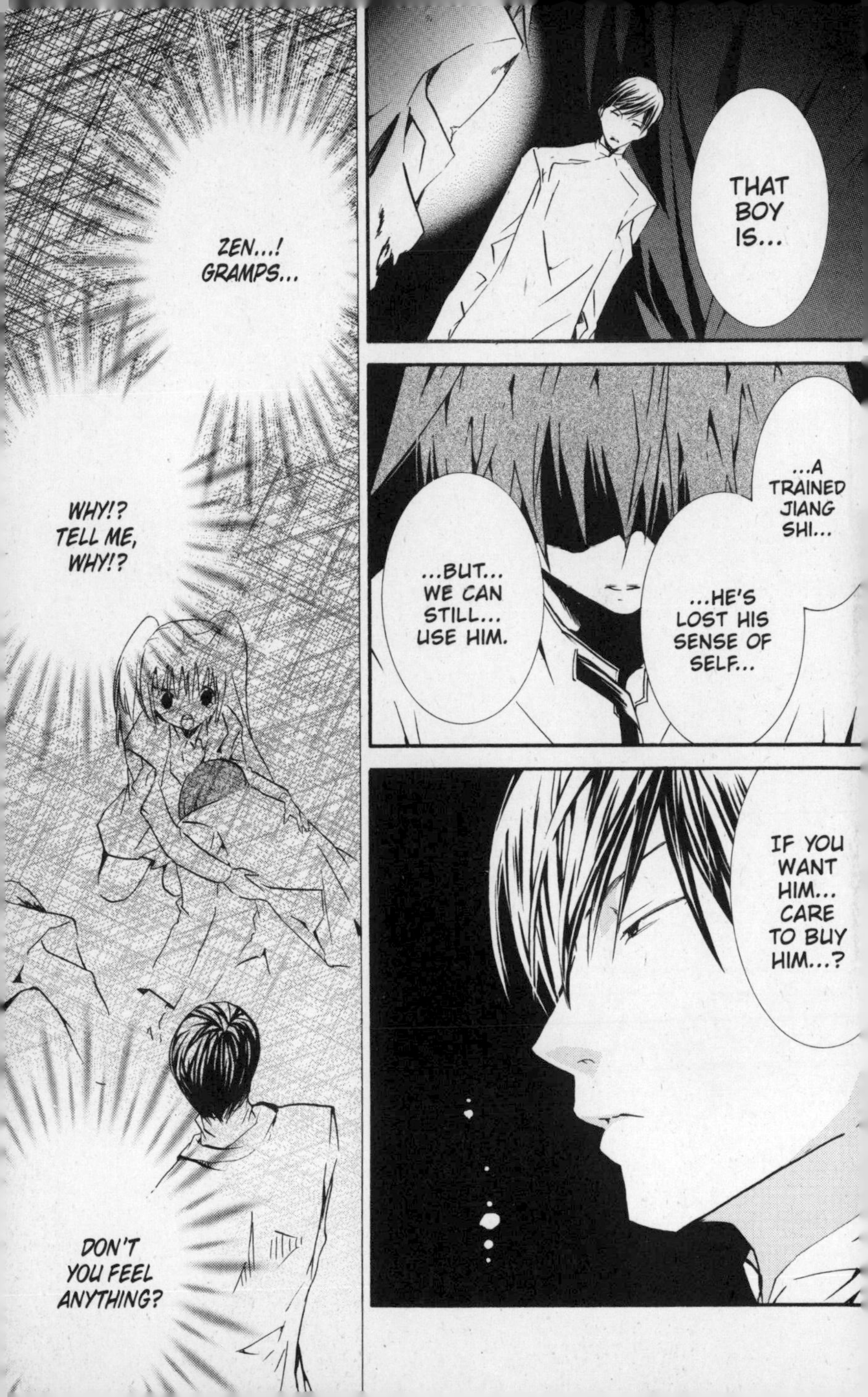
THAT BOY IS...
...A TRAINED JIANG SHI...
...HE'S LOST HIS SENSE OF SELF...
...BUT... WE CAN STILL... USE HIM.
IF YOU WANT HIM... CARE TO BUY HIM...?
ZEN...! GRAMPS...
WHY!? TELL ME, WHY!?
DON'T YOU FEEL ANYTHING?

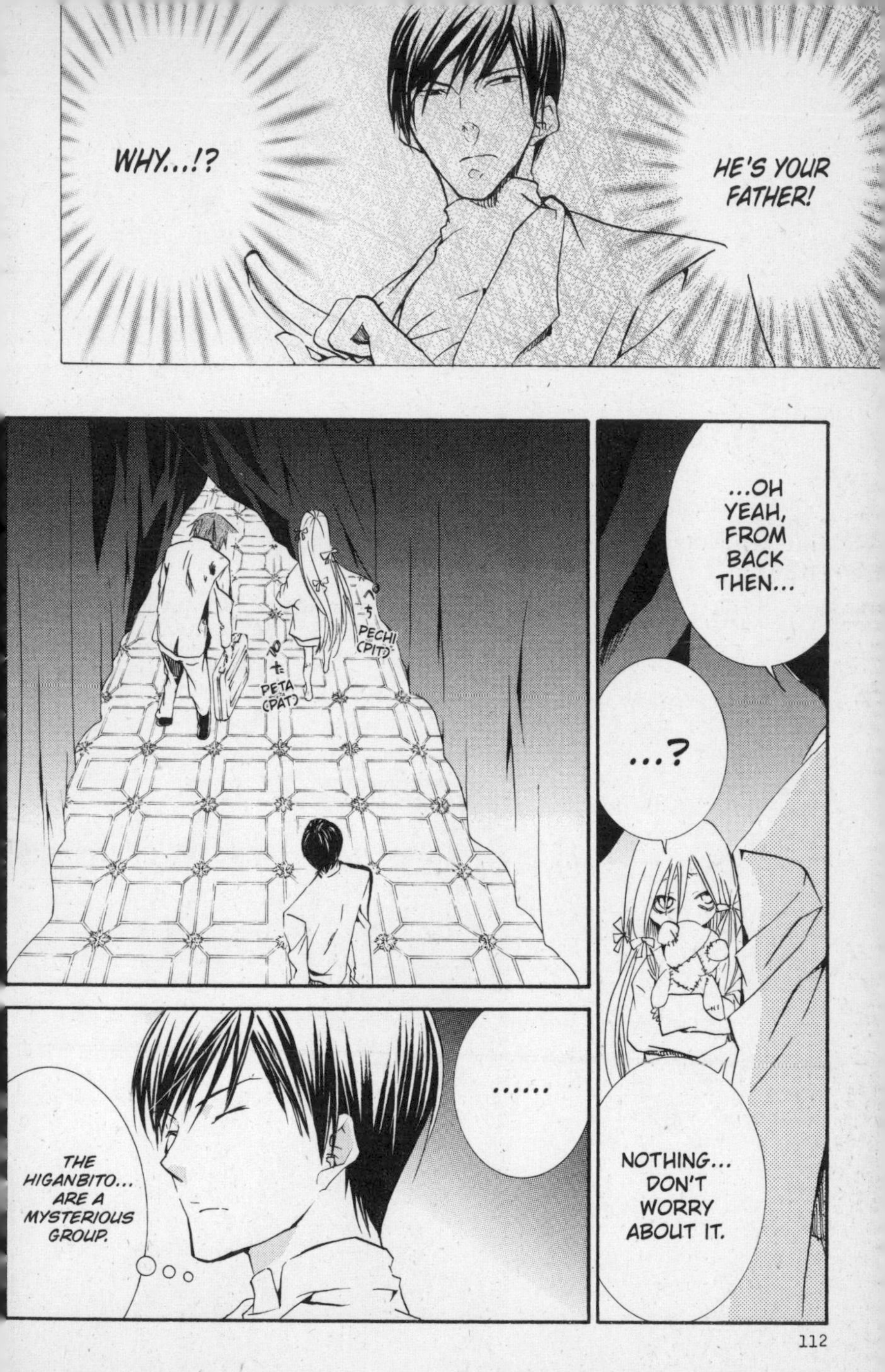

HE'S YOUR FATHER!
WHY...!?
...OH YEAH, FROM BACK THEN...
...?
NOTHING... DON'T WORRY ABOUT IT.
PECHI (PIT)
PETA (PAT)
......
THE HIGANBITO... ARE A MYSTERIOUS GROUP.

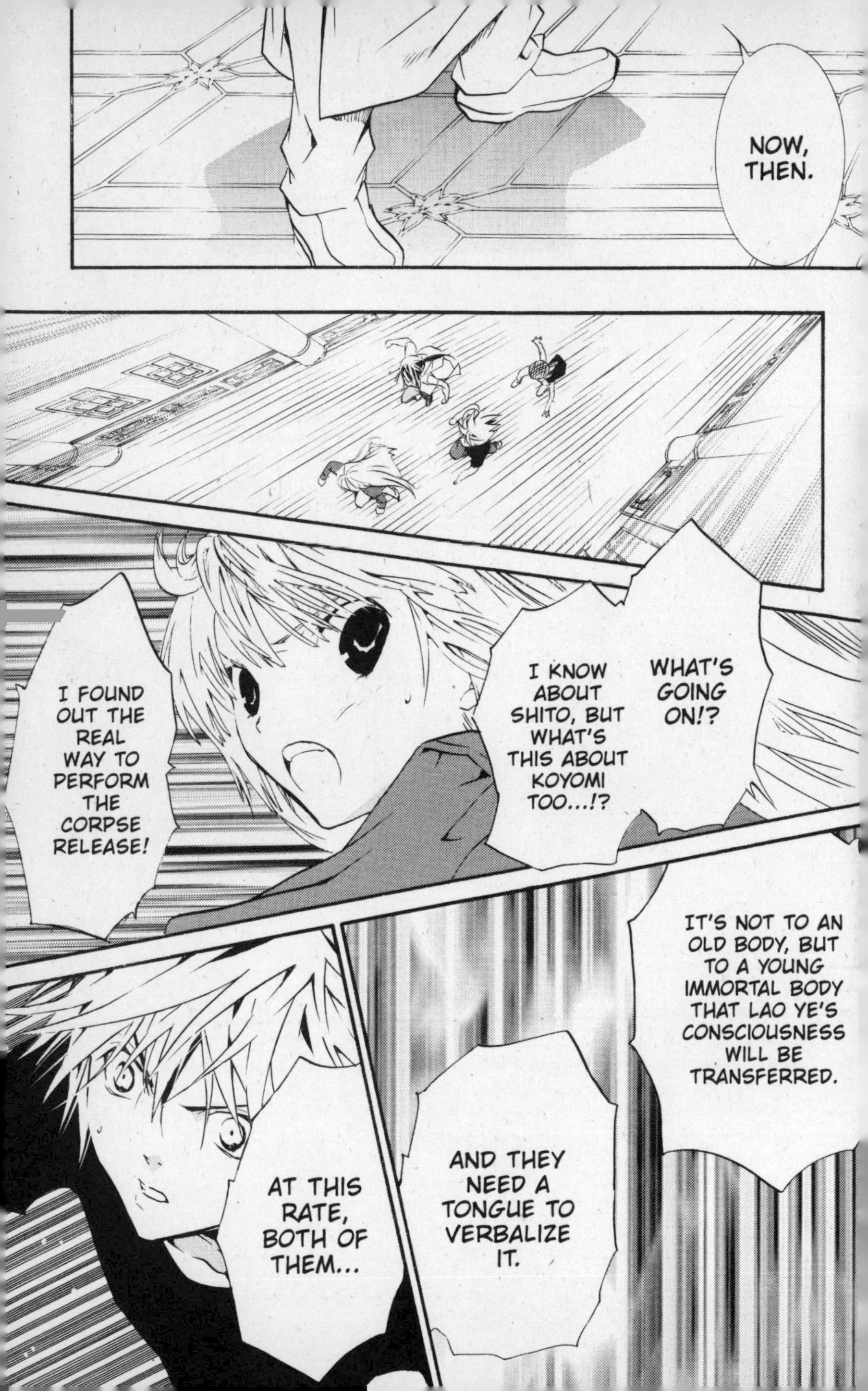
NOW, THEN.
WHAT'S GOING ON!?
I KNOW ABOUT SHITO, BUT WHAT'S THIS ABOUT KOYOMI TOO...!?
I FOUND OUT THE REAL WAY TO PERFORM THE CORPSE RELEASE!
IT'S NOT TO AN OLD BODY, BUT TO A YOUNG IMMORTAL BODY THAT LAO YE'S CONSCIOUSNESS WILL BE TRANSFERRED.
AND THEY NEED A TONGUE TO VERBALIZE IT.
AT THIS RATE, BOTH OF THEM...

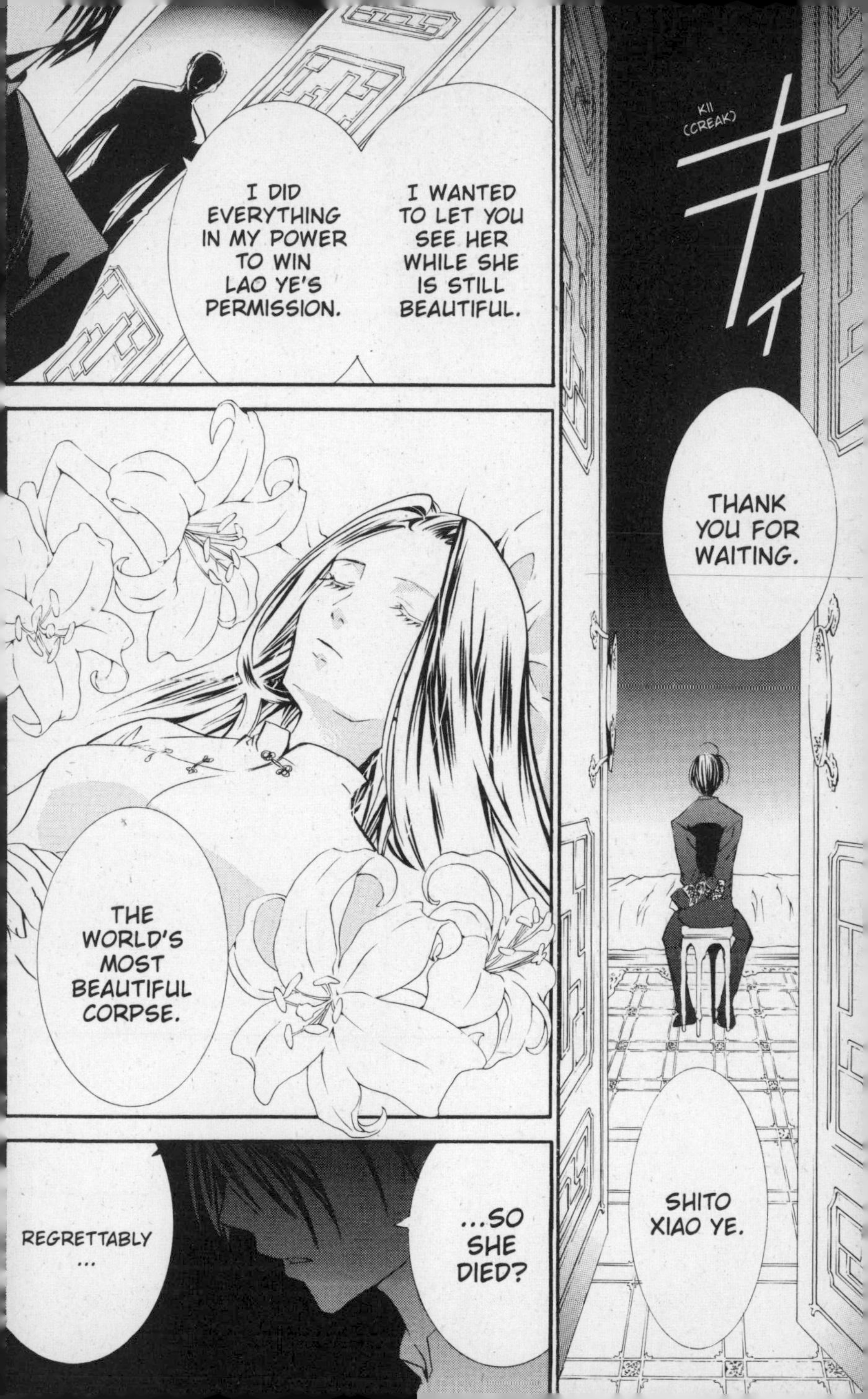
KII (CREAK)
THANK YOU FOR WAITING.
SHITO XIAO YE.
I WANTED TO LET YOU SEE HER WHILE SHE IS STILL BEAUTIFUL.
I DID EVERYTHING IN MY POWER TO WIN LAO YE'S PERMISSION.
THE WORLD'S MOST BEAUTIFUL CORPSE.
...SO SHE DIED?
REGRETTABLY ...

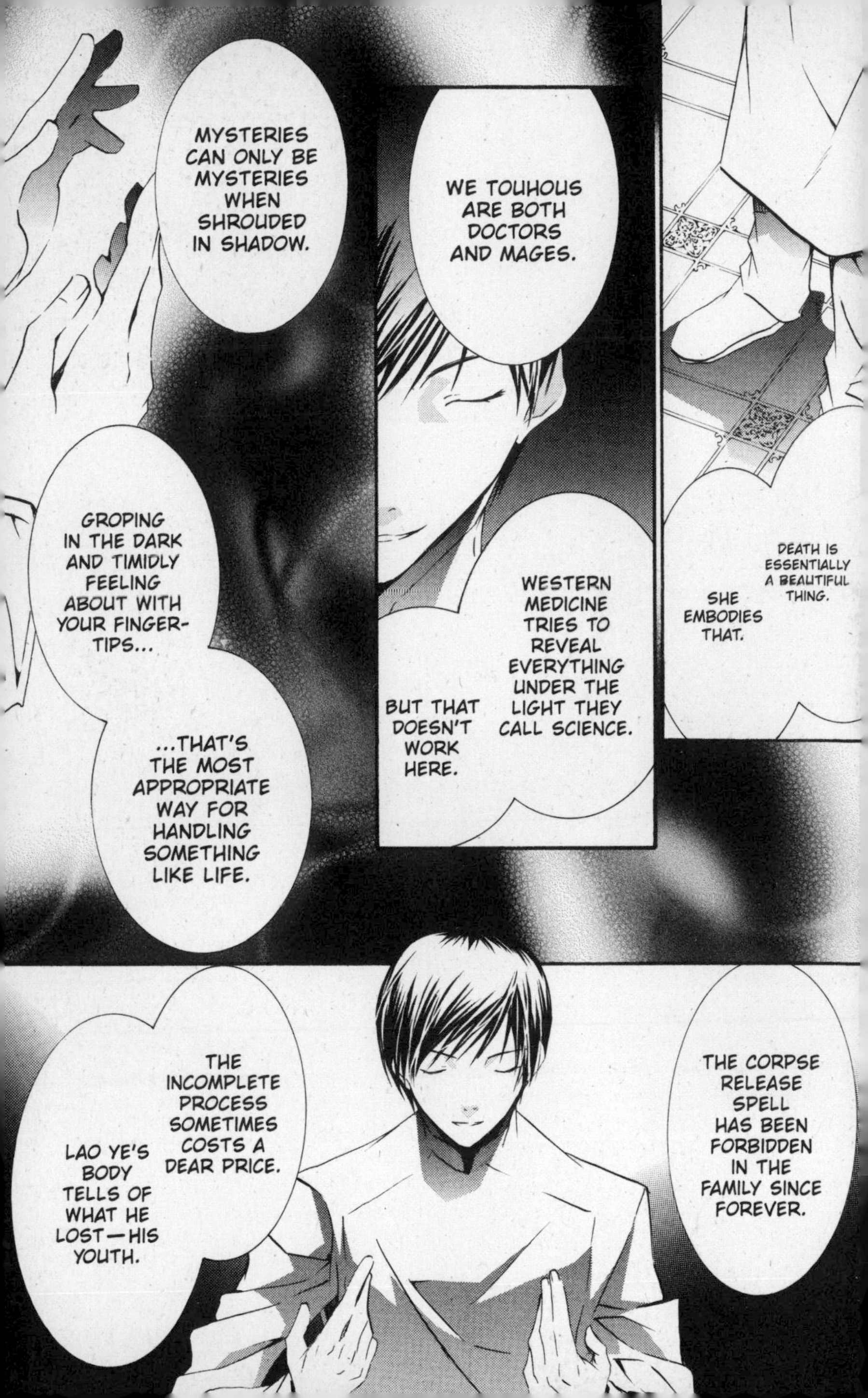
DEATH IS ESSENTIALLY A BEAUTIFUL THING.
SHE EMBODIES THAT.
WE TOUHOUS ARE BOTH DOCTORS AND MAGES.
WESTERN MEDICINE TRIES TO REVEAL EVERYTHING UNDER THE LIGHT THEY CALL SCIENCE.
BUT THAT DOESN'T WORK HERE.
MYSTERIES CAN ONLY BE MYSTERIES WHEN SHROUDED IN SHADOW.
GROPING IN THE DARK AND TIMIDLY FEELING ABOUT WITH YOUR FINGER-TIPS...
...THAT'S THE MOST APPROPRIATE WAY FOR HANDLING SOMETHING LIKE LIFE.
THE CORPSE RELEASE SPELL HAS BEEN FORBIDDEN IN THE FAMILY SINCE FOREVER.
THE INCOMPLETE PROCESS SOMETIMES COSTS A DEAR PRICE.
LAO YE'S BODY TELLS OF WHAT HE LOST—HIS YOUTH.

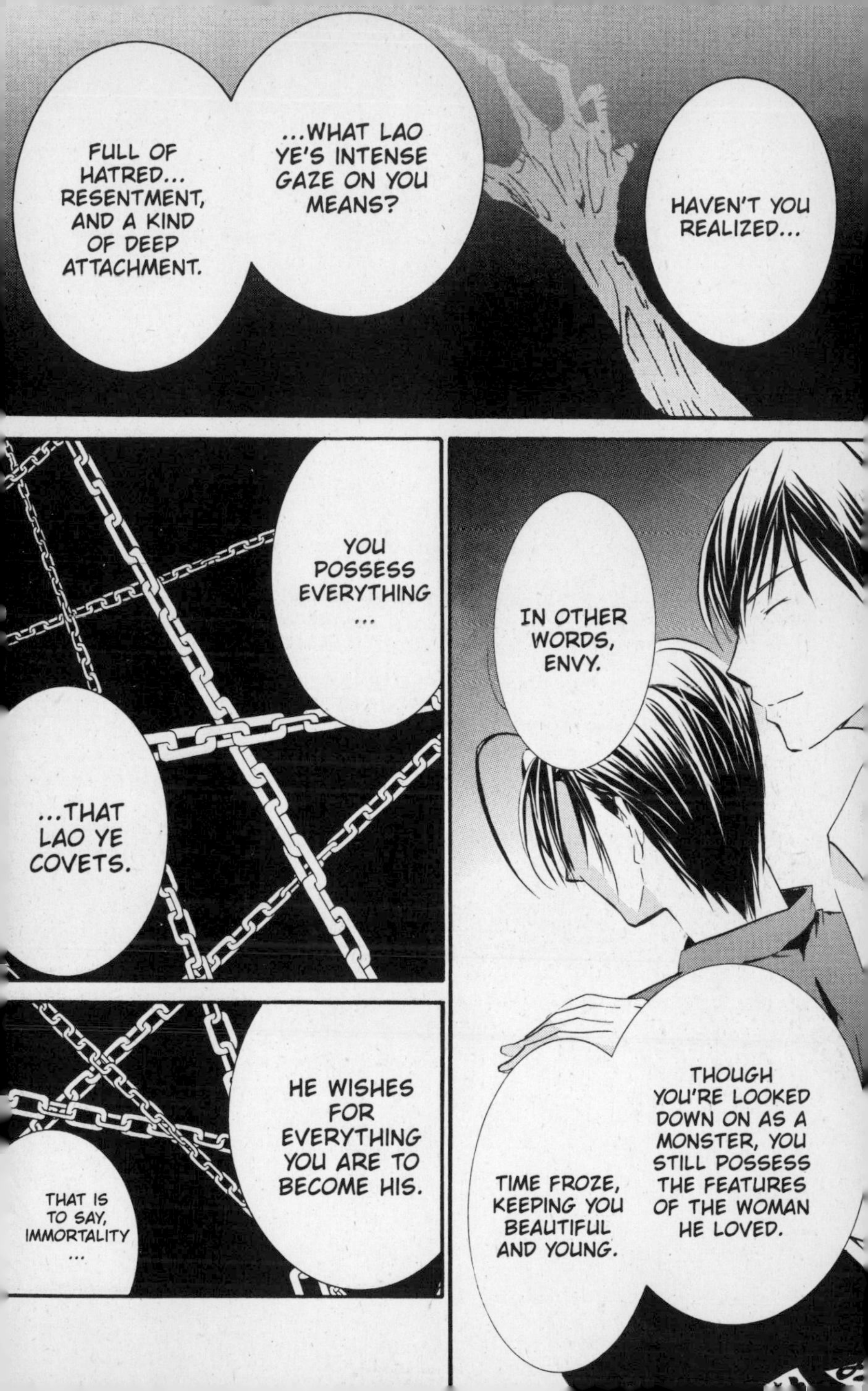
HAVEN'T YOU REALIZED...
...WHAT LAO YE'S INTENSE GAZE ON YOU MEANS?
FULL OF HATRED... RESENTMENT, AND A KIND OF DEEP ATTACHMENT.
IN OTHER WORDS, ENVY.
THOUGH YOU'RE LOOKED DOWN ON AS A MONSTER, YOU STILL POSSESS THE FEATURES OF THE WOMAN HE LOVED.
TIME FROZE, KEEPING YOU BEAUTIFUL AND YOUNG.
YOU POSSESS EVERYTHING ...
...THAT LAO YE COVETS.
HE WISHES FOR EVERYTHING YOU ARE TO BECOME HIS.
THAT IS TO SAY, IMMORTALITY ...

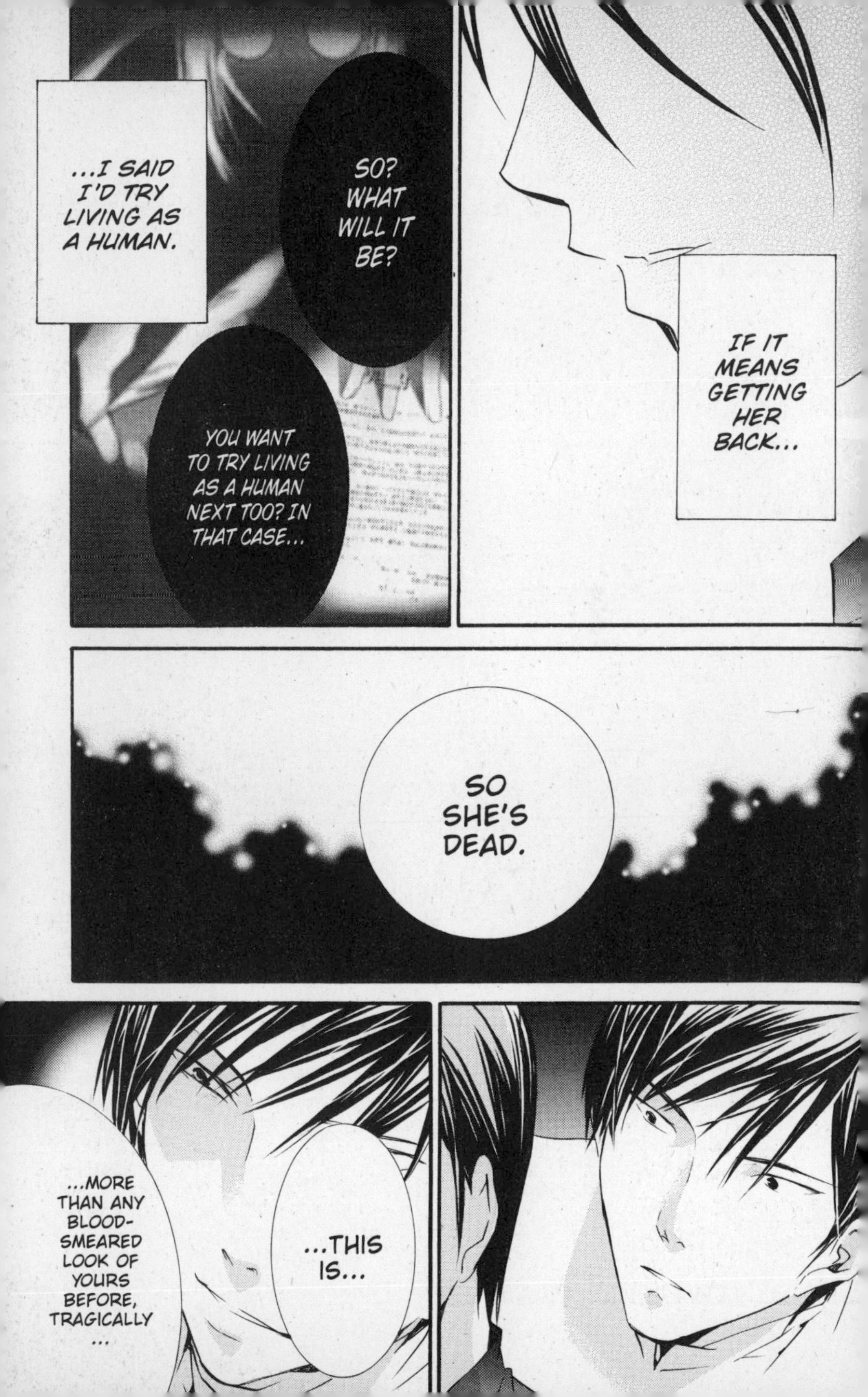

IF IT MEANS GETTING HER BACK...
SO? WHAT WILL IT BE?
...I SAID I'D TRY LIVING AS A HUMAN.
YOU WANT TO TRY LIVING AS A HUMAN NEXT TOO? IN THAT CASE...
SO SHE'S DEAD.
...THIS IS...
...MORE THAN ANY BLOOD-SMEARED LOOK OF YOURS BEFORE, TRAGICALLY ...

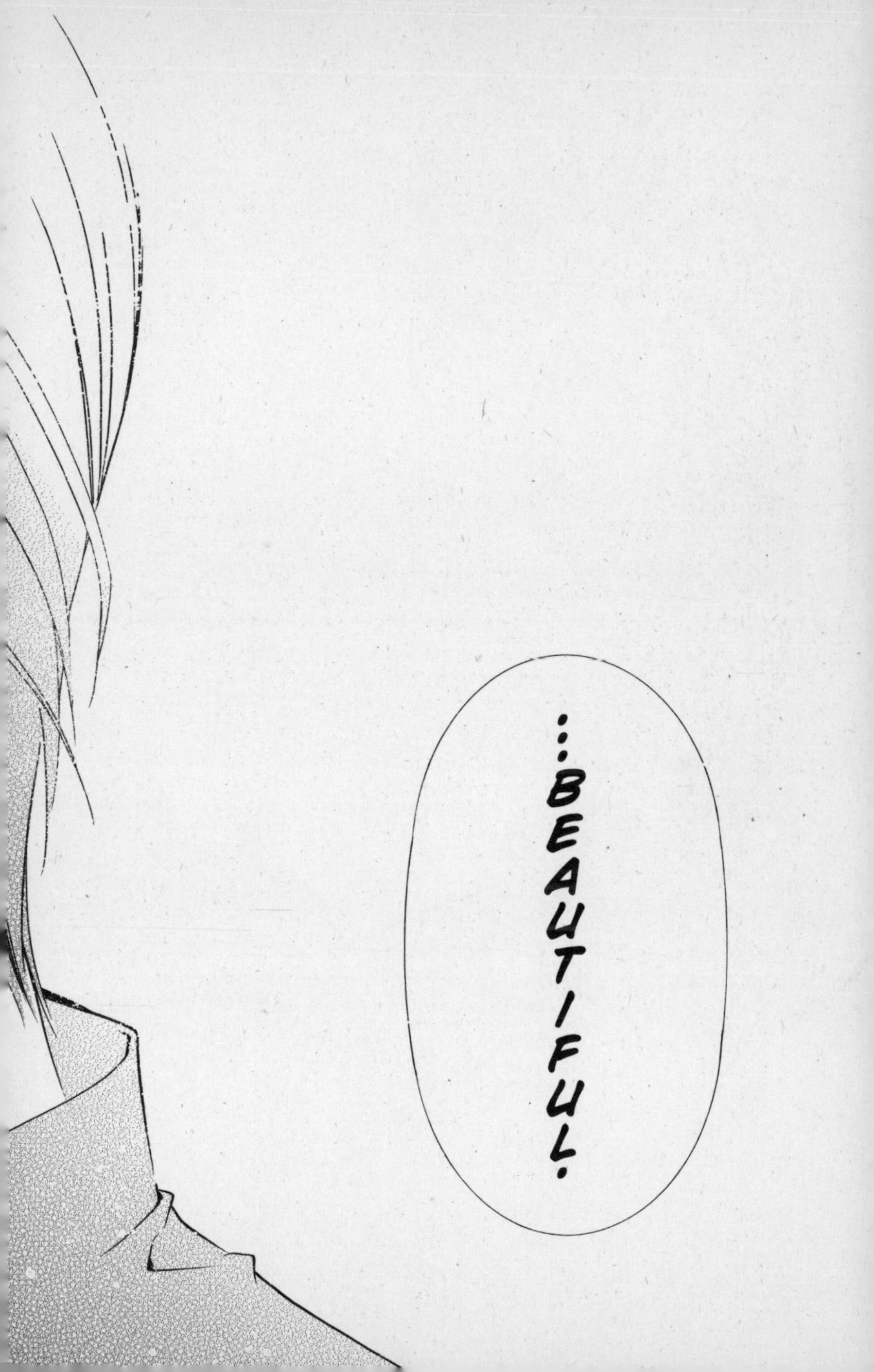
..BEAUTIFUL.

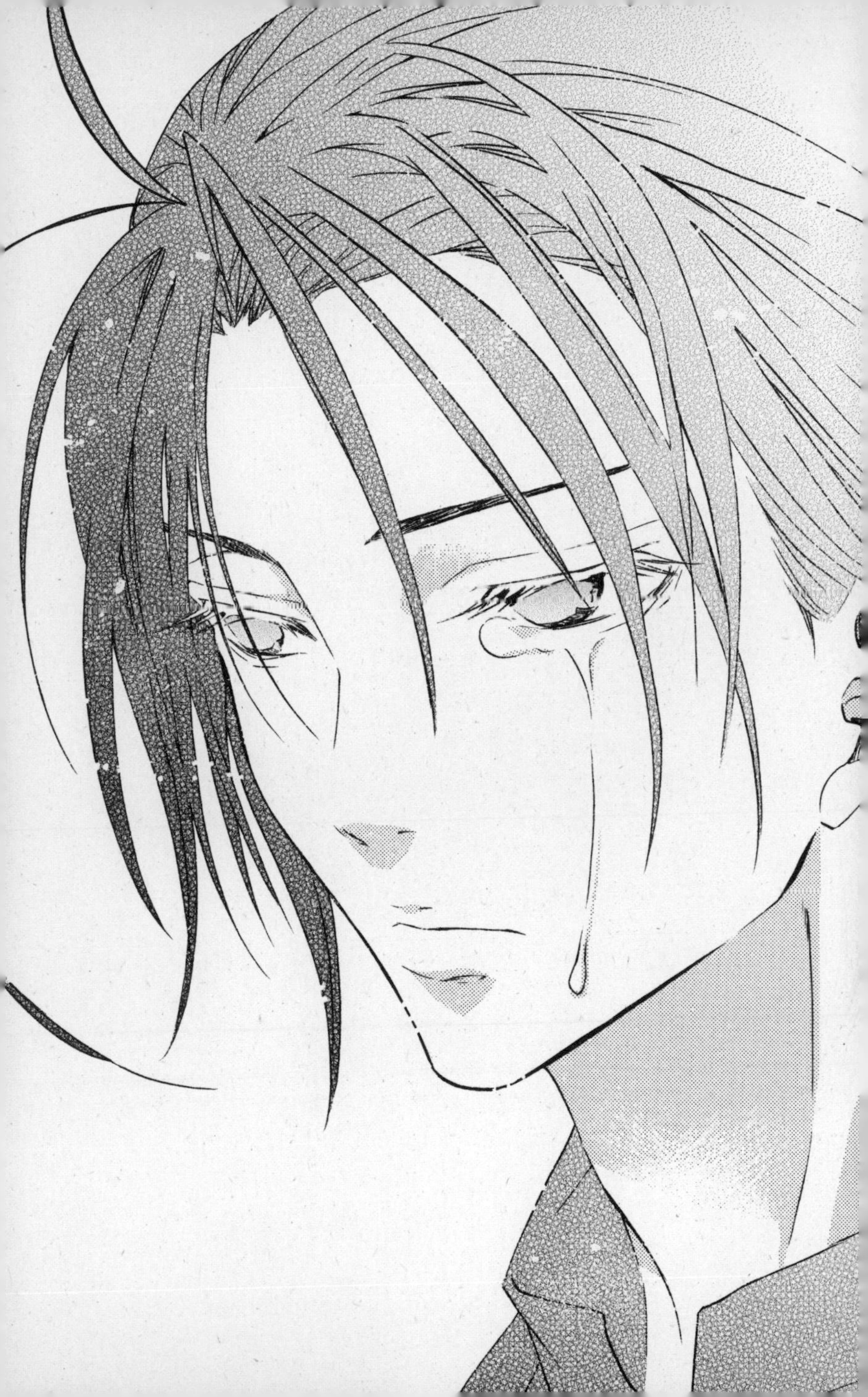

ZOMBIE-LOAN

ゾンビローン

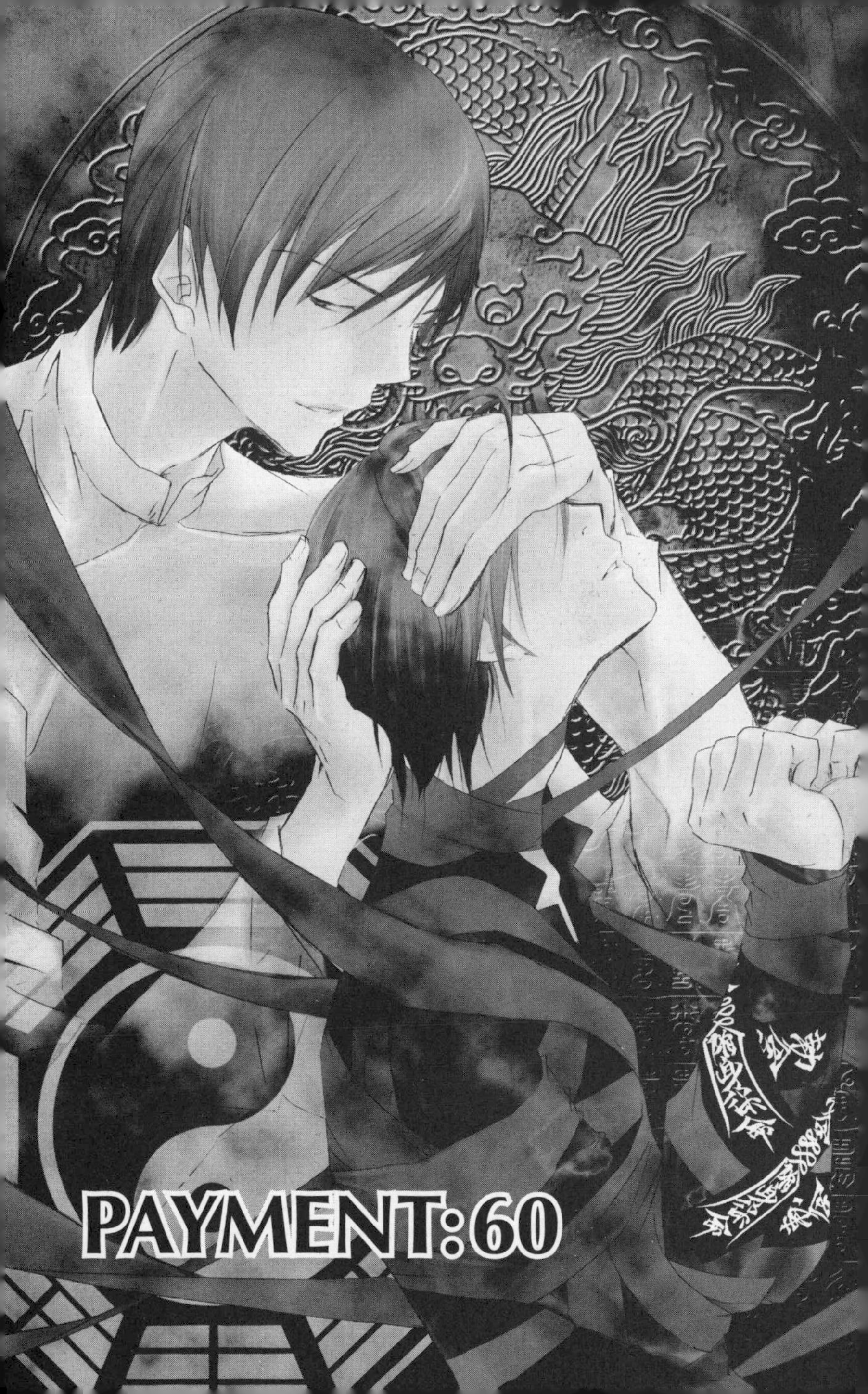
PAYMENT: 60

ZOMBIE-LOAN

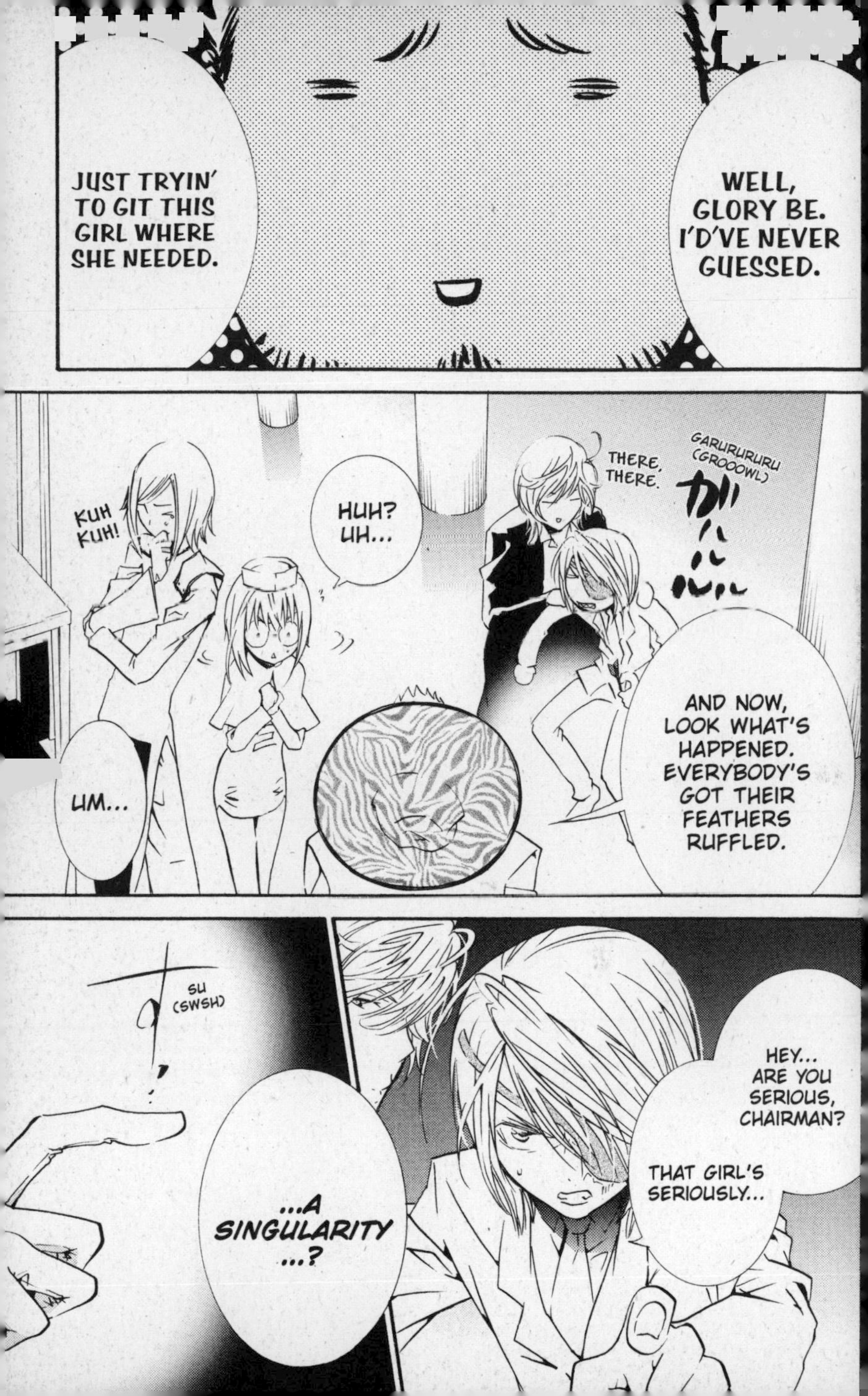
WELL, GLORY BE. I'D'VE NEVER GUESSED.
JUST TRYIN' TO GIT THIS GIRL WHERE SHE NEEDED.
GARURURURU (GROOOWL)
THERE, THERE.
AND NOW, LOOK WHAT'S HAPPENED. EVERYBODY'S GOT THEIR FEATHERS RUFFLED.
HUH? UH...
KUH KUH!
UM...
HEY... ARE YOU SERIOUS, CHAIRMAN?
THAT GIRL'S SERIOUSLY...
...A SINGULARITY ...?
SU (SWSH)

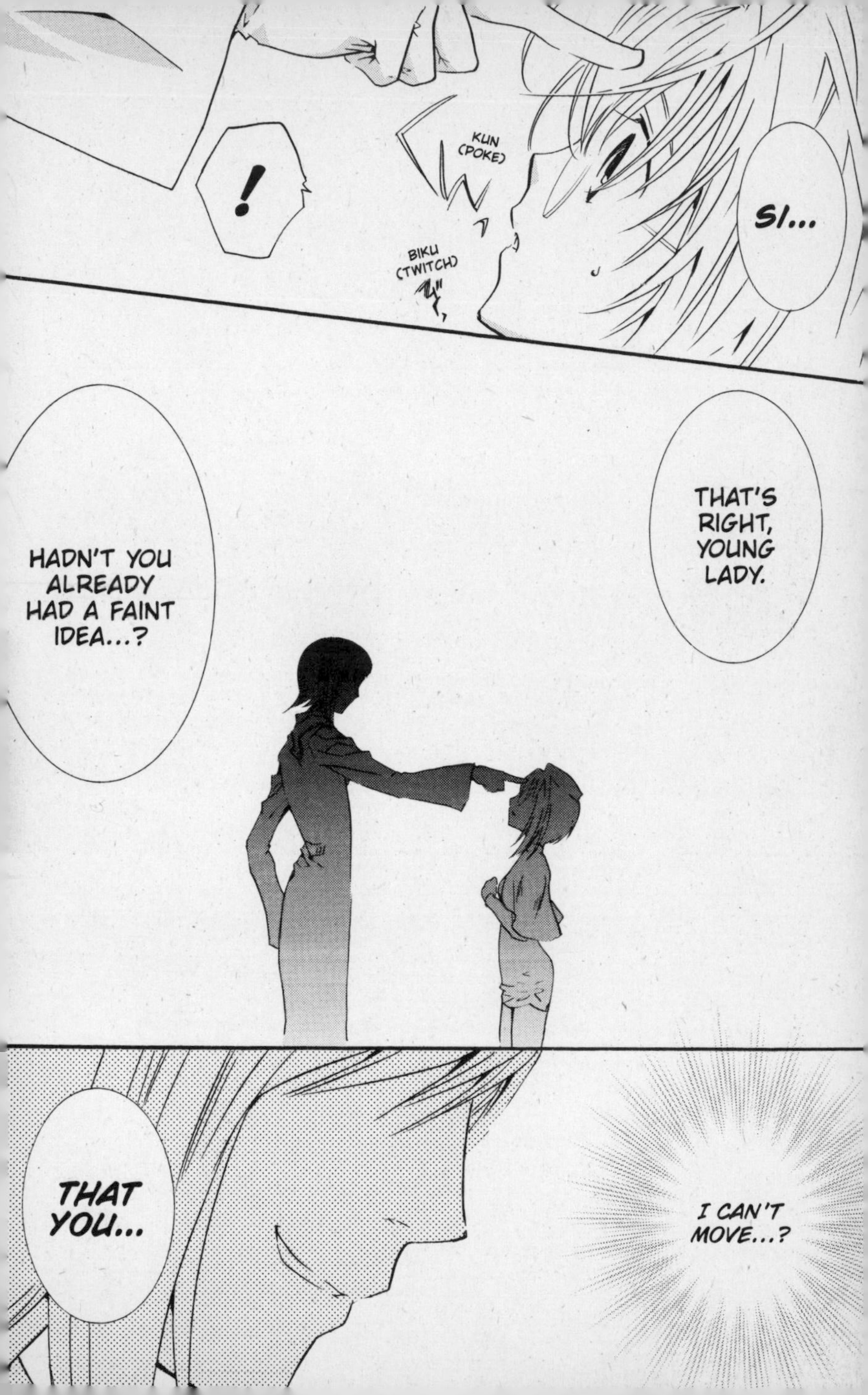
SI...
KUN (POKE)
BIKU (TWITCH)
!
THAT'S RIGHT, YOUNG LADY.
HADN'T YOU ALREADY HAD A FAINT IDEA...?
I CAN'T MOVE...?
THAT YOU...

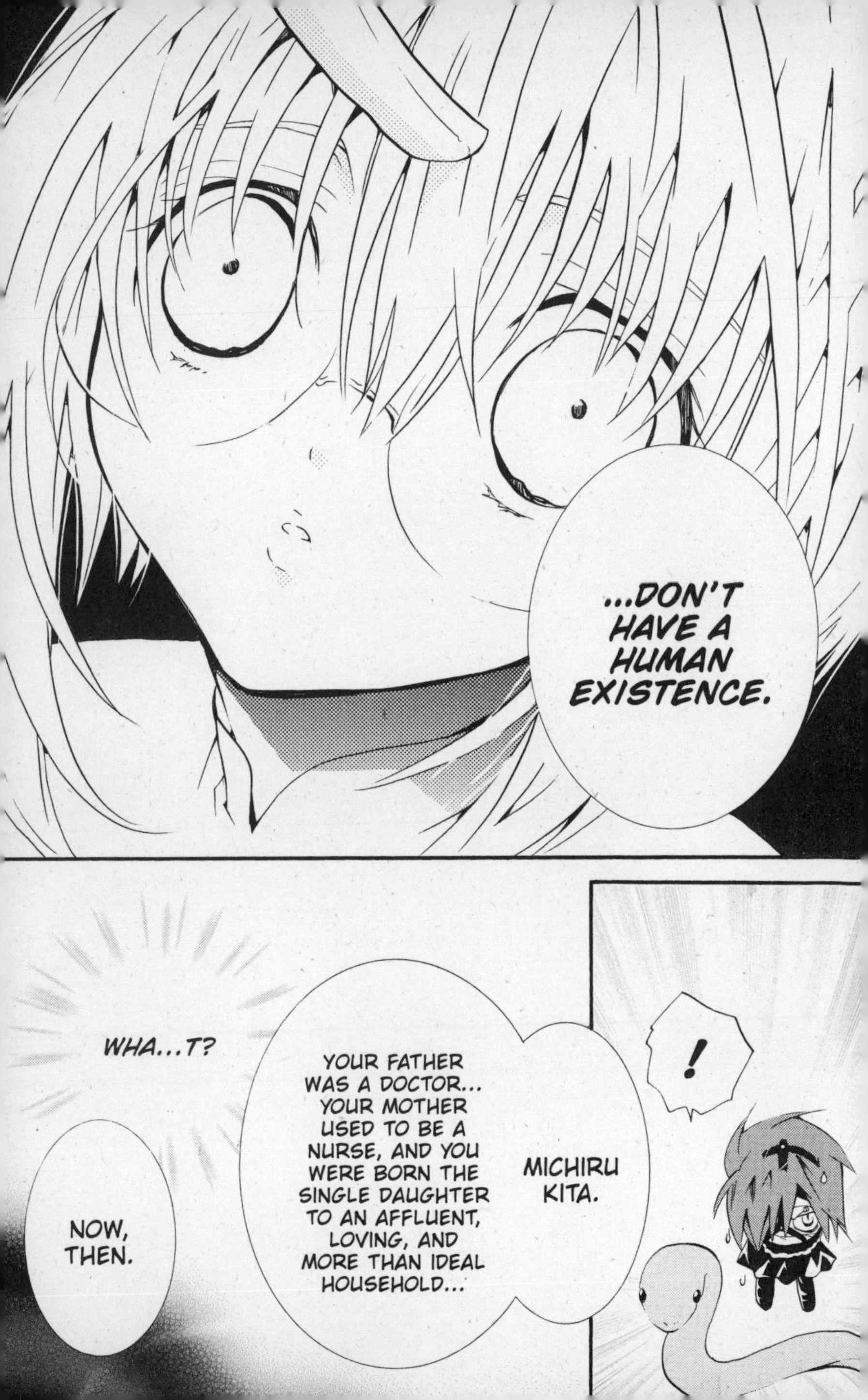
...DON'T HAVE A HUMAN EXISTENCE.
!
MICHIRU KITA.
YOUR FATHER WAS A DOCTOR... YOUR MOTHER USED TO BE A NURSE, AND YOU WERE BORN THE SINGLE DAUGHTER TO AN AFFLUENT, LOVING, AND MORE THAN IDEAL HOUSEHOLD...
WHA...T?
NOW, THEN.

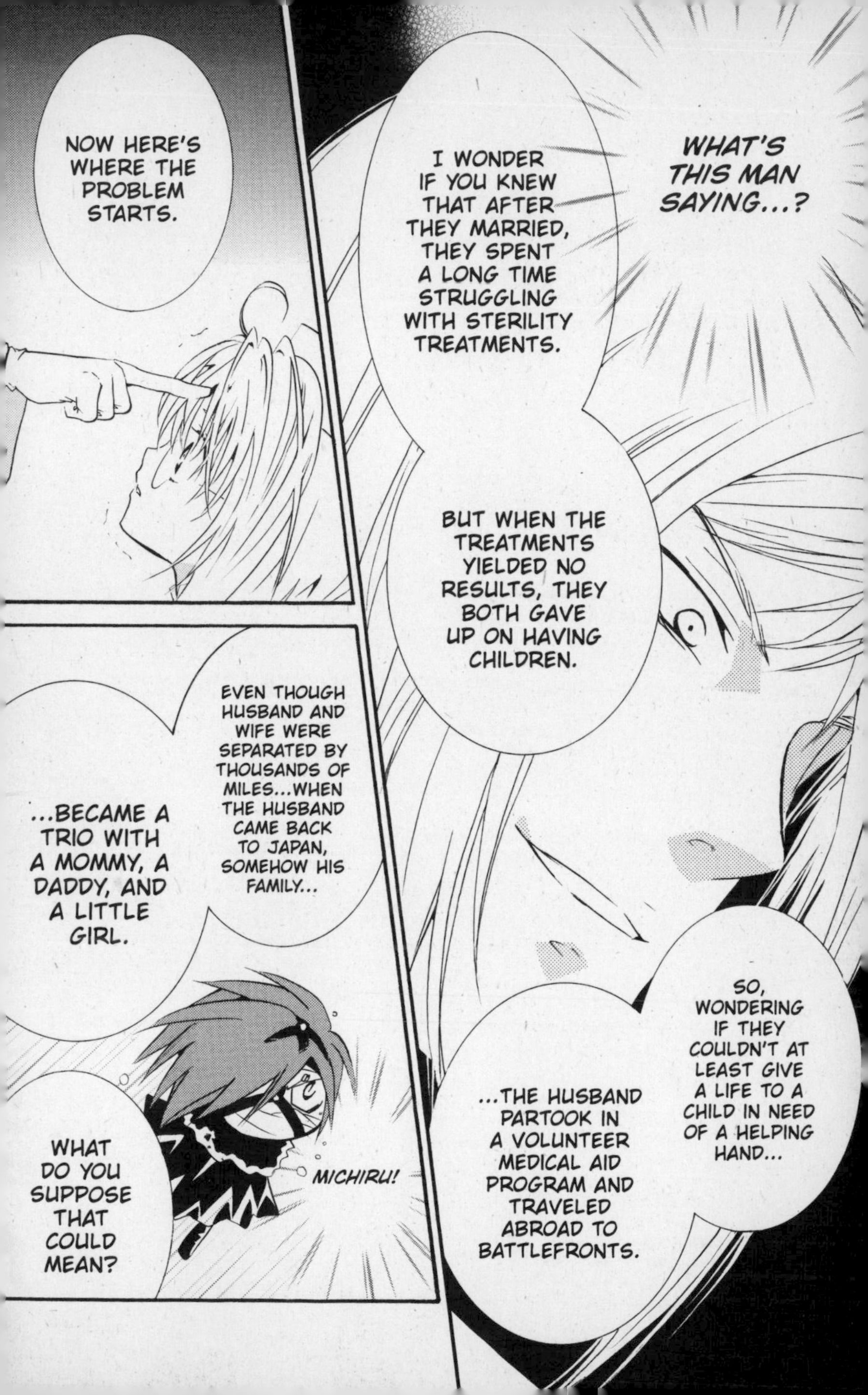
WHAT'S THIS MAN SAYING...?
I WONDER IF YOU KNEW THAT AFTER THEY MARRIED, THEY SPENT A LONG TIME STRUGGLING WITH STERILITY TREATMENTS.
BUT WHEN THE TREATMENTS YIELDED NO RESULTS, THEY BOTH GAVE UP ON HAVING CHILDREN.
SO, WONDERING IF THEY COULDN'T AT LEAST GIVE A LIFE TO A CHILD IN NEED OF A HELPING HAND...
...THE HUSBAND PARTOOK IN A VOLUNTEER MEDICAL AID PROGRAM AND TRAVELED ABROAD TO BATTLEFRONTS.
NOW HERE'S WHERE THE PROBLEM STARTS.
EVEN THOUGH HUSBAND AND WIFE WERE SEPARATED BY THOUSANDS OF MILES...WHEN THE HUSBAND CAME BACK TO JAPAN, SOMEHOW HIS FAMILY...
...BECAME A TRIO WITH A MOMMY, A DADDY, AND A LITTLE GIRL.
MICHIRU!
WHAT DO YOU SUPPOSE THAT COULD MEAN?

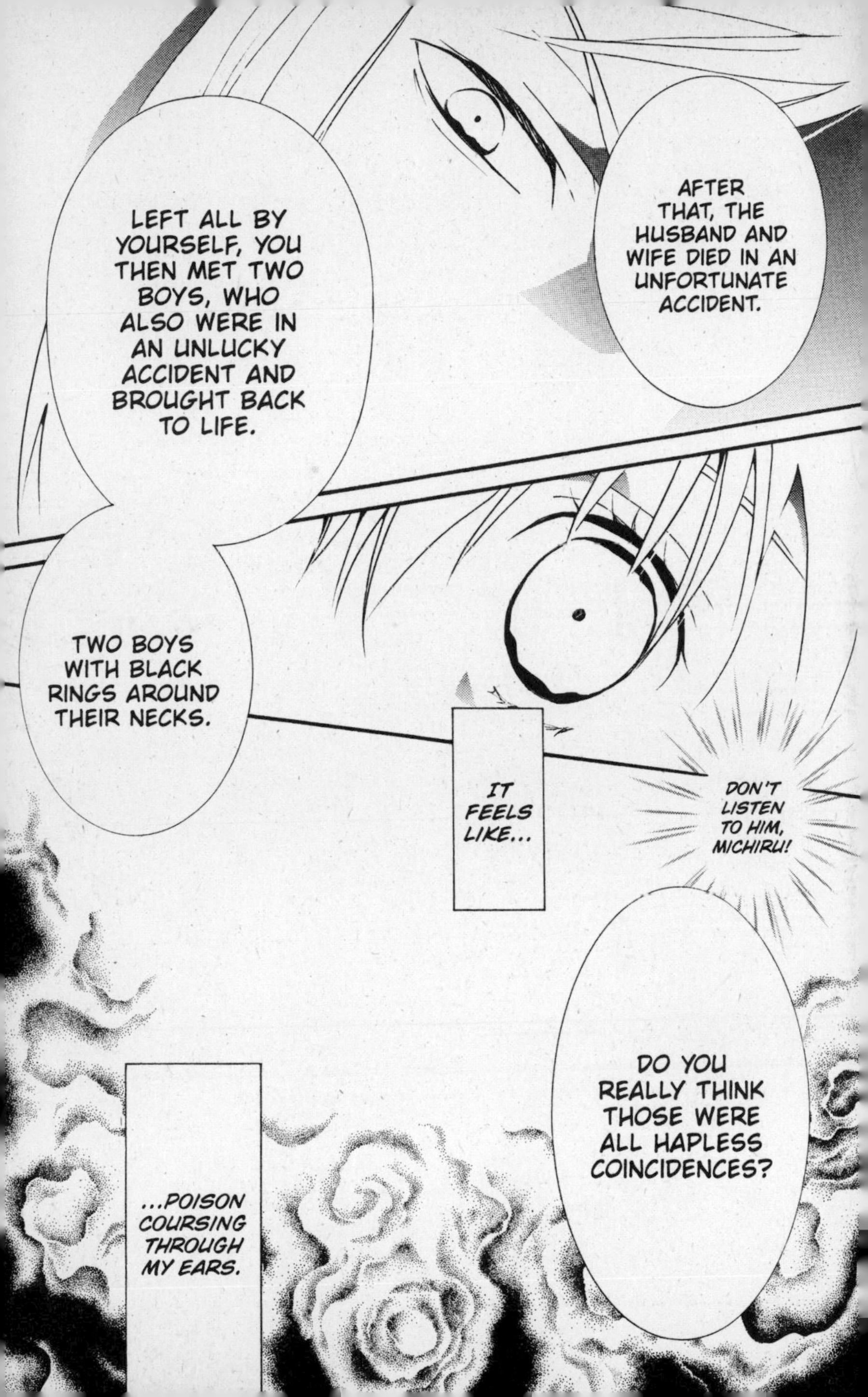
AFTER THAT, THE HUSBAND AND WIFE DIED IN AN UNFORTUNATE ACCIDENT.
LEFT ALL BY YOURSELF, YOU THEN MET TWO BOYS, WHO ALSO WERE IN AN UNLUCKY ACCIDENT AND BROUGHT BACK TO LIFE.
TWO BOYS WITH BLACK RINGS AROUND THEIR NECKS.
DON'T LISTEN TO HIM, MICHIRU!
IT FEELS LIKE...
DO YOU REALLY THINK THOSE WERE ALL HAPLESS COINCIDENCES?
...POISON COURSING THROUGH MY EARS.

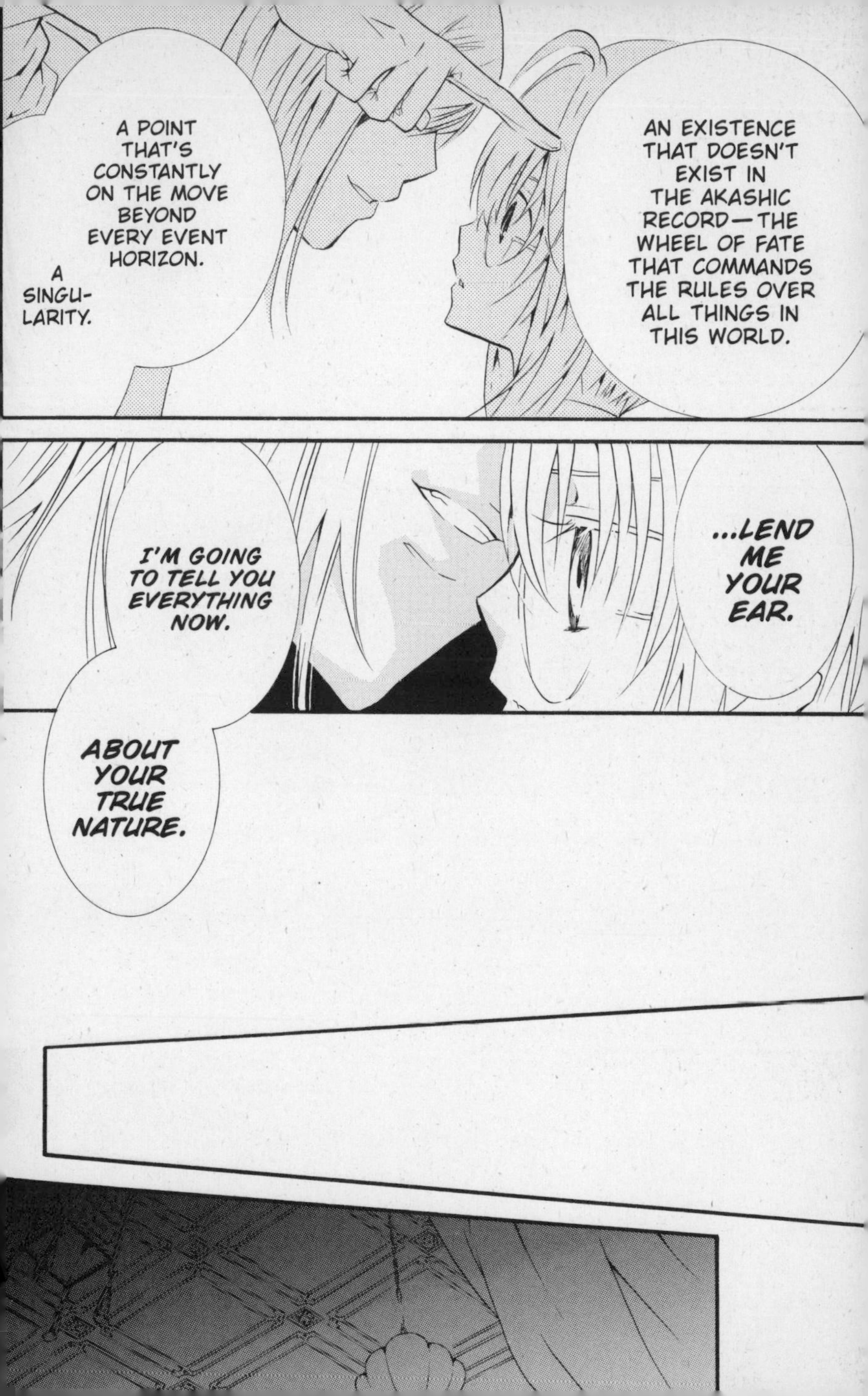
AN EXISTENCE THAT DOESN'T EXIST IN THE AKASHIC RECORD—THE WHEEL OF FATE THAT COMMANDS THE RULES OVER ALL THINGS IN THIS WORLD.
A POINT THAT'S CONSTANTLY ON THE MOVE BEYOND EVERY EVENT HORIZON.
A SINGU-LARITY.
...LEND ME YOUR EAR.
I'M GOING TO TELL YOU EVERYTHING NOW.
ABOUT YOUR TRUE NATURE.

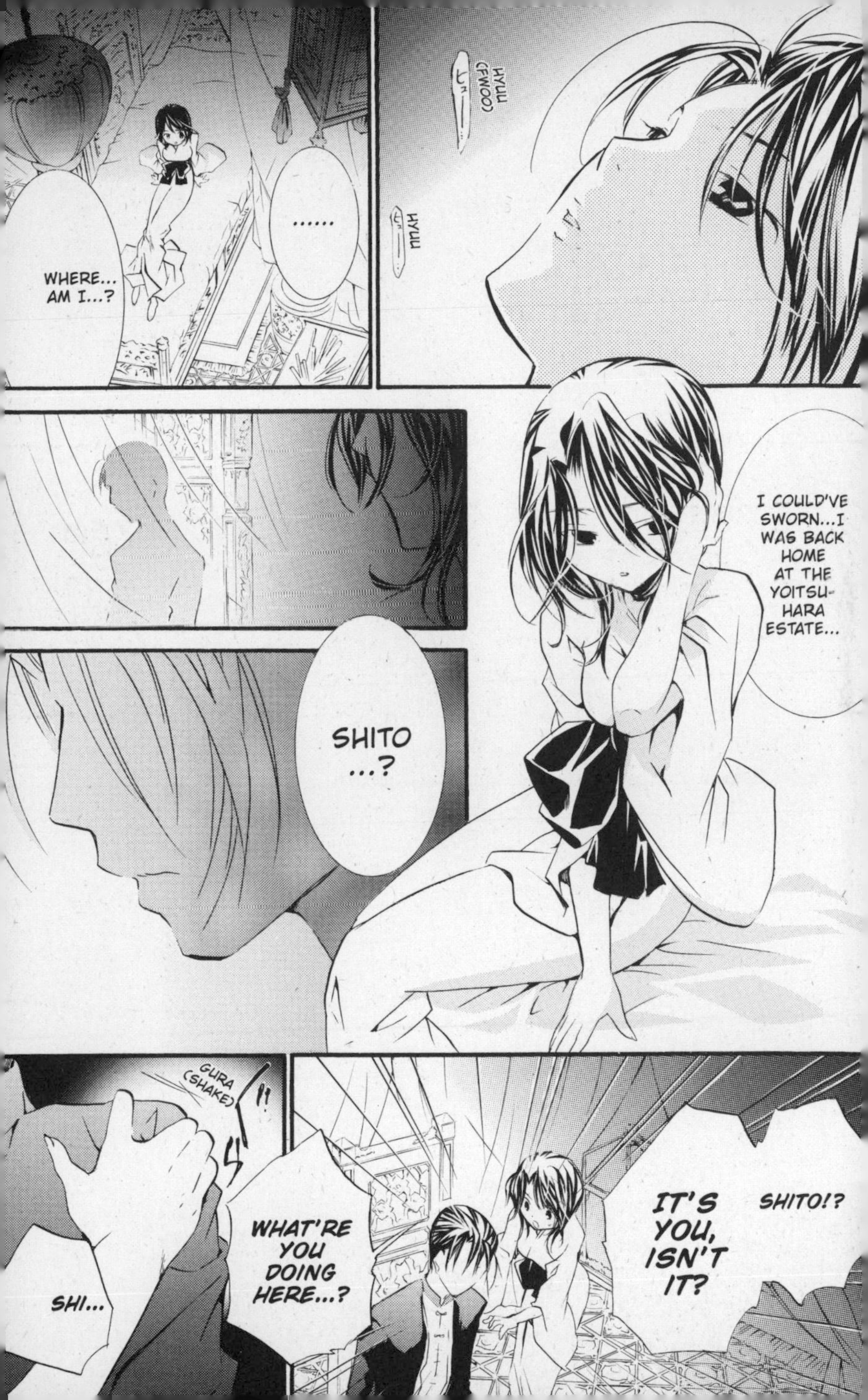
HYUU (FWOO)
HYUU
......
WHERE... AM I...?
I COULD'VE SWORN...I WAS BACK HOME AT THE YOITSU-HARA ESTATE...
SHITO ...?
SHITO!?
IT'S YOU, ISN'T IT?
WHAT'RE YOU DOING HERE...?
GURA (SHAKE)
SHI...

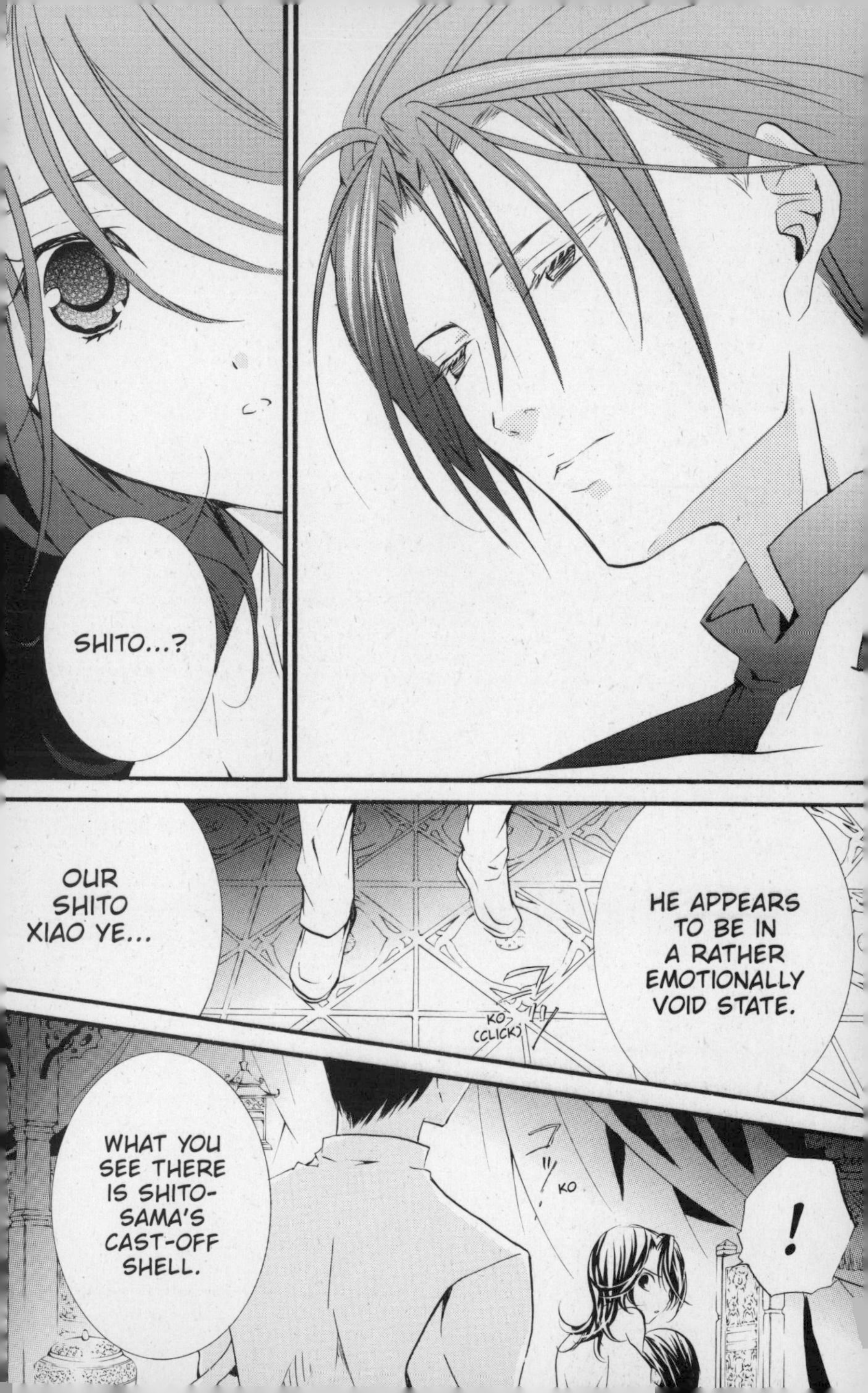
SHITO...?
HE APPEARS TO BE IN A RATHER EMOTIONALLY VOID STATE.
KO (CLICK)
OUR SHITO XIAO YE...
!
KO
WHAT YOU SEE THERE IS SHITO-SAMA'S CAST-OFF SHELL.

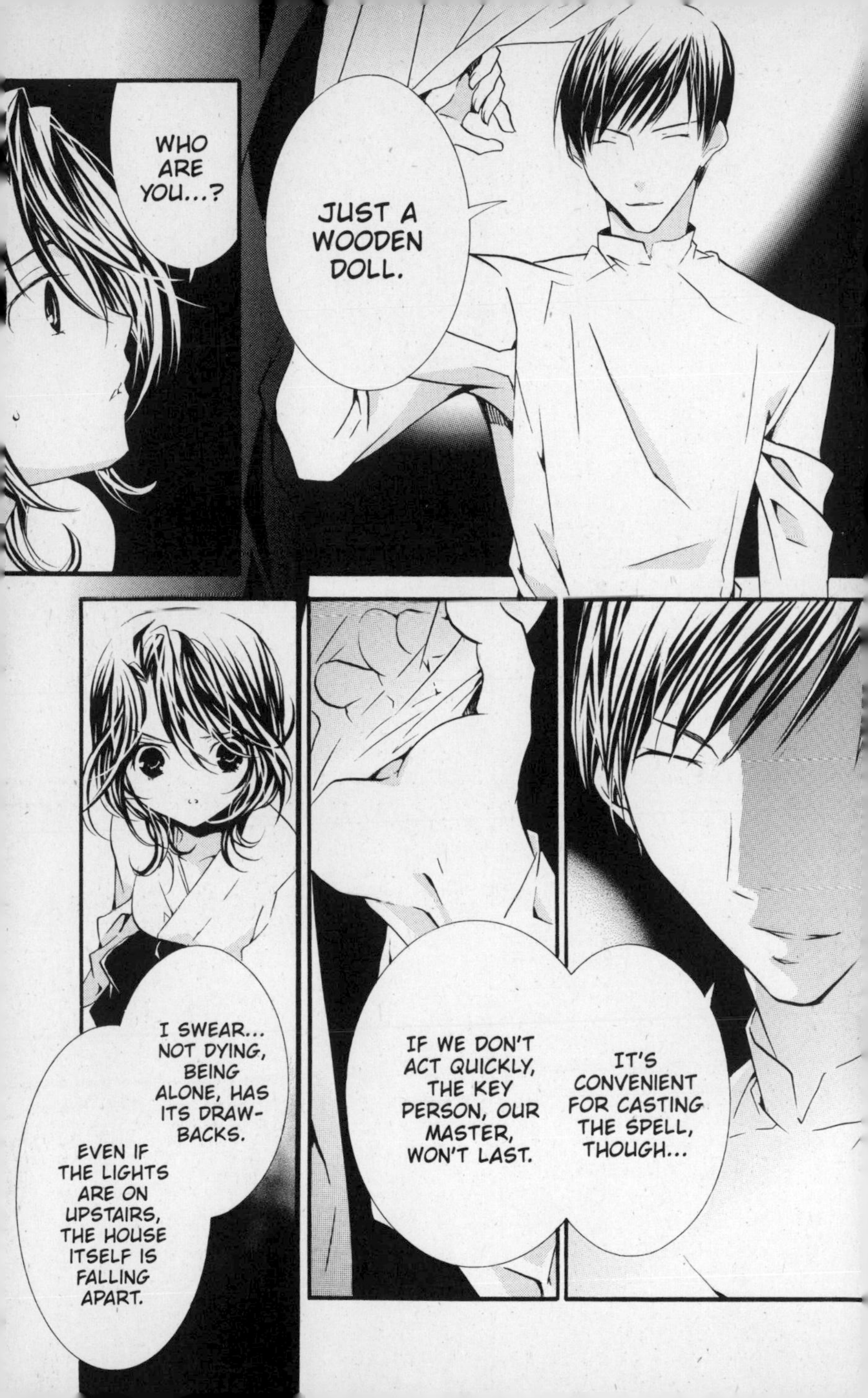
JUST A WOODEN DOLL.
WHO ARE YOU...?
IT'S CONVENIENT FOR CASTING THE SPELL, THOUGH...
IF WE DON'T ACT QUICKLY, THE KEY PERSON, OUR MASTER, WON'T LAST.
I SWEAR... NOT DYING, BEING ALONE, HAS ITS DRAW-BACKS.
EVEN IF THE LIGHTS ARE ON UPSTAIRS, THE HOUSE ITSELF IS FALLING APART.

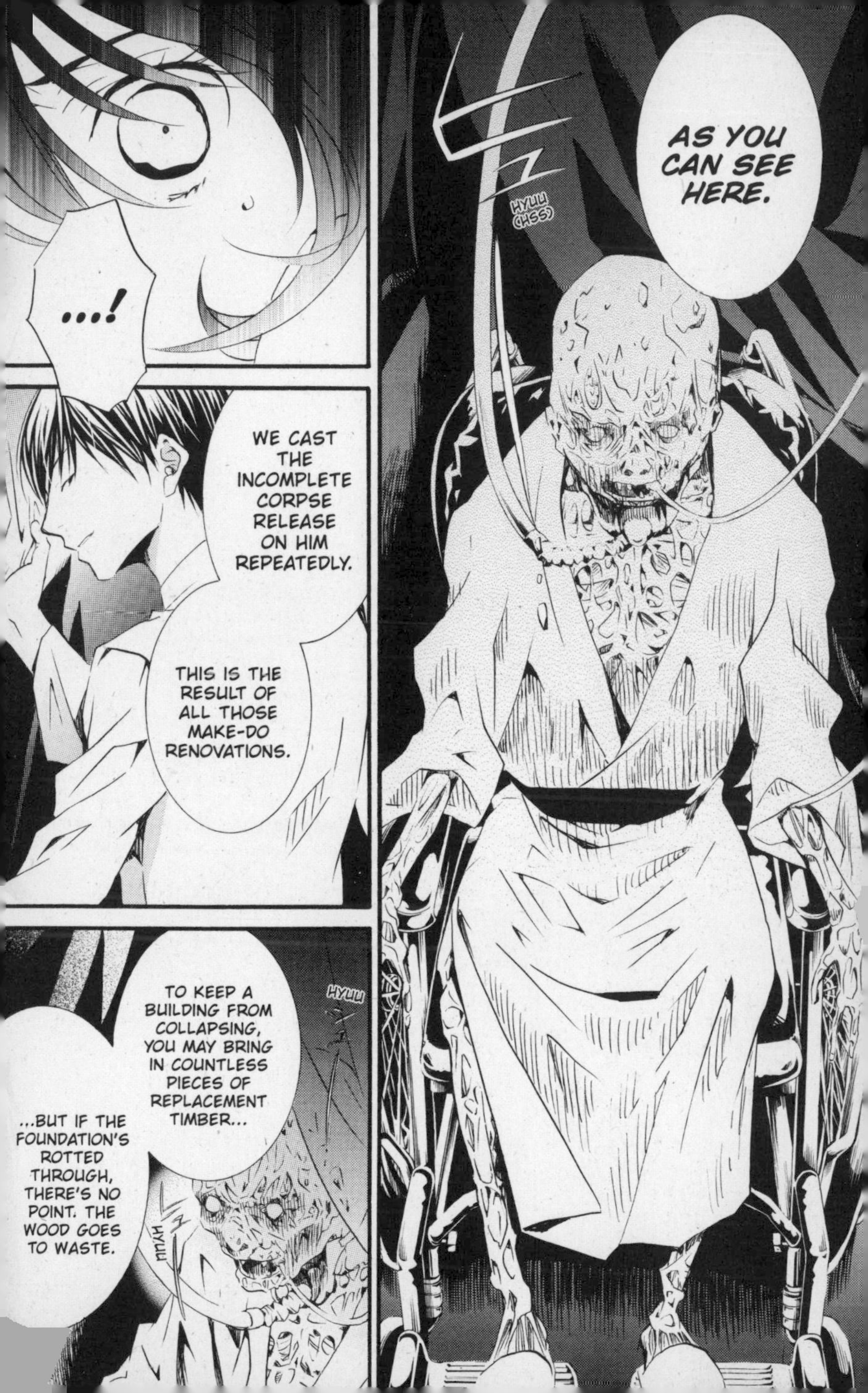
AS YOU CAN SEE HERE.
HYUU (HSS)
...!
WE CAST THE INCOMPLETE CORPSE RELEASE ON HIM REPEATEDLY.
THIS IS THE RESULT OF ALL THOSE MAKE-DO RENOVATIONS.
HYUU
TO KEEP A BUILDING FROM COLLAPSING, YOU MAY BRING IN COUNTLESS PIECES OF REPLACEMENT TIMBER...
...BUT IF THE FOUNDATION'S ROTTED THROUGH, THERE'S NO POINT. THE WOOD GOES TO WASTE.
HYUU

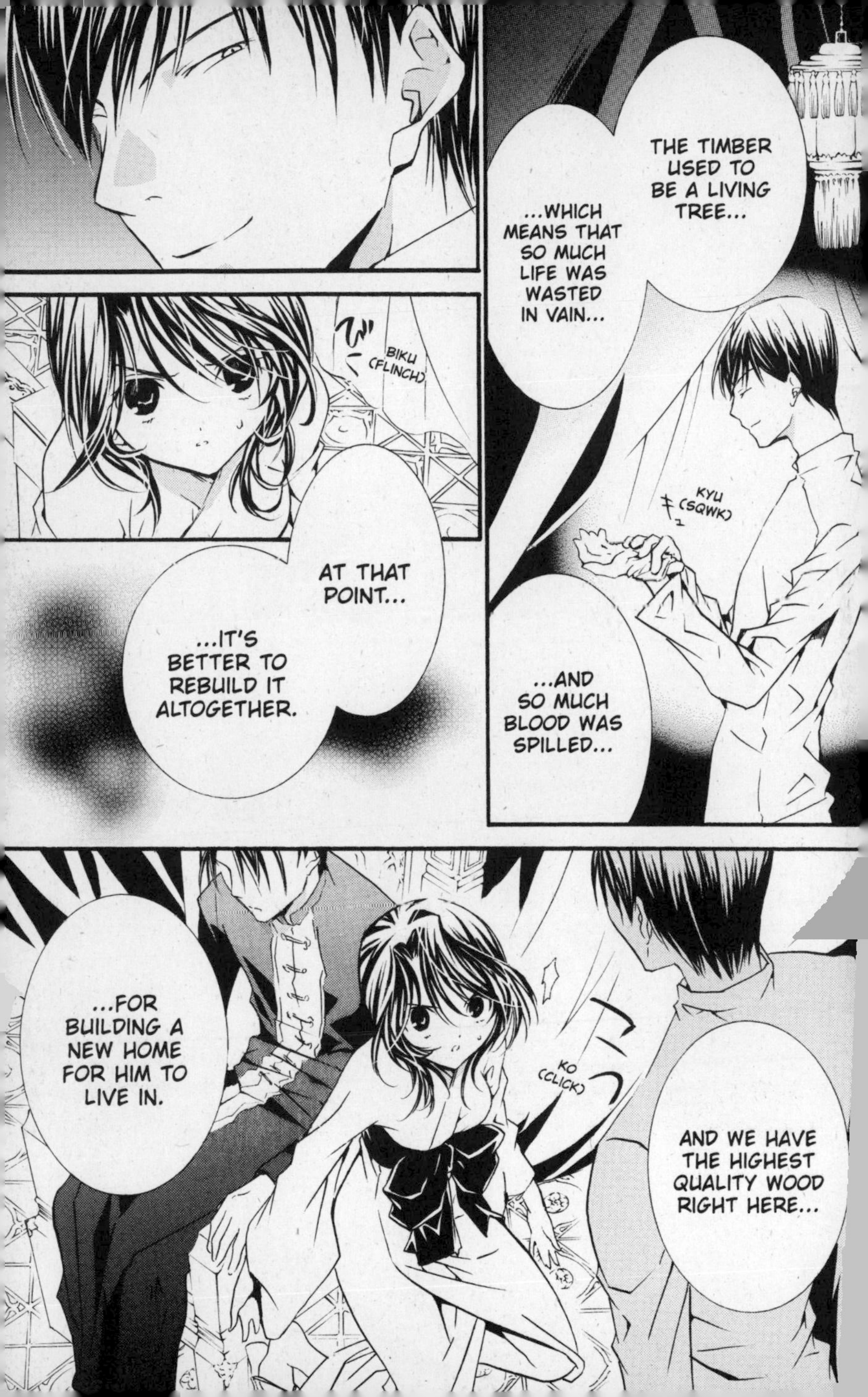
THE TIMBER USED TO BE A LIVING TREE...
...WHICH MEANS THAT SO MUCH LIFE WAS WASTED IN VAIN...
KYU (SQWK)
...AND SO MUCH BLOOD WAS SPILLED...
BIKU (FLINCH)
AT THAT POINT...
...IT'S BETTER TO REBUILD IT ALTOGETHER.
AND WE HAVE THE HIGHEST QUALITY WOOD RIGHT HERE...
KO (CLICK)
...FOR BUILDING A NEW HOME FOR HIM TO LIVE IN.

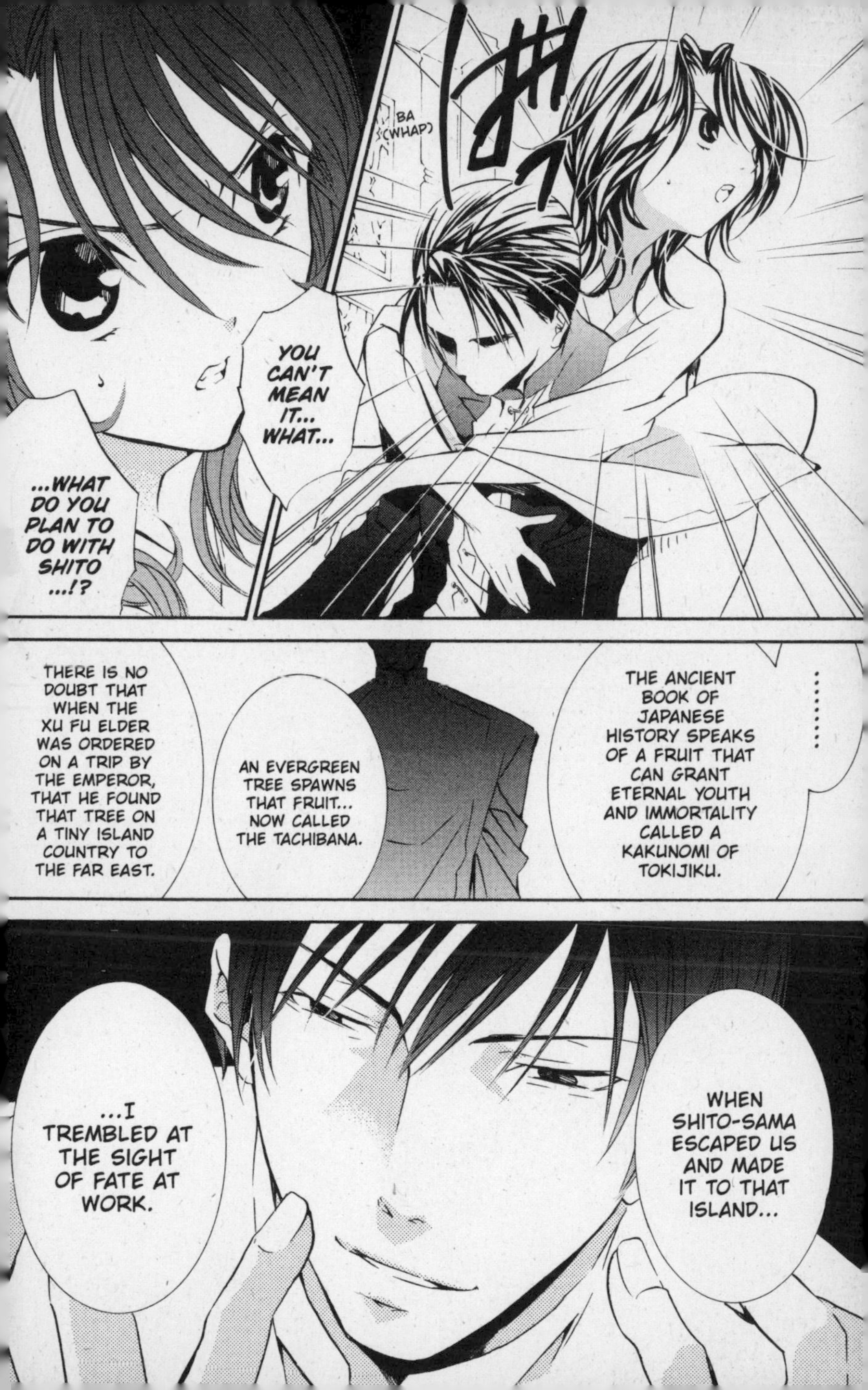
BA (WHAP)
YOU CAN'T MEAN IT... WHAT...
...WHAT DO YOU PLAN TO DO WITH SHITO ...!?
......
THE ANCIENT BOOK OF JAPANESE HISTORY SPEAKS OF A FRUIT THAT CAN GRANT ETERNAL YOUTH AND IMMORTALITY CALLED A KAKUNOMI OF TOKIJIKU.
AN EVERGREEN TREE SPAWNS THAT FRUIT... NOW CALLED THE TACHIBANA.
THERE IS NO DOUBT THAT WHEN THE XU FU ELDER WAS ORDERED ON A TRIP BY THE EMPEROR, THAT HE FOUND THAT TREE ON A TINY ISLAND COUNTRY TO THE FAR EAST.
WHEN SHITO-SAMA ESCAPED US AND MADE IT TO THAT ISLAND...
...I TREMBLED AT THE SIGHT OF FATE AT WORK.

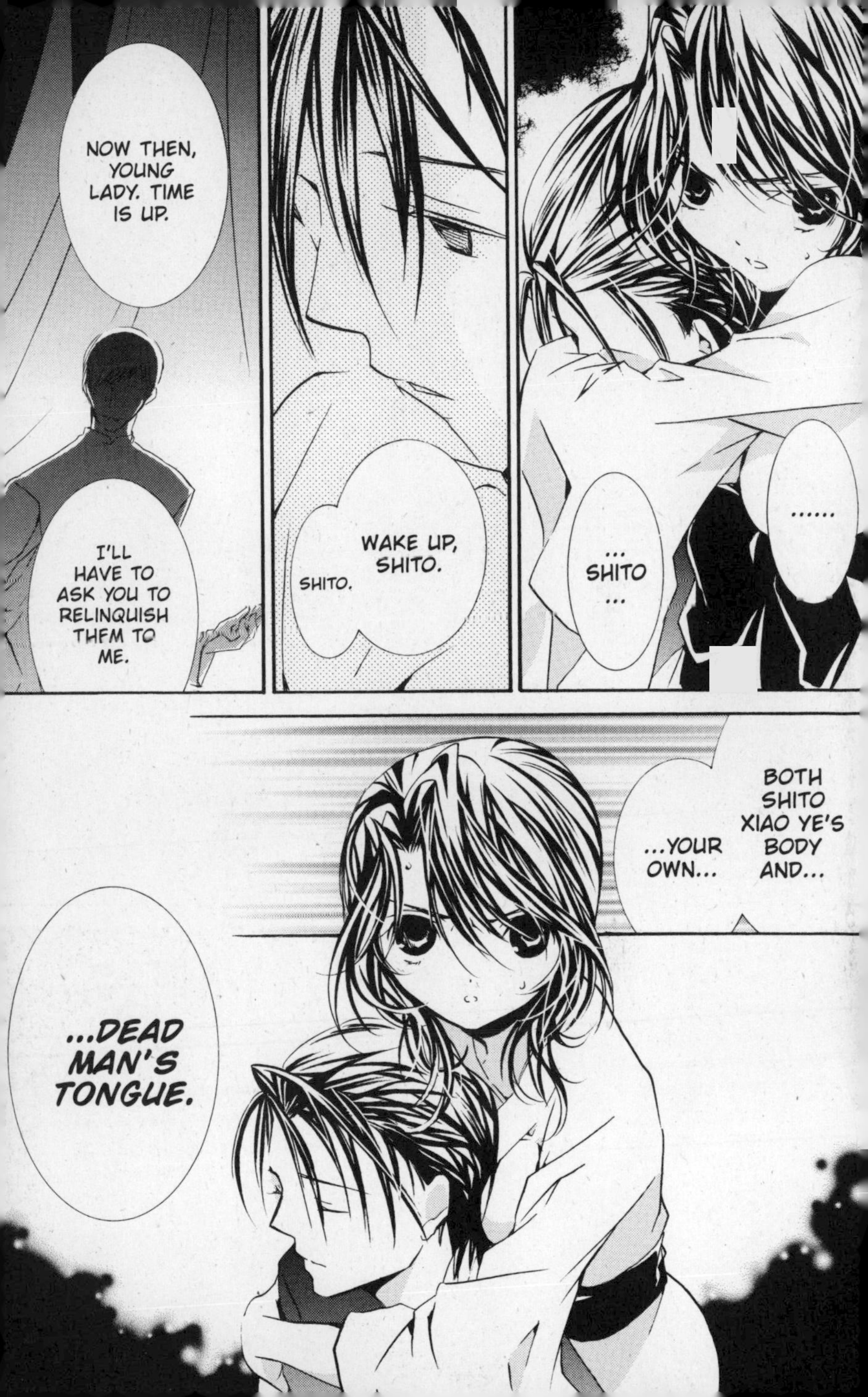
......
... SHITO ...
WAKE UP, SHITO.
SHITO.
NOW THEN, YOUNG LADY. TIME IS UP.
I'LL HAVE TO ASK YOU TO RELINQUISH THFM TO ME.
BOTH SHITO XIAO YE'S BODY AND...
...YOUR OWN...
...DEAD MAN'S TONGUE.

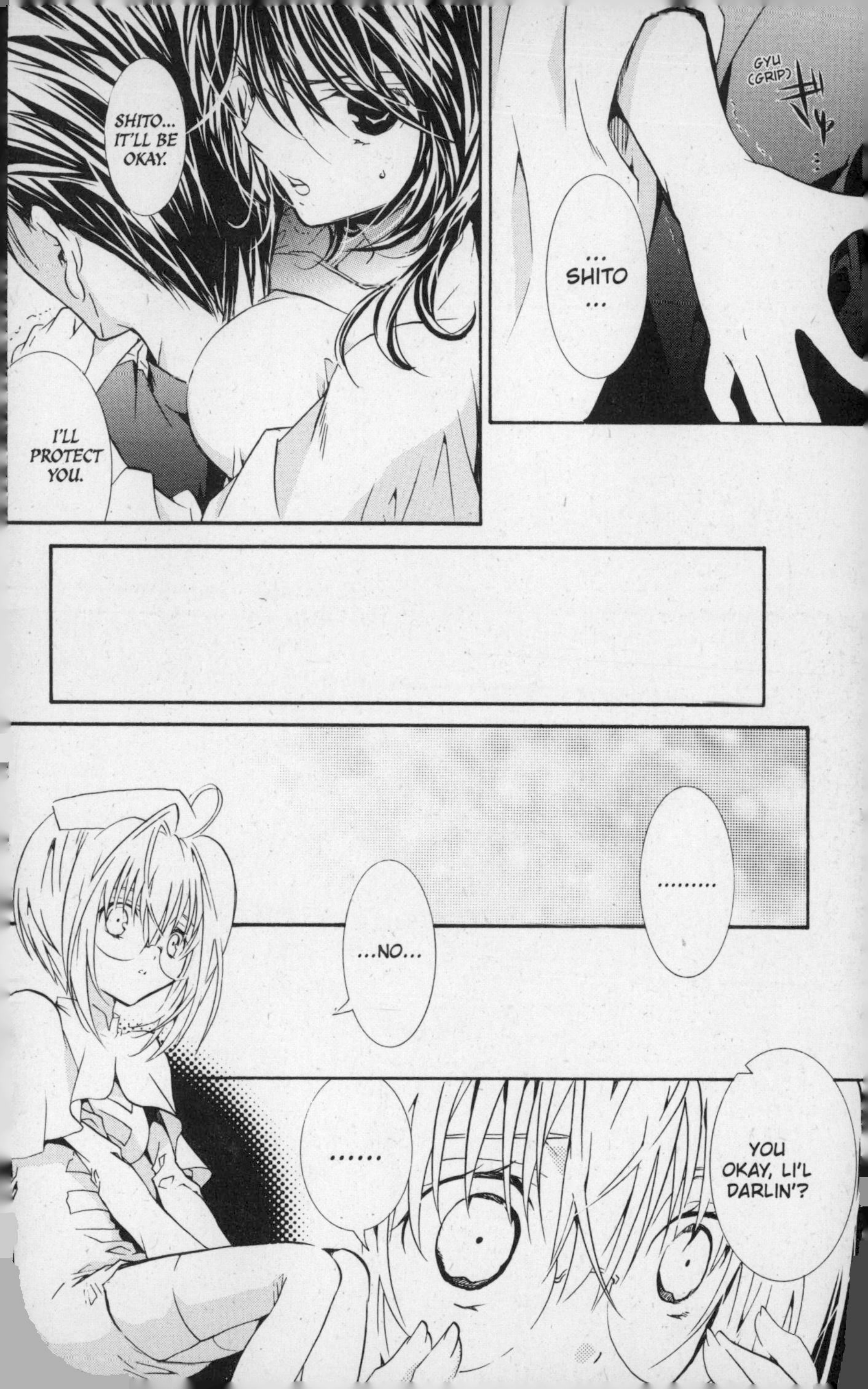
GYU (GRIP)
... SHITO ...
SHITO... IT'LL BE OKAY.
I'LL PROTECT YOU.
....
...NO...
YOU OKAY, LI'L DARLIN'?
......

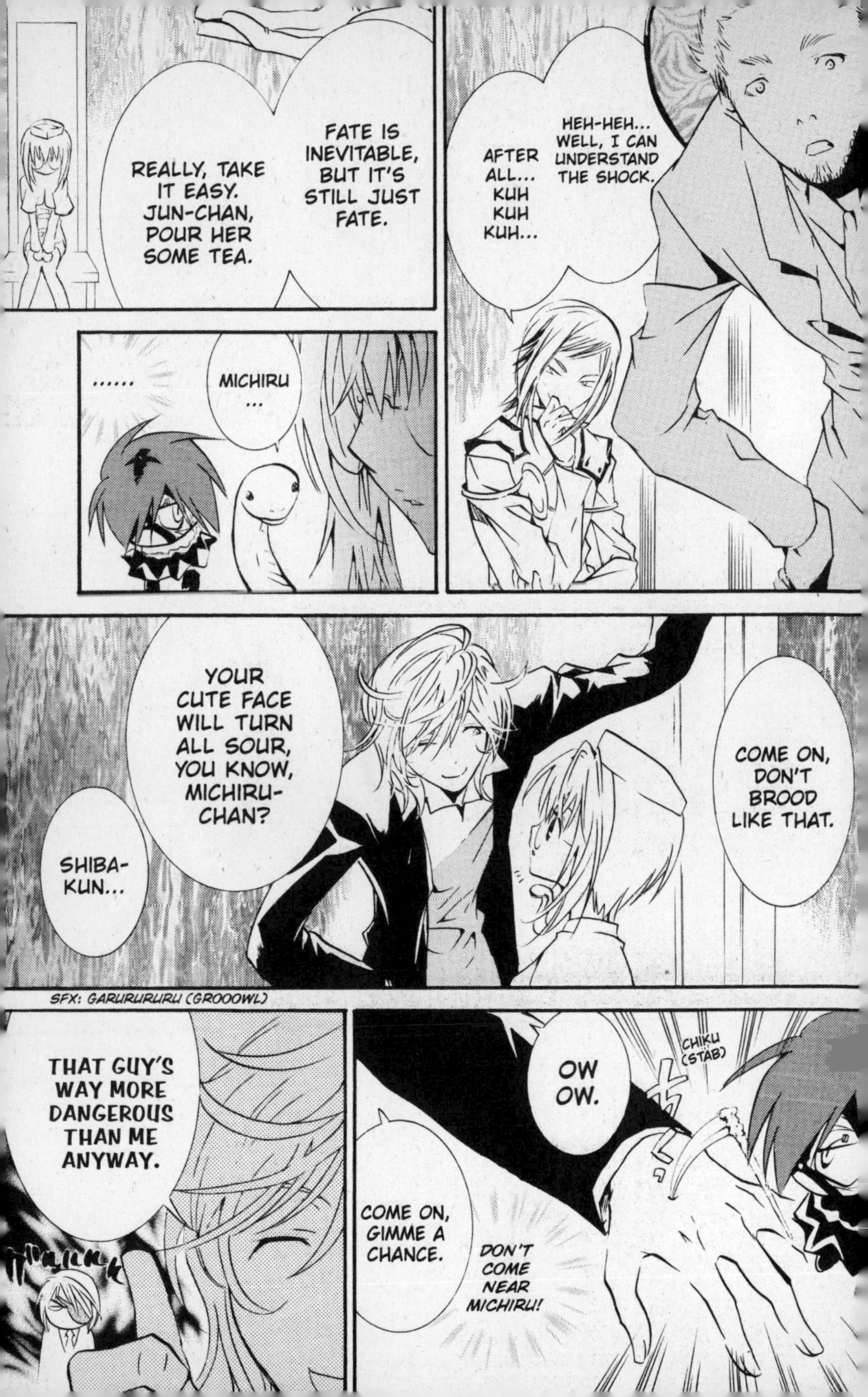
HEH-HEH... WELL, I CAN UNDERSTAND THE SHOCK.
AFTER ALL... KUH KUH KUH...
FATE IS INEVITABLE, BUT IT'S STILL JUST FATE.
REALLY, TAKE IT EASY. JUN-CHAN, POUR HER SOME TEA.
MICHIRU ...
......
COME ON, DON'T BROOD LIKE THAT.
YOUR CUTE FACE WILL TURN ALL SOUR, YOU KNOW, MICHIRU-CHAN?
SHIBA-KUN...
SFX: GARURURURU (GROOOWL)
CHIKU (STAB)
OW OW.
COME ON, GIMME A CHANCE.
DON'T COME NEAR MICHIRU!
THAT GUY'S WAY MORE DANGEROUS THAN ME ANYWAY.

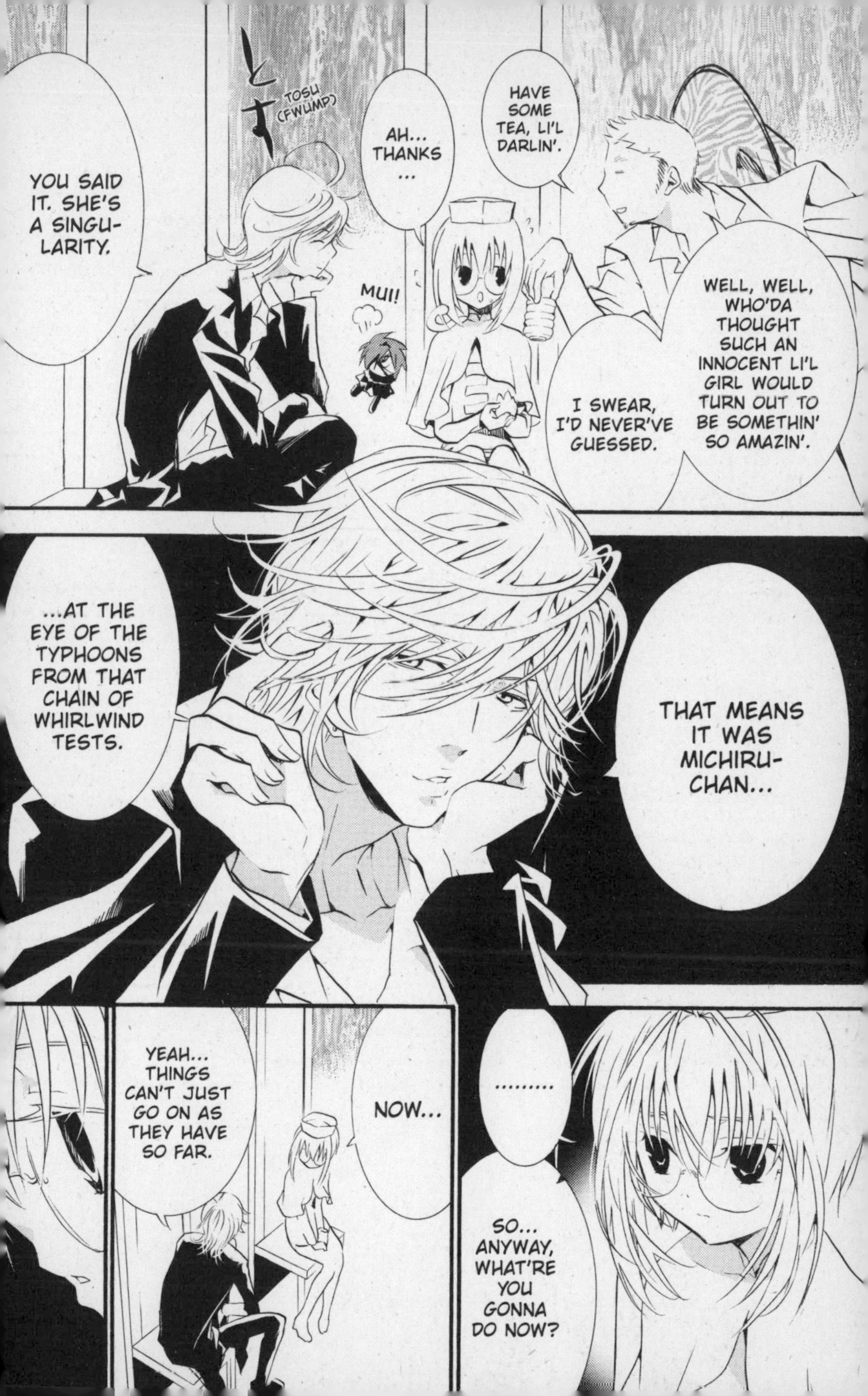
HAVE SOME TEA, LI'L DARLIN'.
AH... THANKS...
WELL, WELL, WHO'DA THOUGHT SUCH AN INNOCENT LI'L GIRL WOULD TURN OUT TO BE SOMETHIN' SO AMAZIN'.
I SWEAR, I'D NEVER'VE GUESSED.
MUI!
とす
TOSU (FWUMP)
YOU SAID IT. SHE'S A SINGU-LARITY.
THAT MEANS IT WAS MICHIRU-CHAN...
...AT THE EYE OF THE TYPHOONS FROM THAT CHAIN OF WHIRLWIND TESTS.
....
SO... ANYWAY, WHAT'RE YOU GONNA DO NOW?
NOW...
YEAH... THINGS CAN'T JUST GO ON AS THEY HAVE SO FAR.

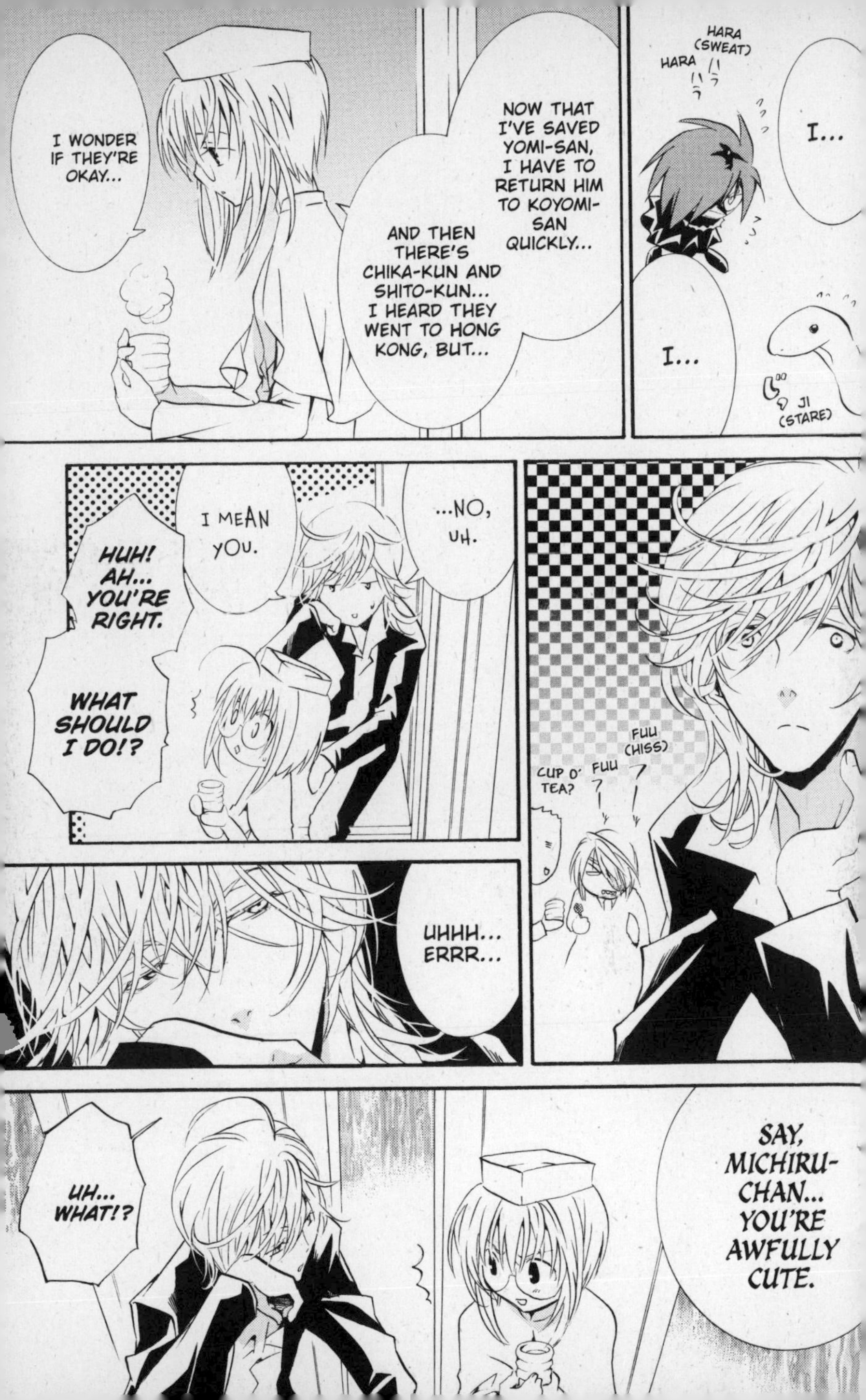

I...
HARA (SWEAT) HARA
I...
JI (STARE)
NOW THAT I'VE SAVED YOMI-SAN, I HAVE TO RETURN HIM TO KOYOMI-SAN QUICKLY...
AND THEN THERE'S CHIKA-KUN AND SHITO-KUN... I HEARD THEY WENT TO HONG KONG, BUT...
I WONDER IF THEY'RE OKAY...
FUU (HISS) FUU
CUP O' TEA?
...NO, UH.
I MEAN YOU.
HUH! AH... YOU'RE RIGHT.
WHAT SHOULD I DO!?
UHHH... ERRR...
SAY, MICHIRU-CHAN... YOU'RE AWFULLY CUTE.
UH... WHAT!?

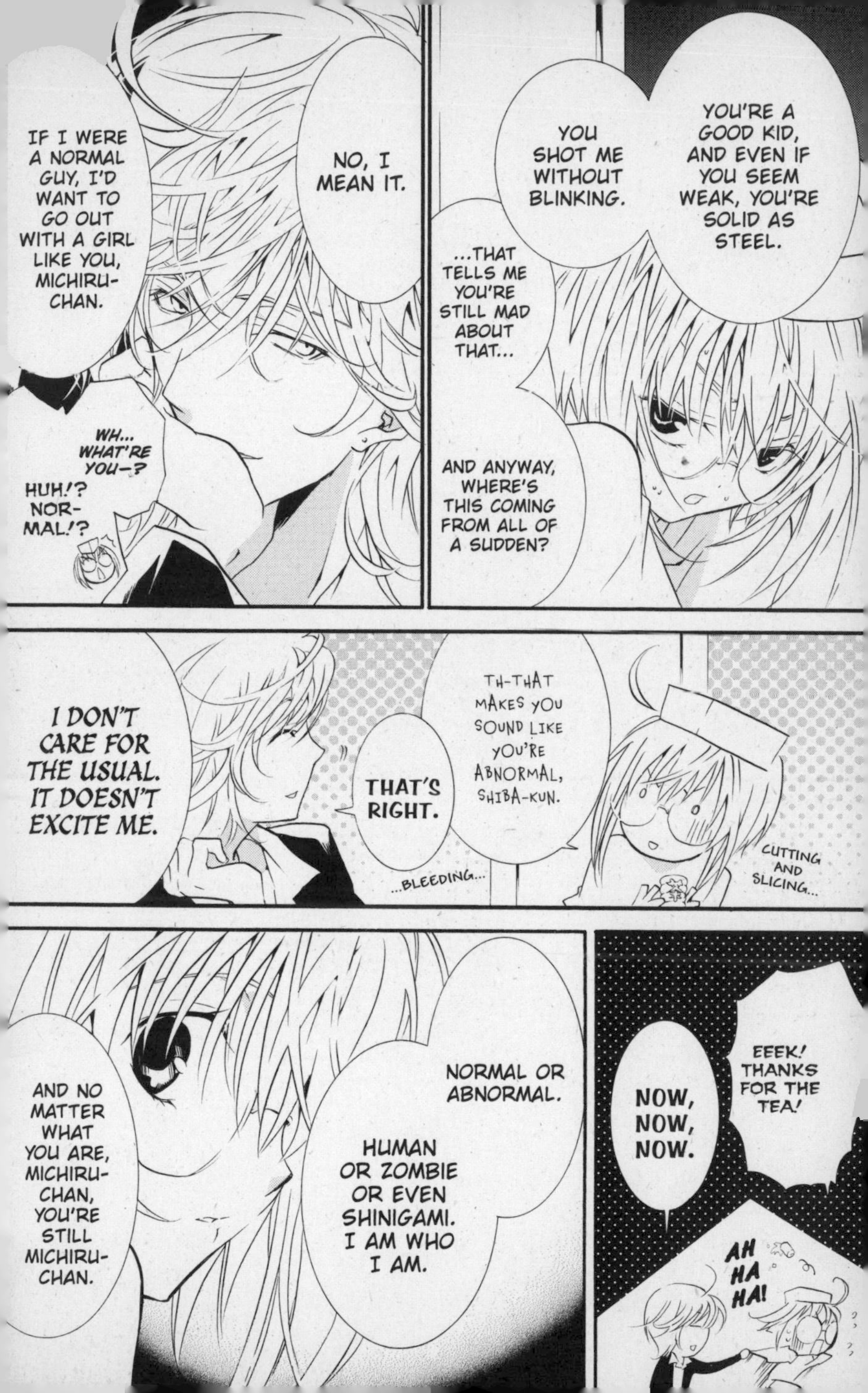
YOU'RE A GOOD KID, AND EVEN IF YOU SEEM WEAK, YOU'RE SOLID AS STEEL.
YOU SHOT ME WITHOUT BLINKING.
...THAT TELLS ME YOU'RE STILL MAD ABOUT THAT...
AND ANYWAY, WHERE'S THIS COMING FROM ALL OF A SUDDEN?
NO, I MEAN IT.
IF I WERE A NORMAL GUY, I'D WANT TO GO OUT WITH A GIRL LIKE YOU, MICHIRU-CHAN.
WH... WHAT'RE YOU—?
HUH!? NOR-MAL!?
CUTTING AND SLICING...
TH-THAT MAKES YOU SOUND LIKE YOU'RE ABNORMAL, SHIBA-KUN.
THAT'S RIGHT.
...BLEEDING...
I DON'T CARE FOR THE USUAL. IT DOESN'T EXCITE ME.
EEEK! THANKS FOR THE TEA!
NOW, NOW, NOW.
AH HA HA!
NORMAL OR ABNORMAL.
HUMAN OR ZOMBIE OR EVEN SHINIGAMI. I AM WHO I AM.
AND NO MATTER WHAT YOU ARE, MICHIRU-CHAN, YOU'RE STILL MICHIRU-CHAN.

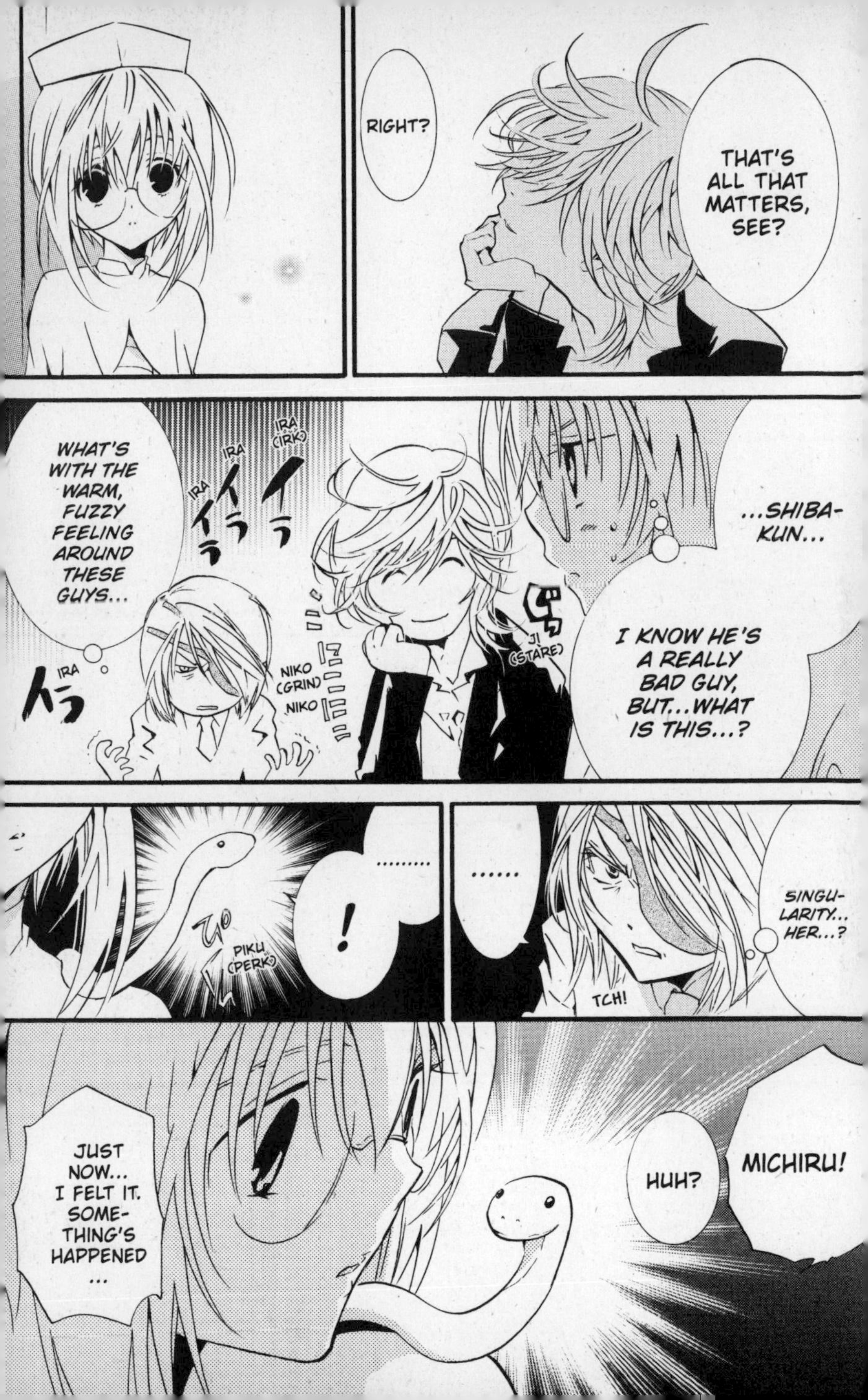
THAT'S ALL THAT MATTERS, SEE?
RIGHT?
...SHIBA-KUN...
I KNOW HE'S A REALLY BAD GUY, BUT...WHAT IS THIS...?
JI (STARE)
NIKO (GRIN)
NIKO
IRA (IRK)
IRA
IRA
WHAT'S WITH THE WARM, FUZZY FEELING AROUND THESE GUYS...
IRA
SINGU-LARITY... HER...?
......
TCH!
....
!
PIKU (PERK)
MICHIRU!
HUH?
JUST NOW... I FELT IT. SOME-THING'S HAPPENED ...

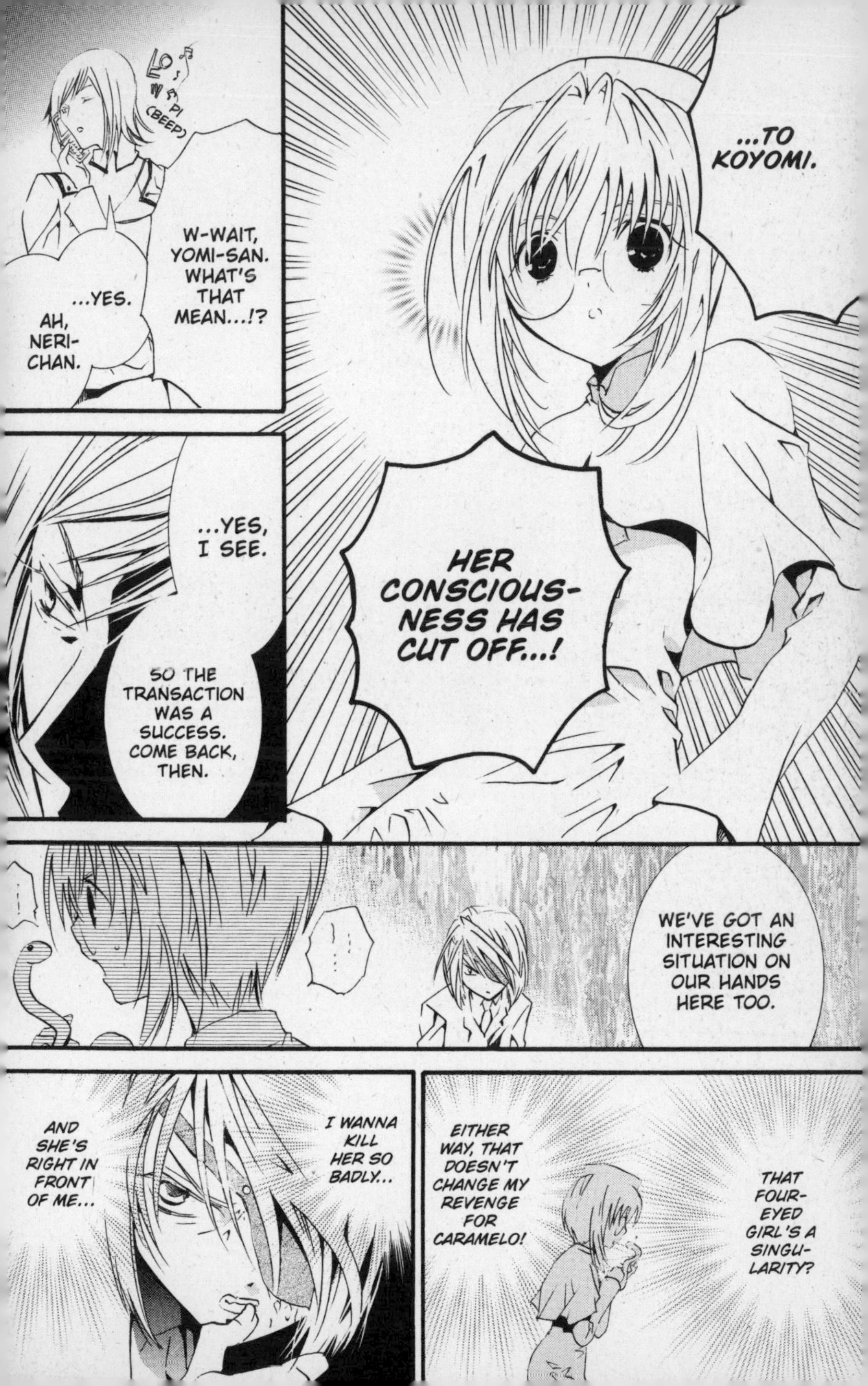
...TO KOYOMI.
HER CONSCIOUS-NESS HAS CUT OFF...!
PI (BEEP)
W-WAIT, YOMI-SAN. WHAT'S THAT MEAN...!?
...YES.
AH, NERI-CHAN.
...YES, I SEE.
SO THE TRANSACTION WAS A SUCCESS. COME BACK, THEN.
WE'VE GOT AN INTERESTING SITUATION ON OUR HANDS HERE TOO.
THAT FOUR-EYED GIRL'S A SINGU-LARITY?
EITHER WAY, THAT DOESN'T CHANGE MY REVENGE FOR CARAMELO!
I WANNA KILL HER SO BADLY...
AND SHE'S RIGHT IN FRONT OF ME...

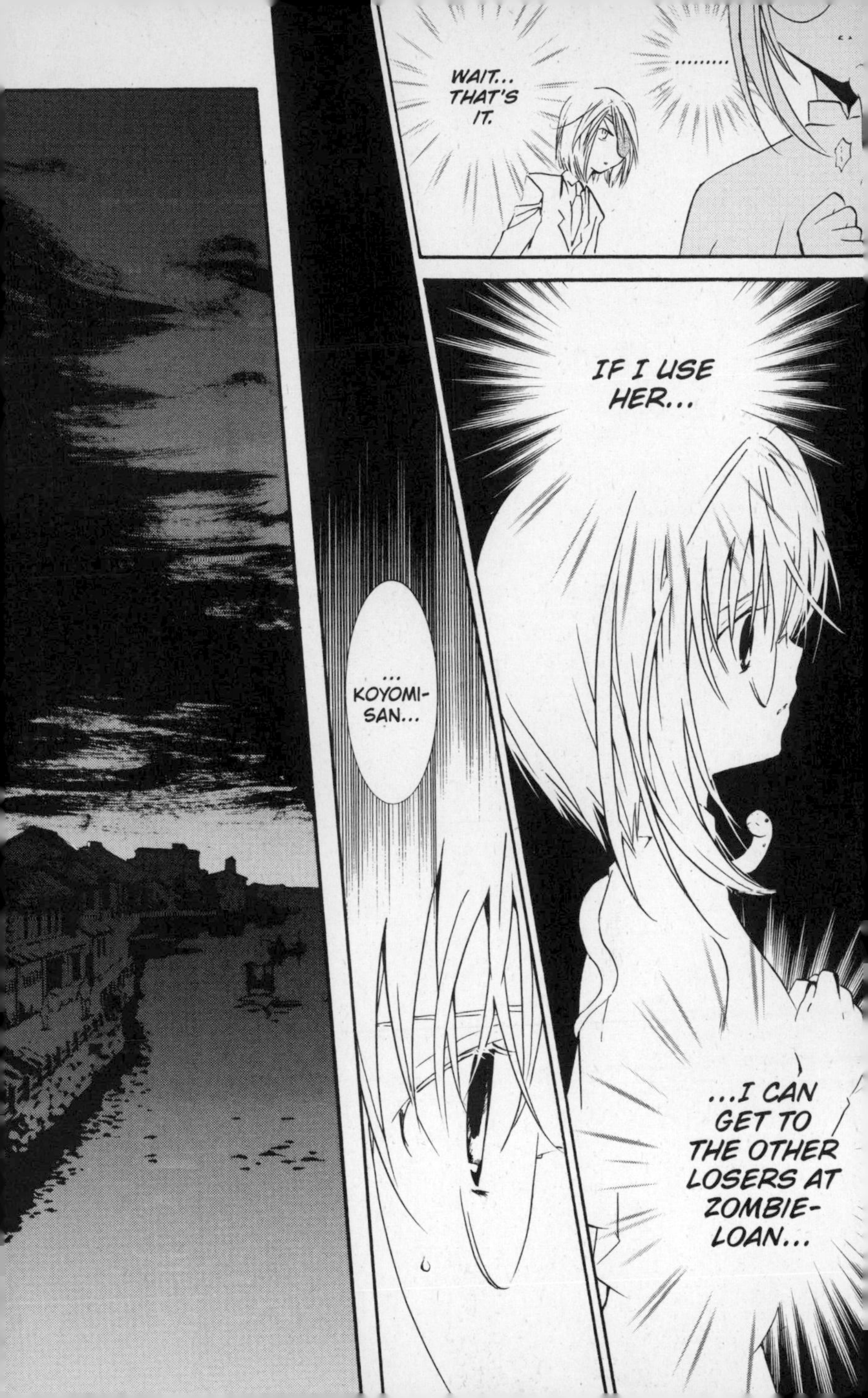
....
WAIT... THAT'S IT.
IF I USE HER...
...I CAN GET TO THE OTHER LOSERS AT ZOMBIE-LOAN...
...KOYOMI-SAN...

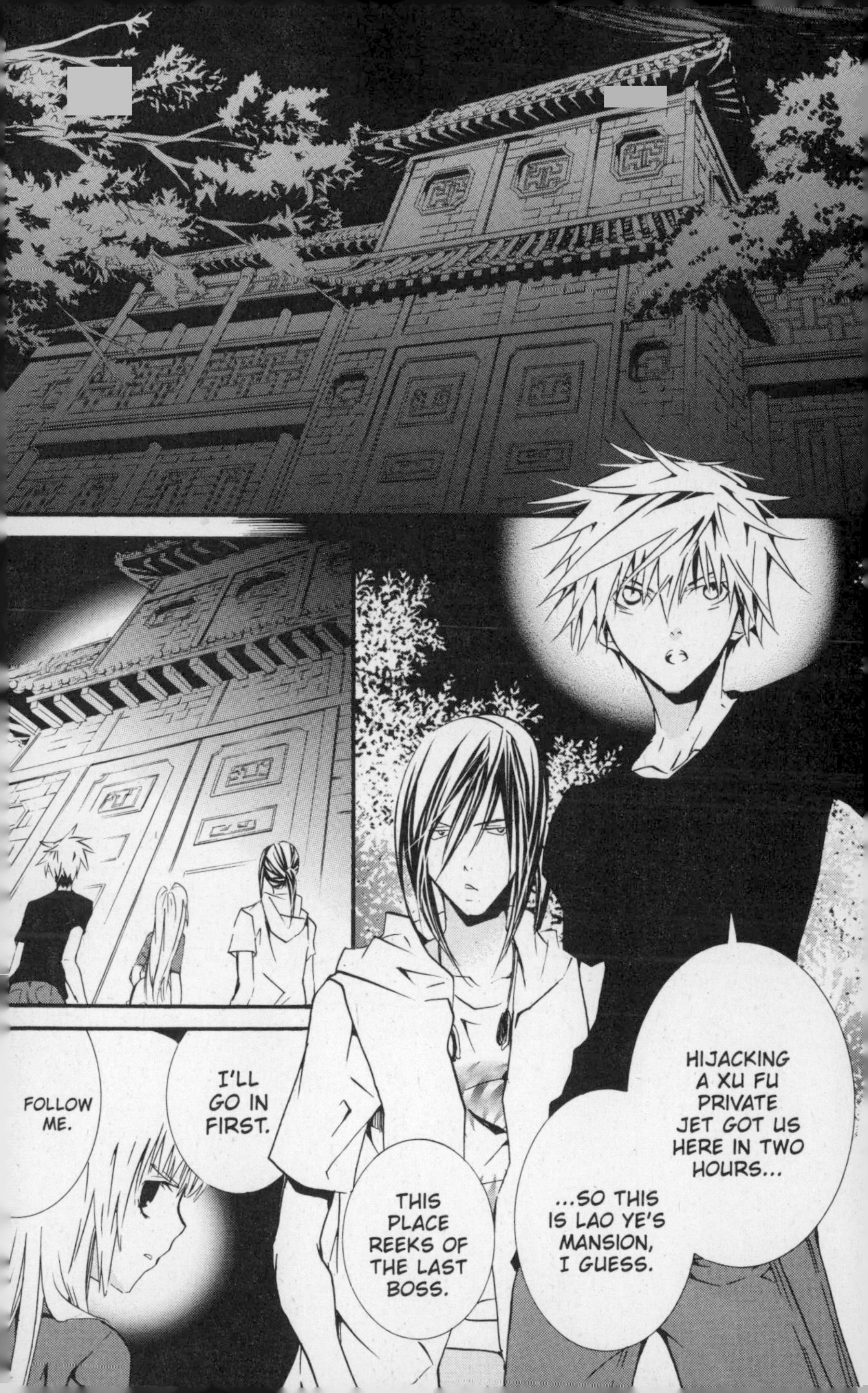
HIJACKING A XU FU PRIVATE JET GOT US HERE IN TWO HOURS...
...SO THIS IS LAO YE'S MANSION, I GUESS.
THIS PLACE REEKS OF THE LAST BOSS.
I'LL GO IN FIRST.
FOLLOW ME.

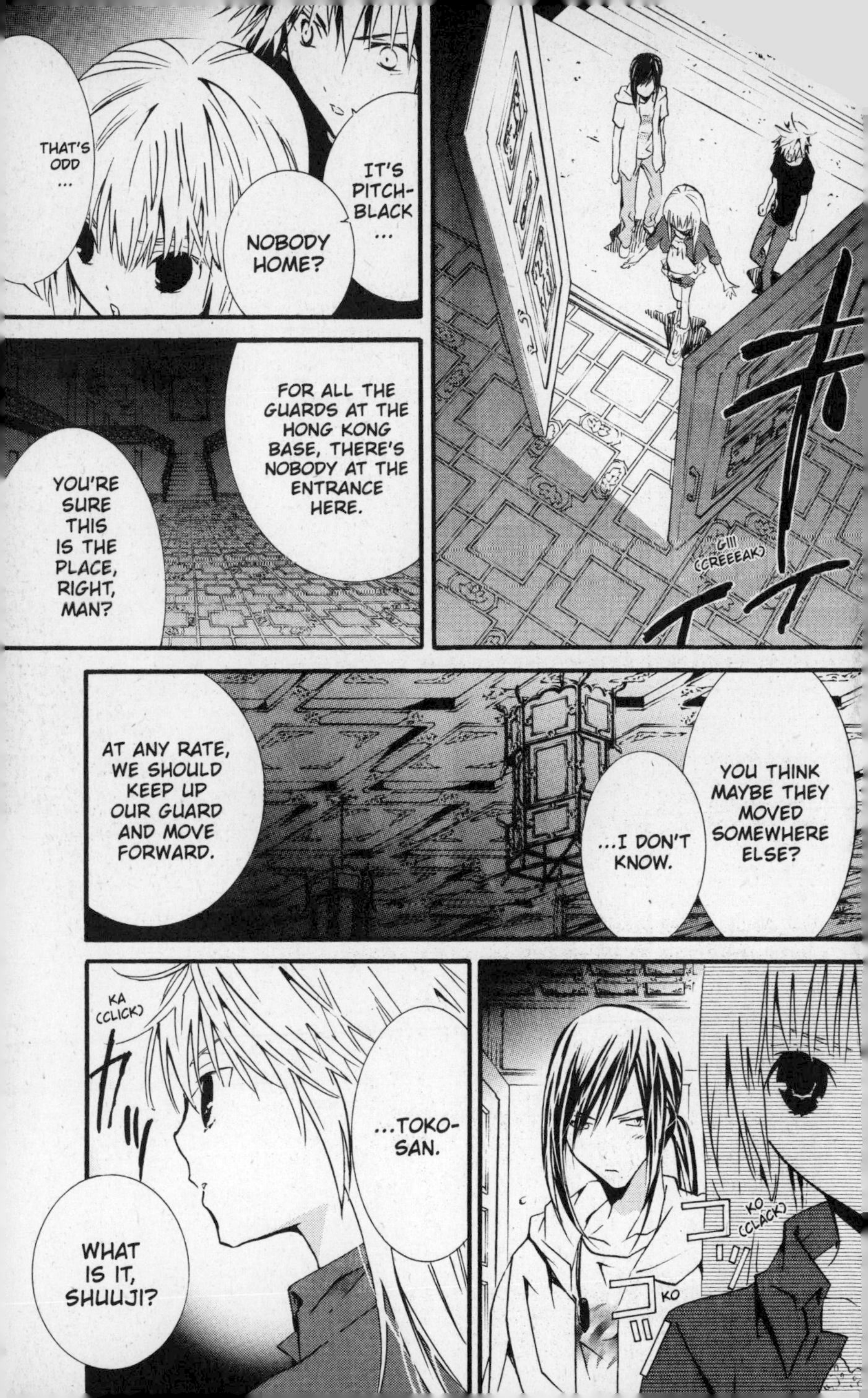
GIII (CREEEAK)
IT'S PITCH-BLACK ...
NOBODY HOME?
THAT'S ODD ...
FOR ALL THE GUARDS AT THE HONG KONG BASE, THERE'S NOBODY AT THE ENTRANCE HERE.
YOU'RE SURE THIS IS THE PLACE, RIGHT, MAN?
YOU THINK MAYBE THEY MOVED SOMEWHERE ELSE?
...I DON'T KNOW.
AT ANY RATE, WE SHOULD KEEP UP OUR GUARD AND MOVE FORWARD.
KO (CLACK)
KO
...TOKO-SAN.
KA (CLICK)
WHAT IS IT, SHUUJI?

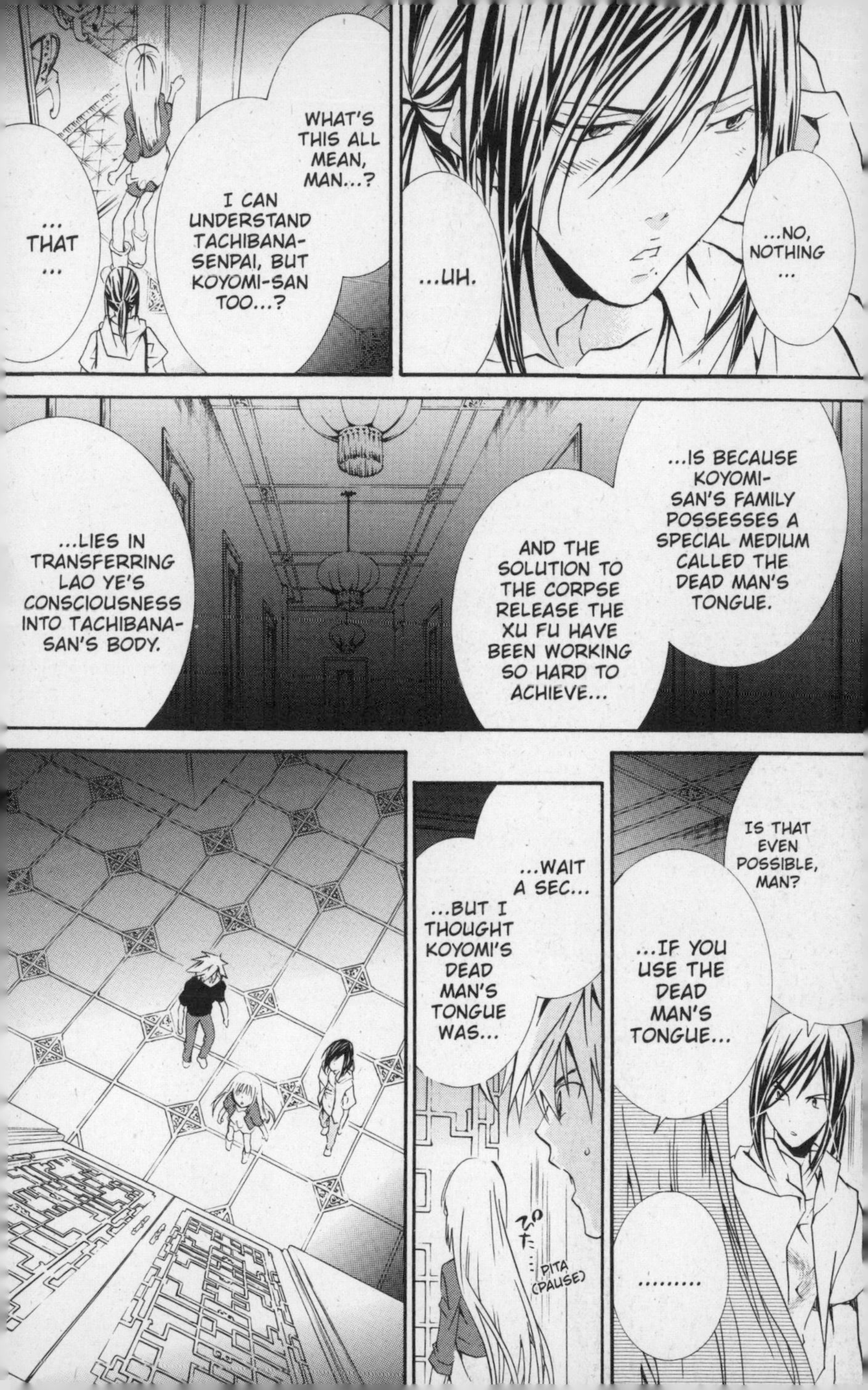

...NO, NOTHING ...
...UH.
WHAT'S THIS ALL MEAN, MAN...?
I CAN UNDERSTAND TACHIBANA-SENPAI, BUT KOYOMI-SAN TOO...?
... THAT ...
...IS BECAUSE KOYOMI-SAN'S FAMILY POSSESSES A SPECIAL MEDIUM CALLED THE DEAD MAN'S TONGUE.
AND THE SOLUTION TO THE CORPSE RELEASE THE XU FU HAVE BEEN WORKING SO HARD TO ACHIEVE...
...LIES IN TRANSFERRING LAO YE'S CONSCIOUSNESS INTO TACHIBANA-SAN'S BODY.
IS THAT EVEN POSSIBLE, MAN?
...IF YOU USE THE DEAD MAN'S TONGUE...
....
...WAIT A SEC...
...BUT I THOUGHT KOYOMI'S DEAD MAN'S TONGUE WAS...
PITA (PAUSE)

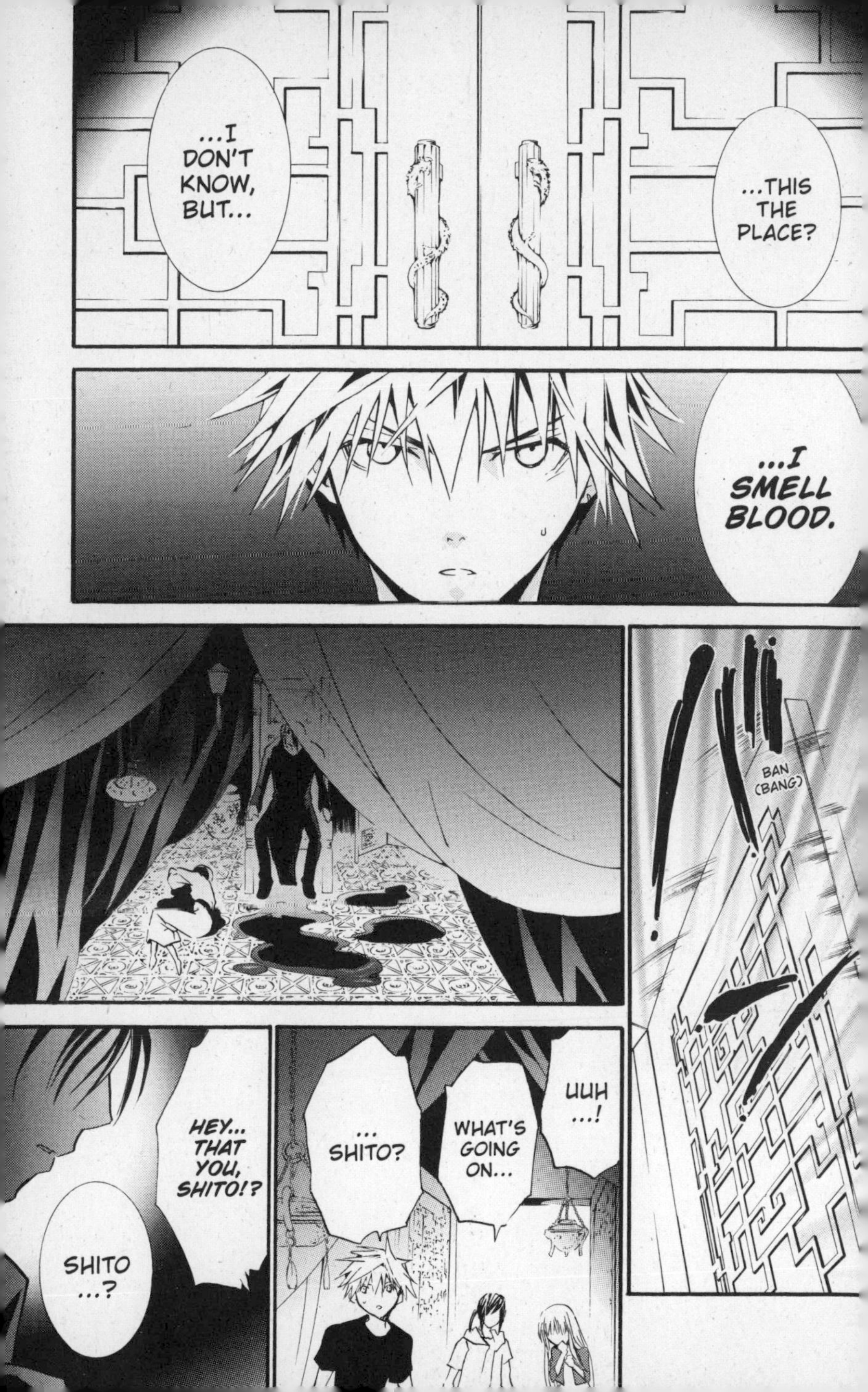
...THIS THE PLACE?
...I DON'T KNOW, BUT...
...I SMELL BLOOD.
BAN (BANG)
UUH ...!
WHAT'S GOING ON...
... SHITO?
HEY... THAT YOU, SHITO!?
SHITO ...?

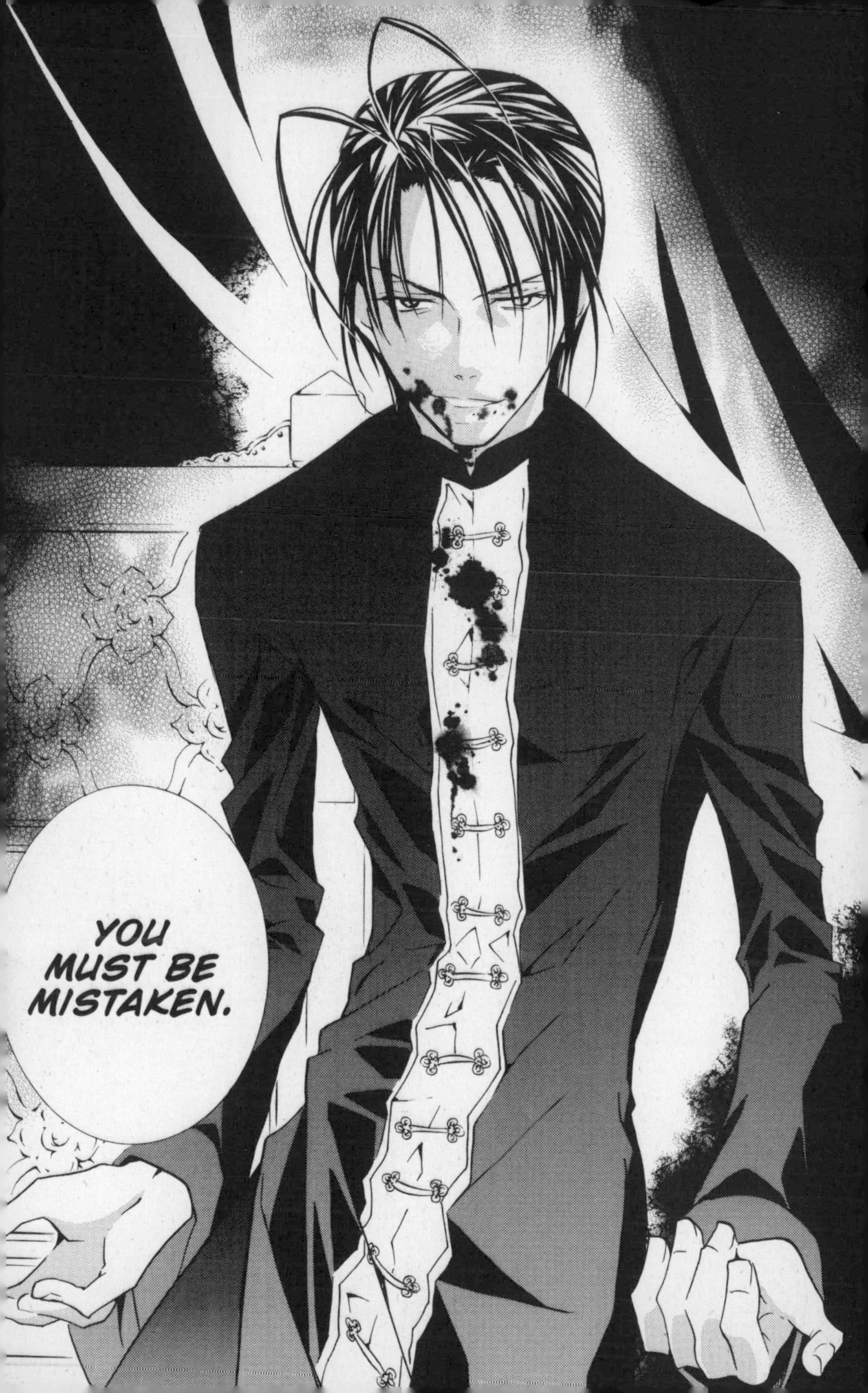
YOU MUST BE MISTAKEN.

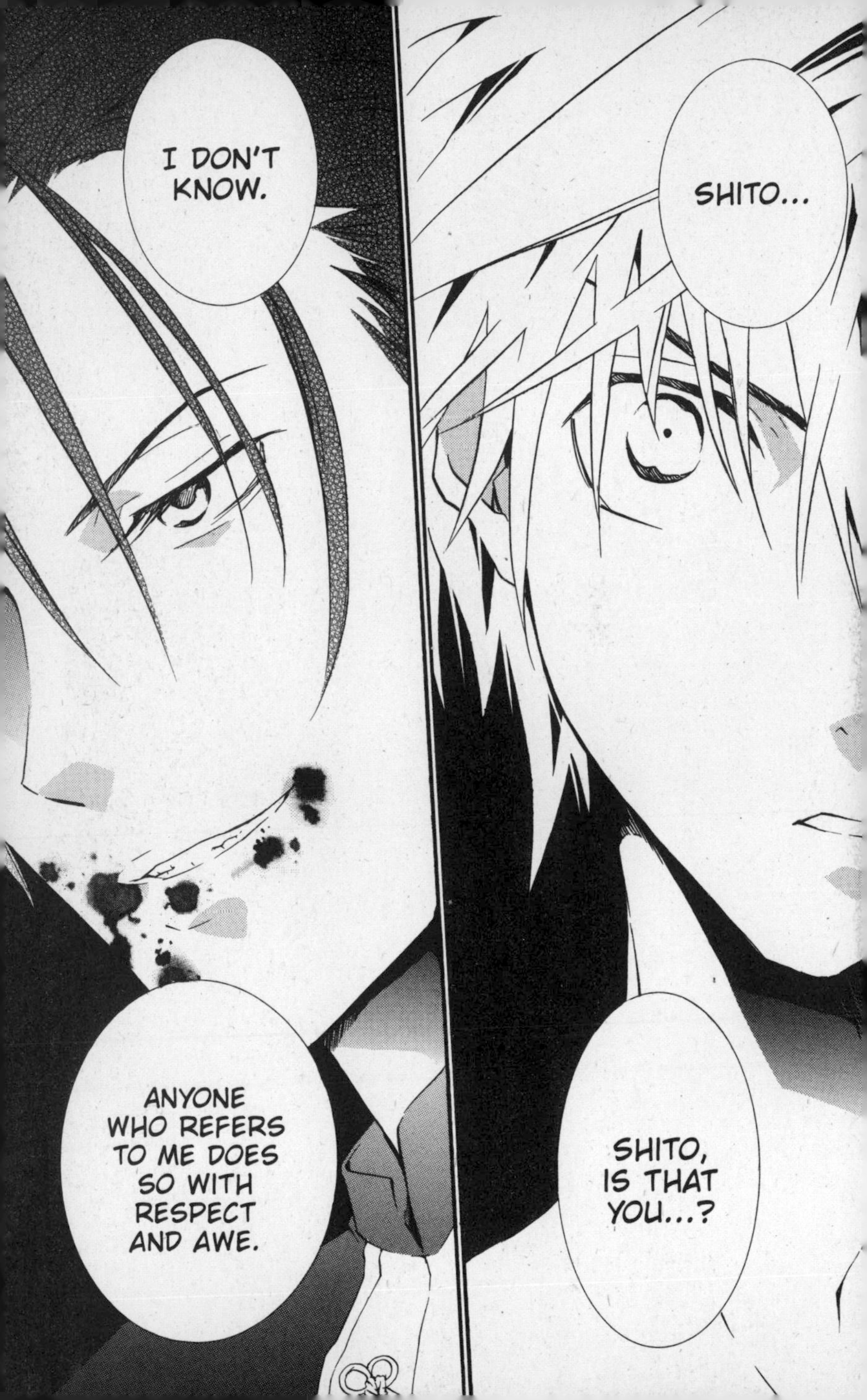
SHITO...
SHITO, IS THAT YOU...?
I DON'T KNOW.
ANYONE WHO REFERS TO ME DOES SO WITH RESPECT AND AWE.

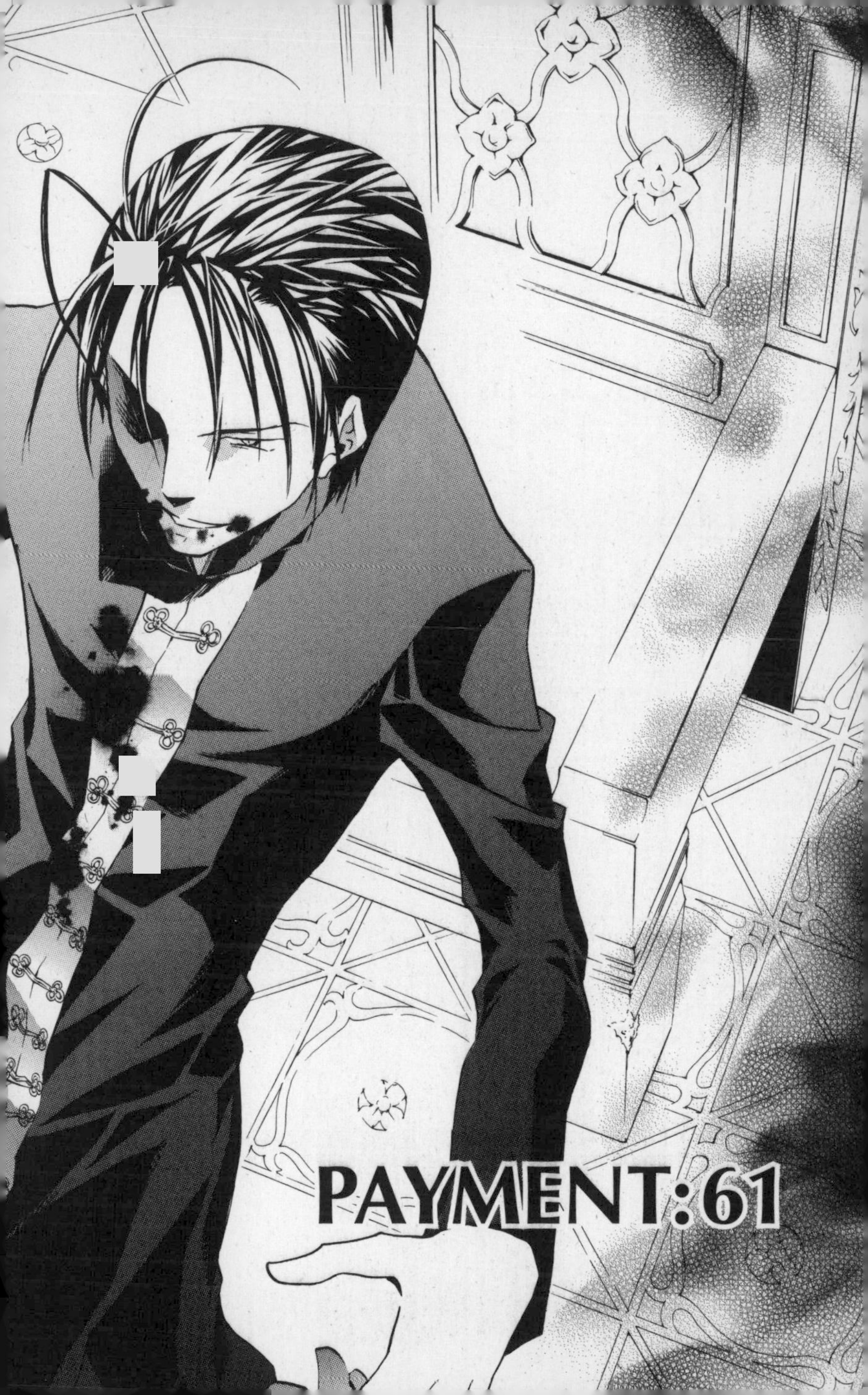
PAYMENT:61

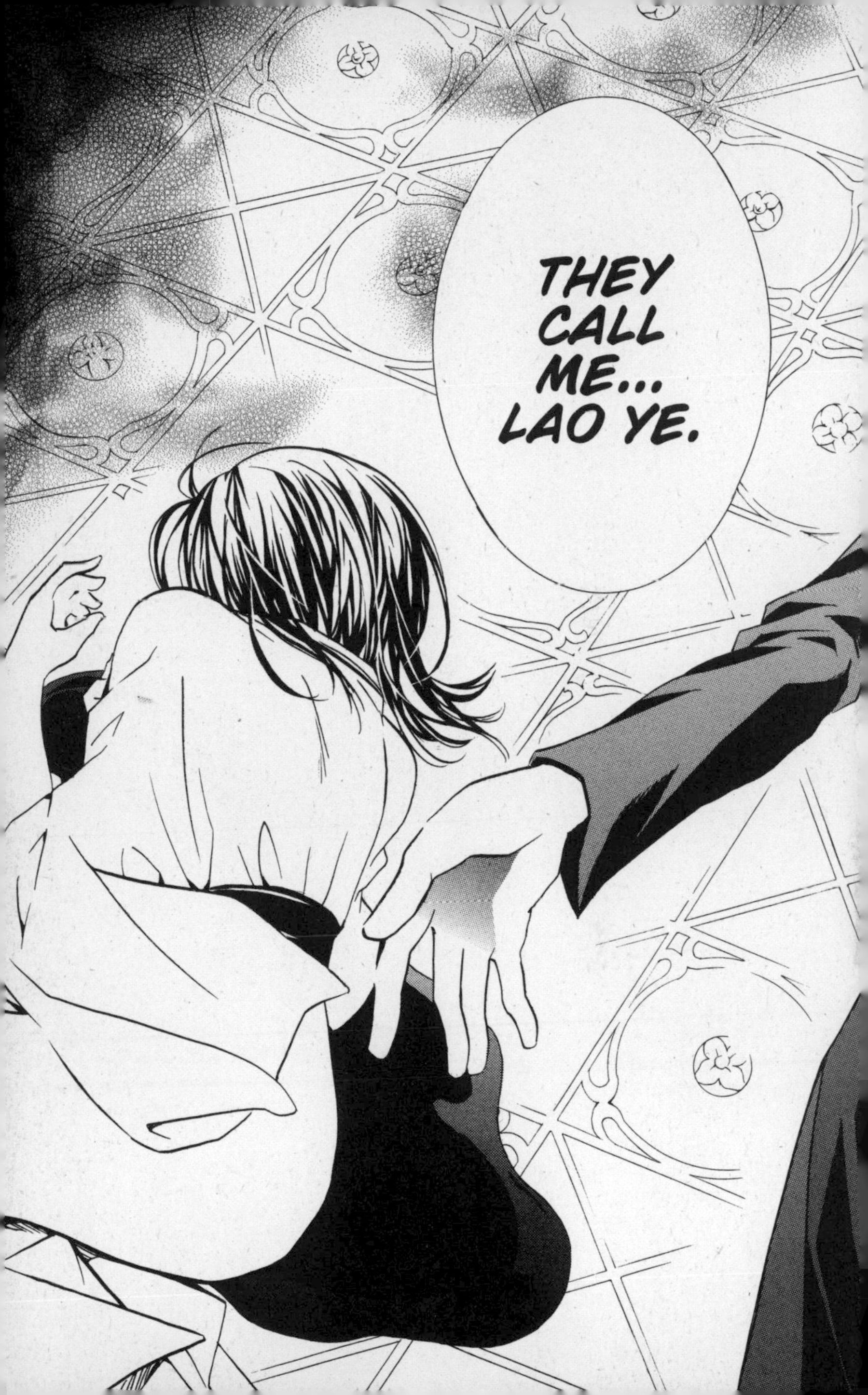
THEY CALL ME... LAO YE.

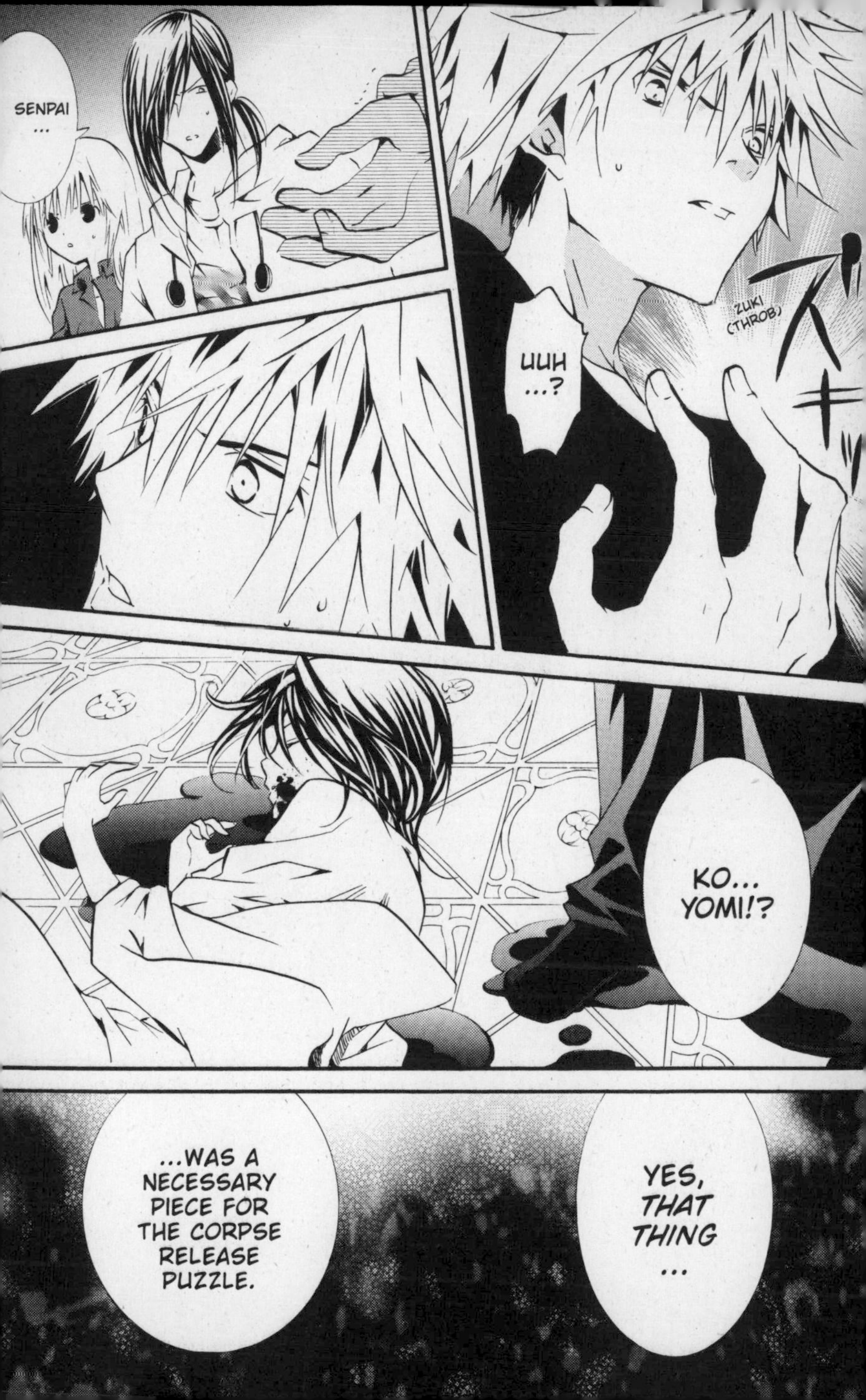
ZUKI (THROB)
UUH ...?
SENPAI ...
KO... YOMI!?
YES, THAT THING ...
...WAS A NECESSARY PIECE FOR THE CORPSE RELEASE PUZZLE.

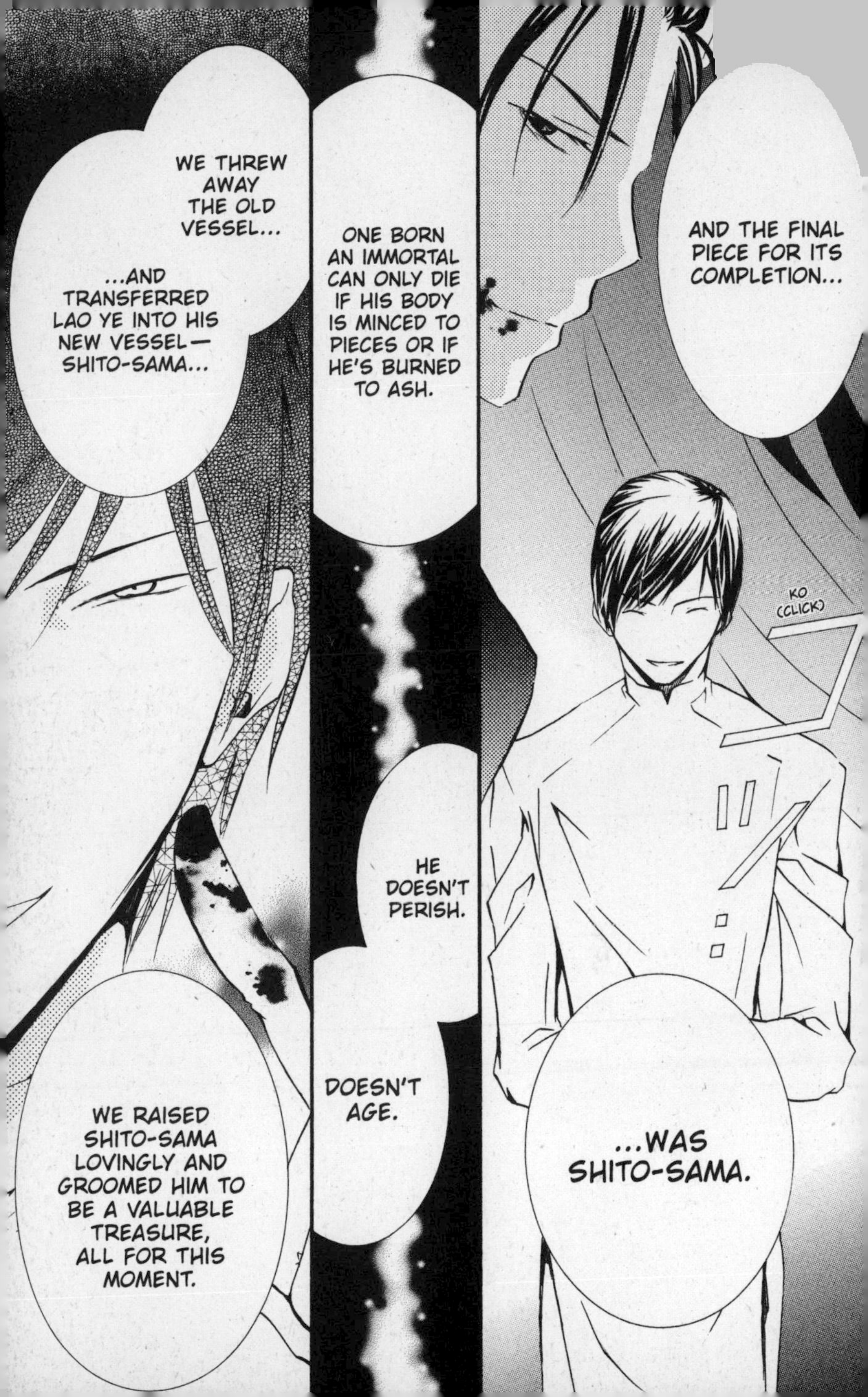
AND THE FINAL PIECE FOR ITS COMPLETION...
KO (CLICK)
...WAS SHITO-SAMA.
ONE BORN AN IMMORTAL CAN ONLY DIE IF HIS BODY IS MINCED TO PIECES OR IF HE'S BURNED TO ASH.
HE DOESN'T PERISH.
DOESN'T AGE.
WE THREW AWAY THE OLD VESSEL...
...AND TRANSFERRED LAO YE INTO HIS NEW VESSEL—SHITO-SAMA...
WE RAISED SHITO-SAMA LOVINGLY AND GROOMED HIM TO BE A VALUABLE TREASURE, ALL FOR THIS MOMENT.

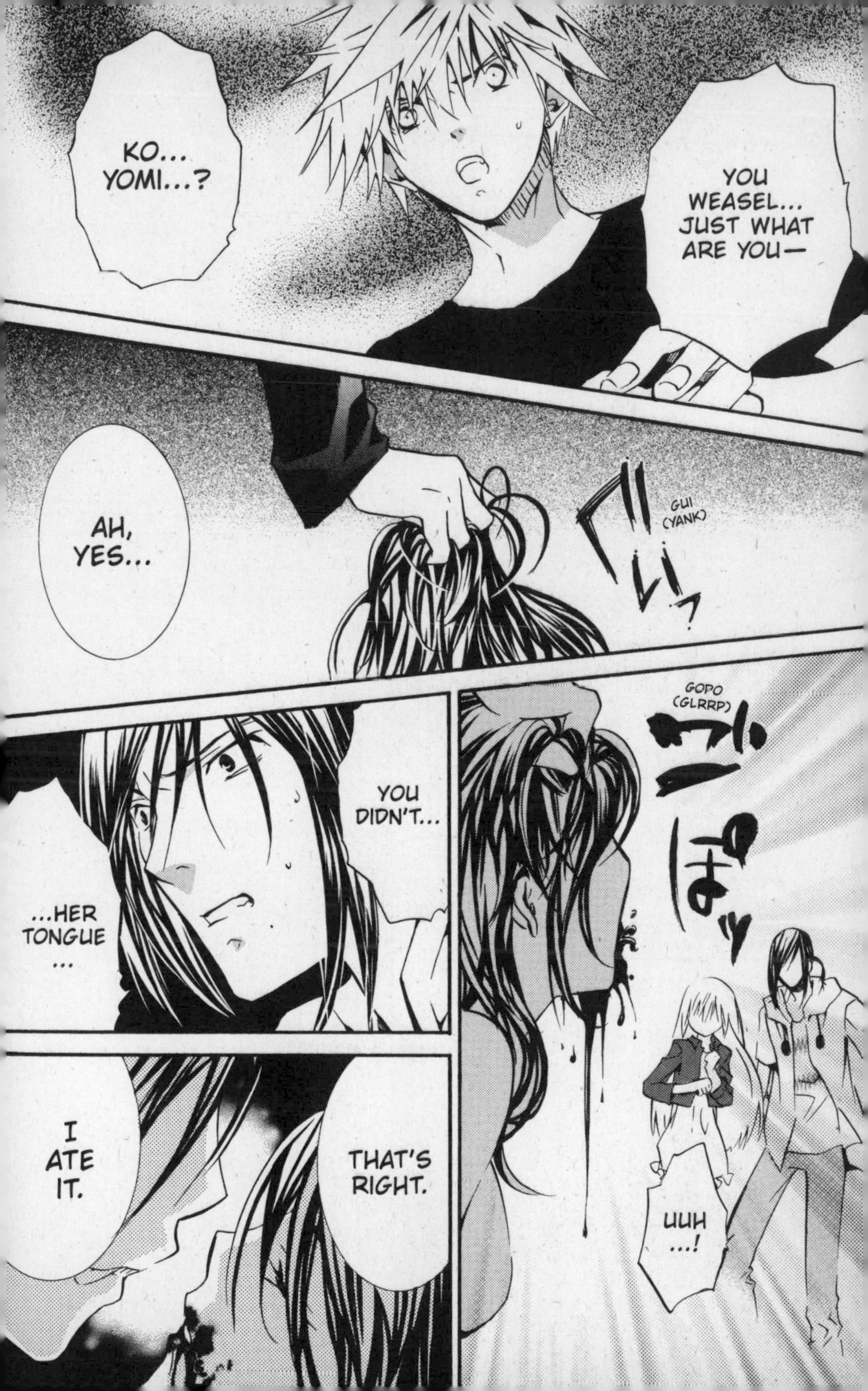
YOU WEASEL... JUST WHAT ARE YOU—
KO... YOMI...?
GUI (YANK)
AH, YES...
GOPO (GLRRP)
UUH ...!
YOU DIDN'T...
...HER TONGUE ...
THAT'S RIGHT.
I ATE IT.

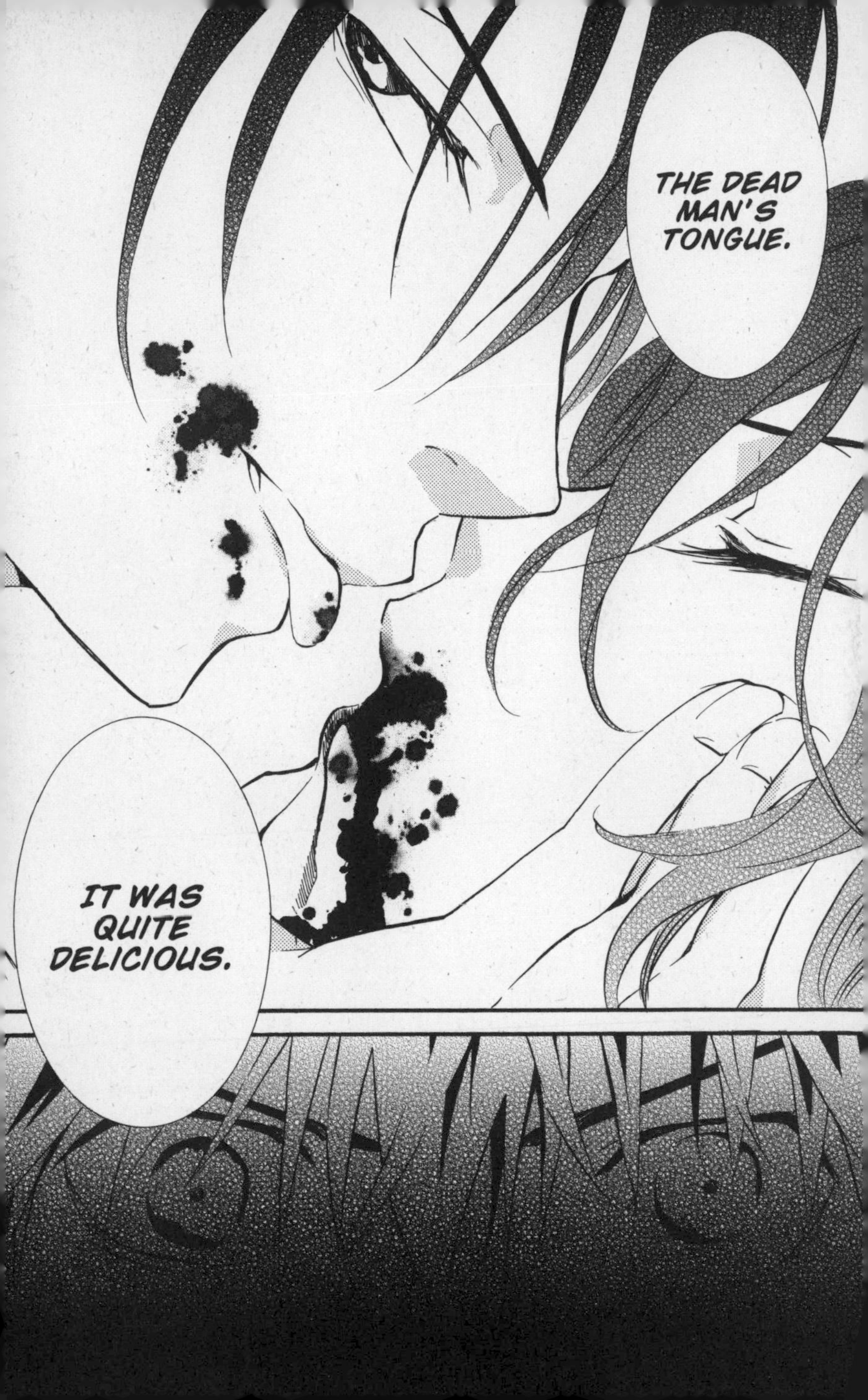
THE DEAD MAN'S TONGUE.
IT WAS QUITE DELICIOUS.

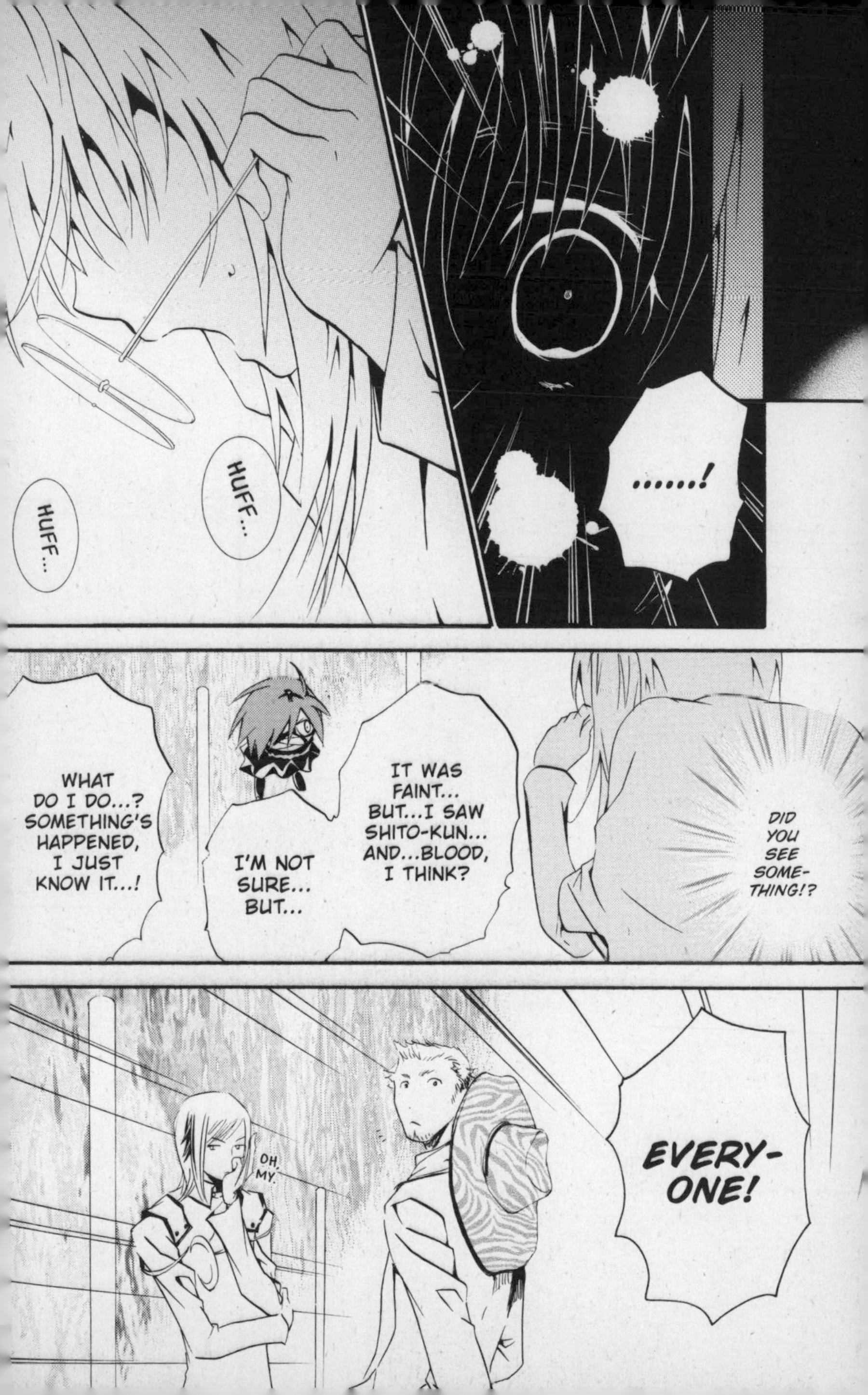
......!
HUFF...
HUFF...
DID YOU SEE SOME-THING!?
IT WAS FAINT... BUT...I SAW SHITO-KUN... AND...BLOOD, I THINK?
I'M NOT SURE... BUT...
WHAT DO I DO...? SOMETHING'S HAPPENED, I JUST KNOW IT...!
EVERY-ONE!
OH, MY.

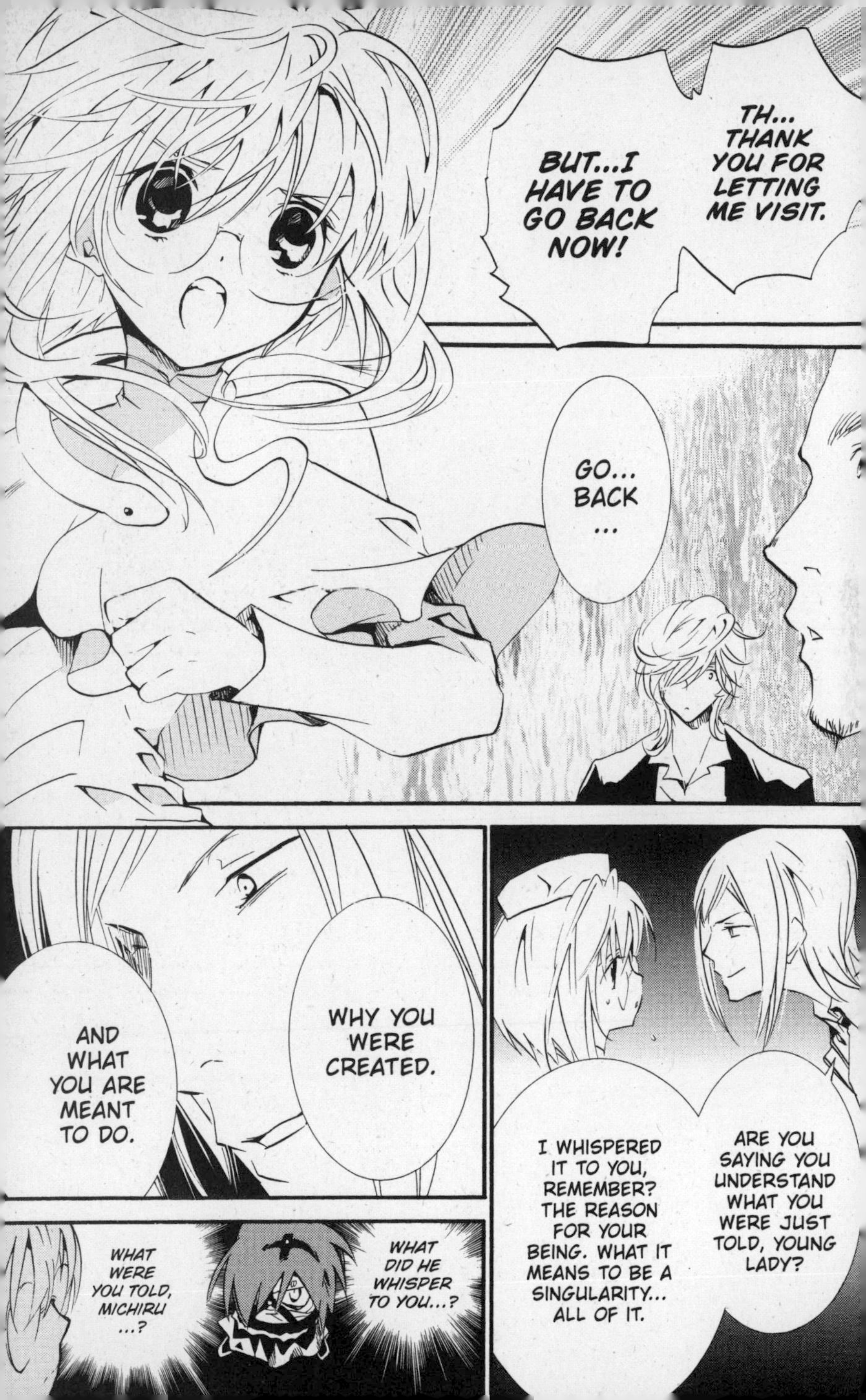
TH... THANK YOU FOR LETTING ME VISIT.
BUT...I HAVE TO GO BACK NOW!
GO... BACK ...
ARE YOU SAYING YOU UNDERSTAND WHAT YOU WERE JUST TOLD, YOUNG LADY?
I WHISPERED IT TO YOU, REMEMBER? THE REASON FOR YOUR BEING. WHAT IT MEANS TO BE A SINGULARITY... ALL OF IT.
WHY YOU WERE CREATED.
AND WHAT YOU ARE MEANT TO DO.
WHAT DID HE WHISPER TO YOU...?
WHAT WERE YOU TOLD, MICHIRU ...?

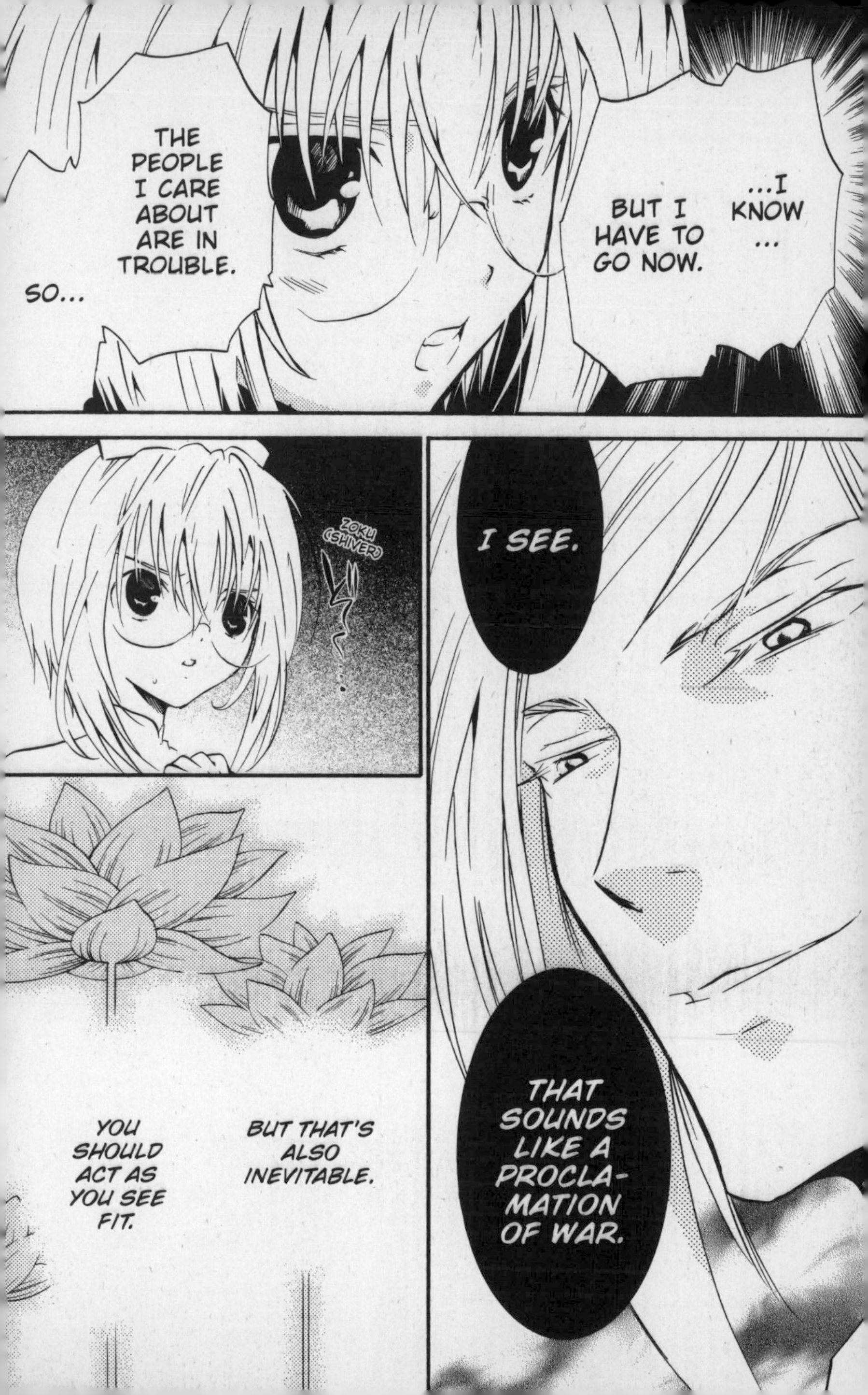
...I KNOW ...
BUT I HAVE TO GO NOW.
THE PEOPLE I CARE ABOUT ARE IN TROUBLE.
SO...
I SEE.
THAT SOUNDS LIKE A PROCLA-MATION OF WAR.
ZOKU (SHIVER)
BUT THAT'S ALSO INEVITABLE.
YOU SHOULD ACT AS YOU SEE FIT.

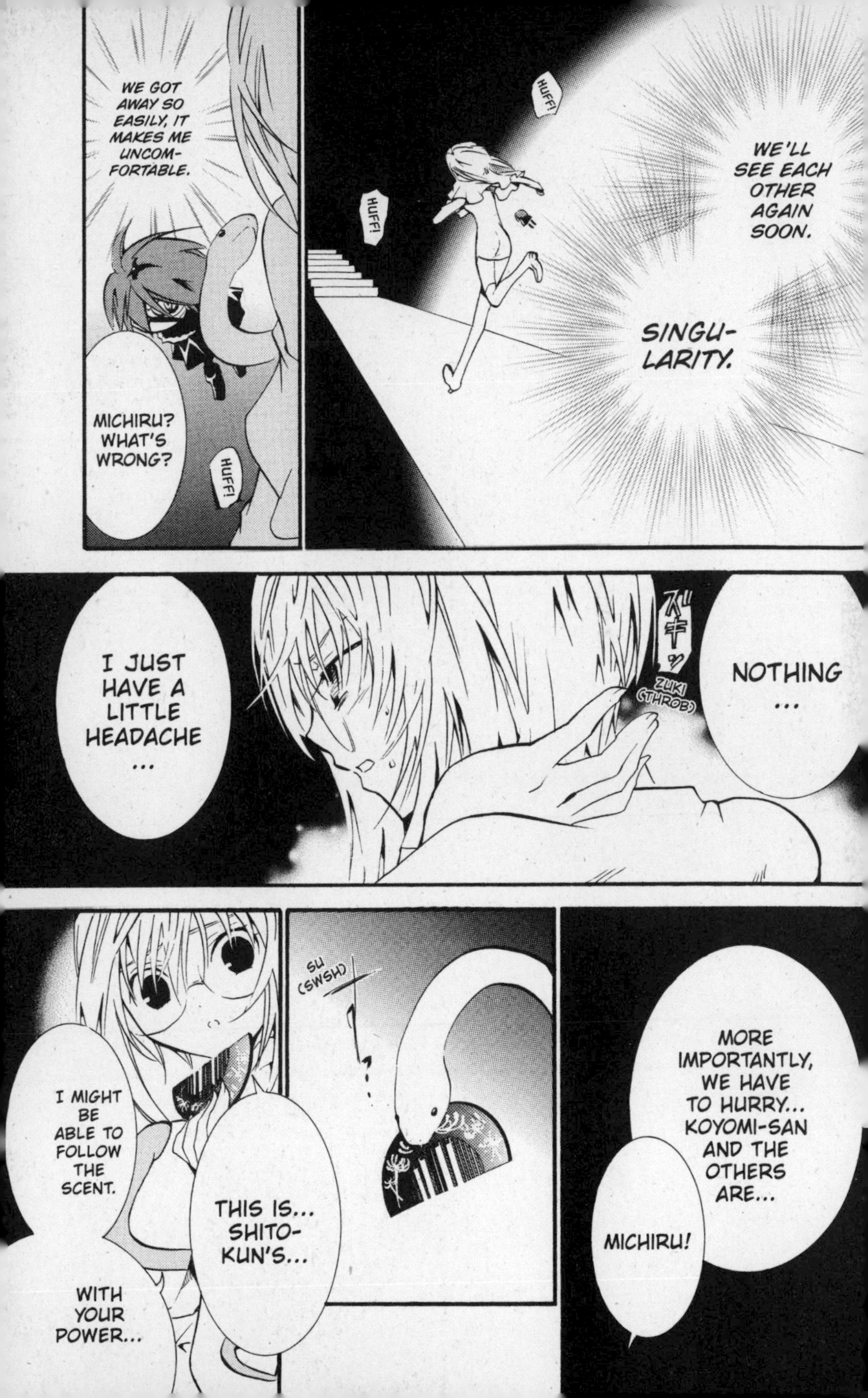
WE'LL SEE EACH OTHER AGAIN SOON.
SINGULARITY.
HUFF!
HUFF!
WE GOT AWAY SO EASILY, IT MAKES ME UNCOMFORTABLE.
MICHIRU? WHAT'S WRONG?
HUFF!
NOTHING ...
ZUKI (THROB)
I JUST HAVE A LITTLE HEADACHE ...
MORE IMPORTANTLY, WE HAVE TO HURRY... KOYOMI-SAN AND THE OTHERS ARE...
MICHIRU!
SU (SWSH)
THIS IS... SHITO-KUN'S...
I MIGHT BE ABLE TO FOLLOW THE SCENT.
WITH YOUR POWER...

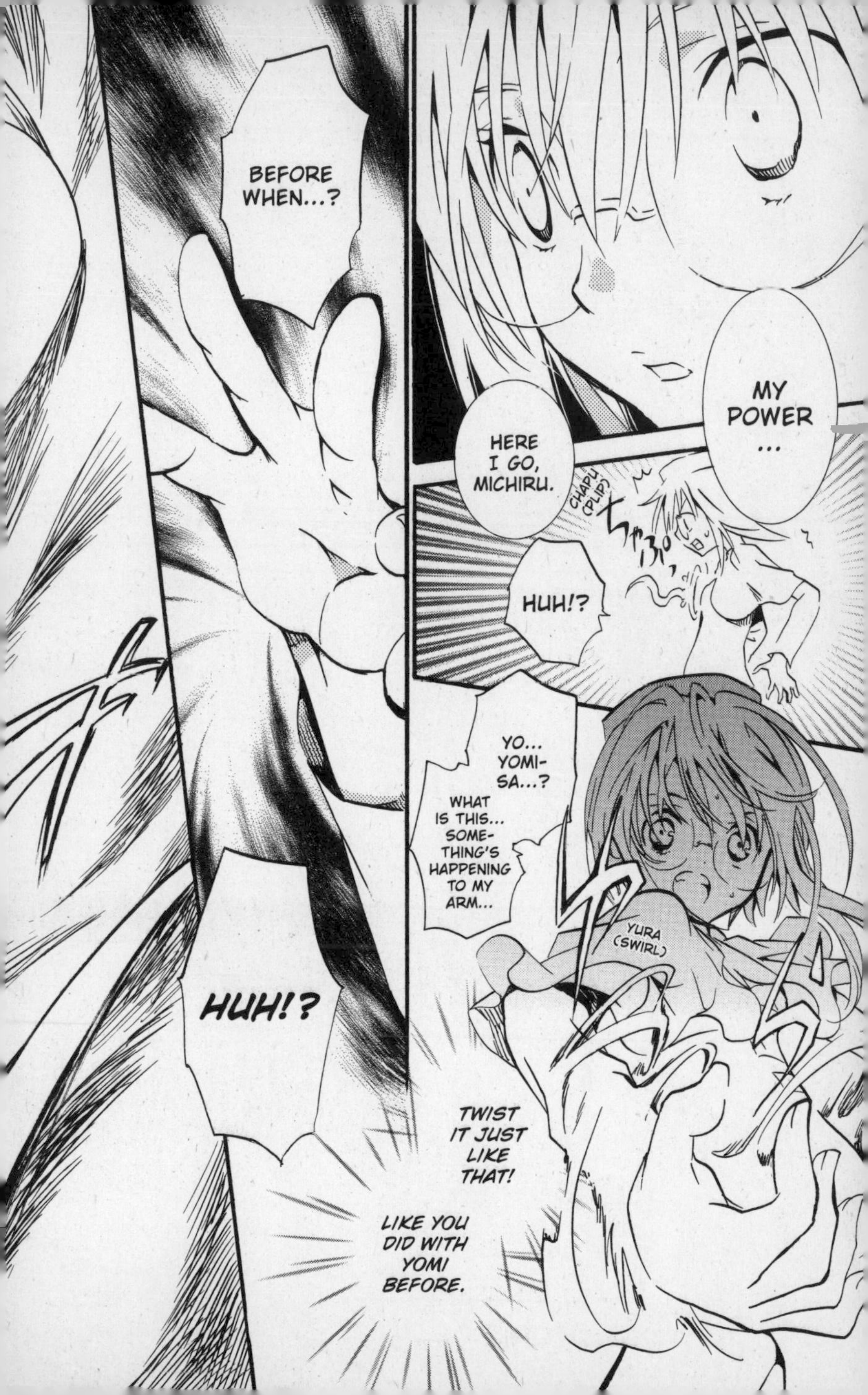
MY POWER ...
HERE I GO, MICHIRU.
CHAPU (PLIP)
HUH!?
YO... YOMI-SA...?
WHAT IS THIS... SOME-THING'S HAPPENING TO MY ARM...
YURA (SWIRL)
TWIST IT JUST LIKE THAT!
LIKE YOU DID WITH YOMI BEFORE.
BEFORE WHEN...?
HUH!?

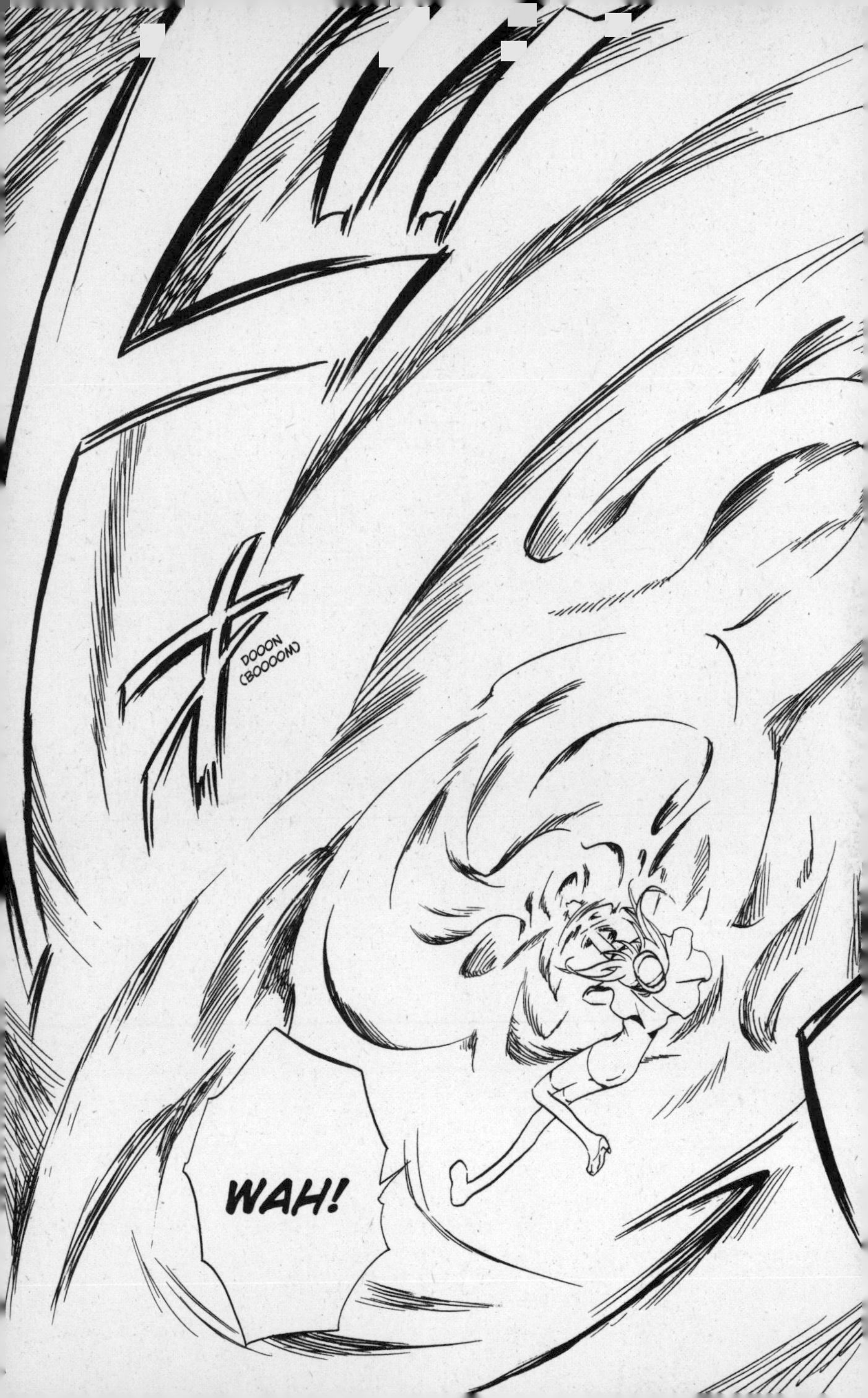
DOOON (BOOOOM)
WAH!

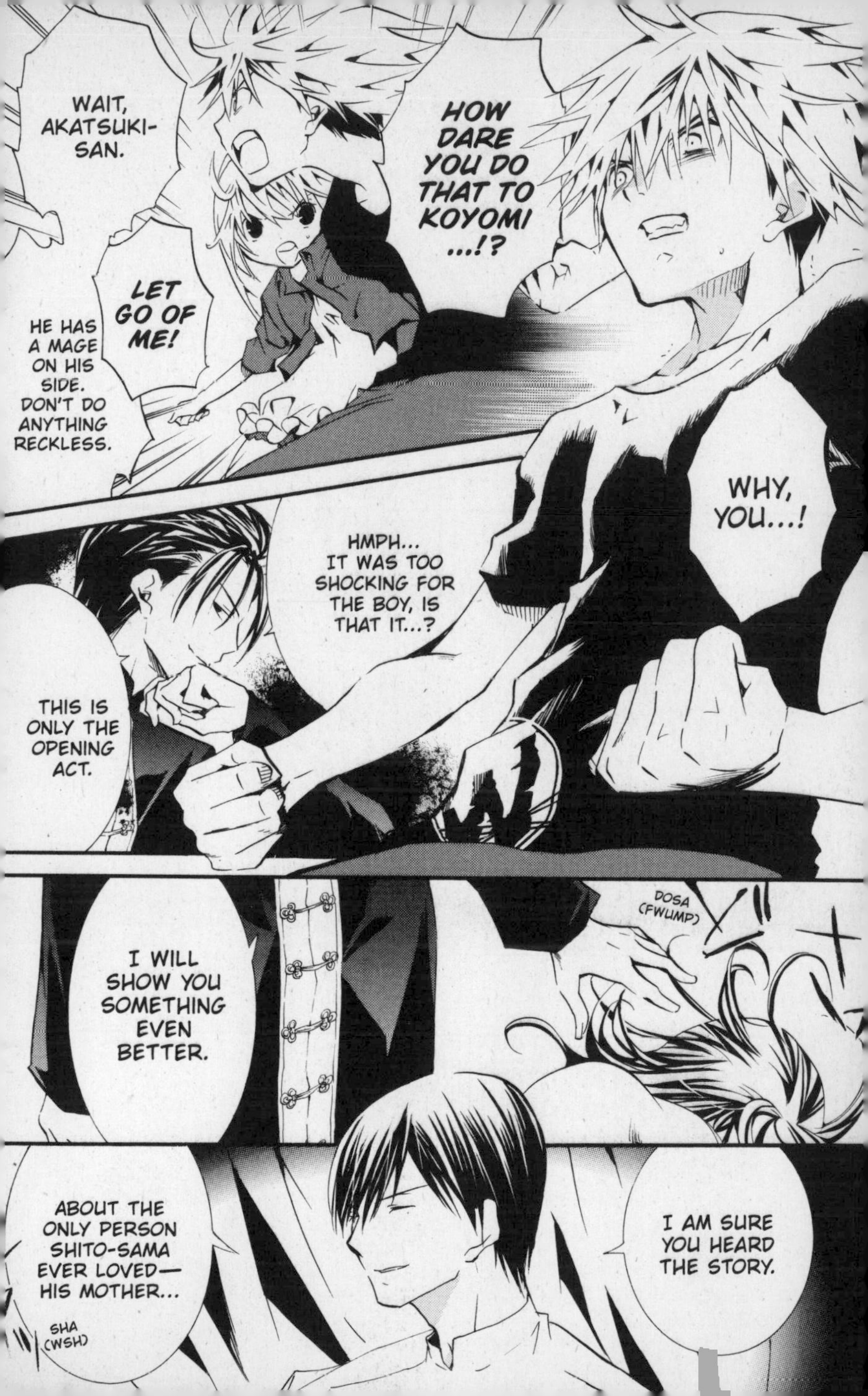
HOW DARE YOU DO THAT TO KOYOMI ...!?
WAIT, AKATSUKI-SAN.
LET GO OF ME!
HE HAS A MAGE ON HIS SIDE. DON'T DO ANYTHING RECKLESS.
WHY, YOU...!
HMPH... IT WAS TOO SHOCKING FOR THE BOY, IS THAT IT...?
THIS IS ONLY THE OPENING ACT.
DOSA (FWUMP)
I WILL SHOW YOU SOMETHING EVEN BETTER.
I AM SURE YOU HEARD THE STORY.
ABOUT THE ONLY PERSON SHITO-SAMA EVER LOVED—HIS MOTHER...
SHA (WSH)

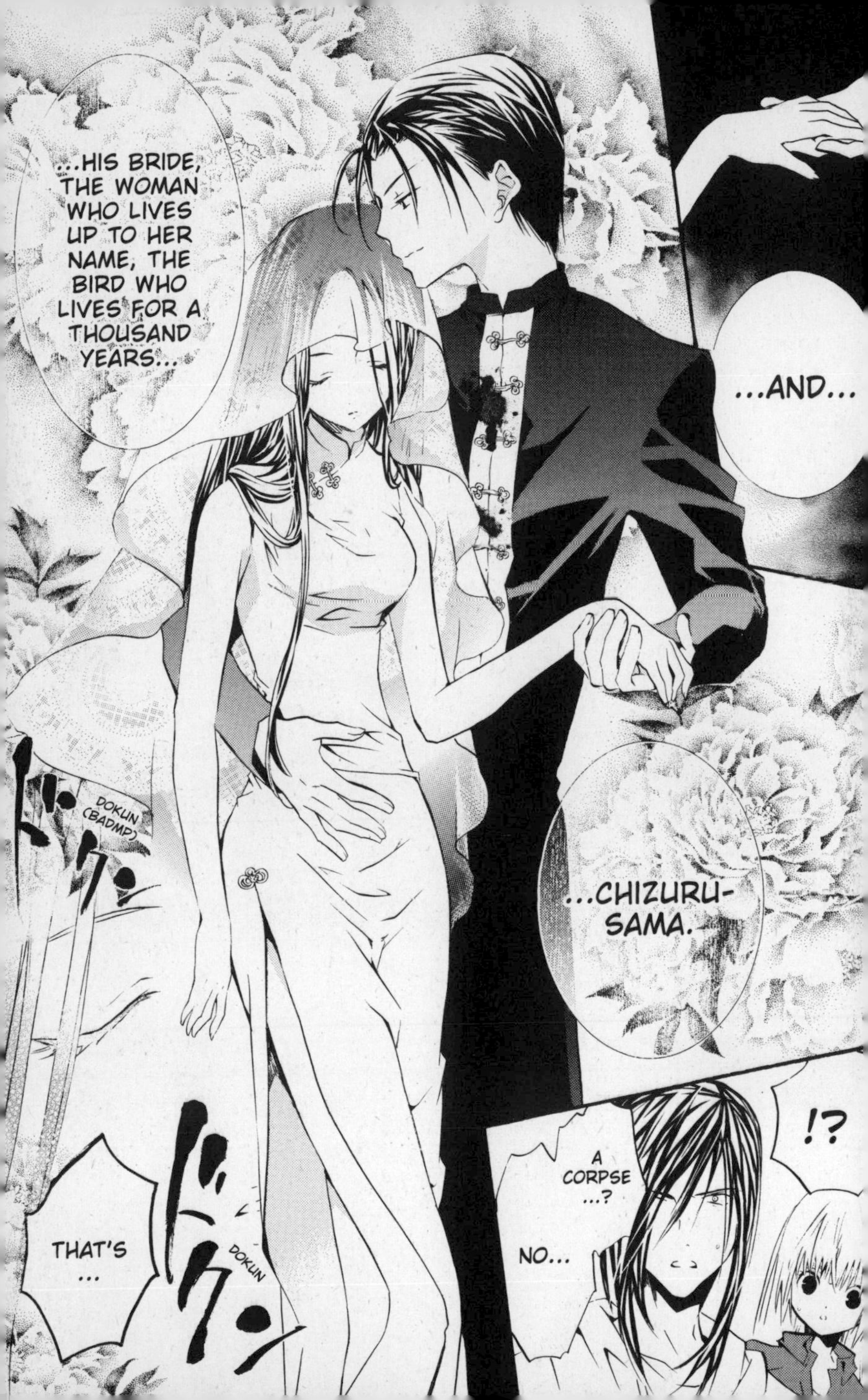
...HIS BRIDE, THE WOMAN WHO LIVES UP TO HER NAME, THE BIRD WHO LIVES FOR A THOUSAND YEARS...
...AND...
...CHIZURU-SAMA.
DOKUN (BADMP)
!?
A CORPSE ...?
NO...
THAT'S ...
DOKUN

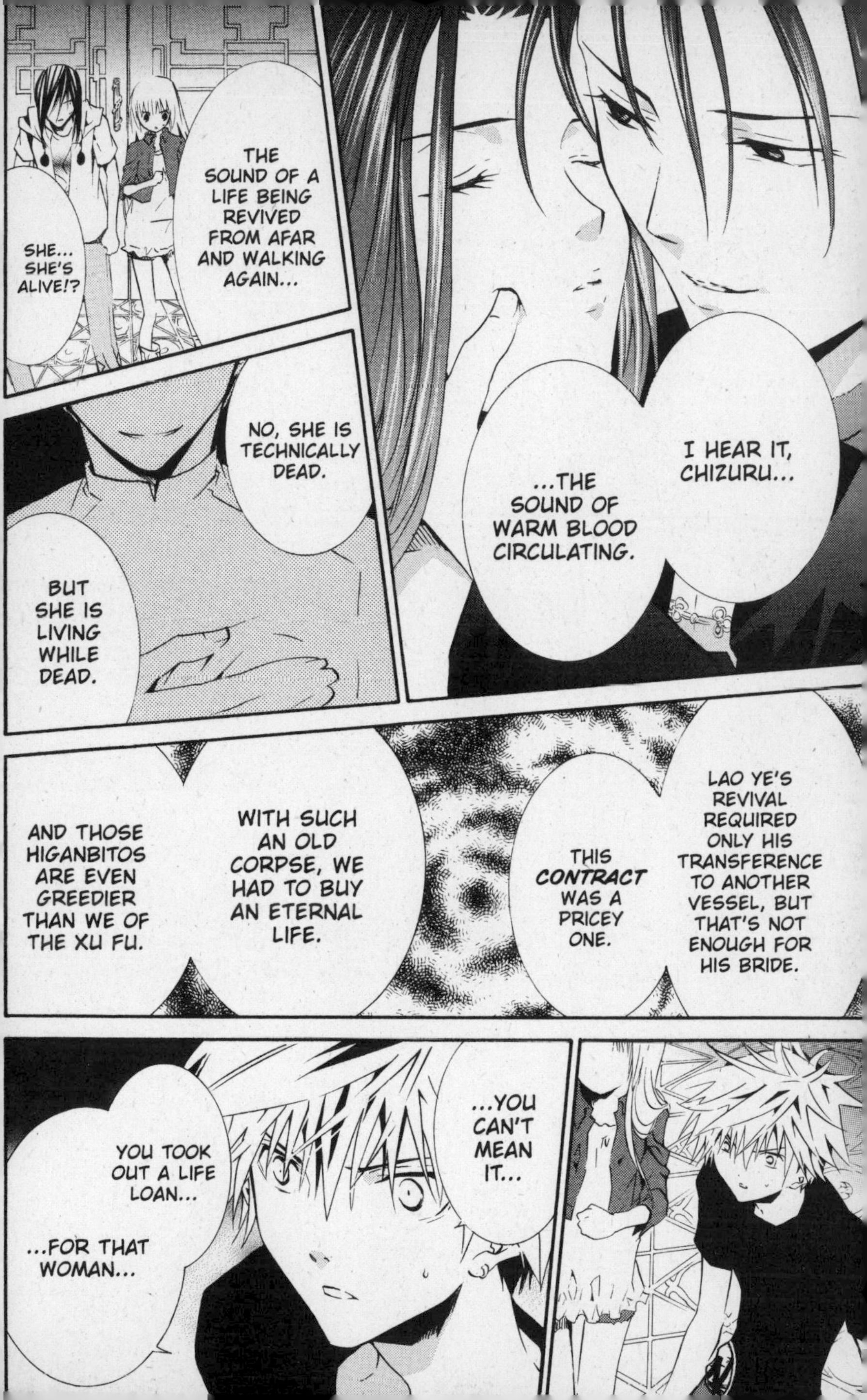
I HEAR IT, CHIZURU...
...THE SOUND OF WARM BLOOD CIRCULATING.
THE SOUND OF A LIFE BEING REVIVED FROM AFAR AND WALKING AGAIN...
SHE... SHE'S ALIVE!?
NO, SHE IS TECHNICALLY DEAD.
BUT SHE IS LIVING WHILE DEAD.
LAO YE'S REVIVAL REQUIRED ONLY HIS TRANSFERENCE TO ANOTHER VESSEL, BUT THAT'S NOT ENOUGH FOR HIS BRIDE.
THIS *CONTRACT* WAS A PRICEY ONE.
WITH SUCH AN OLD CORPSE, WE HAD TO BUY AN ETERNAL LIFE.
AND THOSE HIGANBITOS ARE EVEN GREEDIER THAN WE OF THE XU FU.
...YOU CAN'T MEAN IT...
YOU TOOK OUT A LIFE LOAN...
...FOR THAT WOMAN...

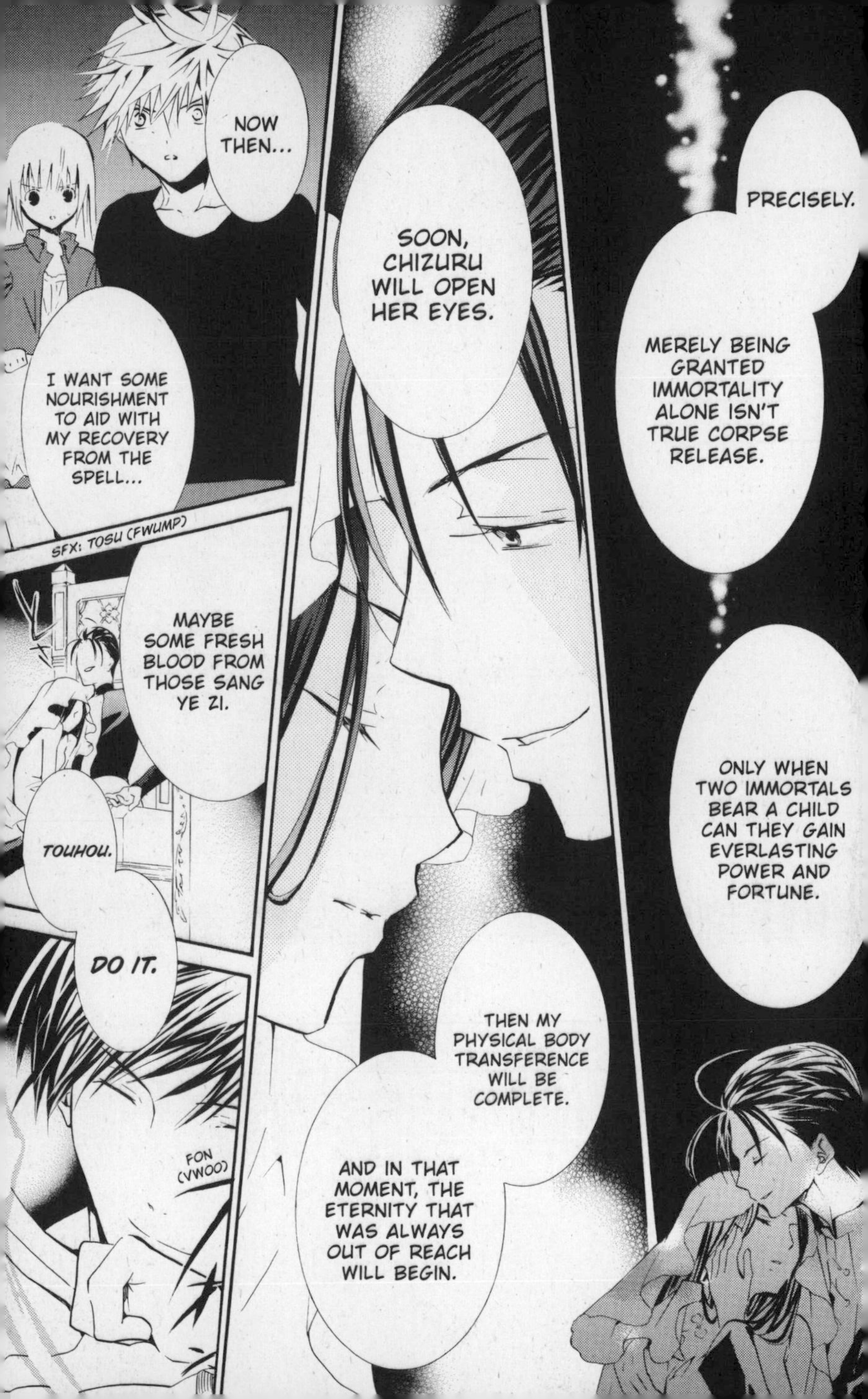
PRECISELY.
MERELY BEING GRANTED IMMORTALITY ALONE ISN'T TRUE CORPSE RELEASE.
ONLY WHEN TWO IMMORTALS BEAR A CHILD CAN THEY GAIN EVERLASTING POWER AND FORTUNE.
SOON, CHIZURU WILL OPEN HER EYES.
THEN MY PHYSICAL BODY TRANSFERENCE WILL BE COMPLETE.
AND IN THAT MOMENT, THE ETERNITY THAT WAS ALWAYS OUT OF REACH WILL BEGIN.
NOW THEN...
I WANT SOME NOURISHMENT TO AID WITH MY RECOVERY FROM THE SPELL...
SFX: TOSU (FWUMP)
MAYBE SOME FRESH BLOOD FROM THOSE SANG YE ZI.
TOUHOU.
DO IT.
FON (VWOO)

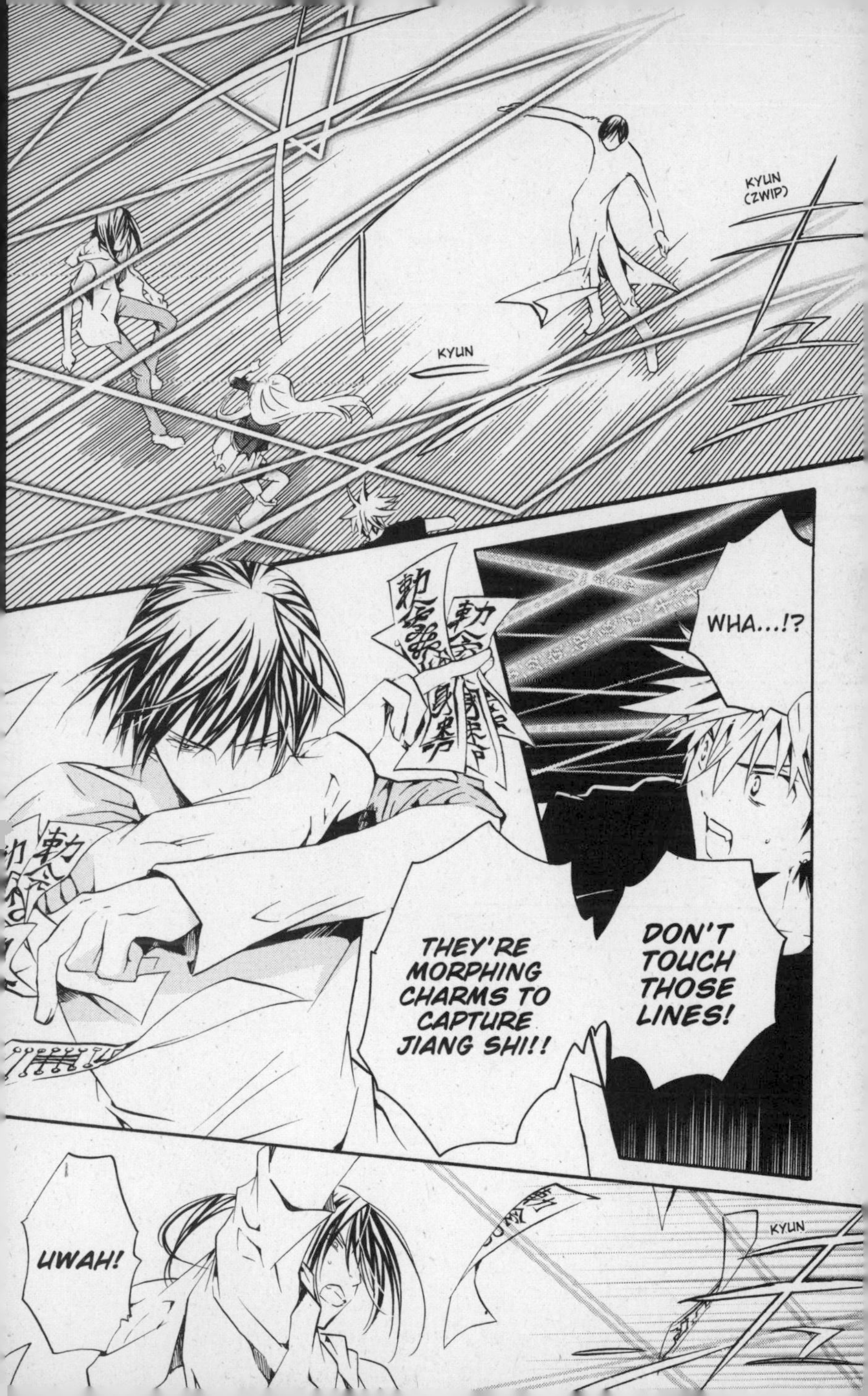
KYUN (ZWIP)
KYUN
WHA...!?
DON'T TOUCH THOSE LINES!
THEY'RE MORPHING CHARMS TO CAPTURE JIANG SHI!!
KYUN
UWAH!

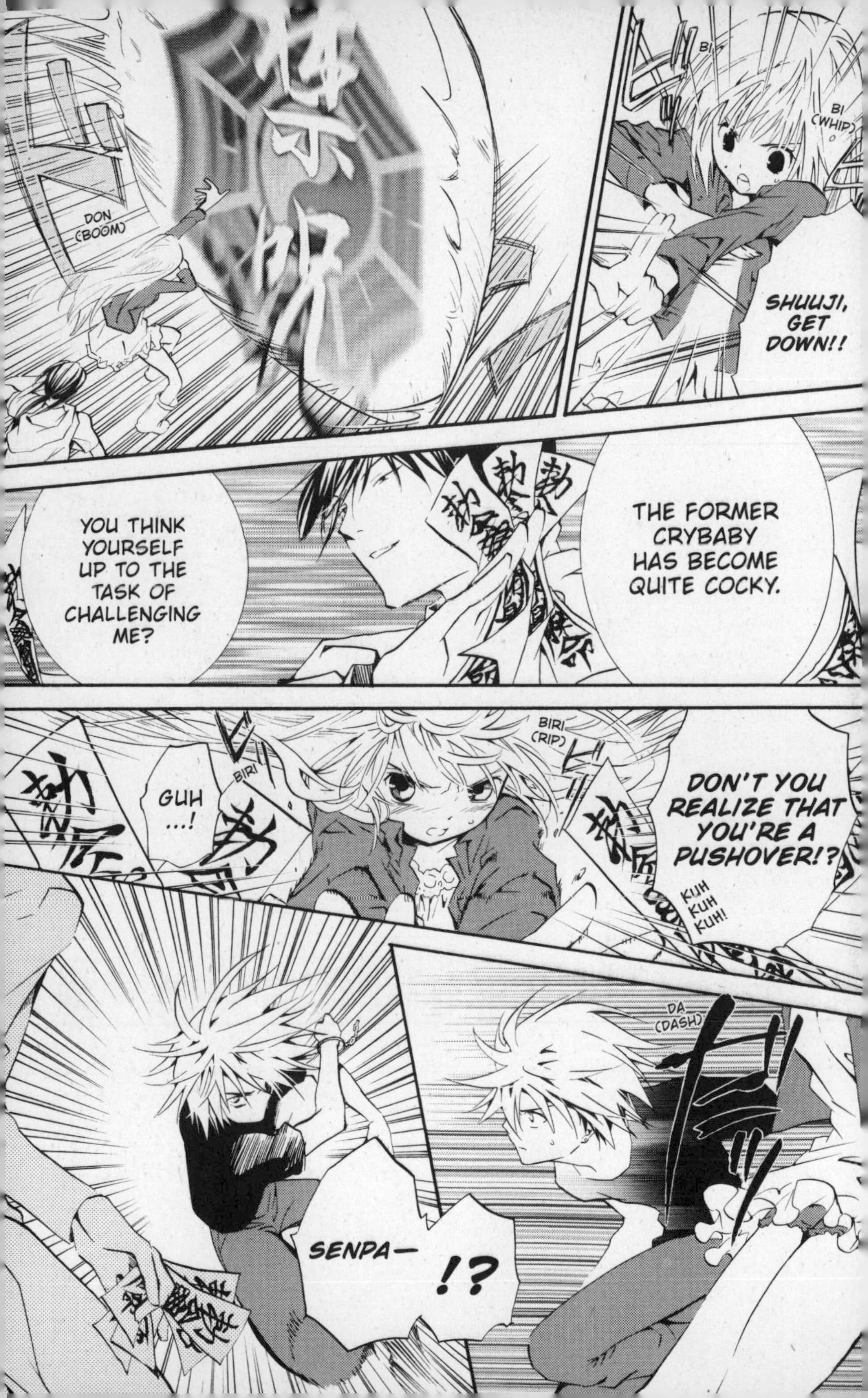
BI
BI (WHIP)
SHUUJI, GET DOWN!!
DON (BOOM)
THE FORMER CRYBABY HAS BECOME QUITE COCKY.
YOU THINK YOURSELF UP TO THE TASK OF CHALLENGING ME?
BIRI (RIP)
DON'T YOU REALIZE THAT YOU'RE A PUSHOVER!?
KUH KUH KUH!
BIRI
GUH ...!
DA (DASH)
SENPA—
!?

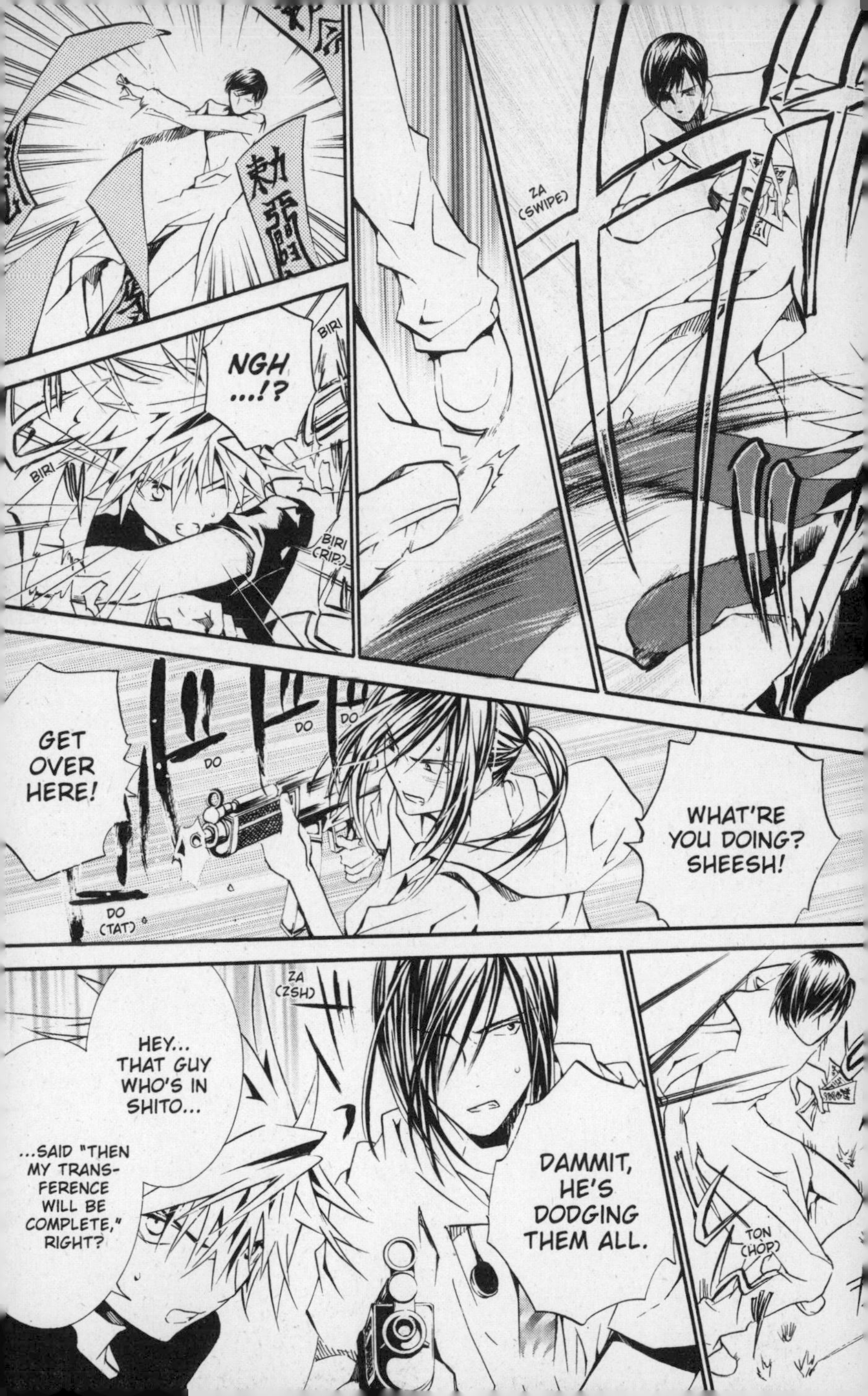
ZA (SWIPE)
BIRI
NGH ...!?
BIRI
BIRI (RIP)
WHAT'RE YOU DOING? SHEESH!
DO
DO
DO
GET OVER HERE!
DO (TAT)
TON (CHOP)
DAMMIT, HE'S DODGING THEM ALL.
ZA (ZSH)
HEY... THAT GUY WHO'S IN SHITO...
...SAID "THEN MY TRANS-FERENCE WILL BE COMPLETE," RIGHT?

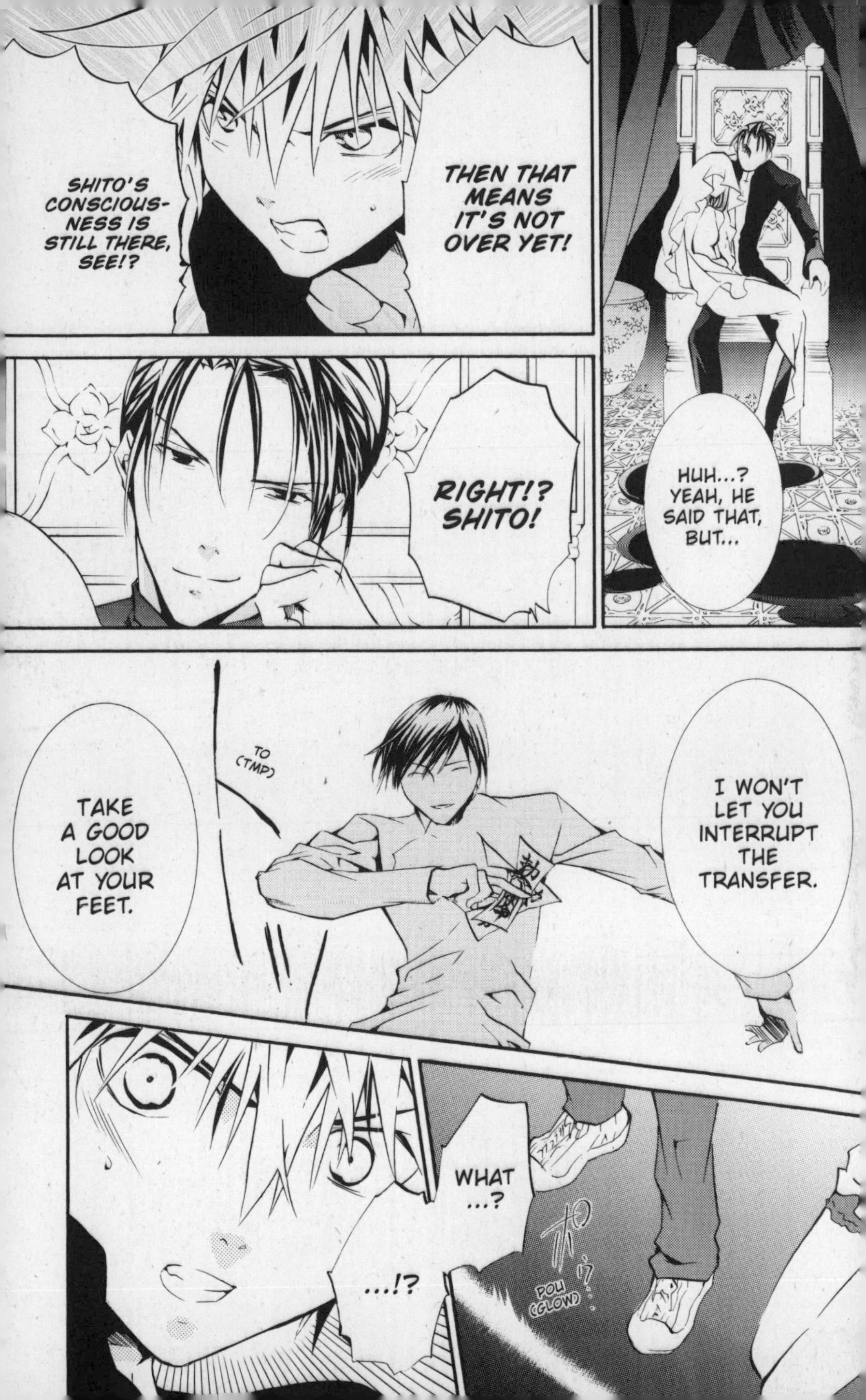
HUH...? YEAH, HE SAID THAT, BUT...
THEN THAT MEANS IT'S NOT OVER YET!
SHITO'S CONSCIOUS-NESS IS STILL THERE, SEE!?
RIGHT!? SHITO!
I WON'T LET YOU INTERRUPT THE TRANSFER.
TO (TMP)
TAKE A GOOD LOOK AT YOUR FEET.
POU (GLOW)
WHAT ...?
...!?

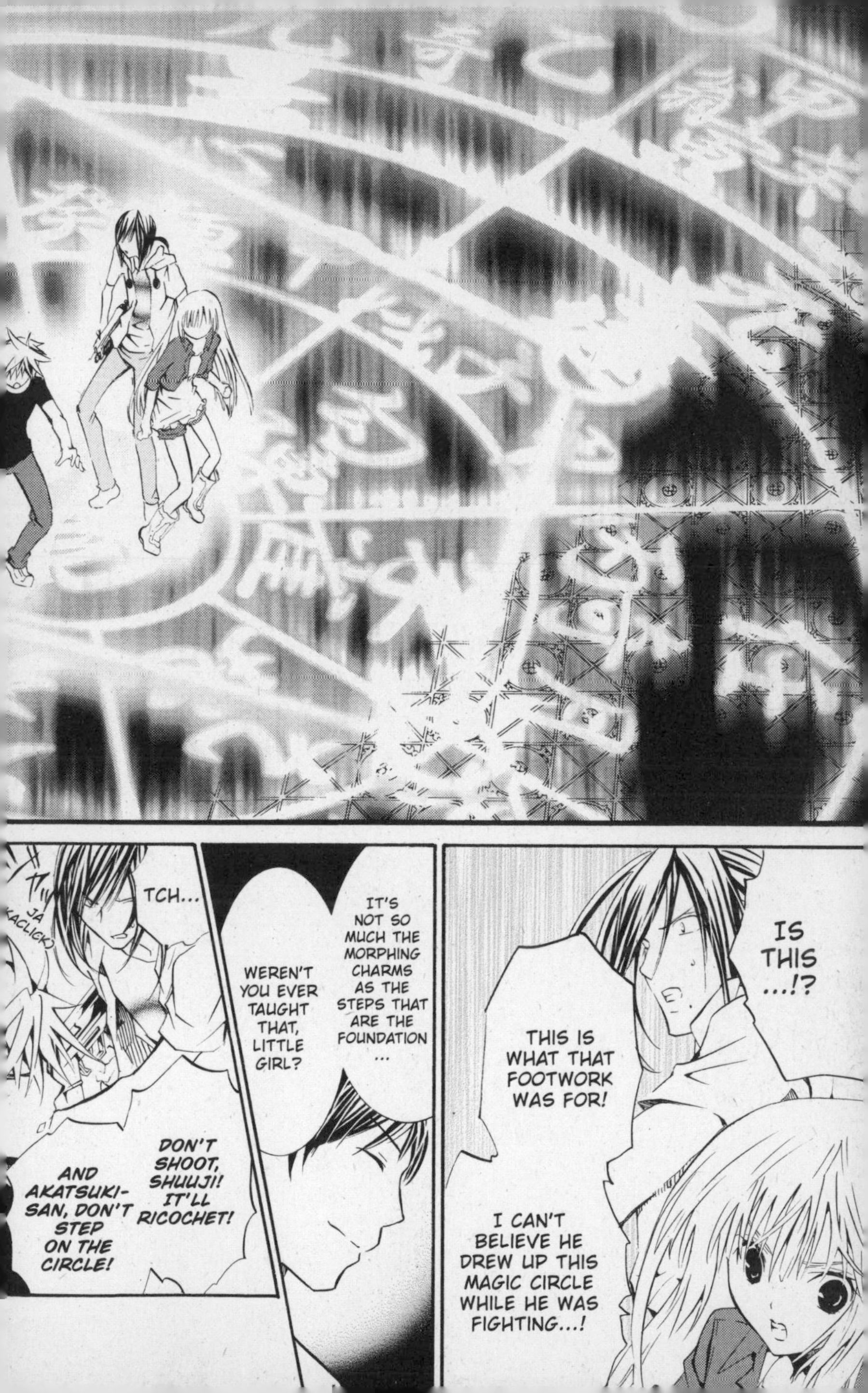
IS THIS ...!?
THIS IS WHAT THAT FOOTWORK WAS FOR!
I CAN'T BELIEVE HE DREW UP THIS MAGIC CIRCLE WHILE HE WAS FIGHTING...!
IT'S NOT SO MUCH THE MORPHING CHARMS AS THE STEPS THAT ARE THE FOUNDATION ...
WEREN'T YOU EVER TAUGHT THAT, LITTLE GIRL?
TCH...
JA
KACLICK)
DON'T SHOOT, SHUUJI! IT'LL RICOCHET!
AND AKATSUKI-SAN, DON'T STEP ON THE CIRCLE!

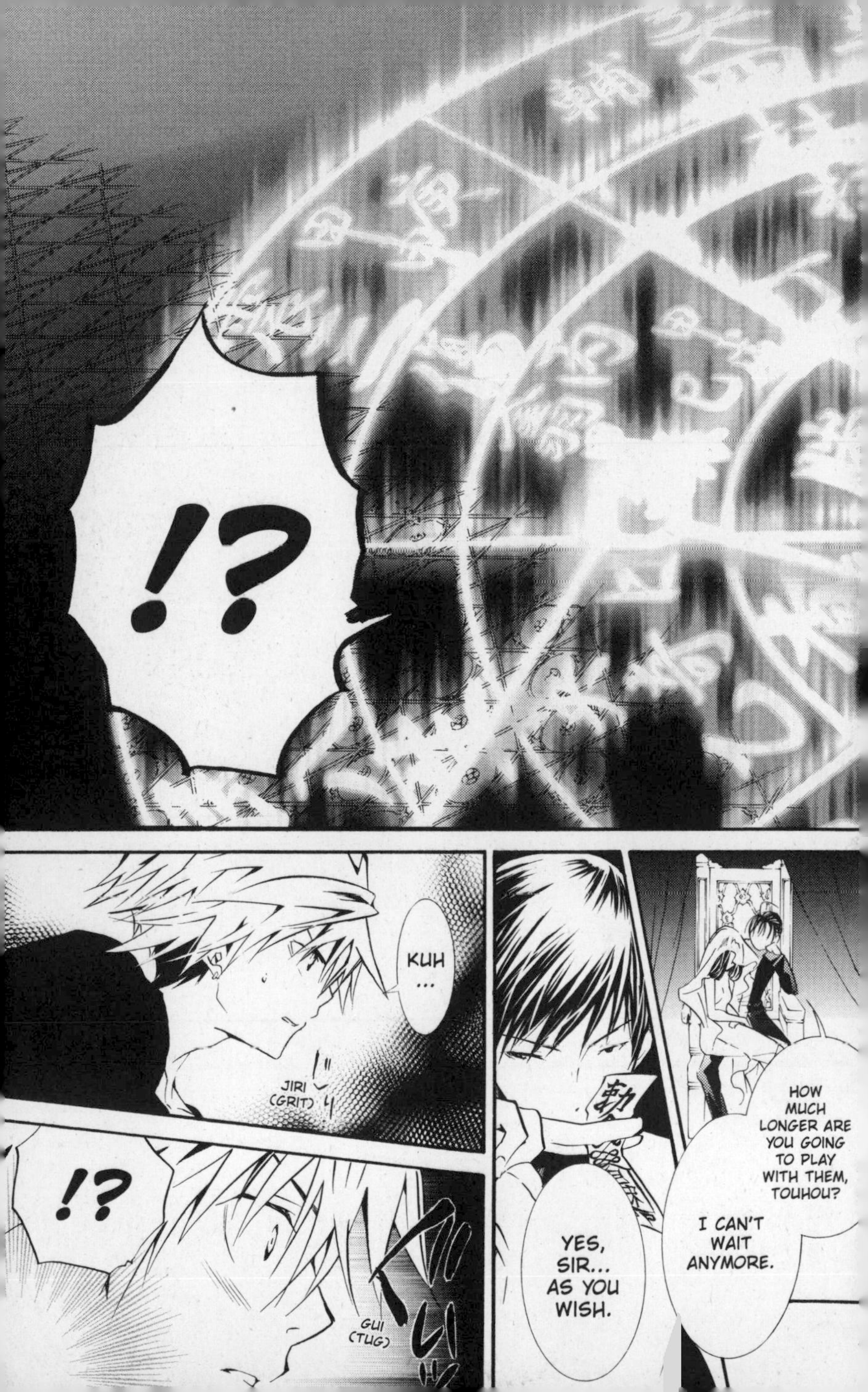
!?
HOW MUCH LONGER ARE YOU GOING TO PLAY WITH THEM, TOUHOU?
I CAN'T WAIT ANYMORE.
YES, SIR... AS YOU WISH.
KUH...
JIRI (GRIT)
!?
GUI (TUG)

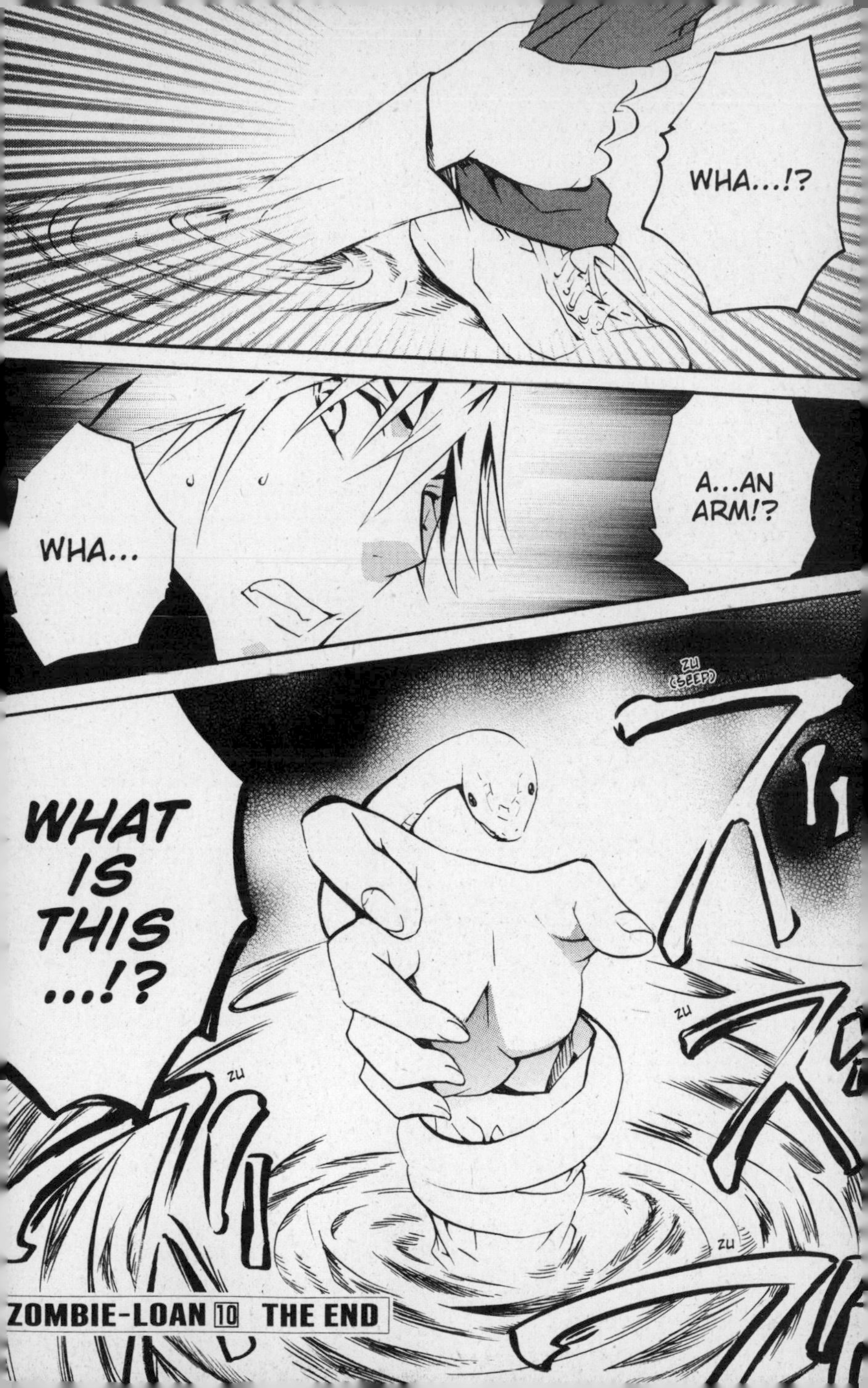

WHA...!?
A...AN ARM!?
WHA...
ZU (SEEP)
WHAT IS THIS ...!?
ZU
ZU
ZU
ZOMBIE-LOAN 10 THE END

TRANSLATION NOTES

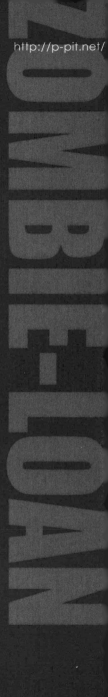

Pg. 5
Har Gow is a traditional Chinese dumpling with shrimp filling served at dim sum meals.

Pg. 11
Huan ying guang lin is the way Chinese shop owners usher in their clientele. "Welcome!"

Pg. 13
Sik zho fan mei a? is Cantonese for "You all done eating?" which is also a common way to greet a friend during the day.

Pg. 14
Ga Jai is a derogatory way for Chinese to refer to Japanese, like how Americans will say "Jap."

The suffix *"ge"* is the same as the Japanese "nii-chan" in reference to an older man friend that you adoringly call "brother."

Pg. 16
Be a good little boy and humbly receive!
He's making fun of how Japanese say "I humbly receive" (*itadakimasu*) before a meal.

Pg. 19
Moumantai means "no problem" in Chinese.

Pg. 98
Jiang shi means "zombie" in Chinese.

Pg. 163
Chizuru means "one thousand cranes" in Japanese. Cranes are associated with longevity for their fabled lifespan of a thousand years.

Pg. 176
Tai xiexie ni le means "thank you so very much."

all produced by
PEACH-PIT
BanriSendou : ShibukoEbara

staff
Nao
Tama
Kinomin
Midori.W
Hitomi.I
Yu.H
Chie
Zaki

special thanks
T.Kuma

...and your reading

to be continued vol.11

ZOMBIE-LOAN

http://p-pit.net/

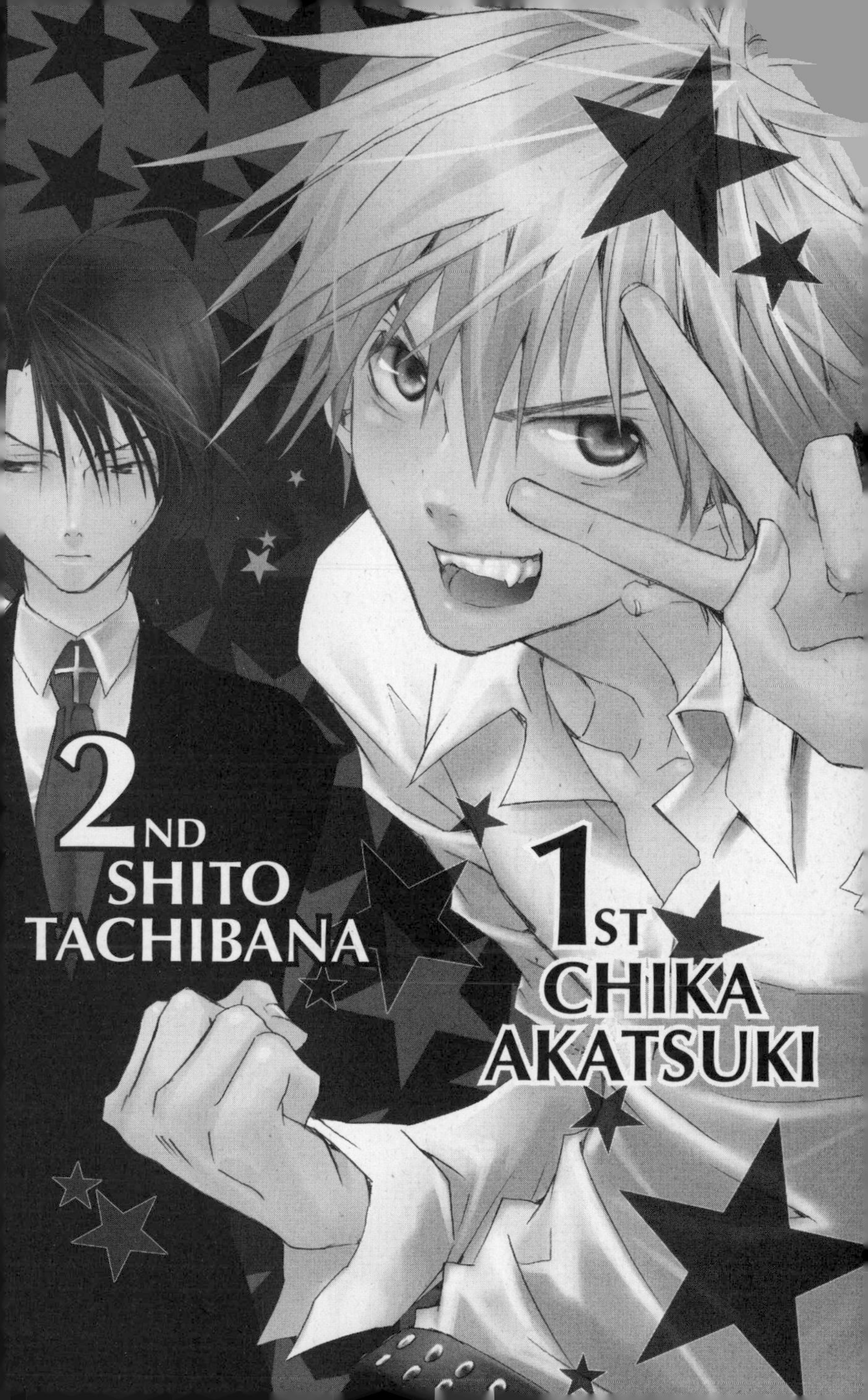
1ST
CHIKA
AKATSUKI
2ND
SHITO
TACHIBANA

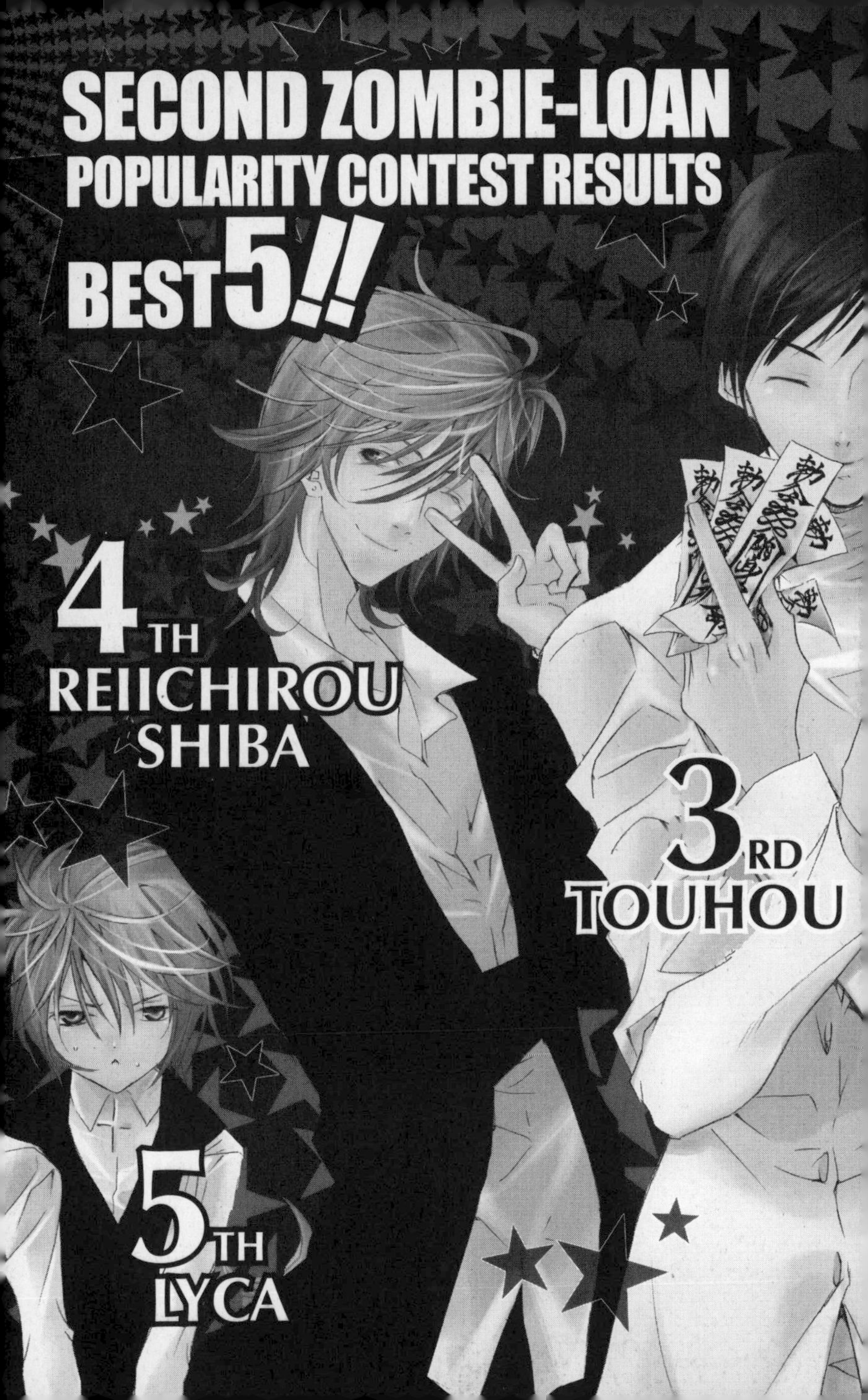
SECOND ZOMBIE-LOAN
POPULARITY CONTEST RESULTS
BEST 5!!
3RD
TOUHOU
4TH
REIICHIROU SHIBA
5TH
LYCA

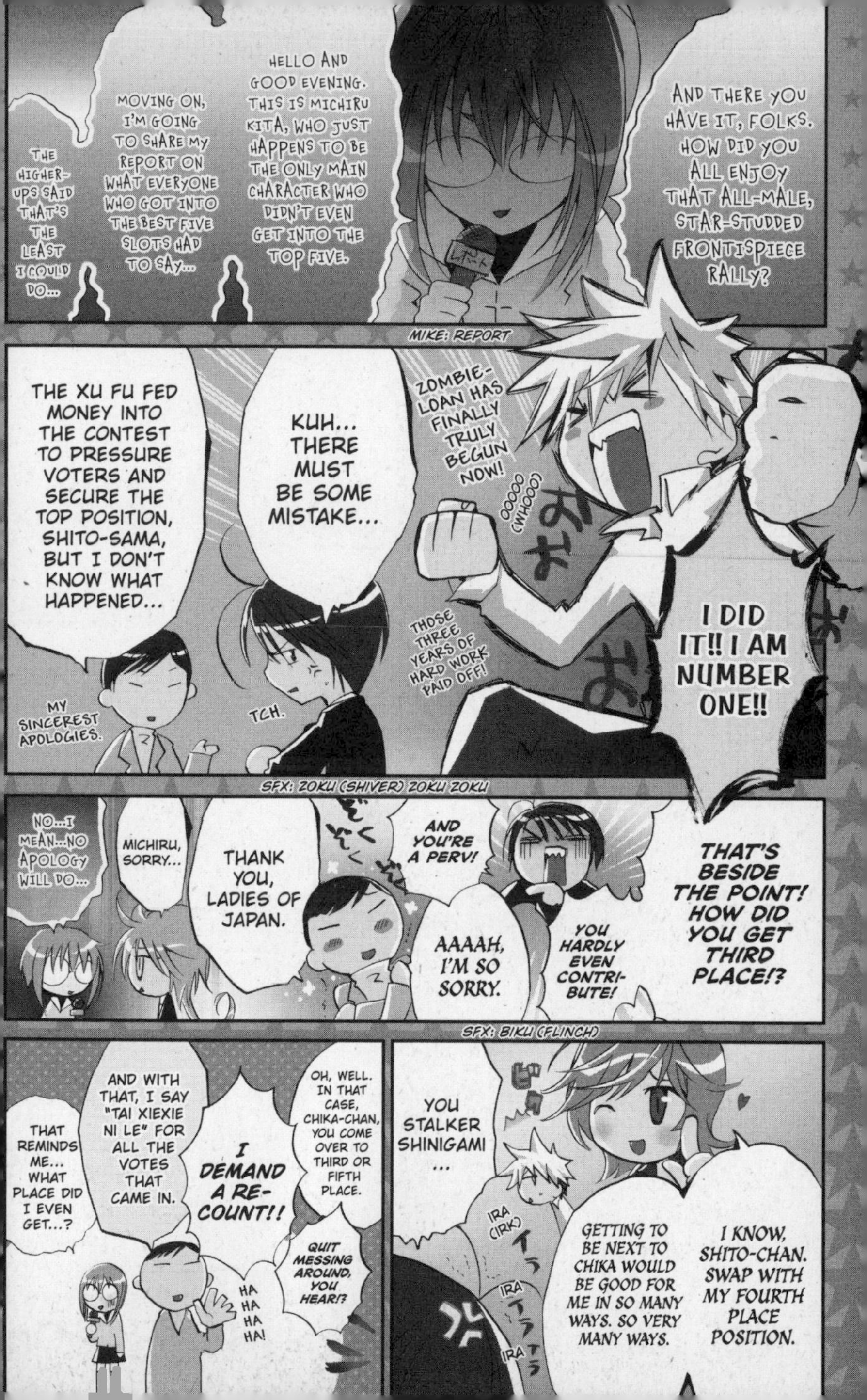
AND THERE YOU HAVE IT, FOLKS. HOW DID YOU ALL ENJOY THAT ALL-MALE, STAR-STUDDED FRONTISPIECE RALLY?
HELLO AND GOOD EVENING. THIS IS MICHIRU KITA, WHO JUST HAPPENS TO BE THE ONLY MAIN CHARACTER WHO DIDN'T EVEN GET INTO THE TOP FIVE.
MOVING ON, I'M GOING TO SHARE MY REPORT ON WHAT EVERYONE WHO GOT INTO THE BEST FIVE SLOTS HAD TO SAY...
THE HIGHER-UPS SAID THAT'S THE LEAST I COULD DO...
MIKE: REPORT
I DID IT!! I AM NUMBER ONE!!
ZOMBIE-LOAN HAS FINALLY TRULY BEGUN NOW!
OOOOO (WHOOO)
THOSE THREE YEARS OF HARD WORK PAID OFF!
KUH... THERE MUST BE SOME MISTAKE...
THE XU FU FED MONEY INTO THE CONTEST TO PRESSURE VOTERS AND SECURE THE TOP POSITION, SHITO-SAMA, BUT I DON'T KNOW WHAT HAPPENED...
TCH.
MY SINCEREST APOLOGIES.
SFX: ZOKU (SHIVER) ZOKU ZOKU
THAT'S BESIDE THE POINT! HOW DID YOU GET THIRD PLACE!?
AND YOU'RE A PERV!
YOU HARDLY EVEN CONTRIBUTE!
AAAAH, I'M SO SORRY.
THANK YOU, LADIES OF JAPAN.
MICHIRU, SORRY...
NO...I MEAN...NO APOLOGY WILL DO...
SFX: BIKU (FLINCH)
I KNOW, SHITO-CHAN. SWAP WITH MY FOURTH PLACE POSITION.
GETTING TO BE NEXT TO CHIKA WOULD BE GOOD FOR ME IN SO MANY WAYS. SO VERY MANY WAYS.
YOU STALKER SHINIGAMI ...
IRA (IRK)
IRA
IRA
OH, WELL. IN THAT CASE, CHIKA-CHAN, YOU COME OVER TO THIRD OR FIFTH PLACE.
I DEMAND A RE-COUNT!!
AND WITH THAT, I SAY "TAI XIEXIE NI LE" FOR ALL THE VOTES THAT CAME IN.
THAT REMINDS ME... WHAT PLACE DID I EVEN GET...?
QUIT MESSING AROUND, YOU HEAR!?
HA HA HA HA HA!

SECOND ZOMBIE-LOAN

POPULARITY CONTEST RESULTS

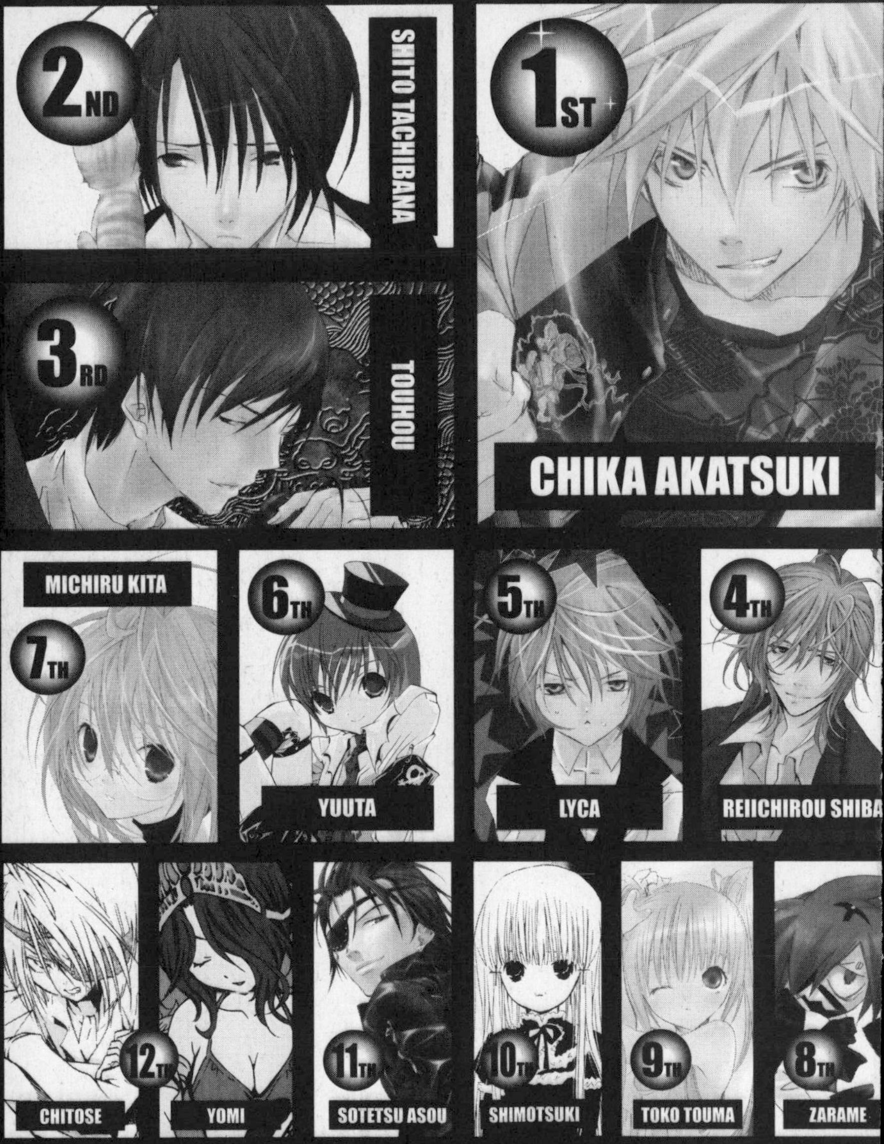
1ST
CHIKA AKATSUKI
2ND
SHITO TACHIBANA
3RD
TOUHOU
4TH
REIICHIROU SHIBA
5TH
LYCA
6TH
YUUTA
7TH
MICHIRU KITA
8TH
ZARAME
9TH
TOKO TOUMA
10TH
SHIMOTSUKI
11TH
SOTETSU ASOU
12TH
YOMI
CHITOSE

#14 ZEN INUBASHIRI #15 KOYOMI YOIMACHI SHUUJI TSUGUMI #17 OTSU SAWATARI MOMOKA AKATSUKI GOLEM GIRL #20 PUNK BOY (FROM PAYMENT 3) #21 BEKKOU KOUME #23 YOSHIZUMI #24 HAKKA #25 YUURI AKATSUKI HONG KUAN #27 UNDERTAKER INFORMER GOLEM MAN YUMI SAITO YUMI'S FRIEND

ZOMBIE-LOAN
10
by PEACH-PIT

Translation: Christine Dashiell
Lettering: Alexis Eckerman

ZOMBIE-LOAN Vol. 10 © 2008 PEACH-PIT / SQUARE ENIX.
All rights reserved. First published in Japan in 2008 by
SQUARE ENIX CO., LTD. English translation rights arranged
with SQUARE ENIX CO., LTD. and Hachette Book Group
through Tuttle-Mori Agency, Inc. Translation © 2010
by SQUARE ENIX CO., LTD.

Yen Press
Hachette Book Group
237 Park Avenue, New York, NY 10017

www.HachetteBookGroup.com
www.YenPress.com

Yen Press is an imprint of Hachette Book Group, Inc.
The Yen Press name and logo are trademarks of
Hachette Book Group, Inc.

First Yen Press Edition: October 2010

ISBN: 978-0-7595-3099-7

10 9 8 7 6 5 4 3 2 1

BVG

Printed in the United States of America